The New Edinburgh History of Scotland

VOLUME 4

The Wars of Scotland

The New Edinburgh History of Scotland

General editor: Roger Mason, *University of St Andrews*

Advisory editors: Dauvit Broun, *University of Glasgow*; Iain Hutchison, *University of Stirling*; Norman Macdougall, *University of St Andrews*; Nicholas Phillipson, *University of Edinburgh*

The Wars of Scotland
1214–1371

Michael Brown

Edinburgh University Press

For Robert

© Michael Brown, 2004

Edinburgh University Press Ltd
22 George Square, Edinburgh

Reprinted 2009, 2010 (twice), 2012, 2013, 2014, 2015

Typeset in 11/13 Ehrhardt
by Servis Filmsetting Ltd, Manchester, and
printed and bound in Great Britain by
Bell & Bain Ltd., Glasgow

A CIP record for this book is available from the British Library

ISBN 0 7486 1237 8 (hardback)
ISBN 0 7486 1238 6 (paperback)

The right of Michael Brown
to be identified as author of this work
has been asserted in accordance with
the Copyright, Designs and Patents Act 1988.

Publisher's acknowledgement
Edinburgh University Press thanks Mercat Press, publishers of
the *Edinburgh History of Scotland*, for permission to use the *New
Edinburgh History of Scotland* as the title for this ten-volume series.

Contents

Maps, Genealogical Tables and Illustrations

Acknowledgements

No book is written completely in isolation. Consciousness of this fact is increased when, as in this case, the book is one volume in a series, and when the scale and ambition of that series are themselves an indication of the continuing and growing interest in the history of Scotland. The completion of this book has made me feel very much part of a team, and the help and advice of John Davey of Edinburgh University Press has, from start to finish, eased my task considerably. In terms of academic guidance and support, I have benefited enormously from the comments of Dr Dauvit Broun of the University of Glasgow and the perspectives – always interesting and often unexpected – of my colleague Alex Woolf. Once again, I find myself happily acknowledging the debt I owe to Dr Norman Macdougall who has been a source of help and encouragement during the writing of this book. I am also happy to record my gratitude to the general editor of this series, Dr Roger Mason, for approaching me in the first place, for encouraging me during its progress, and for his comments on the book during the process of its completion. I trust that the series will continue to flourish under his guidance. Finally, I have depended on the support of my family, Margaret and Robert, who have provided the – always welcome – opportunity to escape the horrors of medieval Scotland for its much pleasanter contemporary guise.

General Editor's Preface

The purpose of the New Edinburgh History of Scotland is to provide up-to-date and accessible narrative accounts of the Scottish past. Its authors will make full use of the explosion of scholarly research that has taken place over the last three decades, and do so in a way that is sensitive to Scotland's regional diversity as well as to the British, European and transoceanic worlds of which Scotland has always been an integral part.

Chronology is fundamental to understanding change over time and Scotland's political development will provide the backbone of the narrative and the focus of analysis and explanation. The New Edinburgh History will tell the story of Scotland as a political entity, but will be sensitive to broader social, cultural and religious change and informed by a richly textured understanding of the totality and diversity of the Scots' historical experience. Yet to talk of the Scots – or the Scottish nation – is often misleading. Local loyalty and regional diversity have more frequently characterised Scotland than any perceived sense of 'national' solidarity. Scottish identity has seldom been focused primarily, let alone exclusively, on the 'nation'. The modern discourse of nationhood offers what is often an inadequate and inappropriate vocabulary in which to couch Scotland's history. The authors in this series will show that there are other and more revealing ways of capturing the distinctiveness of Scottish experience.

Michael Brown has fulfilled this brief admirably. His compelling story of Scotland in the thirteenth and fourteenth centuries places the 'Wars of Independence' in an unusual and illuminating chronological context. He sees them as symptomatic of European processes characterised by the consolidation of royal lordships and the emergence of more intensive and demanding structures of authority. Scotland's very survival as a distinct political entity was threatened during this period. However, in a tightly drawn narrative Dr Brown shows that the wars were more than a matter of 'national' resistance to an external enemy. He uncovers behind them the patterns of conflicting lordships, royal and baronial, Scottish and British, which family rivalries shaped and dynastic ambition ignited. How the Scottish kingdom struggled to maintain its freedom from English lordship has rarely been so well told; the dynamics of that struggle have never been so convincingly explained.

Introduction

The years between the reign of King Alexander II in the first half of the thirteenth century and the accession of the Stewarts in the later fourteenth century, which are dealt with in this volume, have not normally been regarded as a single era in the history of medieval Scotland. Instead the last years of the thirteenth century have traditionally formed a watershed in perceptions of the Scottish realm, dividing two distinct historical periods. The years from 1214 to 1286 are generally seen as witnessing the culmination of developments in state, church and political society which can be traced back to the eleventh century and which were driven by the achievements of the royal line in extending and consolidating the idea and reality of the Scottish realm. The end of this royal line in 1286 and the onset of major warfare and crisis involving the survival of Scotland as a distinct political unit seem to create a very different environment. For the next seventy years, issues of war and allegiance dominated the landscape and resulted in a country which was deeply sensitised to questions of rights and identities. The legacy of this period was to continue to shape the internal character and external relationships of the Scottish kingdom for two centuries after 1350.

If the years from 1214 to 1371 do not form an era of consistent development and static themes, there are nevertheless strong arguments for dealing with this era within a single study. In particular, across Western Europe the decades from the mid-thirteenth to the mid-fourteenth century have been identified as a period of critical importance in the definition of political units. The continued development of certain principalities as centres of administrative and ideological significance in these years marked a decisive stage in their formation as late medieval and early modern states. In the largest of these, such as the French and English kingdoms, this century and a half saw the extension and intensification of centrally-inspired political identities and of the physical reach of royal government. At the same time, often in response to that process, the thirteenth and fourteenth centuries also witnessed developing senses of communal action and identity. For smaller realms the era also involved issues of sovereignty and survival. The growth in the material and ideological power of the great monarchies was accompanied by efforts to extend their lordship over neighbouring lands. In France and the British Isles, the principal royal rulers sought to transform loose traditions of superiority into demanding and inflexible structures of authority. In smaller realms such demands provided tests of political structures and collective identities in which ancient communities survived or experienced absorption by more powerful neighbours. In some of these, like native Wales and Norway, processes of state formation were halted by conquest or loss of distinct structures of royal lordship, while others, like Portugal and, in a more limited way, Brittany, continued to develop as separate societies with their own structures of internal authority and separate status.[1]

The history of Scotland in the thirteenth and fourteenth centuries concerns such issues as they affected one small north-west European kingdom. However, within these wider patterns, it is important to recognise the uniqueness of the Scottish experience and its significance in the longer-term development of a distinct unit of Europe and the British Isles. The 150 years covered in this volume witnessed not two distinct periods, but an era that involved major changes and reversals in the internal and external structures and relationships. These centred on issues of politics and political society and it is one of the principal aims of this volume to discuss the Scottish realm as a complex and changing polity. Throughout the period under consideration, Scotland was both a single kingdom and a collection of diverse lordships and provinces. The implications of this exerted a major influence on the character and development of Scotland. While there existed an assertive sense of Scottish identity, this was fostered and expressed by the central elites of crown and church and represented the interests and perspectives of these groups. It is possible to place too much emphasis on the strength of common, shared political and cultural values in thirteenth- and fourteenth-century Scotland and caution needs to be exercised in prioritising this view of rights and loyalties. During the two centuries covered by this book, the Scottish kingdom remained a composite of lands and communities with considerable variation in their practices and responses to events. The

---

[1] J.-P. Genet, 'Which state rises?', *Historical Research*, 65 (1992), 19–33; S. Reynolds, 'How different was England?' in M. Prestwich, R. Britnell and R. Frame (eds), *Thirteenth Century England*, vii (Woodbridge, 1999), 1–16; R. W. Kaeuper, *War, Justice and Public Order: England and France in the Later Middle Ages* (Oxford, 1988); J. R. Strayer, *Medieval Origins of the Modern State* (Princeton, 1970).

meaning of Scotland and of Scottishness was not necessarily the same to all the king's subjects.

This account represents an attempt to characterise this diversity and to understand the links between it and the development of a centrally-driven sense of Scottish government, community and identity. The conflicts which engulfed the realm at the end of the thirteenth century, and provide the core for the second half of this volume, were not, as the customary, modern label has it, 'the Scottish wars of independence', a national struggle for liberation. The wars were both more and less than this. They were certainly about the defence of the rights of the Scottish crown against subjugation or absorption. During them there developed a greater sense of those elements that constituted collective interests and freedoms. However, these were also struggles for possession of the kingship of the Scots between rivals, and wars which decided, or at least shaped, the character of provincial society in different parts of the realm. To stress a central, monolithic defence of national rights is to place too much emphasis on one element of these wars to the exclusion of others. The narrative and analysis provided here seeks to convey the variations in approach, experience and motivation across Scotland and to widen understanding of the wars and their impact. The principal themes of this book are provided by the survival and adaptation of Scotland in this pivotal period. The experience of the country is considered in a variety of ways. Scotland is discussed as a realm on the fringes of European political rivalries, in particular the developing hostility between the English and French monarchies, which drew in small realms and principalities across the west including Scotland. In addition, Scotland receives consideration as a royal lordship extending across the northern British Isles – including isles and coasts with close connections to Ireland and Wales – and with a political elite whose interests reached well beyond the borders of the kingdom. This kingdom's development as a community with a growing sense of common rights and identity is set alongside its existence as a diverse collection of local societies, held together by variable ties of allegiance to the crown. It is the study of a land in an age of change and conquest.

PART ONE

The Scottish Realm (1214–86)

CHAPTER I

King and Kingdom

L ate on the evening of Thursday, 4 December 1214, King William of
Scotland died at Stirling. Early the next day, a large entourage
departed on the twenty-five mile journey to Scone, near Perth, leaving
the queen, clerics and royal servants to mourn their dead lord. This party,
led by seven earls and the bishop of St Andrews, formed the escort for the
heir to the throne, William's son Alexander, a youth of sixteen. On the
afternoon of Friday, 5 December, Alexander was crowned king at Scone,
'with more pomp and ceremony than anyone before him'. The new king
spent the Saturday and Sunday feasting and holding court before, on
Monday, making the short trip to the bridge over the river Tay at Perth.
Here Alexander met the mourners bringing his father's body for burial
and, with the earls carrying the bier for part of the journey, the cortege
travelled to Arbroath. Two days later, on Wednesday, 10 December, the
old king was laid to rest in the church of Arbroath Abbey.[1]

In a week of celebration and mourning, royal authority was transferred from William, who had ruled the kingdom for nearly half a
century, to his young son, the new King Alexander II. What was
Alexander inheriting? His kingdom was understood less as a territorial
unit than as a collection of rights, customs and communities. At the
centre and at the summit of this network stood the king. For the Scottish
kingdom, the making of a new king, his inauguration, was the most
important ceremony and the most important political act in the realm.
The process of inauguration was rooted in the history of the kingdom
and its ruling dynasty. We know about king-making in thirteenth-
century Scotland from the description and depiction of the crowning of
Alexander's son in 1249 and from the representation of the event on the

---

[1] John of Fordun, *Chronica Johannes de Fordun, Chronica Gentis Scottorum*, ii, 275–6;
Scotichronicon, v, 2–3, 78–81.

seal of Scone Abbey. Scone was the traditional site of a ceremony which gave specific roles to different groups of the king's subjects. It was the responsibility of the earls, led by Fife and Strathearn, to give the king his sword of office and set him on his throne, a seat made of stone. Enthronement on this ancient royal seat was perhaps the oldest part of the ceremony, performed by men who could claim established rights as provincial rulers and heads of an extended royal kindred. Following this, a group of prelates, led by the bishop of St Andrews, the senior ecclesiastic of the realm, received the king's sacred promise to rule lawfully in accordance with custom, gave him a blessing and clothed him in clerical vestments. Finally, the king was proclaimed by his master poet *ollamh rig*. The poet gave the king his wand or sceptre, recited Gaelic verses in his honour and recited Alexander's full genealogy back to Fergus, 'first king of Scots in Albany', and beyond to Gaedel Glas and Scota, the legendary founders of the Scots.[2]

The various components of the ceremony all played their part in the renewal of royal rule in the realm. The figures who were involved reflected different elements within the kingdom and the character of Scottish political society as a whole. The poet who recited the royal genealogy was not acting out of an empty sense of tradition, but enunciating the king's right to rule. The realm which Alexander was inheriting was a land of many lands, an accumulation of varied provinces and peoples. Whilst most European kingdoms could articulate a common identity based on claims to shared descent, on legal or linguistic unity, on being a people, the inhabitants of Alexander II's realm could not do so with confidence. The kingdom of Scots was carved out by rulers whose power was originally centred in the region between the Forth and the Grampian mountains. During the three centuries before Alexander's accession, the kings of Scots had brought other lands and kingdoms under their lordship. Beyond the Grampians, the claims to the kingship from the rulers of Moray were defeated, while south of the Forth, the English of Lothian and the Welsh-speaking inhabitants of Strathclyde were forced under the dominion of the Scottish kings. These kings established themselves as the overlords of the northern third of the island of Britain, rulers of a realm which stretched northwards from the limits of the English realm at the river Tweed and the Solway Firth. However, the provinces won by Alexander's ancestors did not slot together automatically to form a pre-ordained political unit. Geography divided the king's realm rather than

² *Chron. Fordun*, ii, 289–90; Bannerman, 'The King's poet and the inauguration of Alexander III', 120–49; Duncan, *Scotland: The Making of the Kingdom*, 555–8; Duncan, *The Kingship of the Scots*, ch. 7.

holding it together. The natural borders at the Forth and the Grampians retained a significance throughout the Middle Ages. Passing the Forth was made difficult by the Firth or Scottish Sea and by the mosses which spread from its banks further inland. The Grampian mountains limited access westwards from the east coast, and the spur of hills, known as the Mounth, which stretched to the North Sea near Stonehaven demarcated the lowlands of the north-east. The line of coast and upland provided Scotland with its internal shape. The Border Fells, the moors and hills of Galloway and the ranges of the Highlands, Loch Linnhe and the firths of Clyde, Forth, Tay and Moray all divided and defined provincial structures. Galloway and Argyll, for example, were separated from eastern Scotland by the uplands which formed their borders, and they retained strong senses of separate identity and contacts beyond the kingdom. Equally, it was no accident that the political centres of Alexander's realm lay in the coasts and river valleys of the east which, despite the firths and uplands which intruded on them, formed the largest area of low-lying and good-quality land in northern Britain. Ease of access and communication contributed to the formation and maintenance of royal government and authority in these regions.

Geographical and historical factors worked together to provide the basis for the Scottish kingdom which Alexander inherited, but also encouraged the continuation of provincial and regional variations within it. The English-speaking south-east, the Gaelic-speaking east-coast beyond the Forth, and upland or west-coast provinces like Argyll, Galloway and Lochaber differed greatly from each other. The sense of the kingdom as a political unit was slow to develop and not fully complete in 1214. The name of Scotland was not used exclusively to describe the whole kingdom between Tweed and Caithness. It also retained its older meaning as a single province, *Scotia*, the land between Lothian and Moray. The sense remained that Moray, Lothian and Scotland were different lands with the same royal lord. In the twelfth century, even the kings acknowledged the difference. Royal documents were often addressed to different groups – Scots, English, French, Gallovidians or men of Moray – and referred to the land or realm of the king of Scots. However, by 1200 this had changed. The kings addressed all their good men and usually spoke of the kingdom of Scotland, or of the Scots, to mean their whole dominions. The royal genealogy also reflected this change. During the twelfth and thirteenth century it was extended to include the kings of Dal Riata in Argyll and of the Picts from the fifth to eighth centuries in the royal line. This increased the pedigree of Scotland's current kings and their geographical appeal by widening the inheritance they claimed. When he recounted the full list of Alexander's

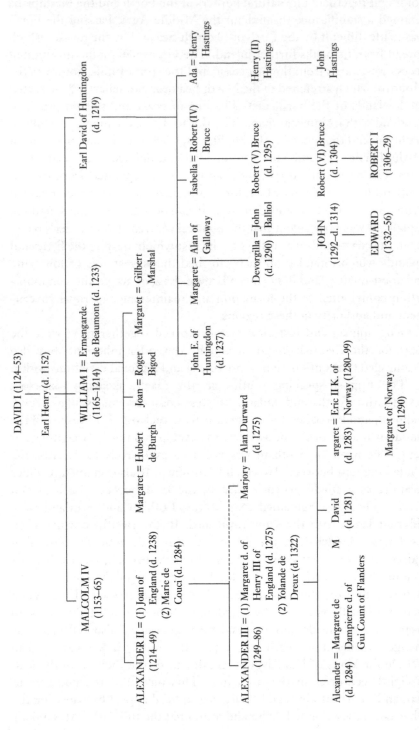

Table 1.1. The Royal House of Scotland 1214–90

kingly forebears, the poet was staking Alexander's claim to be heir to rights which stretched across northern Britain.[3]

The strengthening of the idea that Scotland was a single realm with a single ruler provided the motor for the development of Scottish unity and identity in the twelfth and thirteenth centuries. The heightened status claimed by the kings of Scots as the heads of a unified, stable and defined political society was not an isolated phenomenon. Instead it was part of a process which saw the physical and material increase of royal resources and royal authority and the reshaping of the kingdom's elites. The new king's inauguration and the weeks which followed it provide an illustration of the patterns of change and continuity fostered by Alexander's predecessors.

The ancient custom preserved in the inauguration stressed the king's legitimacy by looking backwards to the origins of Scottish kingship. The ceremony also contained elements through which the king sought sanction in newer forms. There had always been ecclesiastical participation in the ceremony, but the extent and importance of this probably increased during the twelfth century. Under the influence of European movements, which raised the status and defined the values of the Roman Church and claimed greater rights for churchmen in all spiritual affairs, Scottish prelates were accorded a greater role in the inauguration of their king. Alexander's three predecessors, David I, Malcolm IV and William, would all have wished for the church to take a leading role in the ceremony as it did in the coronation of kings in England and France. Full coronation was a rite of the church, conferred on a ruler by permission of the Pope. For another century after 1214, Scotland's kings would seek unsuccessfully to obtain permission for coronation involving the anointing of the new king with holy oil, an act believed to confer spiritual powers on the recipient and linked to full royal status. In the absence of anointing, Scotland's kings added elements to their inauguration which brought it nearer to the full rite of coronation. The role played by the church in administering the king's oath, blessing his accession and clothing him in religious vestments was a way of symbolising ecclesiastical sanction for the new ruler.[4]

The search for the blessing of the reformed church went beyond the inauguration and was symbolised by the old king's burial at Arbroath Abbey. William had founded the abbey, encouraging monks from Kelso to establish a new religious community which he provided with lands and revenues. Arbroath's monks belonged to the Order of Tiron, based in

[3] Broun, 'Defining Scotland and the Scots before the Wars of Independence', 4–17; Broun, *The Irish Identity of the Kingdom of the Scots*, 165–210.

[4] Bannerman, 'The King's poet and the inauguration of Alexander III', 127–30; Duncan, *Making of the Kingdom*, 526, 552–8.

northern France, which had connections with the Scottish royal house going back a century. The foundation of Arbroath Abbey was the latest evidence of the crown's enthusiastic support for the monastic orders and for the reformed church. This alliance of church and crown had reshaped the ecclesiastical government and spiritual values of the kingdom in the preceding century. It gave the leaders of the Scottish church royal political support and financial backing, enhancing the status and wealth of both the secular church, the episcopate and parish clergy, and the monastic movement. It also worked to the advantage of the crown, sanctioning royal authority and, in the eyes of pious kings, safeguarding the spiritual well-being of the realm. The sponsorship of reform linked the kingdom's elites to the intellectual, spiritual and administrative values of the continent. Kings drew on the western church for political and administrative agents, and the royal government was staffed by trained, literate clerics from Scotland, England and beyond, like the Frenchman, William Malvoisin, bishop of St Andrews and a former royal chancellor, who officiated at Alexander's inauguration. Though older elements survived in the church, like the Culdee monks at Abernethy, they were overshadowed by new institutions, like Arbroath Abbey. Most of the revenues of the Abernethy community had been assigned to support this new royal foundation. It was the blessing and support of the reformed western church which the kings of Scots wanted, and it was the recognition by the Pope of a distinct Scottish province of this church during the decades before 1214 which gave an ecclesiastical element to the recognition of Scotland as a political and social unit.[5]

Yet, though the eyes of these recent kings were on the style, glamour and sacred power of this European church and its coronation rituals, in the manner of their inauguration they could not abandon tradition. To do so would have been dangerous and disruptive, raising doubts amongst many of their people about their legitimacy and authority. The provincial character of the kingdom and the roots of Scottish kingship still featured strongly in the role played by the earls who led Alexander to Scone and placed him on his throne. Across thirteenth-century Europe, such magnates acted as the recognised leaders of the community under their rulers, but these earls had a special significance. They were provincial rulers, the heads of earldoms like Fife, Strathearn, Atholl and Buchan which comprised a large proportion of the old Scottish realm. Their old Gaelic title of *Mormaer*, great steward, was still used and they were leaders in war and

---

[5] For the fullest discussion of the changes to the ecclesiastical structure of Scotland and the relations of twelfth-century church and crown, see Barrow, *The Kingdom of Scots*, chs 5, 6, 7, 8.

justice for the Gaelic-speaking communities of their provinces. Later writers even claimed for a group of seven earls the power to make kings, and the part played by this number of earls in Alexander's inauguration may have reflected some basis for these claims.

For all their established rights and power, the earls and the nobility were not unaffected by royal-inspired change. One of the seven earls in 1214 was William Comyn, a lord of Anglo-Norman descent who had acquired the earldom of Buchan by marriage to its heiress. Though the Comyns were unique in 1214, subsequent decades would see new families acquire the earldoms of Angus, Menteith, Atholl and Carrick as part of a wider process which had seen nobles and knights come from England and France to settle in Scotland during the previous century. While incoming lords had received great estates from the crown – like the first Robert Bruce who was given Annandale before 1124 – nobles of Anglo-French descent were also granted lands by earls, adding a new element to the society of many provinces. The settlement of these families was accompanied by the introduction and spread of the structures of land-holding, law and lordship with which they were familiar. These new values had an influence on the established relationship between the king and the earls. The earls around the young king in 1214 were both the heads of native provincial communities and tenants of the crown. They held their earldoms by ancient custom and as fiefs, recognised by the crown in return for loyalty and service. They were present at Scone to claim an ancestral role in the inauguration as well as to perform their duties to their new lord.[6]

The strength of Alexander's inheritance was based not on lands but on the guarantee of support he received from great men and from the structures of royal authority established by his predecessors. A month after the inauguration, with its stress on traditional elements in Scottish society, Alexander held a great court at Edinburgh. Such great courts were a gathering of the tenants-in-chief of the kingdom, the lords who held land directly from the crown. In 1214 these vassals attended court to renew the bond of loyalty and homage to their royal lord, swearing oaths of fealty to the king for their lands or fiefs. The new king also used the court to confirm the chief officers of his household and government, restoring his father's chancellor, chamberlain, constable and others to their positions. This ceremonial assumption of authority by the king before his great vassals had parallels across Europe. Great courts, *Haut Cour* or *Curia*

---

[6] For the aristocracy of twelfth and early thirteenth-century Scotland, see Barrow, *The Anglo-Norman Era in Scottish History*; Stringer, *Earl David of Huntingdon. A Study in Anglo-Scottish History*; Barrow, *The Kingdom of the Scots*, ch. 10.

Regis, provided the focus of realms which had been settled by French-speaking lords. In the decades before 1214, similar assemblies of nobles would have been held in Westminster and Dublin, Rouen and Paris, Palermo and Jerusalem. The title of 'chancellor' for the head of the royal writing office, 'chamberlain' for the king's chief financial official, and 'constable' for the leading officer in the king's army were used in royal and princely governments across Europe. External influence on the form and structure of government was not confined to the king's household. Alexander also inherited a system of local royal officials, the most impor-tant of whom bore the Old English title of 'sheriff'. During the previous century, the kings had established about twenty sheriffdoms, each headed by an appointed sheriff responsible for executing royal orders, adminis-tering local justice and raising men and money for the crown. By 1214 these agents were overseen by justiciars in a system borrowed directly from England by Alexander's three predecessors with the aim of increas-ing the reach and sophistication of their authority. This royal government and the political society it managed increasingly depended on the use of written documents. Royal orders were issued in the form of a system of standardised brieves, the revenues of the crown were accounted for in writing by the chamberlain and the sheriffs at the exchequer, litigants enshrined legal decisions in documents, and kings and their subjects pro-duced charters which formally recorded grants of lands and the services which went with them. King Alexander's charters were authenticated by the use of his great seal, which depicted the king in his two roles: as an enthroned lawgiver and judge, and as a knight wielding a sword in defence of his people. This seal was carried by the chancellor (or his deputy) as the king's chief clerk. While such documents were produced by a small, and largely clerical, literate class, they were recognised and understood by a much larger section of secular society, and it was increasingly common for lords and knights to possess their own seals.[7]

In the officers and administrative practices he inherited from his father, Alexander was not simply taking over a structure which had been imported by twelfth-century kings. Instead, as with so many elements of the kingdom, Scotland's government represented a merging of new with old. Though the language of government had changed and its sophisti-cation had increased, administrative kingship was not introduced to Scotland with Anglo-Norman institutions. Kingly power also rested on customary obligations which went back centuries. The most important element of this was the network of thanages, royal estates with a respon-

[7] *Scotichronicon*, v, 80–1; Barrow, *The Kingdom of Scots*, ch. 3; Duncan, *Making of the Kingdom*, 159–70, 204–11.

sibility to provide the king with supplies of food and with revenues to support him and his household. It is probable that the thanage at Scone and the cluster of other local estates supplied the food for the feasting after Alexander's inauguration. Though, like many of the crown's estates, part of the thanage of Scone had been used to endow religious foundations, Alexander and his son could still draw significant resources from his thanages. The income from these estates was testament to the well-established strength of the Scottish kings in the heartlands of the old kingdom between the Forth and Moray Firth. Despite the major changes which had occurred since 1100, the geographical base of Scottish kingship remained much the same as it had been four centuries earlier. As the continued significance of Scone illustrated, the heart of this realm was in the valleys of the Tay and the Forth.[8]

Above all, the king's inauguration in December 1214 and the great court which followed the next month were the means by which royal lordship was renewed. Like all medieval monarchs, Alexander II's authority was exercised through a series of personal relationships between the king and his chief subjects. The formal terms of these relationships were expressed in the mutual oaths taken by ruler and ruled at the opening of the reign. Royal government provided the framework by which these personal bonds could be maintained in the absence of the king. In Scotland, more than in most thirteenth-century kingdoms, the lordship exercised by the royal dynasty over several generations had been responsible for forming the group which attended Alexander's court. The bishops and abbots, earls and barons, men and women who were present were bound together through common allegiance to Alexander as their lord. But in origin and in outlook, they otherwise remained a diverse group. Even the king's officers confirmed this. The chancellor, William de Bois, was a typical cleric seeking advancement in royal service and joining the king's chapel in the 1190s. The chamberlain, Philip de Valognes, was a younger son from a Norman family with lands and connections across Anglo-French society. He had come north to Scotland in search of land and status and, like other landless younger sons, had won both by serving the kings of Scots. By 1214 he had spent decades in this service. The constable came from a very different background. Alan fitz Roland, lord of Galloway was the ruler of a great province in the south-west. In the previous century Alan's ancestor, Fergus, had been king of Galloway and a rival of the kings of Scots for regional authority. Alan remained a powerful lord, leading fleets and armies beyond the Irish Sea in pursuit of new lands and influence and entering the service of King John of England in

[8] Barrow, *Kingdom of Scots*, ch. 1; Grant, 'Thanes and thanages, 39–81.

the hope of reward. However, despite such ambitions, Alan was an officer and vassal of the Scottish crown and recognised his obligations to King Alexander. While his father's ancestors were powerful princes, his mother's family were loyal vassals and constables of the crown. Alan represented two different aristocratic traditions, and even Galloway had changed from a sub-kingdom into a province of the Scottish realm. What linked Alan with de Valognes was service to the king. To be a royal officer was a mark of pride and status in Scotland, and hereditary officials, like Walter fitz Alan, the high Steward, and Thomas of Lundie, the king's doorward, adopted their ranks of 'Stewart' and 'Durward' as family names. The Stewarts, south-western magnates of Breton descent, and the Durwards, a native family from Angus, identified themselves in terms of their links of service to the crown and their possession of lands and lordships held as royal fiefs.[9]

All the achievements of Alexander's three predecessors as kings of Scots rested on the formation of a single political hierarchy in their realm, with the king at its head. Royal lordship, patronage and government were directed towards the merging of native and new noble lineages and ecclesiastics into a common elite, united by their recognition of the king's authority. In much of eastern and southern Scotland, this process was well advanced by 1214 and extended beyond these elites to the wider population. During the previous century new non-noble settlers had come to Scotland. Most obviously, but not exclusively, they settled in new urban centres, of which the English name of burghs was an indication of the language of the bulk of their populations. By 1214 there were thirty-eight burghs, founded by the king or his chief vassals. The burghs brought new wealth and skills, economic development and extended networks of trade to eastern and southern Scotland. These changes were symbolised by the bridge over the Tay which Alexander crossed en route for Scone in 1214, but which had been built to connect the market and merchants of nearby Perth to their hinterland. As centres of trade and manufacture, and as centres of English-speaking populations, the burghs north of the Forth had a major economic and cultural impact on the Gaelic-speaking communities around them. The process by which the Scots form of English replaced Gaelic in the coastlands and valleys from the Forth to the Ness began with the foundation of the burghs. Similar English and Flemish settlement had taken place in Wales and Ireland during the twelfth

---

[9] For Alan of Galloway and his province, see Stringer, 'Periphery and core in thirteenth-century Scotland', 82–112; Stringer, 'Reform monasticism and Celtic Scotland, 127–65. For de Valognes, see Barrow, *The Anglo-Norman Era in Scottish History*, 23–4.

century. In these lands the settlers, urban and rural, had been accorded a distinct and superior legal status, raising them above the native population. The distinctions between native and newcomer were sponsored and maintained by elites which were exclusively Anglo-French in character. Scotland was different. Whilst King William was said by one English chronicler to prefer men of the French language to native Scots, the former enjoyed no superior status in law. Scotland's recent rulers identified with the values of European kingship, religion and aristocracy and encouraged their nobility to do likewise. However, their aim was not the systematic eradication or relegation of native practice, but, rather, the extension of their own royal lordship, allying new structures and adherents to traditional sources of support. Native Scots continued to attain bishoprics and to serve in numbers as royal officers, while the distinction between second-generation noble settler and native lord was blurred by intermarriage and influence. The arrival of new English, French, Flemish and Breton settlers in the century before 1214 brought not a disruptive additional element into the realm, but personnel, ideas and technologies which enabled the royal house to realise their claims to effective lordship across the kingdom.[10]

Alexander's inauguration and his formal assumption of power displayed the success of this royal lordship. The succession of the young king continued the line of David I's descendants and was a central part of the dynasty's achievement. The smooth succession of David I and his two grandsons to the royal title broke with a past dominated by internecine wars and provided the continuity of leadership which lay beneath the wide recognition and support for their rule. Yet, despite this recent past, the speed of Alexander's inauguration, a day after his father's death, showed that the succession of a new king was a moment of anxiety for many in his realm. Alexander was the first king of Scots to inherit the throne from his father for centuries and his acceptance as king was neither as widespread nor as automatic as the titles and ceremonies of Scottish kingship would suggest. For all the achievements of David I and his heirs, there remained a gap between the claims of the kings of his line to rule throughout northern Britain and the reality of their power.

In 1214 it was not hard to find lords who denied Alexander's lordship or even challenged his right to the throne. The news of King William's death reignited a dynastic challenge to David's line from the house of MacWilliam. Descended from David I's half-brother, Duncan II, who

---

[10] For settlement and identity in twelfth-century Scotland within a wider perspective, see Bartlett, *The Making of Europe, Conquest, Colonization and Cultural Change 950–1350*, 53–4, 83–4, 113–14; Davies, *Domination and Conquest*, 13–15.

had been king for a few months in 1094, the MacWilliams possessed a pedigree to match Alexander's. Donal MacWilliam had claimed the kingship in the 1180s and, though he was killed in 1187, his sons, Godfraid and Donal Ban, returned from exile to renew their challenge in 1211. Repeated royal campaigns led to Godfraid's capture in 1212. He was dragged before young prince Alexander and executed, but Donal Ban remained at liberty and in 1215 stood as a rival to the young king. The claims of the MacWilliams were not empty words. Many Scots recognised them as legitimate claimants to the kingship, and in the 1180s and 1210s they found support and allies across the north and west. By supporting the MacWilliams, lords from these lands questioned the rights, status and legitimacy of the newly-enthroned king and, in early 1215, they joined Donal Ban in fresh warfare against Alexander's supporters.[11]

Like others before them, the MacWilliams were the focus of continuing antipathy towards royal lordship and the forces associated with it. For the new king, war in the north demonstrated that, despite his father's efforts, Caithness, Ross and Argyll had been largely untouched by the lordship of his dynasty and the work of previous kings to build an identity which focused on their primacy and transcended provincial allegiances. While the kings could find allies in the north and west who recognised the advantages of royal rule, localised warfare in these regions had been a feature of King William's reign and would continue for much of Alexander's. Even away from these lands of war, there were many lordships – both where royal primacy had been long accepted, like the earldoms north of Forth, or more recently imposed, as in Galloway – which came only indirectly under Alexander's authority and government. The king's rule was exerted through the earl or lord and local laws and customs were maintained. Although the twelfth-century kings had done much to make Scotland a single realm, the practice of kingship continued to reflect the varied traditions of its different provinces and regions.[12]

In truth, Alexander was not the only king in the northern British Isles. Beyond the western shores were kings in the Hebrides and on Man, as well as many kings in Gaelic Ireland. As Alexander's inauguration showed, Scottish kingship shared many characteristics with the practices of these Gaelic rulers, but by 1214 there was a major difference in status. The power and resources of the kings of Scots and their adoption of the image and practices of European monarchy allowed them greater rank

---

[11] Anderson, *Early Sources*, ii, 404; Anderson, *Scottish Annals*, 330–1; *Scotichronicon*, iv, 465–7; *Chron. Fordun*, ii, 274–8.
[12] McDonald, 'Rebels without a cause', 166–86; Grant, 'The province of Ross and the kingdom of Alba', Oram, 'Fergus, Galloway and the Scots', 117–30.

and recognition than other rulers in the region. While native rulers in Ireland and the Isles became under-kings or *reguli*, the kings of Scots were acknowledged as full royalty, the equal of their neighbours, the king of Norway (nominal overlord of the Hebrides) and the king of England. For all their achievements in their realm, in the eyes of the wider world the status of the kings of Scots was formed by their relations with the English kings and, in particular, the dispute over the claims of the Norman and Plantagenet rulers of England to be the superior lords of the Scottish kingdom. Such rights would have allowed their interference in Scotland and would have made the kings of Scots vassal rulers like the Welsh princes. In the decades before 1214, the Scottish kings had denied this overlordship with general success. Only once had King William recognised this claim. In 1174, as a captive, he had been compelled to accept that he held Scotland as vassal of Henry II, king of England, in the treaty of Falaise. Fifteen years later William had purchased his release from the treaty in an agreement, the Quitclaim of Canterbury, which returned affairs to the pre-1174 status quo. Though this did not mean that England's rulers had abandoned their claims, the issue of overlordship was not pressed by Henry II or Richard I, whose concerns centred on their lands in France. Instead the superiority of the king of England over the Scottish kings was limited to the estates which the latter held in the English realm. The most important of these was the earldom of Huntingdon, which was held by William's brother, David. While these estates formed a bond of lordship between kings and kingdoms, Alexander II also inherited a claim to hold the three northern counties of England. This had obsessed William and led to considerable problems for his kingdom in the form of a disastrous war in 1173–4 and ill-judged diplomacy in the 1190s and 1200s. For good or ill, Alexander, like all rulers in the British Isles, was part of a common world which was headed by the Plantagenet kings of England and lords of Ireland. The arrival of Anglo-French barons and knights in Scotland from the 1120s onwards meant that, from Alexander downwards, the Scottish political class had manifold landed and personal bonds with the Plantagenet dominions. William's recent diplomacy and King John of England's ambitions in Ireland had increased these ties and, as the events of the coming months would prove, meant that the new king of Scots and his realm were a part of a political and cultural world that did not stop at the Tweed but stretched to the Channel and well beyond.[13]

As the new king of Scots, Alexander II was the clearest representation

[13] Duncan, *Making of the Kingdom*, 228–55; Duncan, 'John King of England and the kings of Scots', 247–71.

of his realm. Though the Scots were known in Europe for their distinctive dress and speech, and Scotland stood as a province of the western church, it was the personal freedom of the kings of Scots from the overlordship of the Plantagenet king which ensured Scotland recognition as a separate and distinct political unit in the British Isles. However, Scotland in 1214 was not a closed or fully-defined community of uniform allegiance and structure. The royal lordship which had done much to forge the kingdom did not extend across Scotland and, where it was accepted, it took very different forms, while the contacts between the kingdom's elites and the lands and realms which surrounded it created overlaps between the interests and activities of the Scottish king and those of neighbouring rulers. Over the seven decades from 1214, Scotland's kings, Alexander II and then his son, Alexander III, would continue to define their realm and lordship, closing the gap between their dynasty's claims to dominion across the northern British Isles and the reality of that dominion.

CHAPTER 2

Alexander II

THE FOX CUB

The new king of Scots in 1214 was a red-haired youth of sixteen years. Even in an age when adulthood began early, Alexander was young to rule. However, there was no question of a regency government being established. In expectation of the death of the elderly and infirm King William, Alexander had been rapidly schooled in his future office. The young prince had been involved in the decisions of the royal council, and in 1212 he had gone to London to meet with King John of England, receiving a knighthood from him. In the same year he presided over the execution of Godfraid MacWilliam. The roles played by Alexander as king would relate closely to these areas of activity. He would not act alone. The officers Alexander confirmed in early 1215 and the councillors who advised the king during the opening years of the reign were men with long experience in King William's government. Surrounded by this establishment, the new ruler responded to the challenges and opportunities which confronted his kingship. These problems and Alexander's reactions were shaped by the legacy of his father's long reign.

Challenges and opportunities were not slow to materialise. Word of renewed war in the north must have reached court during the early months of 1215, but over the next three years it was the news from England that dominated the activities of the young king and his advisors. The news from England was bad for its king, John. Defeat in France in the autumn of 1214 had spawned a winter of discontent for the king and his rebellious English barons.[1] The young Scottish king was urged to exploit this situation to extract himself from the position bequeathed him

---

[1] For the civil war in England see Holt, *The Northerners*; Warren, *King John*, 224–59; Carpenter, *The Minority of Henry III*, 1–44.

by his father. In his last years, William's misplaced faith in John's promises had seen him follow the rest of the rulers of the British Isles into the king of England's orbit. In 1209 and 1212 William had surrendered money, hostages and even his daughters in return for hopes of recovering England's northern shires and securing a series of marriage alliances between the two royal dynasties. Meanwhile, King John had forged his own connections with the powerful lords of Galloway and Carrick in south-west Scotland, using their military resources against his enemies in Wales, France and Ireland. When John received the homage of Alexander for his father's English lands, knighted him and sent him home with a force of Brabantine mercenaries to aid William's struggle with his Scottish enemies, the message was clear: though Scotland was formally outside John's lordship, its rulers were within his orbit.[2]

For John and his baronial opponents, the winter of 1214–15 was a period of intense activity. The north of England had long been the focus of dissent and, inevitably, Alexander of Scotland was drawn into this crisis. As lord of Tynedale, he was himself a northern baron, and many leading men in the region were also his vassals in Scotland. When these men came to Alexander's court in early 1215, they were not approaching a foreign king, but were counselling their lord, renewing homage and lobbying at the same time. John's enemies, led by Alexander's brother-in-law, Eustace de Vesci, lord of Alnwick in Northumberland and Sprouston in Teviotdale, were pressing for Scottish military support. Meanwhile, John's friends, including the constable of Scotland, Alan of Galloway, urged Alexander to seek his rights to land and marriages through negotiation. Alexander chose the latter course. When John issued Magna Carta in June 1215, the inclusion of a promise to answer Alexander's grievances indicated the prominence of the Scottish king's vassals at Runnymede, both with John and amongst his enemies.[3]

John's repudiation of Magna Carta forced Alexander's hand. By the autumn of 1215, civil war had resumed in England and the leading northern rebels, de Vesci and another of Alexander's brothers-in-law, Robert de Ros, appealed to him for aid. Alexander was now free from the attacks of Scottish enemies and in mid-October he crossed the Tweed and laid siege to Norham Castle. His intervention brought rapid political gains. The baronial council judged Alexander to be rightful lord of

[2] Anderson, *Scottish Annals*, 328–31; Anderson, *Early Sources*, ii, 372–3; Duncan, *Making of the kingdom*, 241–55; Stringer, 'Periphery and core', 85–8; Greeves, 'The Galloway lands in Ulster', 115–21; Duncan, 'John King of England and the Kings of Scots'.

[3] Holt, *The Northerners*, 63, 66, 125; Stringer, 'Periphery and core', 88–9; *C.D.S.*, i, no. 629.

Northumberland, Cumberland and Westmorland. On 22 October he was invested with them by de Vesci and received the homage of the rebel barons of Northumberland. Carlisle was also ordered to surrender and Alexander was promised payment for his help. But the king's military achievements were less impressive. The siege of Norham proved fruitless and in January 1216 Alexander and his allies faced John's counter-attack. Vowing to drive the 'fox cub' back to his lair, John launched a brutally effective campaign against northern England and Lothian, burning four Scottish burghs and retaking Carlisle and other rebel strongholds. It was only after John returned south that Alexander left his lair again, encouraged by the arrival in Kent of a new leader, Louis, son of King Philip of France. Louis now claimed John's throne and in September, after recovering Carlisle, the Scottish king and the leading northerners travelled south to meet the prince at Dover. At their meeting, Alexander did homage to Louis for the three shires of northern England.[4]

Ironically, the chances of Alexander retaining these lands were dealt a blow by the death of King John in October 1216. The cause of John's son, the nine-year-old Henry III, was much more attractive to the English community than that of his distrusted and discredited father. The defeat of a French and baronial force at Lincoln in May 1217 began the decline of Louis' fortunes, and in September the French prince made peace and left for home. Alexander, who had established effective lordship over Cumberland, was still struggling to secure Northumberland when he heard the news. The peace would include Alexander and another of Louis' allies, Llywelyn ap Iorwerth of Gwynedd, the leading Welsh prince, if they abandoned their war gains. While Llywelyn held out successfully, Alexander sought peace. By December he had surrendered Carlisle and at Christmas entered 'the faith and service' of the English king at Northampton.[5]

While Alexander had failed to achieve his war aims, he had at least avoided a second attack on southern Scotland, and his efforts since 1215 may have earned the respect of Henry III and his ministers, who were keen for peace. However, full normality was not immediately re-established. Henry's government had received the full backing of the Papacy in the recent war and Alexander and his subjects were excommunicated and Scotland placed under an interdict, suspending the powers of the Scottish church. This penalty was not lifted fully until late 1218 and the papacy

---

[4] *A.P.S.*, i, 108, 111–12; Anderson, *Early Sources*, ii, 406–9; Anderson, *Scottish Annals*, 332–4.
[5] Carpenter, *The Minority of Henry III*, 13–49, 68–9; Stringer, 'Periphery and core', 90–2; *C.D.S.*, i, nos 674, 686; Davies, *The Age of Conquest*, 241–4.

continued to support the English view of issues between the two realms. The second problem facing Alexander and his adherents was the recovery of the estates they held from the English king. While Alexander and many lords were quickly restored, some waited years to receive their lands. Cross-border links had drawn Alexander into war in 1215, but the difficult experience of lords with lands in both realms during the conflict probably encouraged them to work against renewed warfare. By 1220 this was also the attitude of the English government, even against the wishes of powerful magnates. William Marshal, earl of Pembroke was forced to abandon lands in the honour of Huntingdon, granted to his family during the war, so that they could be restored to their overlord, the Scottish king. The restoration was part of sustained bargaining between the two governments, beginning in 1219 at the instigation of the papal legate, Pandulph, and culminating in an agreement at York in August 1220. It was to meet the terms of this that Marshal was dispossessed and, at some cost, Henry III's sister, Joan, was recovered from her intended husband. In June 1221 Alexander II married Joan of England at York.[6]

Alexander's marriage encouraged him to seek his other goals peacefully. He renewed his claims to the northern counties and received promises about the marriage of his sisters. Though a marriage between Alexander's eldest sister, Margaret, and William Marshal was rejected – ostensibly because of fears about an alliance between the Scottish king and the greatest English lord in Wales and Ireland – Margaret was married in October. Her husband, Hubert de Burgh, earl of Kent, was of lesser status than Marshal, but was effective head of the English government. The friendship between the brothers-in-law determined Alexander's attitude to this government for the next decade. Between 1223 and 1225, when de Burgh and his allies were at odds with a coalition which included Llywelyn of Gwynedd, the earl of Chester and the claimant to Ulster, Hugh de Lacy, Alexander offered aid to de Burgh in Ireland. His involvement in this conflict was not detached. Hubert's enemy, Ranulph, earl of Chester, was uncle and guardian of John of Scotland. Since the death of his father, Earl David of Huntingdon in 1219, John had been the obvious heir to his cousin, King Alexander. Chester married John to a daughter of Llywelyn of Gwynedd, placing him at the centre of the party opposed to de Burgh. Alexander, who was to remain childless for another fifteen years, may have sensed a challenge. The formal investiture of John with his earldom of Huntingdon, which

<hr />

[6] *Chron. Fordun*, ii, 283–4; Anderson, *Early Sources*, ii, 431–35; *C.D.S.*, i, nos 702–3, 717–18, 722–3, 739–40, 746, 749, 754–5, 758, 760–2, 801–2, 808, 811, 874; Carpenter, *The Minority of Henry III*, 165, 194, 211, 219.

Alexander carried out with great ceremony in 1227, was probably meant to illustrate the renewed unity of the royal house. However, even after this, the Scottish king remained at odds with Ranulph of Chester.[7]

Alexander also demonstrated his support for de Burgh in 1230, when the king levied taxation from Scotland to help finance the expedition which Henry III led to Poitou to try to recover the province from the French king. Though it was agreed that this formed no precedent, it indicated the willingness of Alexander to aid his two brothers-in-law. Alexander's generosity may have been prompted by hopes of a marriage between his younger sister, Margaret, and King Henry. The match was the work of de Burgh who wanted Henry as his brother-in-law. It aroused the hostility of other magnates who saw a second alliance with the Scottish dynasty as serving no purpose beyond de Burgh's advancement. It intensified suspicions of Hubert and led to his downfall in 1232.[8]

The rejection of his sister and the fall of his friend stung Alexander into an increasingly pugnacious attitude to the English king. By 1233 he was lobbying the papacy for the right to a full coronation, while English defensive preparations in the north suggested Henry's growing anxiety. Alexander had allies amongst the English king's other vassals. In the winter of 1233–4, Richard Marshal, earl of Pembroke and lord of Leinster, waged open war against his king in Wales and Ireland. He had the open support of Llywelyn of Gwynedd and now formed a confederation with Alexander. Though the Scottish king's plans were frustrated by Marshal's death in a skirmish with royal forces in Ireland in 1234, Alexander gave refuge to Richard's supporters, allowing them to use his realm as a base for piracy in the Irish Sea. The marriage between Richard Marshal's brother and recently-pardoned successor, Gilbert, and Alexander's sister, Margaret, in August 1235 may have had Henry's permission, but must have reminded him of the earlier confederation. In 1236 Alexander used the match and the threat of an alliance with Llywelyn of Gwynedd to put pressure on the English king.[9]

Despite such threats, by 1236 Alexander recognised that none of his efforts had secured him his claims in northern England. His readiness to negotiate was probably not increased by strident papal letters ordering him to obey his rightful lord, the king of England, but in meetings at Newcastle in 1236 and then in the presence of a papal legate at York in

[7] Carpenter, *The Minority of Henry III*, 245, 260, 343–58; Frame, *Ireland and Britain, 1170–1450*, 36–7, 158–60; Anderson, *Early Sources*, ii, 462; *C.D.S.*, i, no. 975.

[8] *C.D.S.*, i, nos 1,086, 1,113; Vincent, *Peter des Roches*, 268–80, 301–2. Alexander's third sister, Isabella, married Hugh Bigod, earl of Norfolk in 1225 (*C.D.S.*, i, no. 906).

[9] *C.D.S.*, i, nos 1,181, 1,335; Vincent, *Peter des Roches*, 371, 417–18, 438–40; *A.P.S.*, i, 108; Anderson, *Scottish Annals*, 343; Anderson, *Early Sources*, ii, 498–9.

September 1237 agreement was reached. The treaty of York dealt with the territorial relationship between the English and Scottish kings. It did not mention Scotland itself. Instead, Alexander finally abandoned the claim to Northumberland, Cumberland and Westmorland and in return was promised estates in these counties to add to the lordship of Tynedale. The death of John of Scotland earlier in the year meant his earldom of Huntingdon, the traditional landed link between the two kings, was divided between John's sisters and their husbands, becoming less significant and identifiable. Alexander's new lands, which came from the barony of Penrith, renewed the landholding connection and Alexander rendered homage for them to Henry. The Scottish king had surrendered wide claims which he had been unable to enforce, in return for secure possession of lesser lands in the same region. The agreement removed the basis of friction between the two kings and was welcome to the numerous magnates present who recognised both Henry and Alexander as their lords.[10] The improved relationship between the kings survived the death of Queen Joan in 1238 and Alexander's marriage the following year to a French noblewoman, Marie de Couci. In 1242, before he led another expedition to France in pursuit of his lost lands there, Henry sought to renew his kinship with Alexander through the betrothal of his daughter, Margaret, to Alexander's new-born son. Moreover, during his absence, Henry entrusted to Alexander's keeping the same northern counties which the Scottish king had tried so hard to secure.[11]

For twenty years, the issue between the English and Scottish kings had been not the status of Scotland, but Alexander's rights and place as the English king's vassal. Yet the relationship between the two rulers was always coloured by Alexander's kingship and kingdom. The years of tension with the Plantagenets from 1215 also witnessed the rapid extension of the Scottish king's authority in the provinces of his realm which lay furthest from the traditional centres of his family's power. Especially in the north, the young king's inheritance from his father mixed increased royal strength with continued hostility to the crown. King William's wars in the northern provinces of Ross, Moray and Caithness forced submissions and won allies, but animosities persisted. The house of MacWilliam remained at the heart of this hostility. The old king's death in December 1214 had been the spur for renewed warfare. Backed by men from Ross and allies from Ireland and the Isles, Donal Ban MacWilliam raided into

[10] Stones, *Anglo-Scottish Relations*, nos 6, 7; Anderson, *Early Sources*, ii, 501–5; Anderson, *Scottish Annals*, 343–5; *C.D.S.*, i, nos 1,325, 1,329, 1,358, 1,575; Stringer, *Earl David*, 182–9.

[11] Anderson, *Early Sources*, ii, 510, 514; Anderson, *Scottish Annals*, 345, 348–9.

John of Scotland and the Royal Succession

In June 1237, as preparations were laid for the meeting of the kings at York, John of Scotland, earl of Huntingdon died aged thirty-one. Since 1219, John had been King Alexander's closest kinsman. Had Alexander died during the 1230s, the Scottish throne would have passed to his cousin. Rather than the limiting of Scottish interests in England which occurred at York, John's succession would have linked the kingdom to a massive English inheritance, including the earldoms of Chester and Huntingdon. John's death meant not just the partition of this inheritance but also raised questions about the Scottish succession. When Queen Joan died in March 1238, King Alexander was left as a childless widower of nearly forty. As well as seeking a new bride, Alexander may have designated an heir. John's eldest nephew, Robert Bruce of Annandale, later claimed that he had been named by Alexander as heir to the throne if the king died childless. Though the birth of a prince in 1241 calmed such worries, John's death meant that, if the royal line failed, Scotland's king would be found from the offspring of his sisters, amongst them the houses of Bruce and Balliol.

Moray. As in previous campaigns, the king's host found it difficult to defeat an elusive enemy who ambushed their forces and raided crown lands, and it was not a royal force but a rival magnate from Ross, Ferchar mac an t-Sagairt, who defeated Donal Ban in June 1215. Ferchar sent the heads of his enemies to a grateful king.[12] Even this defeat did not end conflict. Sporadic clashes continued in Moray until 1230, but even in 1214 the power of the crown in the north was beyond the reach of its enemies. From Ness to Spey, the coastlands were run by royal sheriffs at Inverness and Nairn, and later at Forres and Elgin, peopled with burghs and guarded by a string of royal castles which stretched to the Cromarty Firth. Though they captured an exposed castle in 1212, the MacWilliams could do no more than raid lands so fully integrated into the king's realm. In these districts the king could also rely on the support of local lords, the chief of whom, descended from David I's Flemish mercenary captain, had taken the name of Murray. By 1214 this Murray kindred provided the king with knights and churchmen: the two bishops of Moray between 1203 and 1242 were members of the family and worked closely with their royal lord.[13]

---

[12] Anderson, *Early Sources*, ii, 404; Anderson, *Scottish Annals*, 330–1; *Scotichronicon*, iv, 465–7; *Chron. Fordun*, ii, 274, 278.
[13] *Scotichronicon*, iv, 467.

The warfare between 1211 and 1215 convinced the kings of the need for a secure hold on the mountainous interior of Moray. Rather than seeking to establish sheriffs over this region, first William and then Alexander acted to bind the men of Moray into their lordship by entrusting the lands to a group of their supporters. With the aid of the bishop, this process was underway in eastern Moray before 1211, but rapid change followed the defeat of the MacWilliams in 1215. While some of those who 'stood with MacWilliam' were formally received into the kings' peace, many lords from the region must have been killed or dispossessed. The new lords were king's men from the east and south, most of whom had served in the recent fighting. In Strathspey the comital families of Fife and Strathearn, and the sons of the former earl of nearby Mar, received lands, but the more exposed districts further west went to men of lesser descent but no less ambition. On the shores of Loch Ness, Thomas of Lundie, the king's Durward, became lord of Urquhart, and Thomas of Thirlestane was granted Abertarff, while the brothers John and Walter Bisset received estates which guarded the southern and western approaches of Inverness. These grants followed a pattern established in previous reigns. The king's charter was often merely a licence for the new lord to occupy his lands, throw up a castle – like those quickly found at Urquhart, Strathbogie and Abertarff – and impose his authority. Alexander relied on his vassals to police their lands and guard the routes down the valleys into the lowlands, without expending royal resources.[14]

This approach was not guaranteed to win the love of these upland lordships. Outbreaks of unrest continued through the 1220s, culminating in 1228 in the burning of the castle at Abertarff and the killing of Thomas of Thirlestane, whose rule may have been especially harsh. Thomas's killer, Gilleasbuig, claimed kinship with the MacWilliams and attracted allies from across the north. The king responded to the renewed challenge by rushing to Moray in person. When Gilleasbuig and his sons were killed in 1229, Alexander set about eliminating the MacWilliams, executing all of the kindred, down to a baby girl, who fell into his hands. With the end of the MacWilliams came the rise of the Comyns. William Comyn had been the crown's workhorse in the north for two decades, acting as justiciar of Scotia and warden of Moray and capturing both Godfraid and Gilleasbuig MacWilliam. Royal favour lay behind William's marriage to the heiress of Buchan in 1212, but after his new success he received fitting reward. In about 1230 King Alexander granted William's son, Walter, the lordship of Badenoch, a massive fief which stretched from Lochaber to the upper valley of the Spey, spanning the key routes from both west and south into Moray. The strategic heart of the province had been entrusted to a single lord and the division of Moray between the crown and its noble adherents had been completed.[15]

To the north of Moray lay the province of Ross and the mainland possessions of the Norse earl of Orkney, Caithness and Sutherland. Though King William had led an army as far as Thurso, he was unable or unwilling to establish a royal presence in the far north. Alexander followed this approach, leaving the region to his allies, the Murrays and Ferchar mac an t-Sagairt. Ferchar was a lord from eastern Ross whose defeat of MacWilliam in 1215 won him a royal knighthood, signifying his importance to the crown in Ross. In the mid-1220s he had received his ultimate reward, the rank of earl of Ross. By the end of the decade he was seeking to establish his lordship in the west of his province. Though outsiders, the Murrays played a similar role further north and by the early 1220s William Murray was calling himself lord of Sutherland. The presence of these neighbours to the south was uncomfortable for Earl John of Orkney and Caithness, and he was further troubled by the demands of Adam, bishop of Caithness for the full rights of the church. Adam's murder by Earl John's tenants in 1222 brought the king north with an army. John was forced to submit, resign part of Caithness and surrender the bishop's killers for mutilation. However, Alexander's goals in the north remained limited and the following year he restored John's lands in return for a fine. More significant was the fact that whilst he was in Caithness, the king and his commanders had presided over the election of Gilbert Murray, a cousin and tenant of the lord of Sutherland, as the new bishop. The centre of the diocese was moved south from Halkirk, a few miles from the earl's stronghold at Thurso, to Dornoch near Gilbert's own lands. When Earl John's own murder in 1231 precipitated a succession crisis in Orkney, Alexander was again happy to see the Murrays benefit by the acquisition of Strathnaver. Orkney and Caithness passed to the earls of Angus and when Alexander created William Murray earl of Sutherland in 1235, it meant that although the crown had no landed stake in the region, the far north was now in the hands of magnates who readily recognised Alexander as their lord.[16]

[15] *Scotichronicon*, v, 117, 143–5; Anderson, *Early Sources*, ii, 471; Young, *Robert the Bruce's Rivals: The Comyns, 1212–1314*, 22–8; Barrow, 'Badenoch and Strathspey, I', 5; *Moray Reg.*, nos 76, 86.

[16] Grant, 'The province of Ross and the kingdom of Alba', 88–126; Crawford, 'The earldom of Caithness and the kingdom of Scotland, 1150–1266', 25–43; *Moray Reg.*, nos 1, 3, 87; *R.M.S.*, i, app. 2, no. 1.

The creation of the lordship of Badenoch in 1230 ended the period of Alexander's major interest in the north. The change was signalled in early 1231 when the king removed the justiciarship of Scotia from the elderly earl of Buchan and gave it to Walter the Steward. Despite its hereditary role, the house of Stewart built its power on the frontiers of royal lordship. Lords of Renfrew and Kyle, the Stewarts had established their hold on the islands in the Clyde by 1200 and by the 1220s Walter was looking to the far shore. Alliances were formed with earls Duncan (Donnchad) of Carrick, Maldouen (Maeldomhnaich) of Lennox and the latter's brother, Aulay, the chief lord of the lands round Loch Long, magnates whose support would help the extension of Stewart's lordship into Cowal, the eastern part of Argyll. Stewart was not the only great lord to look west in the 1220s. Alan, lord of Galloway was a man of ambitions which stretched from north Wales to Lewis. Though he lacked the royal title of his Galwegian forebears, Alan had added the wealth of two major Scottish lordships to the warriors and longships of his native province, while his brother, Thomas, had secured the earldom of Atholl by marriage. The two brothers used these Scottish resources to win power across the Irish Sea.[17]

While both Alan and Stewart were careful to avoid any challenge to their royal lord, Alexander was sensitive to their activities. Argyll was a province where links to the Scottish realm were countered by the interests of the rulers of the Isles. The brief royal campaign to Argyll in 1221, in which Alexander and his army had a rendezvous with a Galwegian fleet, may have been designed to extract formal recognition of the king's lordship from local magnates. However, during the 1220s Stewart's involvement in Cowal and Alan's more overt activities in the Isles brought the Scottish king's vassals into conflict with men whose principal lord was King Hakon of Norway. The consequence of this became clear in the spring of 1230 when a Norse fleet sailed into the Clyde, landed on Bute and stormed the Stewart's castle of Rothesay. The king rushed to Ayr where he found Alan of Galloway ready to lead his longships to sea, but the meeting between them was probably tense. While Stewart was given added powers as justiciar of Scotia in 1231, Alan's relationship with the king deteriorated. During the 1230s, as Stewart drew the men of Cowal into his following, the king established a base for royal authority at Dumbarton, appointing a sheriff and forcing the earl of Lennox to abandon his right to the castle rock.[18]

[17] Barrow, *Anglo-Norman Era*, 68–70; *Registrum Monasterii de Passelet* (Glasgow, 1832), 18–20, 132–3, 209, 212–13; Stringer, 'Periphery and core', 92–6.
[18] *Scotichronicon*, v, 105–07; Anderson, *Early Sources*, ii, 464–5, 471–8; Stringer, 'Periphery and core', 97.

By the mid-1230s many local communities in the west and north had been brought firmly into King Alexander's lordship. This extension of royal rule appears to be primarily the work of lords in his service rather than the king himself. The part played by Alexander was chiefly confined to moments of crisis. In Caithness in 1222, Moray in 1228 and on the shores of the Clyde in 1230, Alexander was quick to appear in person to confront his enemies. However, the king was also responsible for shaping political society in the borderlands of royal authority. Like his forebears, Alexander recognised that the delegation of powers in these borderlands was an essential part of his kingship, vital to reward service and maintain peace. The distribution of lordships amongst his supporters was designed to bolster his rule and varied according to region. In Ross and Sutherland, whole provinces were bestowed on individual magnates, while closer to his own estates, Alexander divided inland Moray between nine or more lords. Badenoch was by the far the biggest of these and the king took care to ensure that it was held by Walter Comyn rather than his half-brother, Alexander, who inherited the earldom of Buchan in 1233. Similarly, the power of the Murrays was divided amongst a large kindred and their ambitions were channelled not into the neighbouring areas of their home province, but north to Sutherland. The king distributed power amongst a group which included councillors like Durward, the Bissets, Comyns, and Stewart. Even a great provincial lord like Alan of Galloway had ties to the king's household and appeared at court. Yet, despite such connections, the power of these lords in the militarised societies of the north and west held potential dangers for the king. Alexander's different treatment of Stewart and Alan of Galloway after 1230 showed the delicate balance between effective marcher activity and dangerous empire-building. The ambition of great men could disrupt as well as enhance royal authority, and the ability to manage powerful magnates and maintain the crown's superiority was the key to medieval Scottish kingship.

ROYAL AUTHORITY AND POWER

For all his reliance on aristocratic support, Alexander II was the king and lord of his realm, and the activities of agents were designed to extend his rights. Though delegation of lordship characterised Scottish political society in the thirteenth century, the centre of government was the king himself, wherever he went. Like his father and son, Alexander II was a ceaseless traveller in his kingdom, matching the rulers of larger lands in the mobility of his household. For example, during 1236, a year without major crisis, the king's journeying took him from Roxburgh to St Andrews, where he spent Christmas as the bishop's guest, to Stirling, before he travelled south to Selkirk and Melrose Abbey. In April Alexander held court in Edinburgh Castle and through the summer undertook progresses to Ayr in the west, Forres and Inverness in the north and, finally, south through Tynedale to meet the English king at Newcastle. Alexander's visits to Ayrshire and Moray in the same summer were exceptional and the king was not often found west of Clydesdale or north of the Mounth. Instead he normally ruled his realm from the dales of Tweed and Teviot in the south, Lothian and the Forth valley, and from Perthshire, Angus and the lower shores of the Tay, moving between major royal castles, his lesser manors and the houses of monks and bishops. These areas were the heartlands of royal authority and royal resources, which provided the kings with the men and money to extend their lordship. Much of Alexander's government was concerned with the management of these regions: the collection of revenues and their dispersal, the issuing of royal instructions and land grants, the judgement of law and arbitration of disputes, all recorded by the staff of his increasingly sophisticated royal household.[19]

However, kingship was not about bureaucracy but personality. The king of Scots and his household clerks could not rule Scotland alone. In 1227 the preamble to one of Alexander's charters stated that he acted with 'royal authority and power' but also with 'the consent, testimony and acquiesence of my bishops, earls and barons'. This was no empty formula. Alexander needed the support of the great men of the kingdom to exercise effective authority. Such support depended on the king's inherited status and respect, but also on personal bonds of loyalty. Progressing through his kingdom allowed Alexander to maintain these contacts. When the king was at Selkirk in January 1236, he was attended by a group including six landowners from the surrounding district. These men were the leaders of the local community and were probably accompanied by lesser men. Such royal tenants were the backbone of royal authority. Amongst the southern knights at Selkirk, Alexander found sheriffs of Roxburgh, keepers of his castles and two royal chamberlains, all of them ready to serve a king they knew as their direct lord. In return, knights and barons like John Maxwell, Thomas Randolph and the Balliols of Cavers obtained lands and status for their efforts. It was a pattern repeated in Lothian and Angus and which did not simply revolve around formal

[19] For Alexander II's itinerary in 1236 and the location of his acts throughout the reign, see Scoular (ed.), *Handlist of the Acts of Alexander II*, 37–40; K. J. Stringer, 'Place-dates of royal charters to 1296: Alexander II (1214–49)' in McNeill and MacQueen, *Atlas of Scottish History to 1707*, 162.

government. Selkirk was on the edge of Ettrick Forest, one of the many royal hunting preserves. The lords present may have accompanied the king on the chase, mixing sport with politics, for the numerous royal documents issued from hunting lodges like Traquair in Tweeddale and Clunie in Perthshire show this was normal practice.[20]

The royal court could have a wider significance than as a meeting-place for the king and local communities. In early April 1236, whilst at Edinburgh, Alexander was accompanied by at least three bishops, five abbots, four earls and ten major barons. Such an assembly suggests that the king had called these lords together for a great court. Amongst other business enacted at this time, the king ratified an agreement settling a dispute between Roger Avenal, lord of Eskdale, and Melrose Abbey. The agreement had been reached the previous year in the presence of the king and his barons in what was called a *colloquium*. Literally, a *colloquium* has the same meaning as a parliament, a term which would appear in Scottish usage after 1286 and gradually assume a precise meaning as an assembly of the Scottish political class with specific powers. However, it is unlikely that in the 1230s assemblies with the title of *colloquia* had a formal composition or purpose, let alone a set function as a meeting of the community. Instead, if the *colloquium* had a specific role, it was probably as a royal court in which the king arbitrated between major vassals. All courts which included a significant proportion of the kingdom's leading lay and ecclesiastical lords represented the ideal of government, with the king seeking and receiving the advice of his 'natural councillors' and settling disputes, bestowing patronage, confirming landed rights and issuing statutes with their consent.[21]

However, none of these functions required the presence of large assemblies. Though, in 1244, the king issued new criminal procedures with the advice of twenty magnates, in 1230 he had made law in association with a much smaller council. Even during the large court which met in April 1236, the king was issuing documents which named only four men as present, suggesting business could be handled by a small group of advisors. Two of these councillors were Alexander's justiciars, Walter Stewart, whose authority covered Scotia, and Walter Olifard, justiciar of Lothian, the king's key legal and political deputies. These officers supervised royal justice by travelling themselves on circuits of sheriffdoms or justice ayres twice a year. The king's journeys to Ayr and Inverness in the

[20] *Liber Sancte Marie de Melrose*, 2 vols (Edinburgh, 1837), i, no. 264; *Registrum de Dunfermline* (Edinburgh, 1842), no. 74.
[21] *Melrose*, i, no. 198; *Facsimiles of the National Manuscripts of Scotland*, i, no. 48; Duncan, 'The early parliaments of Scotland', 36–58, 36–7.

'The Laws and Assizes of the Scottish Kingdom'

Across the realms of western Europe, the thirteenth century was an era of major importance for the development of legal structures. Scotland was not excluded from these changes and, by the latter part of the century, the kingdom was clearly regarded as having its own distinct and defined laws and customs. The records of the kings, itemised in 1291 and 1292, contained manuscript rolls listing 'the laws and assizes of the kingdom' and 'the statutes of King Malcolm and King David'. There was a clear understanding that, just as the political and governmental framework of the Scottish realm had been consolidated and extended by successive kings, so had the laws and legal practices of the kingdom. The maintenance of these laws and customs, as developed and acknowledged up to the late thirteenth century, formed a key part in concepts of Scottish identity and collective interests.

It is ironic therefore that the model for much of this legal structure was provided by English law. Key elements of English legal practice as it developed under the Normans and Angevins were introduced into Scotland by kings and officials well acquainted with the affairs of the neighbouring realm. The formation of a hierarchy of courts and the role of itinerant justiciars in supervising judicial activity in the locality were key features of English practice. So too was the use of juries of 'good and faithful' local men to judge land disputes and accuse criminals. Most striking was the adoption by Scottish kings of the system of standard royal brieves developed by Henry II of England, which facilitated the recovery of disputed land by a plaintiff.

Yet despite this influence, Scottish legal custom diverged from its principal model. No complex structure of central courts or professional lawyers developed after 1200, and Scotland retained its own traditions. The records of the crown reflected these. In the Leges Scocie, a collection from King William's time, chapters were devoted to the laws of Galloway and the code known as Leges inter Scottos et Brettos which specified compensation paid for homicide according to social class. These and other kin-based legal structures continued to exist alongside newer practices without open conflict, perhaps especially in the provinces of the west and north. This was not exceptional, and other special areas of justice continued to develop in the marches and in the Leges Burgorum. There were some isolated examples of tenants seeking English law rather than traditional custom, but the crown was, in general, prepared to see both old and new practices continue under their lordship.[22]

---

[22] MacQueen, 'Scots Law under Alexander III', 74–102.

summer of 1236 probably followed these circuits and Alexander was accompanied in each case by the appropriate justiciar. In normal circumstances the justiciars acted in place of the king, pursuing and judging criminals, hearing appeals from the sheriffs' courts and arbitrating in land cases. Though adopted from Norman England, the justiciarship had a Scottish character by the 1230s. While the kings of England and France headed increasingly complex and professional judiciaries staffed by trained lawyers, the Scottish king still relied on great magnates with wide regional powers as his principal judicial agents.[23]

The greatest issues to come before Alexander and his court concerned the earldoms north of Forth. Under King William the crown had been active in determining the possession of the ancient provinces between Forth and Moray. While William's judgements could appear arbitrary, after 1200 the law of succession became more fixed, relying on Anglo-French practice which favoured primogeniture, the right of the eldest son to succeed his father, and barred bastards. Should the direct male line fail, the claims of the male kin of the earl, strongest in traditional custom, were increasingly overridden by those of the earl's sisters or daughters. The marriage of these heiresses to husbands from outside the earldom became more common as the nobility of Scotland became more integrated under royal lordship. William Comyn's inheritance of Buchan by marriage in 1212 was the first of a growing number of cases where a lord of Anglo-French origin acquired an ancient earldom, though previous examples exist of earldoms passing to new lords of Scottish descent. This trend allowed the king, who possessed rights over the marriage of heiresses, to establish his supporters at the head of provincial communities.

However, in the earldoms of Menteith, Mar and Atholl, opportunities for royal patronage were linked to rivalries which tested Alexander's kingship. Even before he was king, Alexander was involved in settling the claims of two brothers to Menteith and ratifying the resignation of the earldom by the elder, possibly illegitimate brother, in favour of the younger. As king, Alexander chose husbands for heiresses who may have been the daughters of these two claimants: Isabella, the senior claimant, married Walter Comyn of Badenoch, while Mary wed Walter, younger son of Stewart. The king was providing heiresses for his supporters, but in doing so linked them into provincial rivalries with long-term significance. While Stewart inherited only minor lands, Comyn added an earldom to his great northern lordship. By the 1230s, the Comyns held

[23] *A.P.S.*, i, 401–3; *Moray Reg.*, charters no. 11; *R.M.S.*, ii, no. 804; *Cartulary of the Abbey of Lindores* (Edinburgh, 1803), no. 22; Barrow, *The Kingdom of the Scots*, 83–138; MacQueen, *Common Law and Feudal Society in Medieval Scotland*, 49.

two earldoms, Buchan and Menteith, and had ties to two more, Atholl and Angus. Though promoted as the king's friends, the Comyn earls now had their own interests – not always those of their royal lord – and the means to pursue them.[24] In Mar, conflict over the earldom was a legacy from the previous reign. In about 1180 King William recognised Gilchrist as earl, perhaps at the expense of the kin of his predecessor, Morgund. After Gilchrist's death, rival claimants stepped forward: on the one hand were the sons of Morgund; on the other, Thomas Durward, the son of Gilchrist's daughter. Both parties had served the king in Moray. By the mid-1220s they sought royal judgement on Mar. Alexander's solution was partition. Duncan, son of Morgund, became earl and held most of the province, but Durward received an extensive lordship in southern Mar, centred on Coull. A record of the 'composition' between the two men was kept by the king, and in the 1230s Durward's heir, Alan, and the earl's sons appeared together at court and locally. But though public reconciliation had occurred, rivalries persisted. The castle of Kildrummy, built by the earls of Mar as their chief stronghold, and Coull Castle, probably built by Thomas Durward, symbolised this rivalry between competing lords in the north-east.[25]

The death of Thomas of Galloway, earl of Atholl in 1231 prompted a dispute within a third earldom. Thomas had acquired Atholl by marriage to Isabella, daughter of the previous earl, and the couple had a young son, Patrick. However, a year after her husband's death Isabella faced a challenge to her rights as 'legitimate heiress' of Atholl. The challenge came from her sister, Forveleth, who argued that, like lesser fiefs, an earldom should be divided between heiresses. The issue came before the king and his full council. Isabella and her powerful supporters, including Walter Comyn, earl of Menteith, won the day. Despite his decision on Mar, the king judged that earldoms should not be divided and that Isabella was sole heiress. Alexander balanced Comyn's success by giving custody of both heiress and earldom to Alan Durward.[26] The king was playing off his rising stars against each other, and had remarkable success up to 1240 in promot-

---

[24] W. Fraser, *The Red Book of Menteith*, 2 vols (Edinburgh, 1880), ii, nos 5, 7, 8; *R.M.S.*, i, app. 2, no. 4; Young, *Robert Bruce's the Rivals: The Comyns*, 34, 37; *Chron. Fordun*, 293.

[25] Duncan, *The Making of the kingdom*, 187–8; *A.P.S.*, i, 111–12; *Illustrations of the Topography and Antiquities of the Shires of Aberdeen and Banff*, 5 vols (Aberdeen, 1843); iv, 693–4; W. Fraser, *The Chiefs of Grant*, 3 vols (Edinburgh, 1883), iii, no. 6; *Registrum Episcopatus Aberdonensis* (Aberdeen, 1845), i, 17; ii, 268–9, 273.

[26] Anderson, *Early Sources*, ii, 478; *Rental Book of the Cistercian Abbey of Cupar Angus* (Aberdeen, 1879–80), nos 30, 34; *Documents and Records illustrating the History of Scotland*, 40–1; *Moray Reg.*, no. 114.

ing their interests and binding provinces into the structures of royal lordship. He did this by subordinating legal consistency to political advantage
and appeared to reach amicable settlements in all three earldoms.
However, in reality, the king did not end rivalries in these provinces.
Instead he linked them to the ambitions of his own closest followers, creating the potential for conflict at the heart of the royal establishment.

It was in his handling of Galloway that Alexander faced the most direct
reaction to his political judgements. Alan, lord of Galloway died in early
1234 without an heir who was acceptable to the king. He had probably
hoped that his natural son, Thomas, would be named lord of Galloway,
but the king quickly backed the division of the province between Alan's
three daughters. The husbands of these heiresses were the northern
English barons William Forz and John Balliol, and the major Anglo-
Scottish lord, Roger de Quincy, who expected to share all Alan's estates.
The division of Galloway was also in the king's interest. Despite the links
of Alan with king and court and the settlement of knights and monks in
the province, Galloway had never been just another Scottish lordship. Its
traditions of kingship, its laws, its links to the west, its powerful kindreds
all fuelled a sense of identity. Its bishops lay under the authority of York
and the patronage of the lords of Galloway rather than the Scottish king.
Division would allow Galloway to be absorbed into Scotland.[27]

However, in 1234, Gallovidian identity remained strong. The leading
men approached the king and asked that Galloway's unity be preserved
either under the lordship of Thomas or, if he was unacceptable, of Patrick,
son of Thomas of Atholl and nephew of the old lord. Even the direct lordship of the king was preferable to division. Despite these offers, King
Alexander refused to budge. The men of Galloway reacted violently,
attacking the king's lands in the south-west. In response, Alexander led an
army into Galloway in July 1235. As in Moray, the royal host proved cum-
bersome against a mobile enemy and was ambushed as it made camp in
marshy ground. The king was saved by the arrival of Earl Ferchar of Ross
who again showed his skill in war by driving off the Gallovidians. The next
day Alexander offered peace and the leading rebels submitted, but the
king's victory was not final. He left Galloway under Walter Comyn, earl of
Menteith, but Comyn proved unable to prevent his men plundering the
lands and churches of the province and their actions provoked a fresh
rising which drove out the Scottish forces. This time the Gallovidians had
support from across the sea. Thomas, son of Alan, returned from exile
with an army from Ulster and the Isles. Despite this aid, the new rising

---

[27] Anderson, *Early Sources*, ii, 492–4; Stringer, 'Periphery and core', 97–102; Stringer,
Earl David, 103–4.

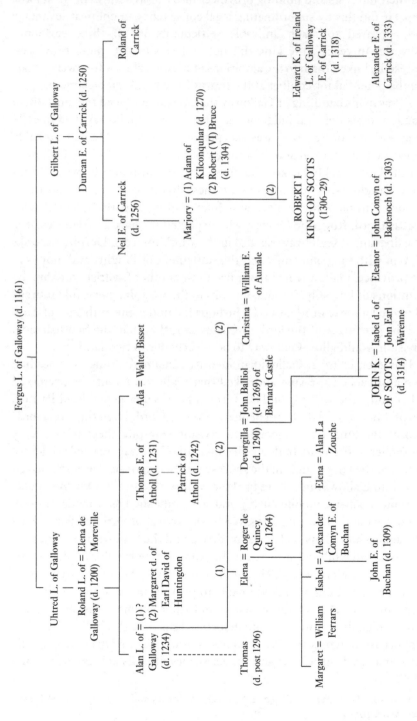

Table 2.1. Galloway and Carrick

ended quickly. The rebels were confronted by the abbot of Melrose, the bishop of Whithorn and Earl Patrick of Dunbar at the head of an army. These southern lords may have offered terms to the Gallovidians, who submitted once more. Thomas was left to face half a century of captivity. His Irish allies met a quicker fate, massacred by hostile Scots.[28]

Galloway, which King William had turned from a kingdom into a province bound to his rule, was now incorporated into the structures of royal government by his son. A sheriff was established at Wigtown, and a third justiciar was appointed to act as the king's deputy in the whole province. The estates held by Alan of Galloway in the province were split amongst their new lords. This dramatic change aroused continued hostility. In 1247 Roger de Quincy, husband of Alan's eldest daughter, who 'oppressed by his tyranny the nobler vassals of the land more than was customary', was forced to flee the province pursued by his tenants. He was only restored with royal help. The leading Gallovidians remained protective of their ancient rights. It may have been a promise to preserve these that quelled the 1235 revolt. The king certainly acknowledged that Galloway had its own 'special laws' and, as part of these, he recognised the rights and role of the captains of the kindreds, the leading nobles and heads of local society in the province. As in many parts of the realm, royal justice functioned alongside native custom. This relative moderation provided the basis for the authority of the crown and its baronial allies in Galloway, but in its captains and its customs the province preserved its separate identity within the Scottish realm.[29]

The fall of the house of Galloway had an impact beyond its homeland. In 1230 Alan and Thomas of Galloway had been amongst the greatest lords of the northern British Isles. Within five years the only free and acknowledged male representative of the dynasty was Thomas's son, Patrick of Atholl. Patrick was still a child in 1235 but, as he approached manhood, many expected him to become 'the great lord of a certain inheritance' including his father's earldom, lands in Ulster and perhaps more. Patrick's claims would have the support of his powerful kinsmen the Comyns, and of Earl Patrick of Dunbar, who was his guardian. Yet many regarded the young lord's claims with anxiety. For Alan Durward, earl of Atholl in the 1230s, Patrick's inheritance of the province would have ended his local influence, and his doubts were shared by his neighbours and allies, the Bissets. Walter Bisset, lord of Aboyne, was married to Patrick's aunt and may have hoped for a share of his lands in Ulster. Whether or not this was the cause, the Bissets saw Patrick as their enemy.

---

[28] Anderson, *Scottish Annals*, 340–2; Anderson, *Early Sources*, ii, 496–8.
[29] Anderson, *Scottish Annals*, 359; MacQueen, 'The laws of Galloway, 131–43.

In the spring of 1242, during a tournament at Haddington, a group of knights led by Walter Bisset's nephew, John, killed Patrick and his retainers in their lodgings, either by trapping them in a burning building, or burning their house to hide the bodies within.

Patrick's murder proved a massive shock to Alexander's authority. At once, the earl of Dunbar took up arms against the killers. Described by one contemporary as 'most powerful among the magnates of Scotland', Dunbar was a man with a large personality and a powerful following in southern Scotland, a lord respected by both the king and his enemies, the Gallovidians. Dunbar's example was quickly followed by the Comyns. Despite the demands of his greatest subjects from north and south, Alexander extended his protection to the Bissets. Walter Bisset protested that the king had been with him at Aboyne the night before the murder and that Queen Marie was still his guest when the deed was done. Despite his public condemnation of the crime, Walter's enemies accused him of ordering Patrick's death. To forestall conflict, the king met with his magnates at Perth in July and agreed to a hearing of the case at Forfar. This effort to keep the peace failed and fighting erupted in the north. The Comyns, led by the earl of Buchan and John the Red, nephew of Menteith, plundered the lands of Bisset and his allies. From Buchan and Badenoch the Comyns were well placed to harry the Bissets' estates in the Great Glen and Strathdee, and Walter was forced to take refuge in Aboyne Castle. The king's justiciars failed to intervene. Following the death of Walter Stewart in 1241, Alexander named two lesser men, Robert Mowat and Philip Melville, as his justiciars of Scotia. If this was an attempt to alter the character of the office and increase royal control over its operation, it had dire consequences. Mowat was an adherent of the Comyns, and neither justiciar acted to restrain the family's depredations. Alexander sacked them and turned instead to Alan Durward. Durward's appointment as justiciar was hardly impartial. He had close ties to the Bissets and was a rival of the Comyns in Atholl. His lands in the north bordered those of Walter Bisset and may also have been attacked. To end these attacks, Durward called out 'the army of Mar', the men of the earldom his father had claimed in the 1220s, and escorted Bisset to safety. As well as performing his office, Durward was renewing this claim to Mar, perhaps after the recent death of its earl, Duncan. His actions aroused the fears of the new earl of Mar, Duncan's son, William.[30]

The crisis of 1242 grew out of the rapid expansion of royal lordship in the previous three decades. The leading participants were those families

[30] Anderson, *Early Sources*, ii, 530; *Scotichronicon*, v, 179–87; Anderson, *Scottish Annals*, 349–50; *Chron. Lanercost*, 49–50; Young, *Robert the Bruce's Rivals*, 38–43.

that had benefited from Alexander's trust and favour in the north. The rivalry between them was fuelled by the king's handling of major issues of land and power in his kingdom. The usefulness of these families to the king was their readiness to take and hold exposed lands on the marches of royal authority. The Comyns, who had ended the MacWilliam threat, and the Bissets, who bought out less determined settlers in the Great Glen after the 1229 uprising, were schooled in the harsh methods of frontier society. The killing of Earl Patrick and the harrying of the Bissets' lands represented the use of these skills in a dispute within the king's circle. Faced with this conflict, Alexander was forced to depend on another magnate clearly involved in northern rivalries. Even when the case was considered by the king at Forfar, the dispute continued. Bisset's oath of innocence was rejected by the 'earls', probably Dunbar, Menteith, Buchan and, perhaps, Mar. Bisset, in turn, refused judgement by local men, offering trial by combat or the king's verdict as alternatives. In November at Edinburgh a third council debated the issue. After long negotiations, it was agreed that Walter Bisset and his nephews should be exiled from Scotland. The decision was reached by political hard-dealing between the king and two powerful factions on his council and in his kingdom.

The dispute demonstrated that the king could not guarantee the obedience of even his closest allies. Ties of family, of political alliance, of private lordship were just as potent and could prove stronger. Links of service to the English king, which many Scottish landholders possessed, could also counter the authority of the king of Scots. Instead of leaving for a pilgrimage to Jerusalem, the Bissets sought out Henry of England in Gascony, complaining to him that Alexander had exiled them because 'he could not allay the presumption of rebels who rose in fury against him'. They embellished this account by suggesting that, as Henry's vassal, Alexander could not exile his magnates without his own lord's consent. The Bissets also fuelled Henry's existing suspicions about Alexander's support for his enemies in Ireland and France. The recent marriage of the Scottish king to Marie de Couci, whose father was 'one of the chief enemies of the king of England' in France, aroused Henry's fears after the failure of his campaign in Poitou. During this campaign Henry had entrusted Newcastle and the far north of England to Alexander, and he was now made aware that the Scots, and in particular the Bissets' enemy, Walter Comyn, earl of Menteith, were fortifying castles in the marches. If Henry expected Alexander to respond to pressure, he was disabused by a letter in which the Scottish king rejected Henry's right to exercise any lordship over Scotland. In the spring of 1244 after his return from Gascony, Henry prepared for war. In July he led an army north to Newcastle; Alexander responded in kind. He called out the host, took an oath of loyalty from its leaders and marched through Northumberland to Ponteland, six miles from Henry. Behind displays of military strength lay a readiness to talk. The kings and many of their magnates wanted a settlement and, in early August, a face-saving deal was agreed. Alexander promised to make no alliance with the enemies of 'his liege lord', the English king, and, in addition, Earl Patrick and Walter Comyn swore that they had no part in attacks on Henry's lands. No reference was made to the rights claimed by the English king in Scotland, but Alexander's promise did indicate the restrictions which his obligations to the king of England placed on Scotland's wider connections. Moreover, the readiness of Henry to claim a role in an internal Scottish quarrel was a mark of his attitude to the realm which his vassal ruled.[31]

Despite this, Alexander had reason to be satisfied with the settlement. After sustained and damaging defiance from his own nobles, Alexander had emerged with his position largely unscathed. The phoney war of 1244 allowed him to summon the host and lead it in defence of his realm. The oaths sworn by his most prominent critics, Dunbar and Comyn, bound them to the negotiated peace. Part of this peace may have been the restoration of the Bissets, who were back from exile by the late 1240s. Atholl itself passed to the murdered Patrick's aunt, Forveleth, and her husband, David Hastings, another royal knight whose claims had earlier been opposed by the Comyns, and their inheritance of Atholl formed part of a redistribution of power amongst those who had supported the king in 1242. The greatest beneficiary of this was Alan Durward, who retained the justiciarship of Scotia and was singled out from his peers by marriage to the king's bastard daughter, Marjory. By contrast, those who had opposed Alexander may have felt excluded from influence. Earl Patrick Dunbar's decision to take the cross in 1247 may have been prompted by the king's attitude. Though the king saw Dunbar on his journey in 1248, he was probably glad to see the earl go. Dunbar's death at Marseilles later in the year may not have been mourned by either the king or the earl's son and heir.[32]

As the greatest lord in the south-east and the king's cousin, Dunbar may have been singled out for royal displeasure. Others involved in the events of 1242 seem to have suffered no lasting penalties. A leading adherent of Dunbar, David Graham, acted as deputy justiciar of Lothian in the 1240s, and the discredited justiciar of Scotia, Robert Mowat, continued to counsel the king. Mowat's allies, the Comyns, remained close to the

[31] Anderson, Scottish Annals, 351-8; Anderson, Early Sources, ii, 536-9; Scotichronicon, v, 185; C.D.S., i, nos 1,621, 1,624, 1,631, 1,637, 1,640-8, 1,654, 2,871-2.
[32] Scotichronicon, v, 179; Dunfermline Reg., no. 77; R.M.S., ii, no. 3,136; Anderson, Early Sources, ii, 551, 571; Chron. Lanercost, 54; Melrose Liber, i, nos 230, 235; MacQuarrie, Scotland and the Crusades, 47-8.

centres of power though their friendship with the king may have cooled. After 1244 Alexander's aim may have been to defuse tensions by turning to a new generation of lords. Both William, earl of Mar and Alexander Stewart had recently succeeded their fathers and now appeared with regularity on the king's council. After the crisis the king was demonstrating the crown's normal ability to call on a wide group of adherents. However, the events of 1242 indicated a change in the character of Scottish politics. Between the 1120s and 1230s, service to the king was the route to lands and lordship for nobles of diverse origins. After 1240 there were no new creations like the lordship of Badenoch or the earldom of Sutherland which represented the crown encouraging its men to extend the realm as a political unit. Instead the opportunity for lords to gain new wealth and status was contained within an established framework and was achieved in competition with other similar magnates. Royal judgements over lands now meant rewarding one lord at another's expense, a situation which could lead to resentment at the king's decision. Kingship increasingly consisted of balancing conflicting interests within the king's own following. For all his apparent resumption of control, Alexander II was probably aware of the continuation of rivalries, which were symbolised by the marriage of the earl of Mar to Elizabeth, sister of Alexander Comyn, earl of Buchan, which occurred about this time. This match drew together powerful northern dynasties who, though major beneficiaries of the king's patronage, resented and feared the rise of Alan Durward. It would need all Alexander's authority to contain such animosities.[33]

It was no coincidence that in 1244 Alexander sought a new outlet for these northern magnates. In that year he began his efforts to buy the Western Isles from the king of Norway. Extension of his royal rights to the Isles was a natural adjunct to the gradual intrusion of Alexander's influence into Argyll. The king's determination to accelerate and extend the westward spread of his authority was probably linked to his desire to provide new areas of opportunity and activity for his powerful lords. In 1249 the king himself led an army to the west to force the submission of Ewen of Lorn. Alexander also intended to carry the war into the Isles and raised a fleet for this purpose. He had only reached the inshore Isle of Kerrera when he fell victim to illness and died, surrounded by his councillors, on 8 July.[34] For a king who had worked hard to extend his lordship by force and persuasion, it was not unfitting that Alexander should die on campaign at the furthest reach of his realm.

---

[33] *Melrose Liber*, i, nos 237, 239; *Scone Liber*, no. 81; W. Fraser (ed.), *The Book of Carlaverock*, 2 vols (Edinburgh, 1873), ii, no. 405; *A.P.S.*, i, 404.
[34] Anderson, *Early Sources*, ii, 539–40, 555–61; *R.M.S.*, ii, no. 3,136.

CHAPTER 3

Alexander III

THE MAKING OF THE KING

On 13 July 1249, less than a week after the death of his father, a boy of almost eight years old was crowned king of Scots as Alexander III. In thirteenth-century Scotland, royal councillors could not afford to be sentimental. Alan Durward, probably accompanied by others who had been with Alexander II in Argyll, deserted the corpse of his dead lord and sped east to be at the inauguration of the new king. Control of the ceremony was essential to Durward. After the open rivalries of previous years he wished to prevent others securing an advantage whilst he was away on the shores of Argyll. When the lords and prelates assembled at Scone, Durward was ready to press his claim to preside over the young king's government. He demanded the right to knight Alexander at the inauguration. As husband of the king's half-sister, justiciar of Scotland and a reputed 'flower of chivalry', Durward sought to be Alexander's mentor and advisor, perhaps even a formal regent. These claims were unwelcome to many of Durward's peers. Some wished to postpone the ceremony, but reportedly 'to prevent a quarrelsome separation into two parties', Walter Comyn, earl of Menteith suggested that the king should be knighted by Bishop David of St Andrews. Posing as a peacemaker, Comyn had blocked the plans of Durward, his established rival. The young king was knighted and crowned with full ceremony in an atmosphere of hastily-restored peace.[1]

This peace was kept during the next eighteen months . Alexander probably remained in the household of his mother, Queen Marie, while royal

---

[1] *Chron. Fordun*, 288–90; *Scotichronicon*, v, 290–7; *R.M.S.*, ii, no. 3,136. The best accounts of Alexander III's minority are Watt, 'The minority of Alexander III of Scotland', 1–23; Duncan, *Making of the kingdom*, 552–76; Young, *Robert the Bruce's Rivals*, 47–61.

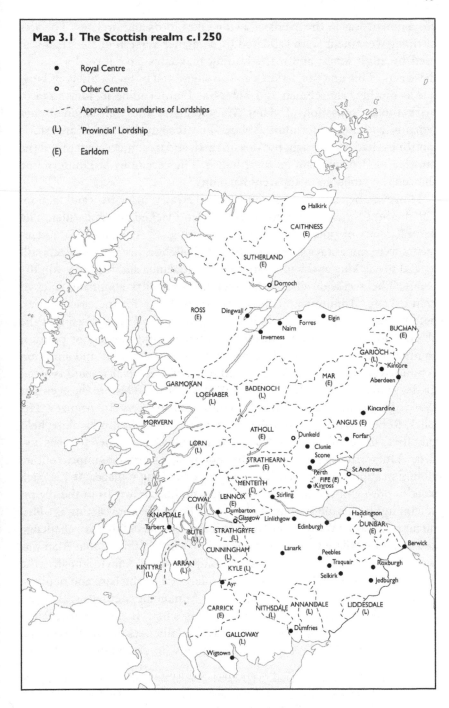

Map 3.1 The Scottish realm c.1250

- •   Royal Centre
- ○   Other Centre
- –·–   Approximate boundaries of Lordships
- (L)   'Provincial' Lordship
- (E)   Earldom

○ Halkirk

CAITHNESS
(E)

SUTHERLAND
(E)

○ Dornoch

ROSS
(E)

Dingwall

Forres   Elgin

Nairn

Inverness

BUCHAN
(E)

GARIOCH
(L)

Kintore

GARMORAN

LOCHABER
(L)

BADENOCH
(L)

MAR
(E)

Aberdeen

Kincardine

MORVERN

ATHOLL
(E)

Dunkeld

ANGUS (E)

Forfar

LORN
(L)

Clunie

Scone

STRATHEARN
(E)

Perth

St Andrews

MENTEITH
(L)

FIFE (E)

Kinross

COWAL
(L)

LENNOX
(E)

Dumbarton

Stirling

KNAPDALE

Tarbert

Glasgow   Linlithgow

STRATHGRYFE
(L)

Edinburgh

Haddington

DUNBAR
(E)

Berwick

BUTE
(L)

CUNNINGHAM
(L)

Lanark

Peebles

KINTYRE
(L)

ARRAN
(L)

KYLE (L)

Traquair

Roxburgh

Ayr

Selkirk

Jedburgh

CARRICK
(E)

NITHSDALE
(L)

ANNANDALE
(L)

LIDDESDALE
(L)

GALLOWAY
(L)

Dumfries

Wigtown

government was in the hands of a council of lords and prelates. The acts of this government were validated by a smaller version of the great seal used by adult kings, and many leading magnates gave formal assent to these acts. This unity of action was also suggested by an assembly of king, queen-mother, churchmen and nobles at Dunfermline in June 1250 to mark the canonisation of Saint Margaret and the translation of her remains within Dunfermline Abbey. The recognition of his ancestor's saintliness had been sought by Alexander II, and its achievement raised the prestige of Scotland and its royal house. The ceremony at Dunfermline showed the kingdom in apparent harmony.[2]

However, beneath this harmony lurked rivalry, insecurity and faction. For the first time in living memory Scotland lacked an adult ruler. The natural focus of political society was missing. If Alexander II's judgements were not always accepted without challenge, his chief subjects still looked to the king as the ultimate source of balance and legitimacy in the realm. The accession of a child created uncertainty about the rules of political life. Ambitious men saw the opportunity for increased power, both on the king's council and in their lands, but all recognised that the absence of royal authority meant the intensity and dangers of political competition had increased. During 1250 and 1251 anxiety and ambition combined to create new alliances and intensify old rivalries and centred on the figures of Alan Durward and Walter Comyn. Despite the events at the king's inauguration, Durward continued to press for primacy. His allies, Robert Menzies and Robert Kenleith, abbot of Dunfermline, held the offices of chamberlain and chancellor, while he continued to act as justiciar. Durward's justice ayres in the north-east were not simply routine administration but showed him acting in the king's place. At his back stood a powerful retinue of barons and knights, drawn from the region and including his old friends the Bissets. The justiciar was acting as a lord intent on power.[3] Walter Comyn and his kin recognised this as a challenge and sought to share their suspicions of Durward, claiming that Alan was seeking a place in the royal dynasty through his wife. A fortnight after the inauguration Walter, his brother Alexander, earl of Buchan, and nephew, John the Red, met with Robert Bruce of Annandale, perhaps seeking an ally with his own claim to be the young king's heir. If this meeting failed to yield results, the Comyns engineered other alliances during the coming months. In March 1251, for example, Walter Comyn and the elderly Earl

<hr />

[2] Simpson, 'Kingship in miniature', 131–9; *Scotichronicon*, v, 296–9; Ash, 'The church in the reign of Alexander III', 31–52; *Paisley Reg.*, 215; *R.M.S.*, ii, no. 804; W. Fraser, *The Book of Carlaverock*, 2 vols (Edinburgh, 1873), ii, 405–6; *Arbroath Reg.*, i, 250; *Aberdeen and Banff Illustrations*, iv, 696.

[3] *Aberdeen Reg.*, ii, 273; *Lindores Chartulary*, no. 80.

Maldouen of Lennox were together at Balloch, and by 1252 the Comyns were operating in partnership with a group of southern barons, among them councillors of the old king like Thomas Randolph, Nicholas Soules, Aymer Maxwell and David Graham.[4]

In the absence of royal lordship, such bands or alliances provided the framework of political life. They did not make conflict inevitable, but strengthened or forged relationships between magnates for mutual support. However, they could add to tensions. To Earl William of Mar, Durward's displays of lordship in the north-east threatened a renewed dispute over his earldom and pushed him closer to the Comyns. To Alexander Stewart and Patrick, earl of Dunbar, the Comyns' involvement in the Lennox and with southern lords suggested the family had ambitions which encroached on their interests, and both magnates were suspicious of Earl Walter and his kin. Though many avoided taking sides, the absence of effective kingship created a climate in which factions flourished and rivalries grew. By mid-1251 churchmen were complaining about the plundering committed by 'ministers' and 'lords' on church lands, a symptom both of local feuding and of growing competition for control of church offices between rival parties.[5]

Three times in the next six years the king's councillors would be removed by force. These rapid shifts of power were driven by the antagonisms of Scottish politics, but the interventions of the English king increased the instability. The Scots themselves sought Henry III's involvement. In 1251 an embassy invited Henry to fulfil the agreement of 1244 and arrange the marriage of his daughter to Alexander III. The wedding was arranged for Christmas at York. However, Henry was incited to take further action by Scots who feared that Durward's hold on power was increased by the departure of Queen Marie to France. On the day after Christmas Alexander married Margaret of England. The wedding prepared the ground for a coup. Walter Comyn and the earl of Mar levelled accusations against the king's councillors. Durward and his allies were forced to flee or face arrest. Henry III backed these moves, and though he stated formally that the dismissal of the king's councillors at York did not prejudice the rights of the Scottish king, he sought an active role in Scotland. As recently as 1244 he had shown a readiness to meddle in internal Scottish disputes. In 1251 Henry wanted not formal authority, but the means to exercise real but informal influence in Scotland. He had knighted Alexander at York and claimed rights as the father of the young

---

[4] *C.D.S.*, i, no. 1,763; *Paisley Reg.*, 171; *Melrose Liber*, i, no. 336; *Dunfermline Reg.*, no. 82.
[5] Watt, 'The Minority of Alexander III', 8–9.

king and queen. He sent north two barons – men with lands in both realms – to act as the guardians of his and his daughter's interests. Like his father, Henry was attempting to bring Scotland into the Plantagenet orbit.[6]

The events at York had given control of council and king to men whose ambitions matched Durward's. Henry's representatives, John Balliol and Robert Ros, were related to the Scottish king, but lacked the standing and following to direct events. Instead, in place of Durward and his allies, Mar became chamberlain, Buchan was named justiciar of Scotia, and custody of the great seal went to a Comyn dependant, master Gamelin. Walter Comyn took no office himself but was clearly a force in a regime which also enjoyed the support of Bishop David of St Andrews and the bishops of Glasgow and Dunblane.[7] The council looked for secular allies. In particular, Alexander Stewart, the key magnate in the west, was wooed by the new government, and Stewart's presence at Stirling in December 1253 with the king, his justiciars and the chamberlain shows a degree of contact. However, many other lords remained both unreconciled and dangerous to the council. In particular, Alan Durward remained a powerful figure. His gifts of land to a kinsman of the earl of Strathearn and fresh contacts with the earl of Carrick show Durward was intent on recovering lost influence.[8]

The key to his comeback was Henry of England. Henry's hopes of influence had been frustrated. His 'link and league' with Scotland failed to provide him with financial or military aid for his continental schemes and, on a more personal level, Henry was angered by reports that his daughter, Queen Margaret, had been 'unfaithfully and inhumanly treated', refused permission to visit her mother and kept apart from her husband. Henry blamed Ros and Balliol for these insults and there were Scots lords ready to encourage his hostility. Among them was Alan Durward, who had won Henry's favour by serving him in Gascony and used this influence to denounce his enemies and promise support for the English king's intervention.[9] In August 1255 Henry came north. Striking against his erstwhile guardians, he seized Ros's lands and sacked Balliol as keeper of Carlisle Castle and sheriff of Cumberland. These posts went to Robert Bruce, and it was Bruce's brother-in-law, Richard de Clare, earl

[6] Chron. Fordun, ii, 290–2; Scotichronicon, v, 298–303; Anderson, Early Sources, 569–70; C.D.S., i, no. 1,848.
[7] Dunfermline Reg., nos 82, 84; Melrose Liber, i, no. 336; W. Fraser, The Lennox, 2 vols (Edinburgh, 1874), ii, 13–15.
[8] Chron. Fordun, ii, 295–6; Scotichronicon, v, 300–3; Melrose Liber, i, no. 322; W. Fraser, The Chiefs of Grant, 3 vols (Edinburgh, 1883), no. 6; R.M.S., i, no. 509.
[9] C.D.S., i, nos 1,888, 1,935, 1,974; Anderson, Scottish Annals, 370–1; Duncan, Making of the kingdom, 563–4.

of Gloucester, who led a force into Scotland with orders to aid King Henry's 'friends' there. In response to this, the Comyns and their allies sought to negotiate. A meeting was held at Edinburgh and another planned for Stirling. Before this could be held, the decisive blow was struck. In early September, Patrick, earl of Dunbar, the greatest lord in Lothian and one of Henry's named 'friends', forced his way into Edinburgh Castle and secured custody of King Alexander and Queen Margaret. When the Comyns gathered an army for a counter-attack, Dunbar, Durward and Gloucester carried the royal couple south to Roxburgh, a few miles from Henry's base at Wark.[10]

During the next fortnight Henry's 'friends' gathered. Walter Comyn was called to appear but refused. On 20 August Henry crossed the border, met his allies and confirmed a document issued in Alexander's name by nineteen magnates. This nominated a new council of fifteen which would govern for the king until he reached adulthood in 1262. The letters also banned the old councillors from office. Walter Comyn and his kin, Mar, three bishops, eleven barons, eight other men and one woman were excluded from government or contact with their king. The letters were issued by a group containing not just Durward's friends but a wide group of magnates, all united by mistrust of the Comyns. Prominent among them were the earls of Fife, Carrick, and Strathearn, Alexander Stewart, Walter Murray and Robert Bruce, but the leading figure of this council may have been Earl Patrick of Dunbar. While these lords were at Roxburgh, distributing royal offices amongst themselves, their enemies remained at large and at the head of an army. Scotland's lords, earls, barons, even bishops and abbots, stood divided into hostile armed camps, apparently on the brink of conflict.[11]

As in 1251, there was no major armed clash. The Comyns disbanded their army and withdrew, Henry III returned south, and the new council sought control of the king's lands and rights. This readiness to step back from the brink raises questions about the character of Scottish politics in the 1250s. Firstly, it suggests that the disputes and divisions since 1249 had not caused a breakdown of basic structures of lordship and authority. Despite his age, King Alexander retained a significance as the focus of government. The men around the king possessed the best claim to act in his name. Changes in the king's keepers meant changes of royal officers. However, control of the young king was not enough on its own to confer legitimacy. As no active source of authority existed within Scotland, then the political class looked outside the kingdom to justify their actions.

[10] C.D.S., i, nos 1,986–95; Anderson, Early Sources, 581–3; Chron. Fordun, ii, 297.
[11] Stones, Anglo-Scottish Relations, no. 10.

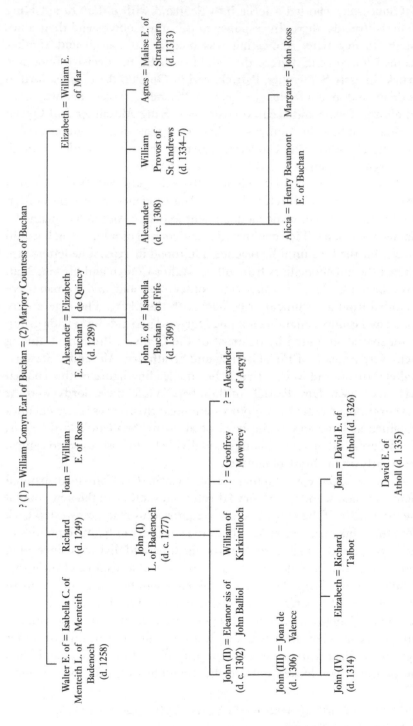

Table 3.1. The Comyns and the Disinherited

Henry III's right to supervise and regulate Alexander's councillors was accepted by Scottish magnates, who recognised the place he held, through his royal rank, his position as lord of the English estates held by the king and many nobles, and through the marriage between the two royal houses. It was equally clear, however, that there were limits to this. In 1251 and 1255 Henry's interventions were accompanied by promises that his actions did not prejudice Alexander's rights, honour or liberties as king. Henry largely kept his promises but it is clear from the pro-Comyn *Melrose Chronicle* that Walter Comyn and his allies denounced the 1255 agreement as being to 'the dishonour of king and kingdom'. This claim was intended to discredit the new council. Defence of their king's full rights was the duty of all his Scottish vassals. The minority council's chief task was to protect the interests of the crown until Alexander could assume the task for himself and resume his father's leadership of the kingdom. Faction obscured, but never obliterated, this fact.[12]

The English king was not the only source of external authority. During the 1250s Scots also looked to the papacy for judgement and support in internal conflicts. The pope's role as protector of the Scottish church was invoked by churchmen, who were themselves part of factional rivalries. In 1250–1, clerics associated with both Durward and his enemies appealed to Pope Innocent IV for support, charging their opponents with crimes and abuses. In 1253 the death of Bishop David of St Andrews prompted attempts by rival candidates to secure papal recognition as his successor. The Comyn-led council's efforts to install Gamelin were initially blocked by opposition from the cathedral chapter, and though Gamelin secured his election in 1254, the change of regime saw him driven into exile and deprived of the lands and revenues of his see, the richest in Scotland. The new regime petitioned Pope Alexander IV to remove him from office, but Gamelin, using his persuasive talents and liberal promises of payment, convinced Alexander to excommunicate the king's council. The pope's punishment was an embarrassing condemnation of the right of the king's officers to rule. Papal judgement was even sought in the secular dispute over Mar. In 1255 Alan Durward claimed that his rival, Earl William, was from an illegitimate line and thus debarred from his inheritance. In the absence of the king to judge the dispute, the papal court, the curia, was used as an alternative source of legal and moral sanction.[13]

Factional conflict was not contained by respect for custom and legitimacy alone. The lack of major violence also reflected the limited power of

---

12 *C.D.S.*, i, nos 1,848, 1,988, 2,002; Anderson, *Early Sources*, 583.
13 Watt, 'The Minority of Alexander III', 8–9; *Scotichronicon*, v, 314–19; *C.D.S.*, i, no. 2,037; Anderson, *Early Sources*, 588–9; Duncan, *Making of the kingdom*, 568–9.

minority regimes. The change of royal councillors had a direct effect on the rights and estates of the crown alone. It did not alter the powers of earls or lords in their provinces. Though churchmen were hounded and an inquest launched into royal finances, the Comyns were able to remain secure in their strongholds, ignoring summonses to answer complaints levelled against them. Even Mar, who faced the government-backed claims of Durward to his earldom, was able to fend off this challenge. Such lords did not need to risk open warfare. Instead they fell back on the support of their men and their friends. After 1255 the Comyns won further support in the north, in particular from Earl William of Ross and Freskin Murray of Strathnaver, and this northern connection provided the means not just to survive, but to undermine the council. During 1256 the English feared civil war would erupt in Scotland between the king and the 'rebels', but conflict was probably limited to clashes between the northern earls and Durward, once again justiciar of Scotia. Feuding may also have occurred in divided local communities. In Fife, for example, Earl Malcolm's support for the 1255 coup put him at odds with his vassals, John Denmuir and David Lochore, and his kinsman, Hugh Abernethy, all of whom actively supported the Comyns, while difficulties may have arisen in Carrick after the death of Earl Neil in 1256 left his young daughter, Marjory, as countess. The Comyns and Mar could exploit such tensions to put pressure on the council, winning new allies and undermining their enemies. During the 1250s the struggle for political leadership in Scotland was won not on the king's council, but in the kingdom's local communities.[14]

By early 1257 the success of the Comyns and their allies in winning support allowed them to draw up terms for 'the peace . . . of our realm' which were sent to the council and Henry III. In August a meeting was planned at Stirling between the king's councillors and their enemies in the presence of an English embassy. Henry wanted a settlement of disputes in Scotland and, having allowed the Comyn faction access to their king, he was probably prepared to accept their return to the council. By autumn 1257, however, it was the Comyns and their allies who rejected compromise. On the night of 29 October Alexander III, now a youth of sixteen, was seized in his lodgings at Kinross by Walter Comyn, earl of Menteith and a force which included local allies like Hugh Abernethy, David Lochore and Hugh Barclay. Though they used the sentence of excommunication passed against the council to justify their actions, the king's captors were motivated more by old enmities and a new confidence in their strength. The overthrow of the 1255 council was, however, a direct challenge to Henry III, and Durward and his friends wasted no

[14] Barrow, 'Wales and Scotland in the Middle Ages', 302–19; *C.D.S.*, i, no. 2,053.

time in seeking English help. By January 1258 Henry was summoning his vassals to join an expedition to 'deliver' Alexander from his 'rebels'. By early April this force was assembling and the English border castles of Wark and Norham were handed over to Durward and his fellow justiciar, Walter Murray, to serve as bases for military action.[15]

Unlike in 1255, the Comyns and their friends were prepared for a confrontation. Over the winter they extended their influence, especially perhaps in the south-west where John Comyn was appointed justiciar of Galloway and secured local support. A large and intimidating Gallovidian contingent was present in the army which the Comyns assembled and led to Roxburgh. Walter Comyn ensured that his party was not without allies. On 18 March an alliance was concluded by named Scottish magnates, headed by Walter, Mar, Buchan and Ross, with Llywelyn ap Gruffydd, the ruler of Gwynedd, who was styled prince of Wales. The alliance was a promise of mutual support against each group's enemies. King Alexander was not party to the agreement and it was recognised that Alexander might force the Scots to break its terms; this clause was understandable given Alexander's growing maturity and the recent changes of political fortune. However, the alliance was not a sign of Comyn weakness. Walter had chosen a useful ally in Llwelyn ap Gruffydd, a rising star. Since 1255 he had established himself as leader of native Wales, inflicting a string of defeats on Henry and the English marcher lords. In early 1258 the English king was preparing for war in the west as well as the north.[16]

Though it had little to do with Scotland, it was Henry's position, not that of Llywelyn or Walter Comyn, which proved vulnerable in 1258. In April, prompted in part by events in Wales, a league of barons formed and in June forced Henry to surrender effective power to them. These events reduced the chance of English forces escalating 'the war and disturbance' in Scotland. Just as a truce was agreed with Llywelyn in June, so the English government sought simply to secure the protection of its Scottish 'friends' until a *colloquium* was held at Edinburgh in early September. An embassy, headed by Henry's baronial foe, Simon de Montfort, went north to attend this council, but when it reached the border it found the Comyns waiting with King Alexander and an army. For three weeks talks were held at Jedburgh, while the Scottish army, once more including Gallovidians, plundered the surrounding country. They acted not simply out of habit but in a conscious attempt to intimidate their enemies.[17]

[15] C.D.S., i, nos 2,077, 2,090, 2,103, 2,113–14, 2,116–21; Anderson, *Early Sources*, 589.
[16] Anderson, *Early Sources*, 591; Barrow, 'Wales and Scotland in the Middle Ages', 311–12; Smith, *Llywelyn ap Gruffydd, Prince of Wales*, 110.
[17] C.D.S., i, nos 2,126, 2,131, 2,133; Anderson, *Early Sources*, 592–3.

It worked. The Comyns agreed to Durward's restoration to the council, but on their own terms. Durward abandoned the justiciarship and his claim to Mar. The council which gained English recognition included Buchan, Mar and Bishop Gamelin, and they and their allies retained the offices seized in 1257. Buchan remained justiciar of Scotia, Mar was chamberlain, and the offices of chancellor and justiciar of Lothian were held by men excluded from power in 1255. The Comyns had ridden their luck, but they succeeded in defending the hold on power which their seizure of Alexander had given them. The rest of the minority saw no challenges to their hold on these offices, and the settlement of the feud between Durward and his enemies ended clashes between rival factions. The struggles of the 1250s had not been about alternative views of the kingdom or its relations with England but about the distribution of power amongst a group of men whose lands and followings gave them a role in government during the king's minority. Such aristocratic interests were an accepted element in Scottish politics. The agreement of 1258 brought lords from both parties onto the council, but it was the Comyns' use of force which had shaped the settlement.[18]

There were other reasons why competition for power diminished after 1258. King Henry's continuing problems with his own subjects ended Durward's hopes of active external support, while the reduction of internal friction was undoubtedly helped by the death of Walter Comyn, earl of Menteith soon after his moment of victory, in October 1258. Walter's demise removed an effective but abrasive figure from Scottish politics. Without him it may have been easier to smooth over past conflicts. However, even Walter had agreed to the inclusion of Durward and two allies on the formal council, a body which also included the less committed figures of Queen Marie and Alexander Stewart. During the next four years royal business was carried out not just by these councillors but by a wider group which included many lords from rival parties. A conscious effort was made to end disputes. Feuds were settled and marriage alliances negotiated between families that had been at odds in previous years. Behind this peacemaking was the awareness that the return of royal rule was not far off. Though Alexander III was now of an age to state his will, formal power rested with his council. When the king visited England in 1260, his leading officers probably remained behind and in control of government.[19]

The adult king could not be held in check. The crunch came in the dispute over Menteith. The death of Walter Comyn without a child

---

[18] Stones, *Anglo-Scottish Relations*, no. 11.
[19] *Chron. Fordun*, ii, 298; Watt, 'The Minority of Alexander III', 18–20.

reopened old issues. In 1259 Walter, younger brother of Alexander Stewart, raised the claim of his wife, Mary, to Menteith against her cousin, Comyn's widow, Isabella. The king judged in Stewart's favour. However, the lands were not granted and many of the royal councillors were unhappy with Alexander's decision. In the autumn of 1260 John Comyn, Earl Walter's nephew, arrested Isabella and her new husband, the English knight John Russell. Comyn accused the couple of poisoning his uncle. John was supported by an impressive group, led by Buchan and Mar but including Durward and the earls of Fife and Strathearn. This group could claim to be acting with authority and condoned John's methods. It forced Isabella to surrender Menteith in return for her release. This action probably coincided with the king's absence in England. In late November 1260 Alexander abruptly left Henry III's court and returned north. His intervention was decisive. By April 1261 Walter Stewart, not John Comyn, was earl of Menteith. The king's display of authority was impressive. Confronted by the king, the leading figures of the minority abandoned John Comyn. Men like Mar, Buchan and Durward had learned the rules of politics under Alexander II and recognised that his son was the principal focus of the realm. They had no reason to see his assumption of power as anything other than a natural renewal of royal leadership. Instead of challenging this, these magnates would seek to benefit from the rule of an adult king.[20]

Alexander, for his part, recognised the need to demonstrate that his leadership worked to the advantage of his great lords. During 1261 he sent an embassy to King Hakon of Norway seeking to purchase a resignation of the Norse king's rights in the Hebrides. Although this approach was rejected, it signalled Alexander's renewal of his father's attempt to extend his rule and his realm westwards. More directly, it gave royal backing to the efforts of his chief vassals into the far west of the Scottish mainland and into the Isles. The events of the minority had confirmed the power of these frontier lords, the Comyns, Stewarts and Durward. By sponsoring war in the west, Alexander was harnessing the interests of these lords under royal leadership. During this warfare, which escalated with the involvement of the Norwegian king in 1263, Alexander depended on the support and cohesion of lords like Durward and Buchan. These magnates acted together as military leaders and the king's lieutenants in the north, confirming the end of old conflicts. Any return to the rivalries of previous decades could have spelled disaster. Instead the

[20] The narrative of this case is given in a papal letter to Alexander III (*Vetera Monumenta Hibernorum et Scotorum Historiam Illustrantia*, ed. A. Theiner (Rome, 1864) no. 237). *C.D.S.*, i, no. 2,225; *Scotichronicon*, v, 322–33; *Charters of the Royal Burgh of Ayr* (Ayr, 1883), no. 11; *Paisley Reg.*, 121.

Treaty of Perth in 1266, which transferred the Western Isles to the Scottish king's lordship, was a personal victory for Alexander. The king had not just added new lands to his realm, he had restored the primacy of royal lordship over his magnates.[21]

GOOD KING ALEXANDER

In later years Scots looked back on the reign of Alexander, 'our king', as an era of peace and plenty, of wine, gold and games. Between the early 1260s and the mid-1280s the heartlands of Alexander's kingdom increased in prosperity and enjoyed internal peace under royal leadership and stable, friendly relations with England. In all these things Alexander benefited from forces which had been at work for decades but, as events would show, their continuation was not automatic. After his death his subjects came to recognise that Alexander's Scotland represented the fullest development of the high medieval kingdom, as both realm and royal government.[22]

The strength of a medieval government was measured in its ability to organise for war. The war with the Norse also demonstrated Scottish military capacity in Alexander's reign. Between 1261 and 1264 the king and magnates raised and led forces to both defend and extend their lordship. In 1261 and 1262 the earls of Ross and Menteith led separate efforts to extract lands and submissions from the kindreds of the Isles and the far west. In 1263, in response to 'the coming of the Norsemen', the arrival of King Hakon with a fleet in the Hebrides, Alexander organised forces for the defence of his realm, while in 1264 two armies were prepared under the king and his lieutenants for campaigns in the Isles which would exploit the Norwegian withdrawal. These forces were assembled by different means. The men whom Earl William of Ross led to Skye in 1262 were probably from his province, and the army raised by Buchan, Mar and Durward in 1264 included their 'knights and retainers'. However, for the emergency of 1263 the king called on the greater resources provided by the 'common army' and contingents raised by knight service. In the confused fight at Largs, 'the foot-followers of the country' and local knights were quickly assembled to drive off parties of Norse. They fought under the joint command of the sheriff of Ayr and the chief local lord, the

[21]   Duncan, *The Making of the kingdom*, 577; *E.R.*, i, 11, 19; *Scotichronicon*, v, 349.
[22]   A verse epitaph, written shortly after Alexander's death and beginning 'Qwhen Alexander our kynge was dede, That Scotland lede in lauche and le', suggests an early origin to the view of the reign as an era of peace (Clancy, *The Triumph Tree, Scotland's Earliest Poetry*, 297).

brothers Walter, earl of Menteith and Alexander Stewart. From Inverness to Dumfries, similar forces under royal officers and magnates probably stood ready to meet an attack from the sea.[23]

The Scottish king did not rely solely on unpaid forces but supported them with small paid contingents. In particular, during 1263 and 1264 the king maintained a body of household knights and sergeants, perhaps totalling sixty armoured horsemen. This body would not have been insignificant on the battlefield, and both English and French kings retained similar household troops. The king also paid to ensure the defence of his realm. The chain of royal castles was strengthened. Last-minute building work was carried out at exposed sites like Ayr, Wigtown, Dumfries and Inverness, and watchmen were employed to warn of attack even at Aberdeen and Stirling castles. The garrisons for these castles were normally provided by the local knights or burgesses but at Ayr, whilst the Norse were in the Clyde, the burgesses refused to serve in the castle. Instead the sheriff, Walter Stewart, raised 120 sergeants, presumably from his family's lands, and these held the castle for three weeks. Royal revenues paid for equipment as well as men. New ships, crossbows, possibly even siege engines were constructed, and food renders and fines of cattle and grain were diverted to feed garrisons and field forces.[24] The performance of these Scots forces was unspectacular but ultimately effective. Against the divided rulers of the Isles and a Norwegian fleet hundreds of miles from home, the combination of the 'common army', the retinues of great lords and paid troops proved sufficient. However, Alexander was aware of the limits of such forces and used the resources of the crown to support them. Like rulers elsewhere in the west, the thirteenth-century Scottish kings were recognising the advantages of paying for war.

The sinews of war were money. In England and France kings raised huge sums to finance their wars and developed bureaucracies to gather and spend this cash. Scotland's kings did not follow suit. The year 1266 ended Alexander's only period of warfare with a rival king, and the sum spent was less than a tenth of the cost of the English king's war against the Welsh in 1276. Alexander III had paid for war from the normal revenues of the crown. The earliest evidence of the scale and character of this income comes from the 1264 records of the exchequer, the court which audited the accounts of royal officials. At the exchequer the king's chief financial agent, the chamberlain, recorded the sums raised by the crown

[23] E.R., i, 5, 11, 19; Scotichronicon, v, 349; Anderson, Early Sources, 607; Cowan, 'Norwegian sunset, Scottish dawn: Hakon IV and Alexander III', 103–31, 122.
[24] E.R., i, 5–6, 10–12, 14–16, 18–19, 22, 24; Duncan, Making of the kingdom, 387–8, 599.

The Army of Thirteenth-Century Scotland

Medieval kings were recognised as the leaders of their people in war and, in thirteenth-century Scotland, the idea of the community in arms had continued significance. Royal armies were still recruited on the basis that individuals and communities had an obligation to serve their royal lord in war. Such 'Scottish service' made up the 'common army', a force which the king could summon from all or part of his realm for a limited time, generally stated to be forty days. This levy had formed the basis of Scottish armies for centuries, providing contingents of freeholders and lesser men normally equipped with long spears or axes, leather helms and small round shields. Only the richest of these would have worn armour of leather or quilted cloth. Yet, as with many aspects of the kingdom's organisation, the century before 1214 had seen new elements introduced to the army. No thirteenth-century royal host was complete without a body of armoured, trained horsemen. Their presence was a mark of the Scottish king's military power. The knight was the symbol of military society in thirteenth-century Scotland, appearing on the seals used by kings and nobles to depict the martial values of the elite. Many nobles held their lands from king or magnate in return for providing knights in their lord's retinue during a campaign, or in his castles at other times. Land grants could also be used to raise non-noble soldiers or sergeants, and specialist archers.

However, though they served on different terms, practical distinctions between the 'common army' and 'feudal' contingents were blurred. A summons to join the army in 1286 included 'all . . . who owed service to the king, either free [feudal] or Scottish'. The men who raised and led the army varied according to district. In the sheriffdoms, royal officials were responsible, but in the provinces of the north and west, contingents were commanded by traditional leaders. These were not always earls or lords and, in Galloway, the heads of native kindreds, the captains, led the Gallovidians in the host. In many cases, however, these distinctions in command were also blurred. The roles of sheriff, feudal lord and provincial leader were often held by the same men. While magnates probably went to war amidst their knights, the armies of footmen raised from their lordships must have been led directly by lesser men, officials or influential freeholders. In its command structure and composition, the army reflected the kingdom. Though limited in range and tactics, it met the military needs of the thirteenth-century kings.[25]

---

[25] Barrow, 'The army of Alexander III's Scotland', 132–47.

and how it was spent. The 1264 exchequer accounted for just under £5,500 spent by the crown. This income came from a number of sources. About a third was from the fines levied in royal courts and from wardships (the revenues of estates without adult lords) and reliefs (succession duties paid by new vassals). The bulk of the king's remaining income came from land. The crown's estates were divided between twenty-eight sheriffdoms, but the greatest concentrations lay in the east and included the thanages of Scotia. Although Alexander and his father continued to grant some thanages as private fiefs, the majority remained as lucrative royal estates, providing money rents and renders of food to the crown. Such rents in kind were common across the royal estates. Originally designed to supply the king's household, much of the produce was sold for cash. However, the king's progresses round his realm still included old thanage centres like Kintore in Aberdeenshire, Cowie in the Mearns and Kinclaven near Perth, and the renders of these estates offset the household's costs. Rents in cattle, pigs, grain and cheese added significantly to the resources of the crown.[26]

From the mid-1260s Alexander's income probably increased, thanks initially to a series of financial windfalls. In the early 1270s seven of the Scottish bishoprics were vacant, the richest, St Andrews, for nearly three years. During vacancies the crown was entitled to the revenues of the bishops' estates and Alexander probably overrode ecclesiastical opposition to secure his rights to this additional income. The king also profited from the absence of adult tenants for long periods in the earldoms of Carrick, Angus, Atholl and, especially, Fife. Fife was one of the richest Scottish earldoms, valued at £400 in the 1290s. Between 1266 and 1284 it lacked an adult earl and its revenues were used to support the king and his family. Towards the latter part of the reign Alexander sought additional income from the burghs. He copied an English innovation by imposing a customs duty on exported hides and wool, and negotiated grants of money from the richest burghs in the form of loans or gifts.[27]

Though they were mostly *ad hoc* payments, these additional sources of income must have raised royal revenues to new levels. Though Alexander's income was less than that of the English and French crown, and little more than that of the greatest English magnates, it was far above that of the richest of his own vassals, rising to perhaps as much as £8,000. In comparable circumstances, the lordship of Ireland produced a normal

[26] *E.R.*, i, 6–7, 10, 25; Duncan, *Making of the kingdom*, 595–602; Grant, 'Thanes and thanages', 61–5; *S.H.S. Misc.*, ii, 24–6.
[27] *Scotichronicon*, v, 380–1; Donaldson, 'The rights of the Scottish crown in episcopal vacancies', 27–35; Stevenson, *Documents*, i, no. 320; Mayhew, 'Alexander III – silver age?', 53–73, 54; Duncan, *Making of the kingdom*, 603–4.

income of £5,000 for the English crown in the 1270s.[28] Of greater significance was the absence of major problems caused by royal financial
demands in Scotland. Alexander III raised his income during a period of
rising prosperity. Loans and customs represented the king's cut of the
growing profits of the wool trade. Loans were balanced by grants of new
powers to burghs, and customs were set at a low level. Alexander's reign
witnessed no rapid growth in the scale or range of the crown's demands
on its subjects. Most significantly, there was no development of taxation
on the goods of the whole population as a means of financing royal activities. The Scottish crown taxed only rarely, for set purposes and from its
tenants-in-chief, in the form of an *aid*. The absence of general taxation
meant that, unlike England, thirteenth-century Scotland saw no challenge to the crown on financial issues from bodies claiming to represent
the whole community of the realm. Alexander III's kingship was part of
a more limited, less demanding tradition than that of the Plantagenets.

Alexander III supported himself from the ordinary revenues of the
crown, 'living of his own', rather than from taxation. His chief expense,
over £3,000 in 1264, was maintaining the king's and queen's households.
The royal couple spent money on wine and gambling, fine woollen cloth,
furs and silk, but the maintenance of the household was not just a question of keeping up the image and style of monarchy. The household was
the centre of royal government. It was an increasingly complex body
which travelled round Scotland with the king. A document from the
1290s sets out the organisation of the king's household, naming eleven
officers and numerous other servants. These officials were divided
between the writing office; the chapel; the finance office; the chamber,
with the last itself sub-divided into four different departments. The
clerks in these departments were paid for their service, and fees were also
given to a body of household knights numbering at least eleven at the end
of Alexander's reign. These knights were not simply a military retinue
but, as messengers and councillors, formed a vital body of royal servants.[29]

King Alexander waged war, collected revenues and enforced judgements without placing heavy demands on his subjects. He could do this
only by depending on the service of his nobility. Professional royal
bureaucrats were limited to a handful of clerics. The rest of the king's

---

[28] For these comparisons, see Prestwich, *Edward I*, ch. 9; Stringer, *Earl David of
Huntingdon*, 191; Altschul, *A Baronial Family in Medieval England: The Clares*, 201–6;
Denholm-Young, *Richard of Cornwall*, 163; Lydon, *The Lordship of Ireland in the
Middle Ages*, 125.

[29] *E.R.*, i, 10; *S.H.S. Miscellany*, ii, 31–43; Stevenson, *Documents*, i, nos 22, 23, 28, 30,
32, 35, 37, 58, 60.

officers, from hereditary stewards, constables and doorwards to household knights, were from families which were royal tenants and subjects.
Even the chief financial officer, the chamberlain, was almost always a lay
magnate like William, earl of Mar or Aymer Maxwell. Beyond his household, the king's government rested on the justiciars and sheriffs. These
posts too belonged to noblemen. In 1264 one magnate, Alexander, earl of
Buchan, was justicar of Scotia, sheriff of Wigtown, bailie of Dingwall and
keeper of the vacant earldom of Carrick and the de Quincy inheritance.
Yet this picture of delegated power is misleading. In the sheriffdoms of
the east and south, where the crown's richest lands and main residences
lay, the king chose a different type of officer. From Inverness and Nairn
down the east coast to Berwick and then west to Lanark and Dumfries,
the sheriffs were barons or lesser nobles. Almost all came from the local
communities they administered. Sheriffs like William Wiseman in
Forres, Simon Fraser in Tweeddale and William Mowat in Forfar were
landowners with strong ties to their sheriffdoms, and many such men
were not the first of their families to hold the office. Although their posts
were not hereditary, nevertheless kings tended to look to the same group
of local families, only occasionally bringing a new man, like William
Sinclair, into the ranks of their sheriffs. In return, these local families recognised the primacy of royal service which, in normal circumstances,
outweighed the alliances between lords which had proliferated in the
minority. Fifteen of the sheriffs in the early 1260s acted as royal councillors and their kindreds were represented amongst Alexander's household
knights. The service and support of these baronial sheriffs was the
bedrock of Scottish royal authority in the thirteenth century. Sheriffs collected royal revenues, mustered royal armies, and enforced royal justice.
More than that, they represented the king and his lordship to the men of
the sheriffdoms, the heartlands of the thirteenth-century realm.[30]

It was only at the fringes of these heartlands that royal government was
delegated to great lords. Earls were only employed as sheriffs in the west,
at Ayr, Wigtown and Dumbarton, where the king saw the need for the
additional resources of magnates like Buchan or Menteith. In the far
west, and the interior of the north, such earls and provincial lords held
direct authority. Here, Alexander's role was to resolve conflict and restore
balance amongst a group which had caused problems for his father. The
same issues reoccurred. In 1269 Alexander had to arbitrate between John
Comyn, lord of Badenoch and his neighbour, the earl of Atholl. Five years
earlier, after a long vacancy, the king had bestowed Atholl on David, lord

[30] *E.R.*, i, 1–34; Young, 'Noble families and political factions in the reign of Alexander
III', 1–30.

of Strathbogie, a kinsman of the earls of Fife. Alexander's choice may have been designed to curb the ambitions of the 'unruly' Comyn, whose lordship bordered Atholl to the north. Comyn's response was to build a castle on his estates at Blair in Atholl and close to Earl David's *Caisteal Dubh*, 'black castle', at Moulin. Alexander stepped in to settle a growing rivalry. His judgement is not known, but harmony was secured when David went on crusade the following year. His death whilst abroad left Atholl to his infant son, the king's ward, preventing any fresh disputes until the young earl grew up.[31]

An earldom without an adult lord was not just a political and financial windfall for the crown. Both Alexander and his father had been lucky that none of their great western adherents – the earls of Ross, the Comyns, or the Stewarts – had suffered a failure of adult succession which would have weakened both their lordship and the crown's influence in unstable frontier regions of the realm. Even in more secure provinces, wardship required the crown to provide direction for communities deprived of their traditional head. Fife, for example, was without an adult earl for much of the two decades from 1266. In these circumstances, it was up to the king to run the province. Alexander's response to this situation was not necessarily in the earls' best interests. When Malcolm, earl of Fife died in 1266, his widow, who retained a sizeable portion of the earldom, was quickly remarried to Donald, son of the earl of Mar. Both Mar and his ally, Buchan, were active in Fife during the late 1260s and retained links with members of the local community, several of whom had participated in their seizure of the king in 1257. These Fife landowners, the most important of whom was Hugh Abernethy, may have welcomed the absence of an adult earl as a chance to forge closer links with other magnates and with the crown. When the new earl of Fife, Colban, died in 1270, not long after he had received his lands, Alexander III took a more direct approach. As Colban's son, Duncan, grew up, his province was assigned to the king's own son, Alexander. Between 1270 and 1284 Fife was treated as crown lands, and the king and his family resided in the earldom.[32]

In Fife, which lay amidst royal sheriffdoms, Alexander exercised direct control; elsewhere he was prepared to delegate his rights. The earldom of Carrick, in the far south-west, was in royal hands for a decade after the death of Earl Neil in 1256. Though the king was the official guardian of Neil's daughter, Marjory, her province was run by Alexander Comyn, earl

[31] *Scotichronicon*, v, 372–3, 376–7.
[32] *Scotichronicon*, v, 356–7, 380–1; *Dunfermline Reg.*, nos 88–9; *C.D.S.*, ii, no. 94; Anderson, *Early Sources*, 684.

of Buchan, who paid a rent or ferme to the king. Buchan's position was a legacy of minority politics. Following Earl Neil's death, the Comyns had forged an alliance with his leading tenants and established local dominance through them. At the same time, the justiciarship of neighbouring Galloway was secured for John Comyn, and in 1264 Buchan inherited a share of the old lordship of Galloway. The king did not regard this extension of Comyn influence as a threat. Though John Comyn was removed from his justiciarship after the dispute over Menteith, he was restored to office in 1266, and at about the same time the king picked a kinsman of the Comyns from Fife, Adam of Kilconquhar, to marry Countess Marjory. The Comyns also sought further allies in the region. In the 1270s John Comyn's son and heir married the daughter of John Balliol, lord of Galloway, a match with enormous consequences for both families and for Scotland. The initial purpose of the marriage was to forge a link between the two leading houses in the old Gallovidian realm.[33]

If the king was happy to see this alliance, other lords in the region were less so. Alexander Stewart, whose family had strong links of kinship with the earls of Carrick, had seen his influence reduced in neighbouring regions since 1256. Further east, Robert Bruce of Annandale could contrast his recent experience with that of the Comyns and Balliols. As landowners in northern England and south-west Scotland, as heirs of the old Huntingdon lands and opponents in the minority, Bruce and Balliol were natural rivals. While Balliol secured new allies, Bruce was forced to extricate himself from a dispute with the king over his rights in Annandale in 1270. If Bruce and Stewart harboured anxieties, direct action came from Countess Marjory of Carrick. Her first husband, Adam of Kilconquhar, had died in 1270 and, according to a later tale, she now abducted the young Robert Bruce, heir to Annandale. However much the widowed countess was attracted by the 'handsome young knight', the marriage also secured her a powerful ally and secured the Bruce family new rank and power in the south-west. The king was not happy with this match. In late 1275 he seized Carrick, dealing directly with lesser men from the earldom, and imprisoned the couple. His hostility was less about lost revenues than the creation of local factions. Significantly, it may have been the Stewarts who persuaded Alexander to restore Robert and Marjory.[34] Events in the south-west in the 1270s showed that the rivalries of minority politics were not completely dead, with the magnates of the region renewing their family's friendships and enmities of 1255. Aristocratic

[33] E.R., i, 5; Scotichronicon, v, 376–7, 382–5; Young, Robert the Bruce's Rivals, 72, 82.
[34] Barrow, 'A kingdom in crisis: Scotland and the Maid of Norway', 120–41, 124–5; Scotichronicon, v, 382–5; R.M.S., i, no. 508.

politics, the patterns of alliances, kinship and competition, retained an importance which would ultimately outweigh the structures of royal government.

The king's containment and management of his greatest subjects, lords and ladies with their own followings, was never easy. It depended on chance and personality. As old rivalries ended, new ones were born. The death of Alan Durward without a son saw the partition of his lands and the end of his divisive claim to the earldom of Mar. Yet this, in turn, removed the basis for the close alliance between the earls of Mar and the Comyns. After the death of his father and Comyn mother in the 1270s, the new earl of Mar, Donald, came to regard his Comyn neighbours as competitors rather than kinsmen. The king had to prevent such competition becoming feuds. The peace for which his reign was remembered was a testament to Alexander's success in this. This success was based less on threat or force, than on established patterns of lordship and reward. Alexander could be forceful. Lesser lords, like Simon, thane of Aberchirder, and greater ones, like the sons of the earl of Dunbar, could find themselves on the wrong end of the king's anger and be forced to beg for forgiveness, but Alexander put none of his magnates beyond the reach of his favour. John Comyn of Badenoch and Robert Bruce, earl of Carrick, who had both incurred the king's hostility, were quickly able to recover his goodwill. Comyn recovered his influence and office, and Bruce was allowed to take possession of Carrick. In 1285 the king even allowed Comyn's son, William, to raise a new claim to Menteith, the issue that had initially caused the rift between them. This time, ironically, the Comyns supported the rights of Countess Isabella, the woman John had imprisoned. The marriage of Isabella's daughter to William Comyn allowed him to challenge Earl Walter Stewart, and, at 'a gret gaderynge' at Scone, the king ordered Stewart to surrender a portion of the earldom to the young couple.[35] Though such judgements did not automatically end disputes, Alexander was a king who sat comfortably at the head of his nobility. The network of royal lordship, forged over a series of reigns, was extended and strengthened to draw in lords from across the Scottish realm. The councils of the last decade of the reign included elder statesmen like the earls of Buchan and Dunbar, and a new generation of magnates like Donald of Mar, James Stewart, Robert Bruce of Carrick and the younger John Comyn of Badenoch. Alexander was above the rivalries of his nobility, and worked with a group who were established leaders of local communities. He employed them in government, recognised their rights and claims and

---

[35] *Scotichronicon*, v, 366–7, 370–1, 382–5, 402–3; Wyntoun, *The Original Chronicle*, v, 138; Grant, 'Thanes and thanages', 58; *National Manuscripts of Scotland*, i, no. 74.

regulated relations between them, demanding their support in traditional and limited terms. The personal lordship of the king, his contacts with this group, remained the basis of Scottish kingship.

The weakening of this royal lordship during Alexander's childhood had led many of his lords to look to the king of England as a temporary, alternative source of direction. In the early 1260s Alexander's assumption of personal authority was accompanied by displays of his freedom from any claims of his father-in-law, Henry III, to be his tutor. On his visit to England in 1260 Alexander pressed for payment of his queen's long overdue dowry, and in 1262 ignored the efforts of Henry III to mediate between him and Hakon of Norway. The treaty of Perth in 1266 secured Alexander the Isles, including Man, on which Henry III had designs. Yet Alexander's relationship with Henry and his son, Edward I, saw no repeat of earlier tensions. When England descended into civil war in 1264, Alexander did not back the English king's enemies, as his father had done in 1216, but openly aided Henry's cause. A contingent of Scots was in the royal army which was defeated at Lewes and its leaders – Robert Bruce, John Balliol and John Comyn – were captured with King Henry. In early 1265 the baronial government sought peace with Alexander but, in response to an appeal from Prince Edward, he was preparing to raise a new force to aid the royalists when he received news of Edward's victory at Evesham. Though there were a number of his vassals amongst the leading rebels, Alexander was a fixed supporter of the king's party.[36]

This support was natural. He regarded the English kings as his kinsmen, lords and friends. Personal contact between the two royal families was more frequent and cordial than at any other period. During the late 1260s Edward visited his sister and brother-in-law in Scotland on two or three occasions, and in the twenty years from 1265 a regular exchange of letters and gifts passed between Alexander and his children and Edward of England. The mutual enquiries about health and fortune made by the 'most hearty' Edward and his Scottish relatives stressed the close family ties which existed between the Plantagenets and the house of Scotland.[37] Alexander III paid visits to the courts of King Henry and King Edward in 1260, 1268, 1274 and 1278. These journeys south were not social calls. Alexander performed his duties as a vassal of the English king. In 1274, accompanied by Queen Margaret, he attended Edward's coronation. His presence contrasted with the absence of Llywelyn ap

---

[36] *C.D.S.*, i, nos 2,219, 2,320, 2,328, 2,377–8; *Scotichronicon*, v, 350–3; Anderson, *Early Sources*, 644, 652.

[37] *Scotichronicon*, v, 354–5, 370–1; Anderson, *Early Sources*, 655; *C.D.S.*, ii, nos 40, 96, 156–7, 185, 204; Stones, *Anglo-Scottish Relations*, no. 13.

Gruffydd, now prince of Wales, who was moving towards conflict with the English king. The outstanding issues and tensions concerning Plantagenet lordship, which led to Edward's first Welsh war in 1276, did not exist between the English king and his Scottish brother-in-law. However, Alexander was not just another vassal. In 1278, when he came south to pay homage to Edward, Alexander demanded an escort of two archbishops and three earls to emphasise his status. As king and baron, Alexander defended his rights energetically. He received special treatment from royal officials in his lands of Penrith and pursued his claim to Huntingdon. More importantly, Alexander carefully guarded his royal rights. In 1274 he obtained Edward's promise that his attendance did not prejudice his position as king of Scots, and in the late 1270s Alexander stood up to his neighbour in a dispute on the border near Berwick. The most striking exchange came in 1278. After Alexander had done homage for his English lands, Edward's councillors reserved their master's right to claim similar lordship over Alexander's kingdom. Alexander rejected these claims saying, 'nobody but God has the right to the homage of my realm of Scotland'. This stance was accepted and expected by Edward, whose aim was to register, not enforce his claim and who sought no conflict with such an established ruler.[38]

With hindsight such incidents can take on a sinister tinge, as evidence of Anglo-Scottish tensions. What probably struck contemporaries, however, was the absence of any crises like those of 1216-18, 1235-6 or 1244. Alexander may have wished to define his lordship more clearly with regard to the English realm. The purchase of the Scottish lands of the de Bohun family and the temporary diversion of the office of constable from William Ferrers to Buchan may suggest a concern over the divided allegiances of many of his vassals. However, as will be discussed later, the king's efforts never amounted to a consistent policy and were a drop in the ocean. Alexander and most of his chief vassals held lands in both realms without problems, and the king was comfortable in an aristocratic world which included the Plantagenet dominions and the kingdom of France. Buying out certain absentees was about the strengthening of the Scottish king's lordship, the key royal policy for generations, not about the loosening of ties between the Scottish crown and nobility and their counterparts in the Plantagenet lands.[39]

The confidence and success with which Alexander maintained the

---

[38]   Prestwich, *Edward I*, 91, 356-7; *C.D.S.*, ii, nos 128, 154, 157, 159; Duncan, *Kingship of the Scots*, 159-64; Stones *Anglo-Scottish Relations*, no. 12; *Scotichronicon*, v, 408-9.
[39]   *Scotichronicon*, v, 374-5, 380-1; *National Manuscripts of Scotland*, i, no. 74; *A.P.S.*, i, 116; Duncan, *Scotland*, 587.

rights of the Scottish crown with regard to his own subjects and other realms should emphasise, rather than disguise, the personal element in the Scottish monarchy. The government of the realm and the defence of its status as subject to God alone depended on the king. The minority had provided a recent lesson of the effects that the absence of an adult and universally-accepted king could have. The future of the dynasty that had created the Scottish realm as a European monarchy was the key to maintaining the security of that realm. In November 1282, as he witnessed the marriage of his son, Alexander, to the daughter of the Count of Flanders, the king could justifiably see the future of his line and the status of his dynasty as secure. His daughter, Margaret, had recently married King Eric of Norway and was soon to produce a child. Yet, within fifteen months, this child, Margaret of Norway, would be Alexander's only direct heir. In retrospect, the decline of the house of Scotland began in 1275 with Queen Margaret's death, but it was the deaths of her children – David in 1280, Margaret in 1283 and Alexander in 1284 – that dealt the king a series of personal blows.[40] The situation was by no means hopeless. At the age of forty-two, King Alexander was younger than either his father or grandfather had been at the birth of their heirs and had made rapid preparations for the succession. Within days of his son's death, the king obtained a promise from his magnates that they would accept the child, Margaret of Norway, as his heir. This was only an insurance policy. In October 1285 Alexander remarried, wedding Yolanda of Dreux, from a French noble family. He hoped that this match would produce a child of his own to succeed him. It was his enthusiasm to return to his young queen that led the king to leave Edinburgh and cross the Forth on the evening of 19 March 1286. Setting out from Queensferry to the royal manor at Kinghorn, Alexander was thrown from his horse and died, his neck broken.[41]

[40] *Scotichronicon*, v, 402–3, 408–13 ; Anderson, *Early Sources*, 679–85; Stones and Simpson, *Edward I and the Throne of Scotland*, ii, 188–90.
[41] Anderson, *Early Sources*, 688–94; *Scotichronicon*, 418–21; *Chron. Fordun*, 309–10.

CHAPTER 4

The Sea Kings

THE KINGDOM OF THE ISLES

The thirteenth-century kings of Scotland viewed the world from the core of their realm in the valleys of the Tay, the Forth and the Tweed. Between 1214 and 1286 the kings sought to establish structures of direct and indirect rule beyond these southern and eastern heartlands by negotiation and by force. To them, the extension of royal lordship westwards and northwards represented the enlargement and tightening of the crown's authority in the fringes of the realm, a legitimate stage in the formation of Scotland as a realm and community which stretched across the northern British Isles. However, Alexander II and Alexander III were not the only holders of a royal title, nor the only source of lordship, in the region. Nor were they the only rulers seeking to extend their authority as superior lords along the coasts and among the islands of the northern and north-western British Isles. If Scotland's kings saw these regions as the frontiers of their kingdom, theirs was not the only perspective. The lands in the west had their own identities and outlooks, distinct from those of the Scottish kings.[1]

The ambitions of the kings of Scots brought them into close contact with the men of the Isles. The islands of the west, from Lewis in the north down through the Hebrides to Islay and south to Man in the Irish Sea, lay under the lordship of the king of Norway. The Isles, or the Sudreys as the Norse termed them, formed the core of a different region. Custom and language in this maritime province reflected the merging of Scandinavian and Gaelic populations and cultures since the arrival of the Norsemen in

[1] The fullest accounts of the Isles in the thirteenth century are McDonald, *The Kingdom of the Isles*, chs 3–5; Duncan and Brown, 'Argyll and the Western Isles in the early Middle Ages', 192–220; Sellar, 'Hebridean sea kings', 187–218.

**Map 4.1   The Kingdom of the Isles and its neighbours
in the thirteenth century**

- - - - - - -   Approximate boundary of lands held
by descendants of Somerled

the ninth century. This distinct identity was recognised not simply by the royal titles claimed by rulers in the region, but by the creation of a single diocese covering the Isles in the late twelfth century. However, this was no separate offshore world. The politics and society of the Isles were bound up with the coastlands which bordered them from north Wales to Caithness. These contacts were strongest with Ulster and Connacht in north-western Ireland, and with western Scotland. Headlands like Kintyre and Ardnamurchan, and mountainous, sea-penetrated districts like Morvern, Lorn and Cowal, had ties of lordship to the nearby islands of Mull, Skye, Jura, Bute and Arran. Similarly, Galloway, Moray and Ross were provinces which looked out west to sea, as well as east to the king's court, and their rulers also had strong ties to the Islesmen. To such men and to sea-going societies from across the north, the Isles were not a peripheral region but the crossroads of a world dominated by ships and sea travel. Sea-routes from Scandinavia, Ireland, western Scotland, England and the continent all met in the Isles, and political ambitions followed. In the thirteenth century, the Isles and their rulers were at the centre of a competition for power between the kings of northern Europe.[2]

The leading men of the Isles in the early thirteenth century came from an extended royal dynasty which had risen to prominence in the conflicts and contacts of these Irish Sea and Atlantic regions. The dynasty's roots lay in the Scandinavian rulers of Dublin, and its founder Godfrey Crovan (Gofraidh Crobhain) had seized Man and the Isles by conquest in the later eleventh century. Kings of the Isles had existed from the tenth century but it was the rule of Godfrey and his son Olaf (Amhlaibh) the Red, who ruled for forty years up to 1153, that provided a recent tradition and unity in the region. This unity ended soon after Olaf's death and would be restored only in greatly-altered form after long years of almost constant conflict. While Olaf's son, Godfrey, held the title of king of the Isles, he had a rival in the great Somerled (Somhairle), probably a noble of Argyll. Somerled claimed kingship for his own sons by Ragnhild, Godfrey's sister: Dugald (Dubhghall), Ranald (Raghnall) and Angus (Aenghus). From the first two of these would spring the principal kindreds of the Hebrides over the following centuries: the descendants of Dugald, the MacDougalls, and of Ranald, the MacDonalds and MacRuairis. Somerled himself bore the titles *Ri Innse Gall* (king of the Isles) and *Ri Airer Goidel* (king of Argyll), and his line remained in direct competition with that of the Godfreysons. Godfrey's descendants ruled in Man, Skye and Lewis, and the sons and grandsons of Somerled held sway in Uist, Mull, Islay and Jura as well as in the coastlands from

---

[2] McDonald, *Kingdom of the Isles*, 10–20.

Kintyre through Lorn, Morvern and Garmoran. Each of these two rival branches tended to recognise a single holder of the kingship but the character of politics in the Isles during the opening years of the century was set by competition between and within these growing kindreds.[3]

The offspring of Somerled and of Godfrey of Man did not exercise power over settled realms or in conditions of peace. The division of the Isles between them had never ended the rivalry of the two lines. The plundering of Skye in 1209 by Somerled's grandsons, Donald (Domhnall) and Ruairi (Ruaidhri), demonstrated continuing friction. The coming decades would see this intensify as various descendants of Somerled sought to exploit the problems of the Manx dynasty. These problems were the result of rivalries between the sons of King Godfrey of Man, Ranald (Rognvald or Ragnall) and Olaf the Black (Olav or Amhlaibh). Similar rivalries divided the descendants of Somerled and caused major conflicts. Leadership of the dynasty was probably established by diplomacy backed by considerable use of force. By the 1210s the most aggressive leaders were the brothers Donald and Ruairi. They inherited the conflicts of their father, Ranald, with his brothers, Dugald and Angus, and were probably responsible for the killing of Angus and his three sons in 1210, eliminating a whole branch of the kindred of Somerled.[4]

Angus's death removed a potential rival for the kingship, which was probably held by Ruairi. It was also a part of the process by which the descendants of Somerled secured lordship in the many Isles and coastal districts of the west. Successful leaders like Ruairi established their rule over the Isles, extinguishing, supplanting or relegating rivals. The same process of change was probably also happening at a lower level. Lesser lords and kindreds, dependants or neighbours of the two principal dynasties, seem also to have established themselves in this period. Powerful families from the later middle ages, like the MacLeods in Skye and Lewis or the MacLeans on Mull, probably emerged as locally significant groupings between 1150 and 1250. Certainly in Argyll the brothers Sween (Suibhne), Ferchar and Gilchrist, the principal nobles in Cowal and Knapdale, were the progenitors of the MacSween, Lamont and MacLachlan families which had long and eventful histories ahead of them.[5] Such lesser lords were already important in the west. Around 1200 Sween possessed the resources to construct the stone stronghold of

[3] Duncan and Brown, 'Argyll and the Western Isles', 195–8; McDonald, *Kingdom of the Isles*, 33–6, 44–7; Sellar, 'The origins and ancestry of Somerled', 123–42.
[4] Anderson, *Early Sources*, ii, 231–2, 378, 382, 387, 456–60 (account from the Chronicle of Man); McDonald, *Kingdom of the Isles*, 85–6.
[5] Sellar, 'Family origins in Cowal and Knapdale', 21–37.

Galleys and Galloglaich

In a region of islands and mountainous coasts, the ship was the prime means of transport, trade and communication, a weapon of war and an instrument of government. Power was measured in galleys which were the descendants of Viking longships. Depictions on seals and carved stones show them with posts at bow and stern, equipped with oars and a single sail. While Hakon IV's flagship in 1263, *Kristsuden*, carried 300 men, the galleys found in the Isles were much smaller, with crews of between a dozen and 100 men. Similarly, though Hakon and Alan of Galloway could command fleets of over 100 ships, Olaf of Man had only thirty vessels in the 1220s, and raiding fleets were probably smaller still. Rulers gathered such fleets through ship-service, the obligation of lesser nobles to provide galleys for their lords' use. In 1264 Magnus of Man promised to supply his new lord, Alexander III, with ten ships on request, and the Scottish kings probably imposed similar obligations on the Hebrideans. The island lords in turn levied service from lesser men. War and politics in the Isles depended on the movement of fleets and the control of anchorages where galleys could be securely beached at night or in poor weather. The castles built in the region guarded such harbours, and the importance of fortified islands like the MacDubgall stronghold at Cairn-na-burgh off Mull is evidence of the link between castle-building and sea-power.

The military prowess of the Islesmen was not confined to the seas. On land they enjoyed a fearsome reputation as raiders, allies and especially as mercenaries. Their best employers were Gaelic Irish lords. Hebrideans had long served such masters as bodyguards, but during the later thirteenth century there was an increase in the numbers of Islesmen serving in Ireland. Exiles from the wars of the Isles, like the Meic Suibhne (MacSweenys), settled as professional soldiers in Ireland and were retained by lords with land grants. These Hebridean warriors, from the 1290s known as *Gallóglaich* (foreign soldier), became a permanent feature of Irish warfare and society. Armoured in chain mail or padded coats and wielding long swords, spears or axes, they provided a core to Irish armies which could withstand English horsemen on the battlefield. The *Gallóglaich* were a factor in slowing the spread of English lordship in Ireland after 1250 and survived as a military caste into the sixteenth century. In both ships and men, the Isles remained a heavily militarised society in the late thirteenth century.[6]

---

[6] Rixson, *The West Highland Galley*; Hayes-McCoy, *Scots Mercenary Forces in Ireland*; K. Simms, 'Gallowglass', in S. Connolly (ed.), *Oxford Companion to Irish History* (Oxford, 1998), 217.

Figure 4.1. Dunstaffnage Castle in Lorn was the most sophisticated of the group of stone castles built in Argyll and the Hebrides between 1150 and 1300. Its three towers may suggest the influence of mainland castle-building styles.

Castle Sween in Knapdale. His example was followed by other lords during the first half of the thirteenth century, above all the descendants of Somerled. Ruairi was probably responsible for the castles at Mingary and Tioram, while his cousins, the sons of Dugald, had perhaps five strongholds by the 1240s, the most important of which was Dunstaffnage in Lorn. Squat and thick-walled, with few towers and simple gateways, like Dunstaffnage and Mingary, or adaptations of natural island refuges, the castles of the sea kings were constructed as instruments of military lordship. Sited to protect anchorages and to police lochs, these castles acted as bases from which their lords could maintain their authority and dominate the sea-routes on which control of the Isles depended.[7]

The concentration of castles in Argyll and the Isles symbolised the character of the region – militarised and unstable – in the thirteenth century. The strength of lords like Ruairi and the sons of Dugald was measured in castles, retinues of skilled soldiers and galley fleets. Lesser lords and kindreds switched allegiance between leaders whose authority lacked clear legitimacy or deep roots. The endemic warfare of the western seas was not simply driven by such ambitious leaders. The Isles and the coasts were

[7] McDonald, *Kingdom of the Isles*, 235–43; *R.C.A.H.M.S., Argyll*, ii 2, no. 287; Simpson, 'Castle Tioram, Moidart, Inverness-shire; and Mingary Castle, Ardnamurchan, Argyll-shire', 70–90.

unproductive lands. Though oats were grown on many islands, the ground was better suited to pasture and the staple products of the region were cattle and sheep, producing meat, wool, hides and cheese. On the poorer isles, like Lewis, hunting and fishing were vital means of supplementing the fruits of farming. This harsh environment produced people raised in traditions of seafaring and warfare. Piracy, plunder and the profits of war were signifi-cant sources of wealth to the Islesmen. The general desire for such wealth encouraged leaders to engage in raiding and war, within the Isles and beyond. The military culture this fostered made the Hebrides and nearby coasts a society that produced soldiers in large numbers and exported them to the surrounding lands as allies, mercenaries or raiders. War was one of the chief forms of contact between the Islesmen and their neighbours. In Ireland and Scotland fleets and soldiers from the Isles had long been an element in war and politics as allies and invaders, part of the web of con-nections that bound the Isles to the surrounding regions. The kings of the Isles and the lesser kindreds of Argyll had ties of blood to rulers from Ross to Connacht, and the place of the Islesmen in northern Europe was also determined by claims of overlordship. Though using royal titles, the lords of the Isles were regarded as *reguli*, under-kings, like the Welsh princes or most Irish kings. They owed allegiance to overlords. The Sudreys were in the realm of the king of Norway, and Argyll was within the Scottish kingdom. During the twelfth century such claims of overlordship had little impact in the west. The thirteenth century would prove very different.[8]

The demands of royal lordship were felt with increasing force in the Isles from 1200. However, the first king to seek direct lordship in the region was neither Norse nor Scots but King John of England. The crea-tion of the lordship of Ireland as a dominion of the Plantagenets in 1171 represented a major shift in regional power. In 1210 John came to Ireland to assert his authority in this lordship and specifically in Ulster. For this purpose he sought allies from the Isles. The brothers Donald and Ruairi fought in his service, and Ranald of Man was given lands in Ulster. Man, on the sea-route from England to Ireland, was offered protection and, though the collapse of John's position in 1215 cut these ties, the English kings retained ambitions in the region. Both Norse and Scots kings fol-lowed John's example. In 1209 an expedition from Norway harried the Isles until Ranald paid homage to King Sverre and renewed the lapsed payment of tribute to him.[9] In 1221 the Scottish crown intervened

[8] For contacts between the Isles and the surrounding communities in the thirteenth century, see Duffy, 'The Bruce brothers and the Irish sea world', 55–86.
[9] Anderson, *Early Sources*, ii, 380–1, 393; A. O. Johnsen, 'The payments from the Hebrides and the Isle of Man to the crown of Norway', 18–34.

directly in the west. Though King William had been happy to accept
John's exertion of influence in areas which were supporting his enemies,
the MacWilliams, his son took a more direct approach. In 1221 and 1222
Alexander II led expeditions to Argyll. The first was halted by bad
weather and the second lasted only a few weeks, but these campaigns
showed the royal banner in the west. The king left a castle at Tarbert on
Kintyre, and on his road east founded a burgh at Dumbarton as royal
bases on the sea-route to Argyll.[10]

The campaign may have had a disproportionate impact on political
relationships in the west. Alexander's efforts may have been directed
against Ruairi, son of Ranald, and while he was forced to flee, others – the
sons of Dugald and Sween and his brothers – submitted to the king. The
submissions seemed to have confirmed these families as lords in Argyll.
In particular, the MacDougalls' association with Lorn and nearby Mull
seems to date from the years after 1222 and to have had some royal
support. The foundation of Ardchattan Priory by Duncan (Donnchad),
son of Dugald, represented the patronage of Valliscaulian monks
favoured by the king, and suggests some identification with the crown.
Yet even beyond Alexander's direct reach, the aftermath of the campaign
saw the formation of more limited but defined lordships in the region. It
may have been between the 1220s and 1240s that Donald, son of Ranald,
secured the lordship over Islay and parts of Kintyre which would remain
with his descendants, Clan Donald. The loser in the process was Ruairi,
son of Ranald, who seems to have lost lands and lordship in the south;
whether he retained influence in Garmoran and the Uists – later the lordships of his line, the MacRuairis – is unclear. Whether it was the aim of
the king's efforts, the 1220s and 1230s saw the fragmentation of the lands
of Somerled amongst his heirs.[11]

The 1222 campaign signalled the arrival of King Alexander as a factor
in the politics of the Isles. However, it would be nearly three decades
before the king returned to Argyll. After his intervention, Alexander was
prepared to see royal interests upheld by the activities of great magnates
in his service. The Stewarts had long performed this role in the Firth of
Clyde. By the 1220s they controlled the Isles of Arran and Bute, securing

---

[10] Stringer, 'Periphery and core', 85–7; *Scotichronicon*, v, 104–7; Dunbar and Duncan,
'Tarbert Castle, a contribution to the history of Argyll', 1–17, 2–3; Sellar, 'Hebridean
sea kings', 201.
[11] Sellar, 'Hebridean sea kings', 201–3. The date at which clear territorial associations
were established in the Isles by different branches of the royal line is unclear. It
probably had not occurred by the 1220s, but in the 1240s Ewen, son of Duncan, was
clearly associated with Lorn, suggesting the beginnings of more regional power-bases
amongst these kindreds.

the latter with a great castle at Rothesay, and were looking across the kyles to Cowal. In the north, Alexander's man was Ferchar, earl of Ross. By the mid-1220s Ferchar was extending his lordship across to Wester Ross, bringing him to the borders of Garmoran and Skye.[12] The greatest adherents of the crown in the west were the brothers Alan and Thomas of Galloway, proven leaders whose interests stretched from Connacht to Man. Galloway had always been closely linked to the Isles, and it shared the same Norse-Gaelic society, plunder-based economy and warriors and galleys. It was with a force of these that Alan and Thomas supported Alexander's Argyll campaigns just as, a decade before, they had assisted John in Ireland. Though the lordship of the Scottish king was a major element in the career of these, primarily Scottish, lords, the interests of the brothers extended beyond Alexander's kingdom and influence. King John had given Alan and Thomas extensive fiefs in Ulster, and the maintenance of these, and the search for power amongst the Isles, was a continuing element in their activities. Even in 1221 Thomas was not simply fighting for the king. On behalf of his ally the king of Connacht, he also defeated a Hebridean fleet sailing to Ireland.[13] For Thomas and Alan of Galloway, and, to a lesser extent, Walter Stewart and Ferchar of Ross, service to their royal lord was combined with the search for greater power on the fringes of his realm. It was not always a comfortable combination.

In the 1220s competition between these regional lords would lead to the clash of rival overlords. In the north, the war raised by Gilleasbuig MacWilliam involved Ruairi, son of Ranald. Ruairi's involvement was the opening round of a conflict with Ferchar of Ross which would continue between their families for over a century. A second dispute centred on Ulster: in an effort to seize the earldom of Ulster, Hugh de Lacy allied with the powerful Ó Neill kings of Tir Eoghan (Tyrone) and overran the lands of Alan of Galloway in the province. His campaign probably involved men from the Isles, and fighting extended into the Hebrides. Despite the support of Scottish and English kings, Alan was unable to recover his lands from de Lacy and it was his desire to renew the struggle which encouraged his intervention in the dispute over the kingdom of Man.[14]

This dispute had seemed settled. King Ranald had allowed his brother, Olaf, to return from exile, had granted him Lewis and arranged Olaf's

---

[12] Duncan and Brown, 'Argyll and the western Isles', 203; Anderson, *Early Sources*, ii, 404 (Chronicle of Man); Grant, 'The province of Ross', 122–3.

[13] Stringer, 'Periphery and core', 84–8, 95; Duffy, 'The Bruce brothers and the Irish sea world', 60.

[14] Duffy, 'The Bruce brothers and the Irish sea world', 69; Frame, *Ireland and Britain*, 158–60; Stringer, 'Periphery and core', 93–5; *C.D.S.*, i, no. 890; *Scotichronicon*, v, 117, 143–5.

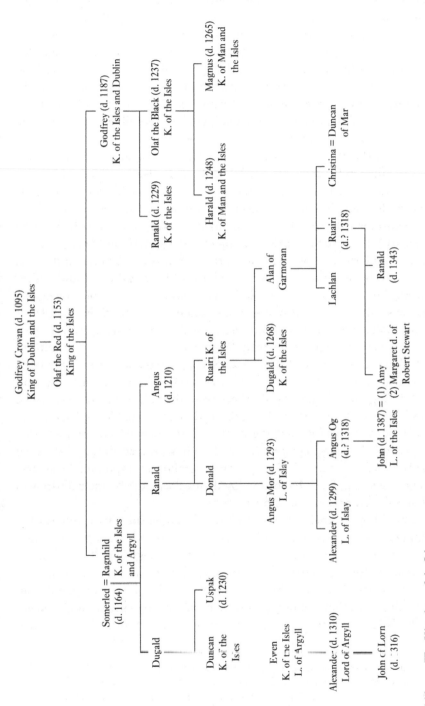

Table 4.1. The Kingdom of the Isles

marriage to his own wife's sister. However, in 1223 Olaf repudiated his bride and married the daughter of Ferchar of Ross. With an eye on the Isles, Ferchar supported Olaf against his brother, and in 1224 Ranald was forced to divide the northern Hebrides with him. Ranald now sought his own ally and found Alan of Galloway ready to offer aid. Alan's backing came at the price of a marriage between his son, Thomas, and Ranald's daughter, which gave Thomas a claim on the kingship of the Isles. Despite the military power of the Gallovidians, this alliance alienated the Manxmen. In 1226 Olaf expelled Ranald from Man and, though two years later Ranald was restored by Alan and a 'great army', in early 1229 he was killed in battle by his brother.[15] Ranald's death did not end Alan's involvement. He now sought Man as a kingdom for his son, ending his feud with Hugh de Lacy to concentrate on his new target. In the face of this continued threat, Olaf sought his own protector. In early 1230 he sailed to Norway to his overlord, King Hakon IV. Olaf found preparations already underway for an expedition to the Sudreys. Hakon had decided to assert his lordship in the west, and a fleet of longships would gather tribute, extract submissions and make kings who would recognise Hakon's rule. The expedition would be led by these under-kings, Olaf of Man and from the house of Somerled, Uspak, son of Dugald. The targets of the fleet were Uspak's kinsmen, 'Somerled's race, who were unfaithful to Hakon', and the men of the king of Scots who sought power in the Isles. The fleet would spend a year in the west, killing, imprisoning and plundering those who refused to recognise the rule of Hakon from Skye to Kintyre, and singling out Uspak's brothers, the MacDougalls, for particular attention. However, the climax of the expedition came in May 1230 when the Norse entered the Clyde. They ravaged Bute and stormed the Steward's castle of Rothesay. Alan of Galloway responded by assembling a fleet and, faced by the Gallovidian galleys, the Norse withdrew to Man, sailing home the next spring.[16]

The fall of Rothesay showed King Alexander and his magnates the dangers of their westward ambitions. Hakon too was seeking to tighten and extend his rule in the region through his vassals and could strike against the Scottish kingdom. Alexander II had come to Ayr to support Stewart in late May 1230, but the Norse identified not the king, but Alan of Galloway as their leading enemy. Scottish magnates had sought power in the Isles and in the 1220s Ferchar of Ross and Alan of Galloway had

[15] Anderson, *Early Sources*, 456–60, 465–6 (Chronicle of Man).
[16] Anderson, *Early Sources*, 471–8; McDonald, *Kingdom of the Isles*, 88–91; Sellar, 'Hebridean sea kings', 202. Alan had ended the feud with Hugh de Lacy by marrying Hugh's daughter (Anderson, *Early Sources*, 467).

backed rival claimants to Man. The ambitions of Alan in particular were a factor in the Nórse expedition. To Alexander the whole crisis seemed the result of Alan's wars against Olaf of Man, which grew themselves from the interests of Gallovidian lords in the unsettled lands of the Isles and Ulster. The deaths of Alan and Thomas of Galloway in the early 1230s allowed Alexander to sever these ties. The king's break-up of Galloway was opposed by Alan's son, Thomas, the claimant to Man. Thomas had the support of Alan's allies in Ulster and the Isles, and these regions provided him with an army. The defeat of this force in 1235 allowed Alexander to divide Galloway between royal officers and trusted lords. It also gave the Scottish crown access to the ships and men of Galloway and to a new frontier with the Isles.[17]

However, the king's intervention in Galloway was exceptional. Elsewhere in the west, royal influence continued to rely on magnates. Earl Ferchar of Ross and Walter Comyn, lord of Badenoch, both leaders in the war over Galloway, were also the king's men in the north-west. These lords and their heirs would secure and police provinces that stretched to the western shores. Strongholds like Inverlochy Castle, built by Walter Comyn's successor as lord of Badenoch, John the Red, to control access to the Great Glen from the Isles, cemented these north-western lordships. As the fighting in 1230 had shown, however, the most sensitive area of the west was Argyll. Both the earl of Strathearn and Walter Stewart extended their influence into the province during the next two decades, Stewart helped by his appointment as justiciar in 1231. With royal support Stewart recovered from the Norse attack and built a new castle at Dunoon in Cowal, and by his death in 1241 he had begun to forge peaceful contact with local magnates. Where the justiciar formed relationships, however loose, the king could follow. By the late 1230s and early 1240s men from Argyll, including the lord of Lorn, Duncan MacDougall, had appeared at Alexander's court seeking royal protection and recognition.[18]

Yet this kind of influence was not concrete. Nor was it unchallenged. The events of 1230 had shown King Hakon's determination for greater power in the Isles, even though his expedition was not an unqualified success. Uspak, Hakon's choice as king of the Hebrides, had died during the campaign, allowing his brother, Duncan, to recover influence. Though Olaf ruled as king of Man until his death in 1237, his son, Harald, refused to seek Hakon's recognition for his succession. Hakon responded with

[17] Stringer, 'Periphery and core', 97; Anderson, *Early Sources*, 476–7, 492–9.
[18] *Paisley Reg.*, 127, 132; *Charters of Inchaffray Abbey* (Edinburgh, 1908), 65–8; McDonald, *Kingdom of the Isles*, 93–4.

force, sending another fleet to the Isles which drove Harald from Man, and for two years the island was ruled by Hakon's agents. When Harald travelled to Norway in 1239, he received Man back in the form of a royal grant, defining Hakon's lordship further. Relations between the kings improved in the 1240s, and in 1247 Harald returned to Norway, this time to marry Hakon's daughter and receive greater authority. By late 1247 even Hebrideans were looking to Hakon's court. Rivalries amongst the descendants of Somerled had been stirred by the death of 'MacSomurli king of Argyll' in battle in Ireland. This leader was probably the veteran Ruairi, long recognised as the senior lord of his dynasty. Following Ruairi's death, his son, Dugald, and his kinsman, Ewen (Eogan), son of Duncan of Lorn, took their claims to the kingship of the Isles to Norway. Hakon rewarded them both but chose Ewen of Lorn to be king.[19]

This king-making occurred amidst growing tensions between Hakon and Alexander II. Since 1244 Alexander had been trying to induce Hakon to resign his rights in the Isles with offers of money. As Norse political influence increased in the west, the Scottish king recognised that it weakened his own lordship in Argyll and the surrounding regions. Hakon refused the offer, responding by strengthening his bonds with the lords of the Isles. In turn Alexander brought pressure of his own to bear on the Islesmen. He was helped by the drowning of King Harald of Man as he returned from Norway and by renewed warfare over Man, Skye and Lewis, which removed Hakon's main western allies. In 1249 Alexander raised an army and fleet from across Scotland and led it into Argyll. Faced by this host, Ewen MacDougall met the king. Alexander offered Ewen new lands on the mainland if he would surrender Mull and the other isles he held from Norway. Ewen refused to break his recent oath to Hakon, and Alexander was preparing to pursue MacDougall into the Isles when he fell ill. The Scottish king died on the Isle of Kerrera, between Argyll and Mull.[20]

FROM KINGS TO BARONS? SCOTLAND AND THE ISLESMEN

Alexander died on a campaign which aimed, illegally some said, to seize Ewen MacDougall's lands and challenge Norse lordship in the Isles. Though it did not reach the main islands, the expedition had driven Ewen

[19] Anderson, *Early Sources*, 507, 512, 533, 546–50 (Chronicle of Man and King Hakon's Saga); Johnsen, 'Payments from the Hebrides', 26–7.
[20] Anderson, *Early Sources*, 539–40, 554–9 (King Hakon's Saga); Duncan and Brown, 'Argyll and the western Isles', 207–10; McDonald, *Kingdom of the Isles*, 98–102.

from Lorn, establishing royal authority over the church of Argyll and installing a royal bailie in the region. The minority which followed Alexander II's death would only be a temporary relaxation of Scottish royal interference in the west. Ewen's experience demonstrated the difficulties of the Islemen, and in particular the descendants of Somerled, caught between two demanding overlords. In the 1240s and 1250s the lords of the Isles sought ways to survive and flourish in this situation. War and plunder had been traditional routes to power in the Isles, and the Islesmen continued to pursue them. In 1250 Ewen MacDougall sought compensation for his expulsion from Lorn by attempting, unsuccessfully, to seize Man in alliance with Magnus, a younger son of King Olaf. He and other Islesmen also looked to Ireland as their arena. In 1247 Ruairi, son of Ranald, had been killed fighting for the Ó Neill and Ó Domhnaill against the English. His son, Dugald, enjoyed greater success, plundering the English settlers of Connacht in 1258. Dugald's prowess impressed the Irish. In 1259 the Irish king of Connacht, Aed Ó Conchobair (O'Connor), married Dugald's daughter, receiving a retinue of 160 warriors as her dowry. A parallel alliance was made between Ewen MacDougall and Brian Ó Neill, the claimant to the Irish High-kingship. Ó Neill certainly won Hebridean support. Both Dugald, son of Ruairi, and Angus (Aenghus), son of Donald, aided the wars of Ó Neill and Ó Conchobair against the English. For the Islesmen, this warfare maintained alliances and retinues in a world which had begun to seem more constrictive.[21]

Even whilst this freebooting continued, the Islesmen had to recognise the continued reach of royal governments in their region. In 1253 Ewen MacDougall and Dugald MacRuairi once again attended Hakon's court and Magnus of Man secured the kingship by visiting Norway to do homage. The Norwegian king's influence in the west was now actively supported by Henry III of England who regarded Hakon as a valuable ally. Magnus of Man had placed his kingdom under Henry's protection and in 1256 was knighted by the English king. Henry's interests included the Hebrides. In 1255, following his establishment of a new Scottish government, Henry took Ewen MacDougall under his protection and promised that the Islesman would be restored to his lands in Lorn which had been seized by Alexander II in 1249. The direct concerns of the English king in the region concerned Ireland. The security of the English lordship of Ireland was increased by royal influence in the Isles. During

---

[21] Anderson, *Early Sources*, 567–9, 594–5 (Chronicle of Man); *The Annals of Connacht* (Dublin, 1996), 88–93; Duffy, 'The Bruce brothers and the Irish sea world', 68–9; Sellar, 'Hebridean sea kings', 194; *C.D.S.*, i, nos 2,041, 2,185.

the late 1250s Henry was particularly keen to prevent Hebridean support reaching their kinsmen amongst the Gaelic leaders of Ulster and Connacht. The king's protection of Ewen was probably given in return for the latter's good behaviour. It contrasted with Henry's hostility towards Angus, son of Donald, and Dugald, son of Ruairi, the active allies of Ó Neill and Ó Conchobair.

Ewen's readiness to seek such protection was significant. In the circumstances of the 1250s and 1260s, patronage – and not private war – was the only way to recover his Scottish lands. He was restored by the Scottish crown in the late 1250s, but only after agreeing to pay a huge annual rent for Lorn. This would almost certainly make Ewen a debtor of the crown, vulnerable to renewed royal hostility and more sensitive to the pull of Scottish royal authority in future events.[22] The settlement imposed on Ewen showed that Scottish ambitions in Argyll had survived the minority of Alexander III. The desire to extend royal rule westwards was not driven by the individual will of the king. By the early 1260s many leading lords, the Comyns, Strathearns, Rosses and Stewarts, had vested interests in Alexander renewing his father's interest in the Isles. In 1261 a fresh attempt was made to buy Hakon's rights in the Isles. Even before this was rejected, new pressure was exerted on the region by Scottish magnates. Walter, earl of Menteith, younger son of the old Steward, inherited his family's interests beyond the Clyde and forced Dugald MacSween to resign lands in Knapdale to him. Further north, war was taken to the Isles. In 1262 Earl William of Ross crossed to Skye and ravaged the island.[23] In response to these attacks, Hakon prepared to lead a fleet of over 100 ships to the Isles. The presence of a Norse king in western seas for the first time since 1102 was intended to cow opposition, win allies and show Scottish vulnerability. In the summer of 1263 Hakon led his fleet into the Hebrides, having raided Caithness and Moray as he passed. The main body sailed into the Firth of Clyde and anchored off the Cumbraes, while raiding parties plundered the coasts and reached as far as Loch Lomond. The challenge to the Scots was considerable. Rothesay and Dunaverty castles were taken, while garrisons were alerted as far afield as Aberdeen, Stirling and Dumfries. However, Alexander and his councillors kept their nerve. Negotiations were opened and, as autumn arrived, served to delay Hakon. When a confused fight erupted

---

[22] Anderson, *Early Sources*, 576–8, 587 (Chronicle of Man and King Hakon's Saga); *C.D.I.*, i, no. 3,206; *C.D.S.*, i, nos 2,014, 2,046; *A.P.S.*, i, 115; Duncan and Brown, 'Argyll and the western Isles', 211–12.

[23] Anderson, *Early Sources*, 601–6 (King Hakon's Saga); Campbell, 'MacEwens and MacSweens', 272–84; Barrow, *The Anglo-Norman Era in Scottish History*, 68–9.

Hakon IV and the Norwegian Realm

To Scottish chroniclers, the campaign of Hakon of Norway and his 'pirate ships' in 1263 was the last attack of the savage Norsemen. However, Hakon was no Viking. Instead, he was a ruler from the same mould as Scotland's kings, extending the reach and strength of his crown. Hakon ascended the throne as a child in 1217, in the midst of long-running warfare between rival regional and aristocratic factions, and it took twenty years before he was free to enhance the image and reality of royal authority. Hakon patronised the reformed church and formalised administration. His coronation in 1247 gave the Norwegian crown the full royal status still denied to Scotland's rulers. Hakon also looked to the Norse settlements beyond the sea. The extension of his lordship in the Sudreys was only one part of this. In Orkney Norwegian influence persisted and the islanders provided ships for Hakon's fleets. By contrast, Iceland had a tradition of self-government, but during Hakon's reign Norway began to intervene in Icelandic disputes, a policy which culminated in 1262 with the Icelanders accepting his rule. Even Greenland came under greater Norse influence. With such horizons, Hakon's ambitions in the Sudreys seem more realistic.

at Largs in early October, the Scots levies repelled the Norse shipmen. Though hardly a great victory, it was sufficient.[24]

The real struggle was for the allegiance of the Islesmen, since Hakon needed to secure their support. He received enthusiastic help from Magnus of Man and from Dugald and Alan, the sons of Ruairi. Others, like Angus Mor of Islay, gave more grudging service, while Ewen of Lorn refused to help, and remained in Scottish allegiance. Other lords made a similar choice, encouraged by the widespread hostage-taking of the Scots king. As Hakon prepared to leave the Isles, he rewarded his allies, but his grants were an empty gesture, the last flickerings of Norwegian lordship. Hakon never reached Norway, dying as he wintered in Orkney. Even before his death many were aware of his expedition's failure. Hakon had not secured his lordship in the Isles. In his absence, his supporters were left exposed to the attacks of the Scottish king and lords. The decisive blows were struck in 1264. At least three expeditions were prepared against those who had aided Hakon. The earls of Buchan and Mar and Alan Durward led an army to the Hebrides, plundering and killing in

[24] Anderson, *Early Sources*, 608–37 (King Hakon's Saga); Cowan, 'Norwegian sunset, Scottish dawn', 103–31.

revenge for the previous year. A second expedition, perhaps led by the earl of Ross, repeated the tactic in Caithness. Alexander himself made ready a fleet to sail against Man but at Dumfries he was met by King Magnus who submitted to the Scottish king. Angus of Islay and others followed suit, but it was the agreement of King Magnus to become Alexander's vassal which symbolised the collapse of Norse lordship in the Isles. Man passed under the Scottish king's rule. Though the indomitable Dugald mac Ruairi fought on, and ended his life in Norwegian exile, the efforts of the Scottish king and his men forced the new king of Norway, Magnus Hakonsson, to recognise defeat. In 1266 the treaty of Perth assigned lordship over all the Isles to the kings of Scots in return for cash payments.[25]

Scottish silver could not obscure the Norwegian defeat. This defeat had been caused by three years of sporadic warfare during which Alexander III never even set sail for the Isles. The Scottish king's victory lay in the submission of the Islesmen. The early 1260s had shown these men the relative power of their overlords. Hakon's expedition had been impressive but, in the face of distance and autumnal storms, it was also a doomed and isolated episode. Alexander weathered the Norse attack and had the means to strike back against Hakon's allies until they submitted. With his magnate adherents enthusiastically backing royal aggression in the west, Alexander did not need to take the field to win the war. Despite Dugald MacRuairi, Hakon had no similar power-base in the Isles. By 1263 Ewen of Lorn had already chosen Scottish lordship. His neighbours followed his example as the best means of protecting their lands in the Isles and Scotland. Alexander's victory also depended on English inaction. The kings of England had been long-standing protectors of Man, and Henry III probably resented the surrender of the island to his son-in-law. However, embroiled in internal crisis, Henry could only watch as the balance of power in the Irish sea was altered.

What had Alexander won? The treaty of Perth transferred the Isles to the Scottish realm and ended Norwegian lordship in the west. It did not ensure the effectiveness of the Scottish kings in the region. From the first, Alexander wanted more than distant overlordship. Even before the treaty was agreed, the Scots king tightened his grip on Man, forestalling English ambitions in the island. In 1265 King Magnus of Man died. His realm was given by Alexander to his own infant son and Man was run by royal bailies. Man had been turned into a lordship of the Scottish crown. Its inhabitants probably resented this change. In previous years they had

---

[25] Anderson, *Early Sources*, 647–9; *Scotichronicon*, v, 346–7; *A.P.S.*, i, 420; Lustig, 'The treaty of Perth: a re-examination', 35–57.

opposed attempts by Hebridean and Gallovidian lords to exert control on the island and they met Scottish royal rule with similar hostility. In 1268 Alexander sent an expedition to Man to fortify the island against 'the assaults of rebels'. Seven years later the Manxmen chose Godfrey, son of Magnus, as their king and expelled the Scottish king's men. Alexander responded by raising a force from Scotland, Galloway and the Hebrides which landed on the island and crushed Godfrey's forces. Royal rule was re-established and the Manx realm was dismantled. Skye was granted to William earl of Ross, whose family coveted the island and, nominally at least, Lewis became a royal lordship.[26]

In the Isles, where the descendants of Somerled continued to dominate, the impact of Scottish lordship was harder to see. Most obviously the title of king of the Isles, borne by Ewen of Lorn and Dugald, son of Ruairi, in preceding decades, was suppressed. Only the Scottish king ruled in the region and under his lordship the two decades from 1266 were ones of relative peace. During these years Alexander confirmed the hold of the leading Hebrideans on different parts of the Isles and Argyll, and drew them into his service. Ewen of Lorn's son, significantly named Alexander (Alasdair), and Alan, son of Ruairi, were amongst the leaders of the attack on Man in 1275. In 1284 the same lords and Angus of Islay attended a royal council at Scone. By this point the king clearly regarded Alexander MacDougall of Argyll at least as a reliable vassal. By the early 1280s he was acting as the royal agent in the Isles, responsible for collecting the king's rents in Kintyre, Argyll and Lewis. As well as showing the king's trust in him, this appointment indicated that in the far west royal authority rested on the resources and influence of the leader of one of the old royal dynasties of the Isles. This relationship was hardly exceptional in the north and west, where the king's interests were often linked to those of great magnates. Moreover, just as such Scottish magnates extended royal lordship westwards before 1266, so it was these noble dynasties that forged the strongest connections with the Islesmen in the later thirteenth century. Marriage linked Alexander MacDougall to the Comyns of Badenoch and the earls of Strathearn, whose lands bordered Lorn, while Angus of Islay possessed looser connections with his neighbours, the Stewarts and earls of Carrick.[27] Such alliances drew the lords of the Isles into Scottish political society. However, 1266 did not mark a clear break with the past for the Hebrideans. Their involvement in an attack on Man was nothing new, and in the 1240s and 1250s Islesmen had made rare

[26] Anderson, *Early Sources*, 657, 672–3; Anderson, *Scottish Annals*, 382–3.
[27] McDonald, 'Images of Hebridean lordship in the twelfth and early thirteenth century: the seal of Raonall MacSorley', 129–43; *A.P.S.*, i, 424.

appearances at both Scottish and Norwegian courts. The extension of
Scottish overlordship did not turn these magnates into simple barons nor
did it alter their horizons and ambitions. Though Ewen and Alexander
MacDougall focussed on Lorn and the Scottish mainland, they still
maintained their longships for trading and raiding. Other kindreds also
looked seawards. The wars of the 1260s produced refugees and adventurers who saw Ireland as a field for their skills. After his kin had
been expelled from Knapdale by Walter, earl of Menteith, Murchadh
MacSween launched a career as a mercenary in Ireland. Though this
ended with his death in the earl of Ulster's dungeons, his family established themselves in Ireland as a dynasty of professional soldiers. Lords
who survived the upheaval, like the MacRuairis and Clan Donald, continued to go to Ireland as allies, and in the early 1290s Angus of Islay supported branches of the Ó Neill and Ó Domhnaill in their conflicts with
the earl of Ulster, as he had done forty years before. As kingmakers,
raiders and mercenaries, the activities of the Islesmen in Ireland lay
beyond the Scottish king's reach.[28]

Though these routes to power were still well-travelled in the 1290s, the
thirteenth century had witnessed the extension of new political and cultural influences into the Isles, linking the rulers to the Scottish kingdom.
The descendants of Somerled were not just warlords. They journeyed on
pilgrimages to England and perhaps beyond, they employed clerics who
recorded their acts in Latin charters, and they authenticated these charters with seals bearing images not just of galleys, but of mounted knights.
The knight and the galley represented the merging of Norse-Gaelic tradition with new influences in the Isles and it became normal for these sea
kings to seek knighthood for themselves. The desire to tap into the
culture and values of the European mainland was a product not of the
growing pull of Scottish society, but of the spread of Anglo-French influences throughout the British Isles. In the Isles, moreover, such changes
did not obscure traditional images of power. For example, Angus fitz
Donald, knight, was also Aenghus Mor, the recipient of a bardic praise
poem which called him 'heir of Mannanan', the sea-god, 'branch of
Tara', and 'Norsemen's king' whose raids brought 'a tide of blood lapping
Inse Gall'. The flattery of patrons by Irish poets is not reliable evidence
of their power, but does show the continued strength of cultural ties
between the Isles and Ireland. Moreover, while Anglo-French influences
penetrated the west, families like the Stewarts absorbed Gaelic culture

---

[28] *Annals of Connacht*, 148–9, 183–9; Duffy, 'The Bruce brothers and the Irish sea
world', 73–4; McKerral, 'West Highland mercenaries in Ireland', 1–29; Hayes-McCoy,
Scots mercenary forces in Ireland, 4–35.

Ulster and Scotland in the Thirteenth Century

The Ulster coast lay a short voyage from both Galloway and the Hebrides, and between the fifth and seventeenth centuries the narrows were passed repeatedly by settlers and soldiers. Change in one region affected its neighbour. In the late twelfth century English adventurers carved out the earldom of Ulster, bringing knights and colonists north and interfering in the realms of the Ó Neill and Ó Domhnaill further west. For the next 150 years the turbulent history of the earldom was linked to the politics of western Scotland. Hebrideans and Gallovidians were involved in the warfare which removed Hugh de Lacy, the second earl, in 1210 and the campaign by which he recovered his province in the 1220s. After de Lacy's death in 1243, the English crown saw Ulster as a base for interference in Scotland. The exiled Scots Walter and John Bisset were given lands in Ulster by Henry III of England and engaged in warfare against their enemies across the North Channel, most notably men from Galloway. The challenge that Brian Ó Neill mounted to the Ulster colony in the 1250s encouraged the English king to give the earldom to Walter de Burgh. By 1290 Walter's son Richard, 'the Red Earl', had lands across Connacht and Ulster and the service of many Irish kings. The defence of this lordship would continue to link Ireland to the Scottish realm throughout the coming decades of warfare.[29]

---

and language. How else is Walter, earl of Menteith's nickname of *Ballach*, the 'freckled', by which he was known even in official records, to be explained? In the islands and coastlands of the west, naming patterns and structures of lordship were exchanged in both directions.[30]

The rulers of the Isles moved in a world dominated by magnates of Gaelic, Norse or Frankish origin, speaking a number of languages and borrowing from several cultures. The Stewarts, Comyns and Rosses, the MacDougalls, MacRuairis and MacDonalds were all part of this society. However, the Isles remained distinct. To mainland Scots the Hebrideans remained an alien and threatening presence. The leaders of the Islesmen ruled militarised societies, of which the inhabitants waged war as a profession. The treaty of Perth had put this society under the lordship of the kings of Scots and though Alexander III experienced no major problems in the west during his later reign, the extension of his realm did not necessarily add to its strength or unity. The Isles were referred to as a separate

---

[29] McNeill, *Anglo-Norman Ulster*.
[30] McDonald, 'Images of Hebridean lordship in the twelfth and early thirteenth century', 129–43; Clancy (ed.), *The Triumph Tree*, 288–91.

part of the kingdom, and with Alexander's death in 1286, the brief period of easy royal dominance came to an abrupt end. Within five years, the English had seized Man and war had been renewed in the Hebrides. In the coming decades a new struggle for dominance would be fought in the west, with the Scottish crown largely reduced to an onlooker. This struggle ended the process of integration of the Isles into Scotland on the terms understood by Alexander III, creating a situation that emphasised the military power and political autonomy of the region. Even before 1286, such factors were never far from the surface. The pressure of rival royal overlords had forced the Islesmen to submit to, first, the Norwegian kingdom and then the Scottish kingdom, but the Hebrideans were never lords being drawn from the periphery to the core. Instead the Isles remained at the centre of their own world, with their own values and political structures. In the century from the 1280s, this world, and not the heartlands of the Scottish kingdom, would represent the most dynamic and assertive power-base in the northern British Isles.

CHAPTER 5

Lords and Communities: Political Society in the Thirteenth Century

KINGSHIP AND THE COMMUNITY OF THE REALM

To understand thirteenth-century Scotland as a political society, it is necessary to step back from the discussion of events which has dominated the preceding chapters. The activities of Alexander II and Alexander III and those of their subjects did not occur in an ideological vacuum but were shaped by established values and structures. The character and organisation of political life, its key issues and the level of participation in government and politics all underlay the successes and difficulties of Scotland's rulers. This concentration on wider interests and structures provides a balance to discussions of Scottish politics that overemphasise either the strength of isolated self-interest or of a monolithic sense of common ideals and identity.

Despite the above, the obvious starting-point for a discussion of Scottish politics is kingship. To inhabitants and outsiders Scotland was most easily defined as a kingdom. The sense of being a realm and a people was built and developed by a royal dynasty. The consistent aim of the kings was the creation of a common political society with limits that matched the borders of their own authority. This process was completed under Alexander II and III. By the 1270s the king of Scots stood at the summit of a political hierarchy which extended across northern Britain and the Isles. Their superior lordship was publicly and peacefully accepted by knights of Lothian, Scottish earls and the heirs of the sea kings. Allegiance to the king defined Scottishness for lords and communities with different languages, customs and outlooks. This identification of Scotland with the monarchy was consciously fostered by the royal dynasty. Kings sought new methods of adding glamour to this family history. By seeking the canonisation of Queen Margaret, her descendant, Alexander II, wished to benefit from an aura of reflected saintliness. For kings who still lacked the spiritual power confirmed by the full rite of coronation, this link to the divine was especially welcome. The saint's new shrine in Dunfermline Abbey symbolised the new status of the royal line. Elsewhere in western Europe such divine associations were exploited by rulers to emphasise the religious aspects of their kingship and made it more difficult for their subjects to challenge their authority. The canonisation of Margaret heightened the status of Scotland's kings in their dealings with their own vassals and with the kings of England.[1]

Both Alexander II and his son were keen to proclaim and protect their full rights within Scotland. Like other rulers, they saw their kingdom as their lordship, their property, a view accepted by subjects and neighbours alike. During the 1250s Henry III of England and all Scottish parties were aware of the importance of maintaining the rights of the young Alexander III in his realm. If these were harmed, it would lead 'to the dishonour of king and kingdom'. The young royal lord personified the Scottish realm, and the maintenance of his rights was the accepted duty of all parties during the minority. However, recognition of this fact was the recognition of the power of adult kings to rule. Royal authority in thirteenth-century Scotland was not confined by constitutional restrictions, and the kings did not regard themselves as limited rulers. When Alexander II reportedly described those who challenged his judgements as 'mice' not 'lions', he showed a confidence in his rights and a disdain for his subjects which is not usually associated with Scotland's thirteenth-century rulers. His son demonstrated a similar attitude when he intervened to enforce his will over the earldom of Menteith in 1260. Alexander III overturned the decision of an impressive council which he regarded as acting 'in defiance of the authority of the king'. Ten years later Alexander again defended 'our royal power with all its rights and liberties' when he secured the ecclesiastical revenues of Annandale. The rights of Robert Bruce in his lordship were overridden by a king who saw them as the fruits of his ancestors' generosity and as being secondary to his own prerogatives. In Scotland, law was made by the king's word. The royal court was the highest legal authority in the realm and royal justice, provided by the king and his officials, was growing in competence and geographical range. As feudal lord of his realm and as heir to the ancient traditions of Scottish monarchy, the king could demand the military and financial support of his subjects and, as we have seen, did so with success throughout the decades from 1214 to 1286. In the face of his acknowledged rights

---

[1] For the circumstances and significance of Margaret's canonisation, see Ash, 'The Church in the reign of Alexander III', 31–52.

and powers, it was hard for the king's subjects to defy or ignore royal demands for service and obedience.[2]

This picture of untrammelled royal power is, however, misleading. Theoretical authority was tempered by custom and pragmatism. It has been stressed in the previous chapters that thirteenth-century Scottish politics were free from the kind of disputes over royal authority found in contemporary England. Excessive demands by the crown for money or military service did not become major issues in Scotland. Similarly, questions of arbitrary or partisan kingship, the undue influence of a small or alien-dominated clique, were limited to the minority of Alexander III. The decade from 1249 witnessed the appointment of formally-constituted councils to run the king's government, and the exclusion of undesirable advisors from office. These efforts parallel attempts to control royal government in England, starting with Magna Carta and producing the reform movement of 1258. However, the English movements were sparked by the demands of adult kings; similar approaches in Scotland were a product of the absence of such a ruler and the difficulties this caused. As adults, neither Alexander III nor his father had faced sustained challenges to their choice of officers. For their part, these Scottish kings chose their councillors and agents from a wide group. Their appointments to office followed traditional patterns which respected claims of status and inherited right. Kings who maintained their government and realm by making only limited demands on their subjects, and whose political choices and activities followed familiar and unadventurous paths were well-placed to avoid conflicts over their authority. Thirteenth-century Scotland was not free from displays of royal greed and ambition or from grievances about royal actions, but these occurred in an atmosphere of general goodwill between the kings and their chief subjects.[3]

Issues of counsel illustrate that Scottish political life was not just about royal authority and its aims. Kingship was not the only framework for the realm. Across Europe the idea of kingdoms as communities was also articulated during the thirteenth century. In England, for example, critics of Henry III identified themselves as the defenders of the 'commune' of England against the king's misrule. The Scots were also aware of this term and its uses. After the death of Alexander III in 1286, the phrase 'community of the realm' was employed to claim the collective authority

[2] Anderson, *Early Sources*, 583; *Scotichronicon*, v, 180–3; *Vetera Monumenta Hibernorum et Scotorum Historiam Illustrantia*, ed. A. Theiner (Rome, 1864), no. 237; *National Manuscripts of Scotland*, i, no. 74.

[3] For resistance to royal authority in thirteenth-century England, see Holt, *Magna Carta*; Treharne, *The Baronial Plan of Reform*; Treharne and Sanders, *Documents of the Baronial Movement of Reform and Rebellion*.

of the political class seeking to govern in the absence of a king. Communal
ideas stressed the notion that a kingdom was not simply the lands and
subjects of a king but a common society with structures and laws which
applied to both ruler and ruled. In Scotland, as elsewhere in Europe, the
sense of this notion long pre-dated its formal expression. Most obviously
the pressure on kings to look to their subjects for advice, support and
consent for their actions reflected the need for communal action.[4]

In thirteenth-century Scotland these rights and roles were not shared
equally. It was only the advice and support of their greatest subjects that
kings sought regularly. Scottish politics rested on the identity and interests of this group and their relations with the crown. Although it included
the prelates of the church, the bishops and abbots, whose concerns will
be discussed in the next chapter, the character of this top rank rested on
the great secular magnates of the realm. Though many of these also had
lands and allegiances in the Plantagenet dominions, such lords still
regarded themselves as part of Scottish political society by virtue of their
estates in the realm and their homage to the king of Scots. Chief among
these nobles were the earls. The title of earl lifted its holders above the
rest of the nobility. The earls retained a special importance as provincial
lords and as a group with traditional powers of making and counselling
the kings of Scots. In practice, however, the thirteenth century was an era
of major change for the earldoms. Between 1200 and 1286 five earldoms
passed to new families, two new earldoms were created, and two, Mar and
Menteith, experienced periods of partition between co-heirs. There was
also great variation in power and importance between earls. The earls of
Dunbar, Strathearn and the Comyn earls of Buchan appeared consistently among the leaders of the nobility, while the interests of others, like
the earls of Ross and Lennox, remained focused on their provinces. Like
other families, the importance of these comital dynasties depended on
personal factors. Two minorities during the 1260s, 1270s and 1280s saw
the decline in influence of the earls of Fife, the most senior and one of the
richest noble lines in Scotland.[5]

Below the earls the rest of the higher nobility is harder to define. The
title of baron was used for perhaps 200 lords with powers of justice in
their estates. Not surprisingly, huge variations existed within this group.
At the top were the holders of great lordships, the Bruces in Annandale,

[4] Reynolds, *Kingdoms and Communities in Western Europe*, 250-331; Prestwich, *English Politics in the Thirteenth Century*, 129-45.

[5] For status and incomes of earls in the thirteenth century, see Young, 'Noble families and political factions', 11; Young, 'The Earls and Earldom of Buchan in the thirteenth century', Grant and Stringer, *Medieval Scotland*, 174-202; Duncan, *Making of the kingdom*, 426-43.

the Stewarts, the Comyns of Badenoch and the Balliol lords of Galloway. In terms of resources, these magnates stood on a par with the earls. Beneath them it is harder to make such clear distinctions but there were another thirty or so noble families whose lands, local importance, offices and regular attendance at politically-important occasions mark them out as consistent members of the political class. The landed wealth of David Graham, the administrative duties of the Maxwells, the inherited rank of the Abernethys, and the frequency with which such lords appeared on royal documents indicate the importance of these lesser figures. The nobles who assembled at Scone in 1284 to recognise the succession plans of Alexander III included the bulk of this aristocratic group. All thirteen earls were named as present, as were twenty-four barons, amongst them three great Hebridean magnates. Despite the changes in personnel that had occurred over the decades since 1214, the bulk of these lords were from families who were well-established members of the political elite of the realm. The disappearance of the Durwards and Avenals, and the rise of the Cheynes, Grahams and Sinclairs does not disguise general continuity. In the earldoms continuity was fostered by the crown. The earls of Scotland retained roles as provincial leaders and their survival as such led kings to preserve their titles and lands. In most cases partition of earldoms between heiresses was not permitted, and they were not allowed to lapse. By maintaining the number and dignity of the earls, Alexander II and Alexander III were preserving the shape of the higher nobility.[6]

The lords present at Scone in 1284 were not there simply to hear and obey their king. They were to be consulted as the leading men of the realm concerning the succession to the throne. Alexander II may have similarly taken counsel about naming an heir in the late 1230s.[7] Like questions of the succession, formal agreements with their neighbours and requests for financial aid were also made by the kings of Scots with the advice and support of prelates and magnates. This political class was understood to exercise collective authority in the absence of the king. Instead of naming a single regent, in the 1250s and 1280s the Scots preferred royal lordship to rest in the hands of a council of leading men. While politics in Alexander III's early reign were dominated by the rivalries of ambitious lords and factions drawn from this political elite, as we have seen, there were also shared, communal values at work. All parties recognised the importance of preserving the customs and relationships

---

[6] *Foedera*, ii, 266–7. For a lucid discussion of the structure of the fourteenth-century baronage, see Grant, *Independence and Nationhood*, 122–37.
[7] Stones and Simpson, *Edward I and the Throne of Scotland*, ii, 144–5.

which formed their common political society. They would not bargain these away in pursuit of immediate political advantage.

However, communal activity in Scotland did not manifest itself solely in the shared values and objectives of the crown and its leading subjects. The events that followed Patrick of Atholl's murder in 1242 reveal the potential for conflict. Though the 'earls', a group including at least four great magnates, looked to the king for justice, they also felt it was legitimate to harry their enemies, the Bissets. When the Bissets sought royal judgement, the 'earls' demanded that the case be judged by a local jury. They attended the king's court with a huge following which made clear their demand for the Bissets' execution, a vocal and threatening alternative to the king's lesser sentence of exile. Their actions reflect an understanding that justice was not a royal monopoly. The practice of bloodfeud, the rights of kin and local community to partake in the judgement existed alongside the king's law. The dispute over Menteith in 1260 revealed similar sentiments. An impressive group of at least fourteen leading magnates did not accept Alexander III's recognition of Walter Stewart's right to the earldom.[8] These men were not acting simply as greedy opportunists, but as a significant proportion of the leading men of the realm. Their actions were presented as being a fresh judgement on the case. Though Alexander III successfully overrode their actions and demonstrated the power of the crown, the episode was proof that collective political and judicial action was not always initiated or controlled by kings.

LOCALITY AND LORDSHIP

Such clashes between royal and aristocratic interests showed the potential for tensions, but they were not a regular occurrence. Relations between the kings and their greatest subjects were largely free of major disputes. The fifty or so lords and prelates closest to the king were mostly the heirs of men whose status had been achieved or confirmed in alliance with the crown. Yet this group only represented the summit of Scottish political activity. The political life of Scotland involved a much wider group of men and women who had a share in the structures, customs and relationships that, alongside royal rule, also defined the realm. Ironically, the scale and composition of this wider political class is best depicted in records whose purpose was to mark the end of the Scottish kingdom. In 1296 the officials of Edward I, king of England, recorded with characteristic efficiency the submissions of Scots to their new lord. The capitulation was almost total. The document,

---

[8] *Scotichronicon*, v, 180–5; *Vetera Monumenta*, ed. Theiner, no. 237.

the Ragman Roll, contained the names of over 1,600 men and women. Though headed by the earls, barons, bishops and abbots, the roll named a much bigger group. These were the Scots whose submission to the new regime was considered a matter worthy of formal record. The concern of English administrators to name and obtain the allegiance of large numbers of people was a clear indication that the running of the Scottish realm and questions of justice and politics involved not just the magnates and prelates, but a large and diverse group of lesser nobles and commoners.[9]

Alongside baronial families with occasional roles in high politics, like the Douglases or the de Vaux, were lords of more local significance like Bernard Hadden of Roxburghshire, William Lascellis of Fife, and William Somerville of Lanark. Below these were many more men and women who held lands as minor tenants of the crown or of a lord, like those identified as tenants of the bishop of St Andrews. Some of this tenantry possessed fiefs in return for knight service, the promise to provide a knight for the retinue of their lord. Many, however, held estates for other services or a money rent. Amongst these tenants the distinction between noble and non-noble must have been hard to determine and may well have varied locally. The key division in rural society may have been the one expressed in legal sources between knights, the sons of knights and others who held their land by charter or by hereditary right on the one hand, and, on the other hand, men of peasant birth who farmed land for rent and others who did not have freehold of their land.[10] The local barons, knightly families and freeholders named on the roll were part of a group of perhaps 1,500 to 2,000 individuals with well-established functions in political society.

Examination of these functions takes us deeper into the workings of Scotland as a kingdom. Though they were bound together by a common allegiance to their king, the Scots named on the Ragman Roll did not come from a monolithic and uniform political community. They spoke a variety of languages, recognised differing legal customs and possessed no single, common attitude to the king and his realm. Thirteenth-century Scotland possessed few elements designed to break down such differences. Below the great magnates, there were no formal meetings of the Scottish political class. Unlike in England, where the presence of knights and burgesses in governmental assemblies was a growing, if still far from regular, phenomenon, Scotland's rulers sought no such central gatherings of wide or representative groups of their subjects. For most of these subjects, even from the landholding class, the central institutions, the royal household,

[9] *C.D.S.*, ii, no. 823; Grant, 'Aspects of national consciousness in medieval Scotland', 68–95.
[10] *A.P.S.*, i, 400; Nicholls, 'Anglo–French Ireland and after', 374–5.

and the king's council or the exchequer had a distant and sporadic importance. Politics and society worked at a more immediate level. In reality,
Scotland was composed of many overlapping communities. These communities – provincial, local, of family or lordship – provided the normal
framework for the interests and activities of the political class. History and
geography meant that, despite the achievements of the kings of Scots,
other identities and loyalties existed alongside those of royal lordship and
the community of the realm.

However, the crown had played a part in shaping the structures of local
society. The Ragman Roll recorded the names of Scottish landowners
sheriffdom by sheriffdom. It is likely that during the century before 1296
many Scots identified themselves with their sheriffdom, the local unit of
royal government. In many cases sheriffdoms had been formed from geographical or historical districts and drew significance from this. The three
sheriffdoms of Lothian retained a common identity through the administration of a single sheriff, while several others shared official and provincial names. The sheriffdom of Lanark was the district of Clydesdale;
Roxburgh was Teviotdale; Kincardine was the Mearns; and Forfar was
Angus. New administrative unity overlay older senses of locality. Though
the sheriffdoms of the far north and west were more recent, from
Dumfries and Roxburgh to Elgin the sheriffdom provided the framework
for public activities.

These activities were undertaken principally by local barons, knights
and freeholders. The military and judicial obligations of these men gave
a collective importance to lesser landowners in the sheriffdom and
beyond. Those who held fiefs for knight-service were bound to provide a
knight or serjeant for the crown. According to a charter of the 1220s, the
knights of Roxburghshire were expected to serve for forty days a year,
either in the royal army or in the standing guard in Roxburgh Castle (or
to pay money in place of these duties). In other sheriffdoms the king's
knightly vassals had similar duties in the defence of the realm. Other
tenants had their own military duty, to provide men from their estates
for the common army. Like the men of Forfar raised by Alexander II for
his campaign to the Isles in 1249, contingents were raised according to
sheriffdom and served under local royal officials. While such service was
rare in the thirteenth century, the holding of 'wappinschaws', the mustering of local men before the sheriff to display their equipment, probably
occurred regularly, accustoming those involved to view the sheriffdom as
a unit of military organisation.[11]

[11] *R.M.S.*, i, app. 1, no. 55; *Arbroath Reg.*, i, no. 250; Duncan, *Making of the kingdom*,
378–88.

The sheriffdom's key role came not in military matters, but in judicial activity. In much of the kingdom the sheriff's court was the centre of local society. The king's tenants in the sheriffdom, whether they owed knight-service or were other freeholders, were obliged to pay suit at the court, attending its thrice-yearly sessions. The court dealt with a range of legal issues which included both criminal pleas and disputes over lands and rights, and, either in his court or elsewhere, the sheriff was responsible for holding inquests to determine the successor to a deceased tenant. These matters were not simply legal routine. Accusations of crime, disputes over rights and property, and questions of inheritance were included among the major issues of local politics. Nor were those tenants not party to litigation simply bystanders. Cases were decided not by the sheriff, but by juries of 'the good and experienced men of the country'. For example, in 1250 a dispute between the abbot of Arbroath and Nicholas of Inverpeffer was judged by a panel of thirteen men, including a former sheriff, and in 1296 inquests of a similar size were held in six sheriffdoms to determine the successor of Eleanor de la Zouche. Jury service could even involve local men in major political issues. In 1242 the earls wished to have Walter Bisset tried for Patrick of Atholl's death 'by the judgement of the neighbourhood', in the form of an assize of local men, but Bisset refused to trust 'the malice of peasants'. The freeholders and lesser nobles of Scotland had a crucial role in royal justice and could be called to attend not just the sheriff's court but also those of the justiciar or even the king when they were in the sheriffdom.[12]

As we have seen, the kings progressed between residences and lodg-ings largely concentrated in the valleys of the Tweed, Forth and Tay. The royal tenants in these lands must have had frequent opportunity to see their king, and they must have been conscious of the active lordship of the crown and their identity as his men. This identity did not rest simply in the king's presence. The king's castles and courts were the foci of public life. The men who ran this royal government in the she-riffdom were usually from the local community. In Roxburghshire, for example, the known sheriffs and constables of Roxburgh were all local landowners, and this pattern ensured that royal administration was carried out in close contact with the knights and freeholders most involved in its operation. Moreover, these shared obligations encour-aged a sense of community which was obviously strengthened by phys-ical proximity. Families from the same sheriffdom witnessed each other's land transactions, intermarried and engaged in local litigation.

[12] MacQueen, *Common Law and Feudal Society in Medieval Scotland*, 33–54; *Reg. Arbroath*, i, no. 250; *C.D.S.*, ii, no. 824; *Scotichronicon*, v, 182–3.

For these tenants as well as the crown, the sheriffdom formed a defined locality in war, government and social activities. Inevitably the sheriff-dom was not a closed or exclusive community. Even minor families pos-sessed lands and kin beyond their locality, and beyond the kingdom in England. Though the interests of these lesser landowners usually centred on a single sheriffdom, most also had other calls on their alle-giance and activities.

Within the sheriffdoms there existed local societies with their own, even stronger senses of identity. On the Ragman Roll the word 'commu-nity' was reserved for the burgesses of a given burgh. These communities were non-noble societies with defined and proudly-defended rights and status. The thirty-eight burghs in existence in 1214 rose to fifty-two during the century, stretching from Annan to Cromarty. This was not a striking growth in an era of rising prosperity and population, and it sug-gests the defence of their markets by existing burghs and the expansion of these established towns. If so, the burghs were still, in general, small urban centres, with most containing a few hundred people. Aberdeen's population of about 1,000 was equalled or passed by only Edinburgh, Perth and Roxburgh. Amongst Scotland's burghs, Berwick, 'the Alexandria of the north', stood alone. Berwick's population was probably double that of its nearest rivals, and it enjoyed a special status as the kingdom's chief urban centre.[13]

All the burghs had a distinct status. They had been founded with grants of privileges which gave the inhabitants rights to control and profit from local economic activity. In return they paid a ferme or rent to their lord. This was usually the king but about a third of burghs owed their status to magnates, as at Renfrew and Dundee, bishops, as at St Andrews and Glasgow, or abbeys, as at Kelso. The burghs' chief privileges were the right to hold weekly markets and annual fairs and the possession of a monopoly over trade in their hinterland or 'liberties'. As a result, burghs were the centres of distribution and exchange for their districts and acted as *entrepôts* for goods brought to the locality from elsewhere in Scotland or abroad. The burgh's rights also extended to manufacture. During the century burghs increasingly secured monopolies over cloth-making, the most lucrative medieval industry. Berwick enjoyed greatest rights in this field, forming the only major centre of textile manufacture in Scotland. Even at Berwick much of the wool traded in the burgh was exported to the Flemish towns, and most manufacturing in Scotland occurred at a purely local level. From tailors and millers to masons and goldsmiths –

---

[13]   For the identity, status and location of burghs in the thirteenth century, see McNeill and MacQueen, *Atlas of Scottish History*, 196–8.

the last clearly a high-status occupation – townsfolk were both craftsmen and merchants, making and selling their wares from home.[14]

Access to the full rights of burgh life was not open to all, but restricted to the burgesses. Representing perhaps a tenth of the population, the burgesses were property-owners or established families. The rank gave its holder access to the burgh court where cases were decided by the community according to its own laws. The court was also the forum in which the government of the burgh was established. Initially under their lord's administration, by 1200 most burghs enjoyed powers of self-government. Two thirteenth-century texts, the *Leges Burgorum* and the *Statuta Gilde*, shed light on this urban community. Each burgh possessed a chief magistrate – in Berwick, the mayor; elsewhere, either a provost or alderman – whose duties were to represent the burgh and preside over its government. The key functions of justice, finance and economic regulation belonged to the four bailies of the burgh, and it was becoming normal for a council of twelve to be appointed to provide advice and consent for the actions of these officials. Laws, officers and shared interests were the basis for urban identity. This was symbolised by the 'seal of the community', used by its officers to ratify and display the collective actions of the burgh on internal resolutions or external dealings.[15]

The cohesion claimed by the seal was probably not total. Though under the burgh laws the bailies and council were chosen annually by the commune, within the burgess class itself there was an oligarchy of the rich and powerful which dominated office-holding. The introduction of the council at Perth and Berwick may have been designed to cement the control of this group on their burghs. In the same burghs the formation of a guild extended this domination to economic matters. It was specifically directed against the textile-workers and served the interests of those burgesses most involved in the sale of cloth who were concerned to limit the influence of the weavers and fullers. Though the violent tensions found in urban centres elsewhere do not emerge in the Scottish records, it seems likely that urban politics served to secure the dominance of most burghs by their richest inhabitants.[16]

The interests of these burgess communities were not confined to their streets and workshops. The complaint from 1289 that Montrose was obstructing access to the fair of Aberdeen, to the damage not simply of Aberdeen but also of Banff and the whole region, indicates the existence

[14] Ewan, *Townlife in fourteenth-century Scotland*, especially chs 1, 3, 5; Ewan, 'An urban community: the crafts in thirteenth-century Aberdeen', 156–73; Lynch, Spearman and Stell (eds), *The Scottish Medieval Town*.

[15] Ewan, *Townlife*, 40–58; Duncan, *Making of the kingdom*, 481–6.

[16] Ewan, *Townlife*, 58–63; Duncan, *Making of the kingdom*, 488–99.

of rivalries and common interests between the burghs. The special status enjoyed by the burghs was further recognised by the creation of a court of the Four Burghs, composed of representatives from Berwick, Roxburgh, Edinburgh and Stirling, which met to hear appeals from burgh courts. The burghs and their inhabitants remained closely linked with their trading hinterlands which provided them with their customers and much of their population. They also enjoyed a special relationship with the royal government. Kings knew their urban subjects. The chief royal residences were near urban centres, and the king could call on his burgesses for support. In the seventy years from 1214 the burghs became an increasingly-valuable source of income for the crown. Customs levied on goods exported from the realm were accepted by the burghs in return for new privileges, and similar concessions accompanied the frequent loans made by communities to the king. For example, in about 1240 Berwick received new freedoms in return for loaning Alexander II the money to pay his sisters' dowries. By the 1280s it was clearly normal for the king to seek and receive credit from most of his burghs. As the royal household's presence would have brought lucrative business to the burgh, such generosity may not have been motivated by bonds of allegiance alone.[17] The burgesses who negotiated with the king on financial issues came from the rich elite, 'the worthy men' of the burghs. The kings backed these men within their communities, and formed links of patronage with families like the Bernhams of Berwick and the fitzMartins of Perth. The sons of burgesses, like David Bernham and Geoffrey fitzMartin, had access to royal service and, through it, became bishops, while their brothers achieved status within their home towns. For some burgesses, like Alexander *le Saucier*, bailie of Inverkeithing, royal service and urban office-holding could be combined. Though lacking the size and independence of continental towns, the burghs and burgesses were a recognised and influential element in Scottish political society. Their communities, led by men of wealth and power, were accustomed to bargain for their interests with their lords, and had access to the courts and councils of the king.

Burghs and sheriffdoms were communities that, for the most part, were defined by their collective relations with the king's government. Yet much of the kingdom's political class also identified itself in terms of hierarchies and of lordship, as well as in terms of communities. It was lordship that gave shape to medieval society. Scotland itself was less obviously a nation or administrative unit than a royal lordship. The Scots were not simply subjects; they were also king's men, bound by personal alle-

---

[17] Ewan, *Townlife*, 143, 147; Duncan, *Making of the kingdom*, 493–5, 603; Mayhew, 'Alexander III – A silver age?', 54, 60, 67.

giance to serve their royal lord. Yet lordship in Scotland was not exclusively, or even primarily, a royal concept. Scottish society was made up of the relationships between hundreds of lords and their men, their vassals, people and peasants. In a hierarchy headed by the king, these lords themselves were dependants of greater lords. For the nobility the personal and private bonds of lordship were central to the ideals of the aristocracy. The loyalty and honour involved in service to a lord, and the rewards and help owed to a vassal, provided the core values of the nobility across Europe. Ideals like these were testament to the real importance of such relations. Just as kings depended on the support and service of their chief vassals in war and government, so the power of these great lords was not built on land, revenues and rank alone, but depended on men and the bonds of lordship which provided their support.

The magnates of Scotland were surrounded by networks of followers. Like the 'knights and retainers' who followed their lords – the earls of Mar and Buchan and Alan Durward – to the Isles in 1264, they could act as a military force. They also provided political support, as at the trial of the Bissets in 1242, when the earls assembled their adherents to demand the death penalty. In more normal circumstances, they attended their lord in his daily life, administering his household and lands and providing him with noble companionship. The description of Earl Patrick of Dunbar calling his kinsmen, servants, tenants and neighbours together to celebrate Christmas and to witness his reconciliation with the abbot of Melrose, illustrates the way in which aristocratic life occurred against the background of the affinity. The maintenance and shifts of lordship, the mobilisation of adherents in royal or private interest, involved continuous activity, and formed the basis of much local political activity. For both lord and adherents, the aristocratic affinity was a major focus of social and political life.[18]

The character of such followings and the bonds between lords and followers was not uniform or static. Household officials, extended kindreds, tenants, neighbours and allies could all fit within the following, but had very different relationships with their lord. The idea of a magnate attended by his feudal vassals, who held fiefs from him in return for service, is an oversimplification. In thirteenth-century England, the feudal relationship became increasingly just a formal, legal obligation. There is some evidence of the same forces at work in Scotland. The retinue of the constable of Scotland, Roger de Quincy, was dominated by professional administrators and salaried knights, rather than tenants or kinsmen. As a lord with major English lands, whose Scottish estates were spread through the kingdom, it is not surprising that de Quincy maintained a paid retinue

18 *Scotichronicon*, v, 182–3, 348–9; Anderson, *Early Sources*, 486.

which would follow him throughout his possessions. This following was very different to the body of men associated with Alan Durward in his controversial political career. Alongside neighbours and kinsmen of Durward from Angus were a group of tenants from Atholl, who maintained links with Alan after his brief tenure of the earldom. The presence of a group of knights from the Bisset family was equally evidence that the alliance between Durward and the Bissets lasted well beyond the crisis of 1242. This was a political connection, and it was held together not by ties of land or by cash payments, but by shared interests and the protection offered by a powerful magnate to lesser men.[19]

In terms of their affinities, neither de Quincy nor Durward were typical Scottish magnates. They lacked the well-established and geographically-focused followings possessed by many of their peers. By the 1280s the house of Stewart had provided five generations of magnates with lands and influence in the sheriffdoms of Ayr and Lanark. The men associated with the family were often responding to this deep-rooted regional importance. Tenants like the Lockharts, Danielstons and Wallaces, neighbours like the Boyds, Lindsays and Crawfords, and even magnate allies like the earls of Lennox and Carrick attended Walter Stewart, his son, Alexander, and his grandson, James. There was a similar sense of continuity and stability amongst the adherents of the earls of Dunbar in the south-east. Lethams, Gordons, Humes and Corbets were linked to the earls as tenants, neighbours, even cadet branches of the house of Dunbar. This continuity should not be exaggerated. It rested on personal links which could change. David Graham, a vassal and associate of Earl Patrick (VI) of Dunbar, did not renew these close bonds with his lord's son, Earl Patrick (VII). This was an extreme case. Graham had accumulated lands well beyond the south-east and may have been asserting his own rising status as a baron, but his limited involvement with the new earl may also have been linked to tensions within the Dunbar family. Ties of lordship, whatever their territorial basis, needed to be upheld by the good treatment of the lord and the loyalty of the dependant.[20]

The core of the Dunbar and Stewart affinities were the men from their own lands. The Dunbars' earldom, and the Stewarts' lordships of

[19] Simpson, 'The familia of Roger de Quincy, Earl of Winchester and Constable of Scotland', 102–29; Stringer, *Earl David of Huntingdon*, 149–76; *Coupar Angus Charters*, i, nos 55, 61; W. Fraser (ed.), *The Chiefs of Grant* (Edinburgh, 1883), iii, no. 6; *Aberdeen Reg.*, i, 17; ii, 268–9, 273; *R.M.S.*, i, no. 509; Waugh, 'Tenure to contract', 811–39.
[20] Barrow and Royan, 'James Fifth Stewart of Scotland, 1260(?)-1309', 166–94, 188–94; *Paisley Reg.*, 17–24, 59, 86–90, 113, 225; *Melrose Liber*, i, nos 93, 225, 230, 235, 237, 322, 325; *Balmerino Reg.*, nos 21, 23, 24; *Coldstream Chartulary*, nos 1–4, 7, 9, 14–20, 29–30, 33–9, 57; *R.M.S.*, i, no. 251.

Castles and Halls

The most imposing physical reminders of the nobility of thirteenth-century Scotland are the remains of great stone castles. The ruins of Dirleton Castle in East Lothian, of Kildrummy in Aberdeenshire, of Bothwell Castle near Glasgow, and of Caerlaverock south of Dumfries are the most impressive examples of fortified, noble residences from this period. Though Bothwell remained incomplete, and Caerlaverock was fully rebuilt in subsequent centuries, all four retain clear indications of their original character and they possess common features. Each had a circuit of curtain walls strengthened by round towers, with entrances fortified by developed gatehouses. At Caerlaverock this gate complex formed the principal focus of the building, while at Dirleton and Bothwell large, circular drum towers were built as the donjon. These buildings were hardly strongholds thrown up out of military necessity in troubled war zones. They were constructed instead to display the wealth and status of their owners and to provide a setting for aristocratic living, influenced by new fashions from other realms, in particular northern France. At Caerlaverock, Dirleton and Bothwell the lords were not magnates but influential barons – John Maxwell, John de Vaux and William Murray – who had not long been resident in these estates. Their purpose in building was to emphasise their importance and taste in a period of rising incomes. That Bothwell was not completed may reveal the strains that building could place on even the richest lords.

Murray, Maxwell and de Vaux were not typical. Nor were the earls of Mar at Kildrummy. Even simple stone castles, like Coull in Aberdeenshire, built by the Durwards, or *Caisteal Dubh*, constructed by the earls of Atholl, represented an uncommon level of work. Most nobles were content to reside in smaller and less fortified residences. Earth and timber castles continued to be used, as at Cupar in Fife, and were still being built, as the example of the Peel of Lumphanan in Aberdeenshire showed. More common still was the hall house. The biggest of these were two-storey stone halls like Rait in Moray and Morton in Annandale, but most would have been smaller wooden structures, often enclosed by earth banks. These provided residences of status for knights and lesser nobles but also for great magnates. The earls of Fife possessed such a hall at Rathillet, while the earls of Strathearn seem to have resided in halls rather than castles. Even the greatest in the realm could use simple buildings as principal residences.

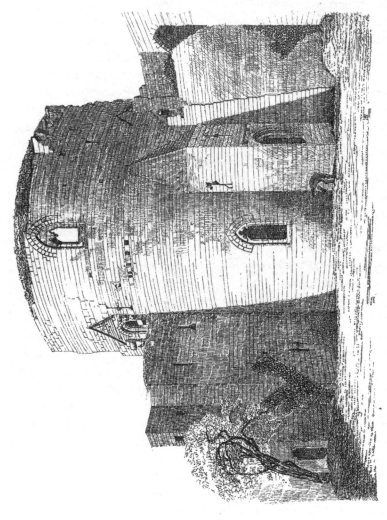

Figure 5.1. The donjon at Bothwell Castle in Clydesdale. Built in the later thirteenth century by William Murray or his son, Walter, it was intended as the centre of a massive castle of enclosure. Despite being the only part of the work completed and being badly damaged in the later wars, it is still an impressive indication of the plans of these lords.

Figure 5.2. **Kildrummy Castle.** Unlike Bothwell and Dirleton, Kildrummy was the residence of a great magnate, the earl of Mar. It was probably built in the mid-thirteenth century as a shield-shaped enclosure defended by four round towers and a gatehouse.

Strathgryfe (Renfrew) and Kyle represented whole districts under the rule of these noble families. The castles of Dunbar, Renfrew and Dundonald were the centres of such private lordships. The lords of these districts had established burghs, like Renfrew and Dunbar, and religious houses, such as the abbey of Paisley (originally at Renfrew) which was a Stewart foundation. Across southern and eastern Scotland there were similar lordships: Cunningham, Liddesdale, Lauderdale, the Durward lordship of Coull, and the Bruce's lands of Annandale. In such districts it was the lord who possessed powers of local justice. Their courts often had jurisdiction in criminal cases and disputes over lands and services outside the authority of the local sheriff. The tenants of such lordships were bound to attend these courts in the same way that the king's vassals presented themselves in the sheriff's court. All baronies possessed some right to local jurisdiction, but the importance of the courts of major lordships had much wider significance and competence. Though the king and his justiciars possessed powers to hear appeals from these courts, in localities under the rule of a great magnate, aristocratic justice was the norm.[21]

Bonds of landholding and service, structures of justice and administration, traditions of loyalty all combined to make lordships into clearly-defined communities of magnates and their tenants. In their lordship of Annandale, the Bruce family enjoyed the service of a particularly close-knit group of knightly families. The Jardines, Torthorwalds, Kirkpatricks, Johnstones and others provided successive Bruce lords with their local stewards and with an entourage of noble servants. Even when Robert Bruce (V) was in France returning from crusade, he was accompanied by a group of Annandale men. Such ties of service could be symbolically depicted in heraldry. The arms of a noble depicted his place in the wider aristocratic world, and when the Johnstones and Kirkpatricks chose versions of the Bruce of Annandale arms, a saltire and chief, this symbolised their close ties to their lords. The Stewart arms of gold with a chequered band of white and blue was similarly copied, not by tenants, but by the Boyds and Lindsays, families with traditional alliances with the Stewarts. By such means were the bonds of lordship advertised and the identity of aristocratic communities strengthened.[22]

The lordships of the Stewarts, Bruces and others were not the only territories under the rule of aristocratic dynasties. The earldoms of Scotland between the Forth and the Grampians possessed even greater status. Lennox, Menteith, Fife, Strathearn, Atholl, Mar and Buchan were seen

[21] MacQueen, *Common Law and Feudal Society*, 42–7, 50–4.
[22] Macquarrie, 'Notes on some charters of the Bruces of Annandale, 72–9; Duncan, 'The Bruces of Annandale', 89–102.

as distinct communities within the kingdom, as was the great south-western province, now divided between Galloway and Carrick. These lands all possessed distinct identities which centred on the rule of their earls and on traditional structures and customs. However, the antiquity of these societies should not be exaggerated. Despite their claims, the status of many earls had been formalised only in the twelfth century. The bounds of their provinces and the composition of the local community had also been altered in recent generations. These changes were often the work of the crown. Like other lordships, the earldoms were not outside the king's rule but were a special part of it. From the perspective of the kings of Scots, the earls extended the structures of royal lordship, albeit indirectly, to communities which were originally on the frontiers of effective kingship. With the exception of Galloway, the traditions of these provincial dynasties made them adherents of the crown.

Yet however recently they had been defined, these provinces formed conscious communities. Their customs and political organisations shared common features but were identified as being the product of local traditions. Like Scotland's kings, many earls claimed authority through distinguished descent. The earls of Fife were traditional heads of Clan Macduff (*Mac-Duibh*), a branch of the royal line, while the rulers of the Lennox claimed to be from an Irish royal dynasty. It was as the head of a kindred that these earls drew much of their power within their provinces. Earls like Maldouen of Lennox issued documents in association with their kinsmen. Even when the native line of earls died out, as in Buchan, their heirs, the Comyns, still linked their provincial rule with the kindred of the old dynasty. In accordance with Gaelic tradition, close kinsmen could expect a significant grant of land from the earl. In the 1220s Earl Maldouen granted much of the Gaelic-speaking west of the Lennox to his brothers, Aulay and Gilchrist, while throughout the twelfth and thirteenth centuries, the earls of Fife established their younger sons as lords within the earldom. These kinsmen were not simply tenants. In several cases, earls conceded much of their customary powers to a relative. In Carrick, Earl Neil created his kinsman, Lachlann, *kenkynnol* or head of the kindred, giving him powers in war and justice, while, in Fife, the name Macduff may have been used to denote a similar role. These earldoms experienced minorities and female succession. The elevation of a chief kinsman may have been intended to accommodate older traditions of lordship which encouraged the inheritance of the best adult kinsman of the earl.[23]

<hr>

[23] Bannerman, 'MacDuff of Fife', 20–38; Young, 'Earls and Earldom of Buchan', 174–202; MacQueen, 'The kin of Kennedy, "Kenkynnol" and the common law', 274–96; *A.P.S.*, i, 89; *Lennox Chartulary*, 62–3, 91–2.

Local custom remained a powerful element in the earldoms and Galloway. The law of Clan Macduff in Fife and the laws of Galloway were distinct legal codes relating to their provinces which survived into the fifteenth century. Before 1300 other provinces probably had similar customs. These legal structures, like those in Wales, Ireland and elsewhere in Scotland, revolved around kindreds. Though in Fife the earl held the title of 'chief of the law of Clan Macduff', the extended family was the crucial level of legal activity and had an obligation to regulate the behaviour and pay compensation on behalf of their kin. In Galloway these local kindreds – the MacLellans, MacDowells and others – were headed by captains. After the province came under direct royal government in the 1230s, a writ was drawn up by the king's clerks which confirmed the position of the captain of the kindred. The officers of the earls and lords, the *judices* or lawmen, the sergeants, the *toischeachdor*, officers who pursued criminals, all worked within this framework of local kindreds. In theory, all freemen of the province would have been part of such a kindred and their obligations would probably have been mediated through this extended family. This extended to military service. The common army service of the men from the earldoms and, even more, from Galloway was performed under the direct leadership of the earl or lord, the head of his kin or the captains of the kindreds.[24]

However, it is probably misleading to generalise too much about these provincial societies. It is certainly misleading to regard them as purely localised in culture and outlook. Earls and their men often had lands and interests beyond their province, and the internal character of these communities was the product of wider influences. As well as being the heads of kindreds, earls were also royal vassals. Their own provinces included not just native kindreds but landholders of Anglo-French descent who owed knight-service or paid money rents for their estates. To these tenants, the earls acted as a feudal lord, holding courts of his vassals and dispensing law and issuing documents in the same manner as other magnates. In provinces like Strathearn or the Lennox, which probably included Gaelic and English-speaking populations in the thirteenth century, and certainly included upland and lowland districts, the earls may have recognised different localities and identities within their province. Yet any such distinctions were blurred. Despite his English descent, Patrick Lindsay was *toischeachdor* of Lennox, while the earl of Strathearn employed the hereditary native *iudex*, Constantine, as his butler. The affinities of the earls included men of both native and Anglo-French

[24] MacQueen, 'The laws of Galloway: A preliminary study', 131–43; Duncan, *Formulary E: Scottish Letters and Brieves*.

origin, who were comfortable in their lordship, while in Galloway both the old dynasty and their successors, the Balliols, acted as the leaders of settlers and established kindreds. Earls certainly continued to see themselves in traditional terms. Even new comital dynasties, the Comyns in Buchan or the Bruces in Carrick, were quickly immersed in local traditions of lordship. By the 1280s Robert Bruce, earl of Carrick was following old customs by fostering out his sons to native lords. The next generation of the Bruce family would inherit the outlook and ambitions of their mother's kin as well as their father's. The mutual antagonism between the men of Bruce's earldom and their neighbours, the Gallovidians, lasted from the twelfth to fifteenth centuries as evidence of the strength of provincial identities. These identities were strong enough to influence newcomers, to survive external pressure and to provide the framework of political life and allegiance for most men of the earldoms.[25]

Bards and Patrons

The cultural influences and contacts possessed by Scots in the thirteenth century were not solely from the Anglo-French world. Traditional connections with Ireland remained unbroken, despite the extension of English lordship to much of the island. A sense of shared heritage between the Gael of Ireland and their kin in Scotland continued to be demonstrated by the passage of poets across the seas between the two lands. Gille-Brighde Albanach left Scotland to write in praise of Irish royal patrons such as Duncan (Donnchadh) Ó Briain, king of Thomond in the second quarter of the thirteenth century. His contemporary, Murdac (Muiredach) Albanach Ó Dailaigh, served the Ó Domhnaill kings in western Ulster before travelling to Scotland, perhaps with a price on his head. In Scotland he enjoyed the patronage of Earl Alan of Lennox and his son Aulay, praising their generosity, possessions and descent from the kings of Munster. Despite the changes in Scotland during recent generations, such lords took pride in their Irish pedigrees and rewarded bards who recalled them. It is wrong to see such contacts as backward-looking or peripheral. Both Gille-Brighde and Muiredach travelled through Europe on the fifth crusade, and their successors continued to move freely across a common cultural world in the western and northern British Isles, receiving patronage from Irish kings, Scottish earls, Hebridean magnates and even Anglo-French lords.[26]

---

[25] *Lennox Chartulary*, 49–50; Neville, 'A Celtic enclave in Norman Scotland, 75–92; Oram, 'A family business? Colonisation and settlement in twelfth- and thirteenth-century Galloway', 111–45.

[26] Clancy, *The Triumph Tree*, 247–83.

The blurring of distinctions based on language, custom and descent was a feature of both the earldoms and the neighbouring districts under direct royal administration. In contrast to Wales, Ireland and elsewhere in Europe, the settlement of new populations had not created a classification of people into colonist and native and structured society in these terms. There was no legal or linguistic fault-line in thirteenth-century Scotland. If a division existed, it was probably formed by geography, economy and patterns of settlement between upland and lowland districts, especially north of the Forth and the Tay. During the thirteenth century the region, which would later be recognised as a distinct highland zone, was showing features in terms of its economy and society that differentiated it from other parts of Scotland. The changes experienced in the century before 1214 had a far more limited effect in the uplands of the north and west. The lack of burghs within this region meant that the influence of urban settlements, so important in linguistic and economic change in the north-east lowlands, was absent from the Highlands. Equally there were few reformed monastic houses whose administration of extensive estates provided the motor for economic and social development in the upland districts of the south. In this highland region, geographical and climatic conditions meant that though grain was grown, greater importance was attached to the herding of livestock, especially cattle, and so the population moved with their beasts between winter and summer pastures. Transhumance of this kind was found in many parts of Scotland but pastoral society probably retained a greater social significance in the Highlands. As in Gaelic Ireland, cattle remained the key measure of wealth and status, and social and political structures in the region may have reflected the needs of pasture. In the western, upland parts of earldoms like Lennox, Strathearn and Atholl, units of land were larger, and they remained based on defined geographical units, glens and loch sides. The fact that, in all three of these provinces, such Highland districts were associated with junior branches of the comital kindred may have been a response to local senses of legitimacy which worked on traditional kin-based structures.

To the west of the earldoms in this highland zone lay other provinces. From Kintyre through Argyll to the interior of Moray and Ross were upland and coastal districts with Gaelic speech and customs. Unlike the highland parts of Lennox, Strathearn and Atholl, these areas had traditionally stood outside the king's reach. The extension of royal lordship over them during the thirteenth century was, as has been shown, often associated with war and disruption. Such change inevitably affected the character of political society. In Moray, for example, upland districts like Glencairnie, Strathbogie, Glen Urquhart and Badenoch were formed into lordships for magnates who aided the crown. Families like the Durwards, Comyns and the earls of Fife were outsiders to their new lands and tenants. Previous lords and local kindreds were probably expelled or relegated in status. However, there is little evidence of widespread changes to local populations or customs. Knight-service does not seem to have been extended to these areas, and new settlement may have been confined to castle-towns around strongholds like Urquhart, Ruthven or Inverlochy. Beyond these, the population probably remained kin-based and pastoral in character, divided between freemen and bondmen (with the latter found as property of the Comyns of Badenoch). Landowners like Gylleroch of Urquhart and Somerled of Boharm were from local elites which probably accepted their place as the tenants of new lords. The Comyns of Badenoch seem to have relied on such men. Their steward of Badenoch in 1234 was Ferchar who was probably from an established kindred. In effect the Comyns acted as overlords. They took the submission of men who were locally important, settled disputes and employed agents to raise revenues and men. They did not seek to impose major change to local customs or the structure of local political elites. The resulting lordship was effective but it rested on relatively shallow roots.[27]

In the parts of Argyll that came under new lords, the approach to the inhabitants could be more forceful. The MacSweens in Knapdale, for example, were initially brought to accept the overlordship of the Stewarts but, during the early 1260s, were expelled from their lands by Walter *Ballach*. In their place, the Stewarts established settlers from their own lordships of Renfrew and Kyle as well as from further east. It was this process that brought a family, the Campbells from the eastern Lennox, to Argyll, as tenants of the crown and the Stewarts. The kings gave grants of lands to similar men in mid-Argyll, but local kindreds like the MacLachlans and the MacNaughtons also retained their importance. Now, however, these native landowners received charters for their estates, specifying knight-, or other, services and altering their status and relationships. In the area of Argyll between the lordships of the Stewarts in Knapdale and Cowal and of the MacDougalls in Lorn, these royal tenants were recognised as 'the barons of Argyll'. The use of this term to describe a mixed group of landowners through their collective status and obligations to the crown is another example of the flexibility and continuing development of ideas of common allegiance and local identity in thirteenth-century Scotland.[28]

[27] Barrow, 'Badenoch and Strathspey, I, 1–15; *Moray Reg.*, nos 83, 85, 86.
[28] *Highland Papers* (Scottish History Society, 1916), ii, 121–9; *A.P.S.*, i, 91; *Inchaffray Charters*, nos 73–4, 85; Sellar, 'Family origins in Cowal and Knapdale', 21–37.

This examination of the local communities of thirteenth-century Scotland reveals two things. First, it indicates the level of political participation across the realm. Political life was not simply about relations between the kings and the small group of magnates and prelates who attended his council. Lesser nobles, knights, burgesses, freeholders and even the richer peasants attended courts and served as jurors under feudal or burghal law, while members of kindreds had roles that were defined in Gaelic customary law. The kingdom relied on the service of this wide group in the maintenance of law, but also in the kingdom's wars. Such roles gave individuals a collective importance within the local societies of Scotland. Lords and officials could not take their service and support for granted. Lesser individuals had their own interests which they expected their superiors to uphold and defend. If, up to 1286, these interests and relationships seemed stable and secure, attempts to alter local custom, as in Galloway in 1235, could provoke a violent backlash. When upheaval came to the whole realm from 1286, local communities would be deeply involved in a similar set of reactions.

This leads directly to the second conclusion. Within the lordship of the kings of Scots were lands of which the customs, structures and identities varied enormously. A burgess of Berwick lived in a very different society to a man from Badenoch or Ross. Differences of language, law and social structure existed across Scotland and even within single provinces or sheriffdoms. However, they all shared an ultimate allegiance to the king of the Scots. In this sense, kingship and royal authority defined Scotland and Scottish identity before 1286. Yet, it is equally important to recognise that kingship and perceptions of Scottishness were themselves defined by the variety and strength of provincial and local societies. Scotland's rulers could never forget that, beneath the common Scottish identity which they fostered, their realm remained a collection of diverse lordships and communities bound together by their own ties of identity and allegiance. By ruling from those areas where royal government was most strongly established, the thirteenth-century kings acknowledged the differences of political tradition which existed within their realm.

While the men from the sheriffdoms of the east and south probably had a strong sense of their ties to the king, such sentiments were, inevitably, less strong where the rule of other major lords intervened. This was not confined to the periphery. Over half of the kingdom was ruled by earls and provincial magnates who provided the focus of local political society. This does not imply a rejection of Scottish identity in these lands, but it must have made the claims of such an identity less immediate to most of the local community. Scotland was not simply a royal-led hierarchy built on a common sense of political and cultural values. Alongside and beneath the shared allegiances of Scottish political society, the earldoms and lordships, the sheriffdoms, burghs and affinities formed networks and communities which attracted the support and loyalty of Scots and were equally part of Scotland. It was the balance between the diversity and decentralisation represented by such groupings and the common ideological focus provided by king and realm that defined thirteenth-century Scotland. In the years of crisis which would follow, this balance would be central to Scotland's survival as a distinct region of the British Isles.

CHAPTER 6

Church and Realm

THE CLERGY OF SCOTLAND

The church was a special community within the Scottish realm. As throughout the Christian world, the clergy were a separate order of men and women with their own privileged place in a society that, virtually without exception, followed the teachings of the western church. The view of this Christian people was that the church was the custodian of their moral, intellectual, spiritual and even their physical well-being. The authority of the clergy therefore pervaded every aspect of life in thirteenth-century Scotland, and the Scottish church played a key role in shaping perceptions of the realm, both internally and externally. In the century and a half before 1214 the character of the church had been altered radically. These alterations had been the product of an era of renewal and reform which, from the mid-eleventh century, had left its mark on the whole of Latin Christendom. People from all ranks of society had engaged in a search for personal spiritual rebirth, following lives of simple piety after the model of the apostles, or endowing those who did with alms. Linked to this quest for the apostolic life were efforts to raise the central authority of the church and the standards of moral behaviour. Driven by a series of reforming popes, the western church was formed into an ecclesiastical monarchy. The reach and rule of the papacy penetrated into the furthest corners of the continent. In one of those corners were the Scots. The Christians of Scotland had been deeply affected by major changes in the practice of worship and in the government and organisation of the church during the twelfth century, changes which received the support of the royal house.

By comparison, the thirteenth century marked the waning of the age of reform in western Europe. The papacy's spiritual credentials were increasingly compromised by its political agenda, and secular rulers and their governments were increasingly able to challenge the authority of the church hierarchy in law and politics. Within the Scottish kingdom the decades from 1214 to 1286 saw the slowing and completion of those changes which had reshaped the church. The most important and enduring of these changes in the twelfth and thirteenth centuries was the establishment of a structure of parishes. Parish kirks and clergy were the bedrock of the secular church, the clerics and institutions whose intended function was to minister to the spiritual needs and maintain the religious and moral orthodoxy of the wider Christian population. The evidence of papal records in the later thirteenth century indicates the existence of nearly 1,000 parishes within the Scottish realm. The creation of this parochial structure was still underway in the mid-century when Bishop David Bernham of St Andrews was recorded as having dedicated 140 churches in his diocese. Though many of these would have been re-dedications of existing parish kirks, the bishop's activities indicate a continuing process of organisation and formalisation. Central to this process were the means to support parish clergy financially, allowing them to minister to their flocks. In Scotland, as across Latin Christendom, this support was based on the payment of teinds (tithes), a levy on the fruits of the parish taken annually from that year's harvest and livestock. The cleric who held the parish was assigned this living in return for the performance of his spiritual duties.[1]

It is important not to idealise this system. Resistance to the payment of teinds was an enduring problem. In 1242 Alexander II ordered his lay subjects not to withhold their dues, while the most spectacular example of such opposition was the killing of Bishop Adam of Caithness by his flock in 1222. Another problem came from within the church. Even while the structure of parishes was being established in Scotland, it was identified as a valuable asset by ecclesiastics. The practice of appropriation, by which parish kirks and teinds were held by individual clerics or ecclesiastical institutions who did not perform their parochial duties directly, was common practice by 1200. It has been estimated that perhaps half the parishes were appropriated, the vast majority held in perpetuity by religious communities, abbeys and cathedral chapters. For example, King William's foundation at Arbroath held thirty-five appropriated parishes, Glasgow Cathedral had the same number, and Kelso Abbey possessed over forty kirks. The growth of a university-trained clerical elite during the thirteenth century probably added to the numbers of absentee parish clergy. In appropriated parishes the duties of the priest were assigned to

---

[1] Ash, 'David Bernham, Bishop of St Andrews, 1239–53', 35. For the existence of parishes and parish kirks by 1300, see McNeill and MacQueen, *Atlas of Scottish History*, 348–60.

a vicar, the benefice and teinds were possessed by an absentee individual or community. Though ecclesiastical authorities sought to ensure that vicars received a sufficient portion, it was inevitable that parochial duties were carried out by clerics of lesser education and status. While burgh churches tended to enjoy sufficient endowments to support a number of clergy, in the bulk of parishes the access of ordinary Scots to the sacraments or spiritual guidance was probably limited by the training and energy of a poorly-rewarded priest.[2]

It would be unfair to suggest that the leaders of the church were unconcerned with these problems or with the standards of worship. Attempts at reform were frequent and came above all from the bishops of the Scottish church. These bishops held authority over sees formed or formalised during the twelfth century from lands and rights possessed by earlier bishops. By the thirteenth century these dioceses were defined territorial units with established boundaries and organisations. Within the Scottish king's realm there were eleven mainland dioceses and one for the Isles. Many of these were based on established provinces: Moray, Argyll, Galloway, Ross and Caithness were even known by their provincial titles, while Glasgow corresponded to the old sub-kingdom of Strathclyde. Less obviously, the bishoprics of Dunblane and Dunkeld covered the earldoms of Menteith, Strathearn and Atholl, and St Andrews included both Lothian and the heartlands of the Scottish kingdom north of the Forth. These dioceses varied greatly in terms of size and wealth. By far the largest and richest were St Andrews and Glasgow. Together they contained nearly half the parishes in the kingdom and their assessed value was more than the other mainland sees combined. By contrast, Brechin was the smallest and lay entirely within the boundaries of St Andrews. The bishop was responsible for the care of his diocese, upholding the functions of the clergy and the structures of Christian life. To this end, the bishops enquired into ecclesiastical practices, issued statutes, and instructed and corrected clergy and laity. The conscientious bishop performed these tasks by holding diocesan synods, like the one called by Bishop Walter of Glasgow at Ayr in 1227. Bishops also maintained their authority through visitations, progresses round their dioceses. In August 1242, for example, Bishop David Bernham of St Andrews progressed through the Angus portion of his diocese, dedicating twelve kirks as part of his activities.[3]

---

[2] *Scotichronicon*, v, 181; Crawford, 'The earldom of Caithness', 28–9; Duncan, *Making of the kingdom*, 299–300; McNeill and MacQueen, *Atlas of Scottish History*, 363–5. For another example of resistance to teinds, see *Glasgow Reg.*, i, no. 139.

[3] Shead, 'The administration of the diocese of Glasgow in the twelfth and thirteenth centuries', 127–50 ; Ash, 'The diocese of St Andrews under its "Norman" bishops', 106–26; Anderson, *Early Sources*, ii, 522.

Cathedral Building

The building of a medieval cathedral was an ongoing process, not a single campaign. Initial construction merged with later extension, maintenance and rebuilding, which meant that such great churches were the products of several generations of labour. At St Andrews, for example, building was effectively in progress from the 1160s until the early fourteenth century. Elsewhere in Scotland, the thirteenth century witnessed the culmination of works at many diocesan centres, undertaken with the objective of constructing churches worthy of bishops and their chapters. Cathedrals like Glasgow and Dunblane retain numerous elements from this period.

Perhaps the most striking of the thirteenth-century cathedrals is Elgin, the seat of the bishops of Moray from the 1220s. As at Glasgow, the impetus for reconstruction came from a disastrous fire in 1270, and during the next two decades Elgin was substantially remodelled. Though now in ruins, the character of this work is retained in the great western door flanked by towers, and in the choir which is lit from the east by two rows of five lancet windows. The octagonal chapter-house attached to the choir provides another fine contemporary feature. Such works display the skills available to Scottish bishops and the influence of English styles on Scottish architecture. Unfortunately, Elgin marked the end of this era. Warfare would sever such cultural links and put the great cathedrals at risk, from natural, not man-made disasters.[4]

There were similarities between the king's government and that of the the bishops. While on progress and in cathedral and synod, the bishop was surrounded by an increasingly complex *familia* of clerks and chaplains. He also delegated powers to officials as judicial deputies. In the ecclesiastical courts of the diocese, whose jurisdiction included all clergy and extended to laymen involved in disputes concerning morality and religion, it became normal for judgement to be given by the official. Ten dioceses certainly had such a law officer by 1300. Like secular rulers, bishops also relied on deputies within the diocese. Archdeacons held quasi-episcopal authority under the bishop, and, by the mid-thirteenth century both St Andrews and Glasgow in recognition of their greater size, had a second archdeacon, covering Lothian for St Andrews and Teviotdale for Glasgow. Below the archdeacons were rural deans responsible for supervising clusters of from ten to twenty parishes and empowered to judge and correct disputes and offences.[5]

[4] Fawcett, *The Scottish Cathedrals*, 29–61; Fawcett, 'Ecclesiastical architecture in the second half of the thirteenth century', 148–80.
[5] Shead, 'The administration of the diocese of Glasgow', 135–7; Ash, 'The diocese of St Andrews', 124–6.

Figure 6.1. The east end of Elgin Cathedral, showing the two rows of lancet windows. In its original form, this end of the cathedral dated from the late thirteenth century.

The centre of the diocese was the cathedral. The location of most of these had been established long before 1200, but in the north it was only in the 1220s that Dornoch was chosen by the bishops of Caithness as their cathedral site and that Elgin became the centre of the diocese of Moray. The wealth and importance of cathedrals required a group of clergy to maintain worship and to administer the cathedral church and its possessions. At St Andrews these duties were performed by a monastic community, living together under their own prior, but this model was not copied in most dioceses. Instead of being run by monks, these cathedrals were run by secular clergy formed into cathedral chapters. During the thirteenth centuries these chapters, their composition and their functions were increasingly formalised. At Aberdeen and Dunblane during the thirteenth century, the local clergy and abbots were replaced in their roles at the cathedral by chapters of canons. Such secular canons lived within the cathedral precincts but, unlike the St Andrews community, had their own houses and possessed their own parish livings. The roles and hierarchy of chapters also developed during the century. By 1300 most had a dean, a chancellor and a chantor. The key task of the chapter was the election of the bishop. Though details of this varied from diocese to diocese, the canons of the chapter always had a major voice in the formal choice of a new bishop.[6]

That the choice was never left entirely to the chapter by the king and others was testament to the importance of the office of bishop. Bishops were not just spiritual leaders, they were also magnates of the realm. The example of the greatest, the bishop of St Andrews, illustrates this significance. The bishops of St Andrews had estates throughout their diocese, and in eastern Fife possessed a concentration of lands and rights in an ancient episcopal holding known as the Boar's Raik. The value of the bishops' lands was around £1,000, making them the wealthiest Scottish landowner after the king. Along with their palace at St Andrews Castle, the bishops held at least nine manor houses across their diocese, of which the favourites were Inchmurdoch near St Andrews, Kirkliston near Edinburgh and Stow in the Borders. To run these lands and residences the bishops employed a number of stewards and bailies, and in the 'Ragman Roll' a group of landowners was named as tenants of the bishop of St Andrews in five sheriffdoms. Around the bishops of St Andrews were households that included knights and squires alongside

---

[6] Dowden, 'The appointment of bishops during the medieval period', 1–20; Barrow, *Kingdom of the Scots*, 212–21; Dilworth, 'The Augustinian chapter at St Andrews', 22–5; Duncan, *Making of the kingdom*, 281–4; Cowan and Easson, *Medieval Religious Houses: Scotland*, 201–12.

clerks and chaplains, as befitted a great lord of earthly as well as spiritual power.[7]

The monastic community established at St Andrews in the 1140s, whilst rare amongst cathedral chapters, was part of a wider movement which had a major impact on the Scottish church and left its mark on the Scottish landscape. The great ruined abbeys which can be seen across the country were established as living examples of the Christian ideal. Men and women left their families to enter these houses and seek the apostolic life in communities of monks and nuns far removed from the secular world. They lived according to set regulations, the rules of St Benedict or St Augustine, which required them to spend their lives in prayer, contemplation and physical and mental labour. Monks could hold no personal property, though their abbey or priory could own lands and goods as a community. Many forms of this apostolic life had developed in the twelfth century and they were embodied in different religious orders. Scotland experienced the full range of these, and their importance demonstrated by the number of abbeys founded between 1100 and 1200. Of the twenty or so major abbeys which were founded, six were from the leading new religious order, the Cistercians. By the early thirteenth century these new orders – the Augustinians, Premonstratensians, Cluniacs and Tironensians as well as the Cistercians – had absorbed or replaced earlier religious communities, such as the Culdee house at Lochleven and the *clerici* of Deer in Buchan, or had been established on new sites in the dales and hills from Galloway to Moray. As well as these male communities there were also nunneries, giving women access to the monastic life. The majority of these houses were also part of the Cistercian order.[8]

Enthusiasm for these houses continued into the thirteenth century. However, while the royal dynasty had led the way before 1200 in sponsoring new monastic orders, founding Holyrood, Kelso, Melrose, Arbroath and other great abbeys, only one – Balmerino in Fife – of the five Cistercian houses established after 1200 was a royal foundation. The others, Deer, Culross, Saddell and Sweetheart, were founded by noble patrons. Alexander II's piety drew him instead to other religious groups. In 1230, with the encouragement of the French bishop of St Andrews, William Malvoisin, the king founded Pluscarden Priory for monks from Val des Choux in eastern France. Within a few years two more houses of

[7] *C.D.S.*, ii, 205. For the 'Boar's Raik' see Taylor, 'The coming of the Augustinians to St Andrews', 115–23. For the lands and residences of the bishops of St Andrews, see McNeill and MacQueen, *Atlas of Scottish History*, 361–2.

[8] Lawrence, *Medieval Monasticism*, 149–205; Barrow, *Kingdom of the Scots*, 212–32.

these Valliscaulian monks had been established in Scotland, by Duncan MacDougall at Ardchattan in Argyll, and at Beauly, probably by the Bissets. In addition, the king and many of his chief secular subjects continued to bestow lands and revenues on existing houses. Alexander's grant of lands in Ettrick Forest to Melrose in 1236 was, for example, important enough to be recorded in the abbey's chronicle, while the Stewarts at Paisley, the Dunbars at Coldstream and the lords and ladies of Galloway in a whole series of religious houses, continued to endow communities which their ancestors had founded.[9]

However, it is undeniable that, after the Valliscaulian priories in the 1230s, there were few new monastic houses. Sweetheart Abbey in Galloway was established in 1273, nearly fifty years after the previous Cistercian foundation, and it would be the last major abbey founded in Scotland until the fifteenth century. Rather than the onset of decline, this should be regarded as a natural end to the exceptional growth of the new orders across Europe. However, it may also be linked to the emergence of new, radical approaches to the religious life in the early thirteenth century. The friars grew up in response to the needs of increasingly-complex Christian societies in Italy, France and Spain. Though they lived in communities and belonged to orders, they were very different from monks. Friars could own no property even as a community. Instead they relied on charity, gifts of money and simple buildings, earning them their name of mendicants (beggars). These friars did not live in enclosed communities away from the world. Instead they went into secular society to minister to the laity, devoting their energy to preaching to lay audiences and hearing their confessions. Both main mendicant orders, the Dominicans (Black Friars) and the Franciscans (Grey Friars), were in Scotland by the early 1230s, probably again with the encouragement of Bishop Malvoisin and the king. Alexander II showed special favour to the Dominicans. As early as 1233 one of them, Clement, was elected bishop of Dunblane, embarking on a radical reform of his diocese and cathedral. Nine houses of the order were founded by the king's death in 1249. During the same period three Franciscan houses were established, and by the 1290s nearly thirty communities from five orders existed in Scotland. In keeping with their aims, these houses were almost all founded amidst the densest populations in the burghs. Berwick, the largest town, possessed five separate houses of

9 Cowan and Easson, *Medieval Religious Houses: Scotland*, 6–10, 72–8, 83–5; Anderson, *Early Sources*, ii, 499; Stringer, 'Reform monasticism and Celtic Scotland: Galloway c.1140–1240', 127–65. The founders of these later Cistercian foundations were Malcolm, earl of Fife (Culross), William Comyn, earl of Buchan (Deer), Ranald, son of Somerled (Saddell), and Dervorgilla, lady of Galloway (Sweetheart), while Beauly was probably founded by John Bisset, and Ardchattan by Duncan MacDougall of Lorn.

friars, while there were two at Perth, Edinburgh, Dundee, Aberdeen and St Andrews. The friars' activities often led to clashes with the secular clergy, who resented the influence these newcomers quickly built up within the laity in Scotland, as elsewhere.[10]

These religious orders attracted Scots from a wide social spectrum, from nobility and burgesses to the illiterate peasants who gained access to the religious life in the harsh guise of lay brothers (conversi) who worked the abbey's estates. However, such religious communities numbered tens, not hundreds of people. Their importance should not be measured in terms of numbers, but in their influence on wider society, as witnessed by the lands and revenues bestowed on them by many benefactors. Such patronage made the great abbeys centres of wealth as well as spirituality. For example, Melrose Abbey held rights to pasture in Ettrick Forest and between the waters of Gala and Leader. With the skilled management associated with the Cistercians throughout Europe, the monks had 12,000 sheep or more on these lands by the late thirteenth century. By exporting wool from these flocks via Berwick to the continent, the monks must have produced a massive income. The epitaph for Abbot Mathew of Melrose in the 1260s dwelt more on his development of the community's wealth and property than on his reputation for piety. In the borders, the religious houses, Melrose, Jedburgh, Kelso, Dryburgh and Coldingham, were the richest landowners. The spiritual and temporal resources of these houses made their abbots figures of political importance, found on the king's council alongside earls and bishops. Despite the strictures of their rule, abbots and friars were bound to play their part in the world. As in much of Christian society, the search for simplicity and genuine piety existed alongside demonstrations of power and material wealth.[11]

SPECIAL DAUGHTER

Scotland's lay and ecclesiastical elites were deeply conscious of the place of the church as a part of Latin Christendom. Change and reform in Scotland came from a desire to conform with the values and ideals of the western church and to receive the blessing of its head, the papacy. Above all, it was the popes who, as God's vicars on earth, determined the position of the Scottish clergy and their flock amongst the churches and

[10] Lawrence, The Friars: The Impact of the Early Mendicant Movement on Western Society; Cowan and Easson, Medieval Religious Houses: Scotland, 114–42.
[11] Melrose Liber, i, nos 174, 198, 257, 264–5; Anderson, Early Sources, ii, 600–1 (though Matthew was deposed by his community). For the estimate of Melrose's flocks see Duncan, Making of the kingdom, 429–31.

Historical Writing in Thirteenth-Century Scotland

The keeping of a historical record was one of the tasks of a monastic community, forming part of the labours required by their orders. The two surviving narratives from thirteenth-century Scotland were produced in this environment and came from one or more of the religious houses at St Andrews and from Melrose Abbey. The narrative survives as the work of a series of monks which begins well before the founding of the abbey and continues to about 1270. It was kept not year by year, but was apparently written up in sections from collections of assembled material. As the prime purpose of the chronicle was as a record of the community, it is not surprising that the focus of many entries was on Melrose. The charter which the monks received from Alexander II in 1236, the deposition of Abbot Matthew by the community in 1261, and the miracles surrounding one monk, Adam of York, were all recorded in the chronicle. However, the monastic chroniclers also looked beyond the affairs of their institution to the surrounding country, the kingdom and the affairs of the Cistercian order and of Christendom in general. The chronicle shows the monks of Melrose to be acutely aware of and involved in contemporary politics and society.[12]

realms under their authority. The abiding statement on this position came in 1192 when Pope Celestine III issued the papal bull *Cum Universi*. This order was presented as 'a pledge of benevolence' delivered in return for the Scots' 'reverence and devotion to the Roman Church'. It accorded the Scottish church protection from external interference in disputes within Scottish bishoprics, or from papal representatives who had not come directly from Rome 'because the Scottish church is subject to the apostolic see as a special daughter with no intermediary'. The bishops of nine sees were directly subject to the pope with no intermediate archbishop. This statement was a clear rejection of the claims of the archbishops of York that Scotland lay within their province. It also blocked the exercise of authority in Scotland by English prelates acting as papal legates. Though scattered bishoprics across Europe enjoyed direct subjection to Rome, the Scottish church was the only province to possess the status of a 'special daughter'. The ecclesiastical province of Scotland did not include the whole of the Scottish kings' realm. The archbishops of York successfully asserted their rights over the bishops of Galloway, aided by local mistrust of the kings and their clerical allies. Similarly, the diocese

---

[12] Anderson, *The Chronicle of Melrose*; Scott, 'Abbots Adam and William of Melrose and the Melrose Chronicle' 161–72.

of the Isles remained under the authority of the Norwegian archbishop of Nidaros (Trondheim) after the acquisition of the Hebrides and Man by Alexander III. Notwithstanding these exceptions, papal recognition of Scotland's provincial status had an enormous significance for both church and realm. The definition of its boundaries and liberties gave the Scottish church basic safeguards against interference from outside the province. However, tensions remained. During the thirteenth century the Scottish church continued to face challenges, if not to its existence as a province, then to its distinctively Scottish character.[13]

Such challenges were inevitable. The Scottish church was merely a province, subject to the authority of the papacy. As the 'mother' of its Scottish 'daughter', the papacy had a right and duty to be involved in the running of the province. The election of Scottish bishops was, for example, subject to papal confirmation, either in Rome or by local prelates appointed to scrutinise the candidate. In 1258 Nicholas Moffat, who had been elected bishop of Glasgow by the chapter, was rejected by the pope in favour of John Cheam, an Englishman at the papal curia, and twenty years later a candidate for the see of Caithness was debarred by local scrutineers. While such interference was rare, the papacy maintained a close interest in the politics of the British Isles and the impact of papal authority was regularly felt by Scottish churchmen in the thirteenth century.[14]

This authority was exercised by the popes' personal representatives, legates and nuncios. Though *Cum Universi* specified that such officials must come directly from Rome, during the next century a succession of legates with authority over the Scottish church were active in the British Isles. The duties of papal legates were not confined to the ecclesiastical sphere. They also played major roles in the relations between English and Scottish realms and, despite *Cum Universi*, both John and his son, Henry III, secured consistent papal support for the English crown in its dealings with subjects and neighbours. This could prove uncomfortable for the Scottish clergy. Alexander II's leadership of the northern English rebels in 1215 placed the Scottish realm and church at odds with the papacy. In November 1216, the legate Guala Bicchieri responded by placing Scotland under an interdict, forbidding the clergy to perform their spiritual duties. When Alexander made peace in December 1217, the clergy

---

[13] Barrell, 'The background to *Cum Universi*', 116–38; Ferguson, *Medieval Papal Representatives in Scotland*, 191–203. The sees included in the province were St Andrews, Glasgow, Brechin, Dunblane, Dunkeld, Aberdeen, Argyll, Moray, and Caithness.

[14] Ash, 'The church in the reign of Alexander III', 39–42; Balfour-Melville, 'John de Cheam, Bishop of Glasgow', 176–86.

were forced to seek absolution 'naked and barefoot'. The bishops and clergy of the king's household travelled to York to face the legate's judgement, some of them being deprived of their benefices – papal authority could not be defied with impunity. The reissue of *Cum Universi* by Honorius III in 1218 was probably prompted by the Scots' insecurity over their liberties after the display of papal displeasure.[15] However, the involvement of legates in the relations between the two realms usually aimed at peacemaking. The marriage of Alexander II to Joan, Henry III's sister, and the agreement which accompanied it was negotiated by the legate Pandulph, while another legate, Otto, presided over the treaty agreed at York in 1237 and the dispute between the kings in 1244. Yet, even whilst seeking peace, papal sympathies lay with the English king. Alexander II was repeatedly ordered by the papacy to make peace as a liegeman of the English king, observing the treaties which the pope claimed obliged Alexander to remain loyal to Henry III. This perception of the Scottish king as a vassal of his neighbour was also behind the rejection of Alexander's efforts in 1221 and 1233 to obtain the full rite of coronation. These indications of the attitudes of their spiritual superior in Rome, and memories of the interdict must have made the Scottish clergy nervous about their status and unwilling to see their royal lord go to war with the English king.[16]

Fears about the liberties of the Scottish church were also raised by other activities. Like other monarchies, the papacy sought to levy taxation and to exercise justice within the provinces of the church. Taxation was usually requested by the papacy to finance crusading activities and in 1200, 1220 and the late 1240s the Scottish church joined other provinces in paying a proportion of its income for the defence of the Holy Land. However, during the 1250s, fresh requests for taxation met with opposition from Scottish clergy who feared that these financial demands compromised their rights and threatened the intrusion of English control with papal support. In 1251 Henry III of England announced his intention of leading a crusade. He received a grant of clerical taxation within his lands and asked that this be extended to Scotland. This request was rejected by Pope Innocent IV as 'completely unheard of' in 'another's kingdom', but in 1254 Innocent reversed that position. He and his successor, Alexander IV, allowed the levying of one-twentieth of Scottish ecclesiastical revenues for six years. Instead of the tax being used to finance a crusade, it was now

---

[15] Ferguson, *Medieval Papal Representatives*, 73–84; *Scotichronicon*, v, 92–101; Anderson, *Early Sources*, 425–6, 431–3.
[16] Williamson, 'The Legate Otto in Scotland and Ireland', 145–73; Ferguson, *Medieval Papal Representatives*, 81–5, 89–96; Stones, *Anglo-Scottish Relations*, 34–7; *C.D.S.*, i, nos 1,265, 1,266, 1,277; *Calendar of Papal Letters* (London, 1893), i, 83; *Foedera*, i, 209.

agreed between the English king and the pope that the money should be used to pay part of the debt owed by Henry to the papacy for the kingdom of Sicily. Henry had bought the Mediterranean realm for his younger son, promising to pay the pope £90,000 for it. Issues of European politics meant that the papacy had a strong financial interest in ordering the Scottish church to raise money for Henry. Although, as with his other dealings with Scotland during Alexander III's minority, Henry promised not to use the grant of taxation as a precedent, the Scottish church raised the issue with the pope as a breach of their liberties and refused to release the money they had raised. Attempts by papal collectors to move the money to London were resisted forcefully.[17]

The legacy of this dispute was still felt in 1265 when a new legate, Cardinal Ottobuono, arrived in England. Ottobouno's principal task was to aid Henry III against his subjects and, despite the royal victory in 1265, the legate imposed a three-year tax of one-tenth on the English church to be given to the king. Alexander III was asked to permit the tax to be extended to Scotland but, although he had actively supported his father-in-law, Alexander refused. A second tax on the Scottish clergy, this time to fund the crusade of Henry's sons, was rejected in 1269. It was only when a general crusading tax was ordered by the council of the western church at Lyons in 1274 that the Scots agreed to make payment. Their earlier intransigence had not pleased the papacy and a special collector of the new tax, master Baiamond, was sent from Rome to assess the income of the Scottish church. Baiamond performed his duties until the late 1280s, producing a new valuation of ecclesiastical income and collecting nearly £18,000 from the church. Though Alexander III refused to allow these funds to be assigned to pay for Edward I's crusading ambitions resistance to the export of the money to England evaporated, after Alexander's death. From the 1250s to the 1280s, the Scottish church experienced not simply more frequent financial demands from the papacy, but repeated efforts to divert this money to the English royal family.[18]

The judicial activities of the papacy were usually less controversial. Legates often arbitrated in ecclesiastical disputes, while papal judges-delegate presided over courts which dealt with appeals and cases in a

---

[17] Ash, 'The church in the reign of Alexander III', 43–4; C.D.S., i, nos 1,798, 1,806, 2,040, 2,065–6. For Henry III's European ambitions in the 1250s, see B. Weiler, 'England and the Empire, 1216–72: Anglo-German relations during the reign of Henry III', unpublished PhD thesis, University of St Andrews (1998), 128–38.

[18] Ferguson, Medieval Papal Representatives, 108–17, Ash, 'The church in the reign of Alexander III', 44–5. For Baiamond's assessment of the Scottish church's income, see Miscellany of the Scottish History Society, vols v, vi (Edinburgh, 1933–9); Watt, 'Bagimond di Vezza and his "Roll"', 1–23.

range of moral and spiritual areas. Before 1286 over 150 cases were appealed from Scotland to papal courts and during the early years of Alexander III even secular issues, like the disputes over Mar and Menteith, were brought before papal courts. This held the potential for tension. In 1261 a papal nuncio summoned Alexander and his magnates to York to hear the case over Menteith. When they refused to come, Scotland was placed under a second interdict. The nuncio had exceeded his authority, and the pope lifted his sentence and appointed Scottish prelates to hear the case, warning them not to infringe the king's rights. However, although Alexander decided the case, the papacy had registered its own legal rights.[19]

The Menteith case and the more sustained tensions over taxation reveal the potential for disagreement between the papacy and its 'special daughter'. Such friction can usually be traced to the perspective of the popes, distant from events, far to the north, sympathetic to the English king's account of events, and inclined to misunderstand the anxieties of the Scottish clergy. These attitudes were present in Pope Alexander IV's provision of the English cleric, John Cheam, to the bishopric of Glasgow in 1259 after a disputed election. To enforce his decision, the pope then appointed two English bishops to secure Cheam's rights against the opposition of the clergy. This opposition was the natural response of clerics who regarded the whole process as infringing their established rights. The Cheam case should not be taken as characteristic of papal insensitivity, however, and even here Alexander IV showed a willingness to smooth over the dispute. In general, the popes dealt with disputes over elections to bishoprics by providing Scottish candidates or allowing a fresh election to take place. The bulls issued by Innocent IV specifying that elections to Scottish sees and law-cases involving Scottish clergy should be held within the province added to the protections given by *Cum Universi*. Though they had to lobby hard for their interests, the Scottish clergy still recognised the papacy as the ultimate guarantors of their status and liberties.[20]

The defence and extension of this status and these liberties within Christendom was consistently pursued by the leaders of the Scottish clergy. Elected within Scotland by chapters of local canons, the bishops who provided much of this leadership were, with very few exceptions, Scottish in allegiance and outlook. They gave patronage to other clergy

[19] Ferguson, *Medieval Papal Representatives*, 104–7, 118–90; Theiner (ed.), *Vetera Monumenta Hibernorum et Scotorum Historiam Illustrantia* (Rome, 1864), no. 237.
[20] Balfour-Melville, 'John de Cheam', 178–80; Ferguson, *Medieval Papal Representatives*, 199–200; Duncan, *Making of the kingdom*, 280.

from within the province and ensured that the resources of the Scottish church, and its direction, were largely controlled by Scots. Resistance to large-scale diversion of revenues and to the provision of offices to clerics from elsewhere was the protection of the rights of Scots against what was regarded as external interference. But there were exceptions to this: in addition to Cheam, two other English clergy held Scottish sees without obvious difficulties, and the Frenchman, William Malvoisin, exerted a major influence on the Scottish church as bishop of St Andrews. At a lower level, a number of benefices were assigned to Italian clergy in papal service who never set foot in Scotland. There may have been resentment at this, but efforts to reduce non-Scottish influence within the church focused, in particular, on the regular clergy. As members of religious orders with houses across Latin Christendom, the monks and friars inevitably continued to operate in a wider ecclesiastical world which involved close links with England. The Scottish Dominicans and Franciscans were considered by their orders to belong to English provinces, while the custom of giving supervisory duties to the founding mother-houses of Benedictine and Cistercian abbeys meant that many Scottish religious communities were inspected by English monks. As offshoots or cells of English institutions, the priories of Coldingham and the Isle of May were even staffed by English monks recruited from Durham Cathedral and Reading Abbey respectively. There are strong indications that these ties provoked opposition from Scottish clergy. In the 1230s and again during the 1260s the Scottish Franciscans sought to establish themselves as a distinct province of the order. Though they failed, the Franciscans clearly sought recognition as a separate Scottish body. In a similar vein, the bishops of St Andrews led attempts to detach the priories of Coldingham and the Isle of May from their English mother-houses, in the latter case successfully transferring the priory of the Isle of May to St Andrews cathedral. During the 1280s the pope conceded that non-Scots should not be appointed to head religious houses in the province, further recognising and extending the rights of Scots to hold the chief offices of the Scottish church.[21]

These efforts to limit influences from outside the Scottish province had consistent, active support and leadership from the crown. Alexander III, in particular, helped to buy the lands of the Priory of May and backed the Franciscans' efforts to detach themselves from the English province. It was Alexander too who refused permission for John Cheam to enter his bishopric. The case illustrated the king's interest in having men from

---

[21] Ash, 'The church in the reign of Alexander III', 34–5, 39; Duncan, 'Documents relating to the Priory of the Isle of May', 52–80; Mackenzie, 'A prelude to the War of Independence', 105–13.

within his realm as the leaders of the Scottish church. Cheam sought the temporalities of his see, estates and revenues without swearing an oath of fealty to the Scottish king. Alexander was not prepared to allow a man who was not in his allegiance to hold the extensive properties of the bishops of Glasgow. Though Cheam eventually agreed to swear fealty, Alexander had strong reasons for wishing the wealth and influence of the church to be in the hands of Scottish-born clergy who would naturally accept his lordship. The king's desire to uphold and extend the Scottish character of the church went beyond landholding. The existence of a Scottish province and the extension of its distinct rights gave an additional dimension to royal efforts to strengthen the identity and status of Scotland as a secular realm free from external lordship. The kings wanted a clerical elite which would continue to support their authority as the rulers of northern Britain, even against the demands of their spiritual masters in the papacy. The interdict of 1217 had shown the Scottish clergy's adherence to their king in the face of papal sanctions and when Alexander II in 1237 and Alexander III in 1269 sought to deny legates entry to their kingdom, they were acting to prevent the pope's representatives exercising greater influence over the Scottish clergy.[22]

In general, both kings had little difficulty in preserving the good relationship with the church which their ancestors had enjoyed. Crown and clergy shared many interests which went well beyond material patronage. The kings defended the status and institutions of the church, and expected to have influence over the clergy and the support of their prestige and resources. This relationship applied not just to the external interests of the church, but also to its place inside the king's realm. For instance, the crown gave vital support to the church's efforts to raise teinds against the hostility of some magnates and communities. In response to the complaints of churchmen, Alexander II summoned a council of earls and barons in 1242, ordering lay nobles to cease harassing clerics and to respect the church's privileges. The most spectacular example of such harassment was the murder of Bishop Adam of Caithness in 1222 in a dispute over teinds. The king's campaign in the far north was undertaken in his role as the defender of ecclesiastical liberties as well as the lion of royal justice, and this conjunction of goals was repeated in Alexander's campaign in Argyll in 1249. With the king was his councillor Bishop Clement of Dunblane, who received royal backing for his efforts to reform the troubled diocese of Argyll. Clement's activities led to the appointment of a series of bishops from his own order, the

[22] Balfour-Melville, 'John de Cheam', 178–80; Ferguson, *Medieval Papal Representatives*, 91–2, 108.

Dominicans, whose missionary skills proved useful in a scattered, frontier diocese. In such regions churchmen appreciated the value of stable royal-sponsored structures of authority, while kings recognised the support that the influence and activities could provide to their lordship. The bishops of Moray granted or leased upland estates to the kings' aristocratic allies in the province, and in Galloway the extensive influence of monastic houses, especially Melrose, was used to aid the establishment of royal peace in the province after 1234.[23]

If the ideological alliance of church and royal house was symbolised and elevated by the canonisation of Queen Margaret, its more practical character was illustrated by the importance of clerics in royal government. The king's chancellor and the salaried clerks of the household writing and financial departments were increasingly numerous and though neither new in Scotland nor different in function from other realms, were another element to the crown's links to the clerical elite. From the kings' perspective, the need to influence the composition of this elite was great and it centred on their powers in the election of bishops. The king needed to be able to ensure the promotion of men he could work with to the leadership of the church. He also wished to use the process to reward his own ecclesiastical servants. Royal rights in elections were limited but important, for example the king could specify when cathedral chapters held the election. Delay allowed the king to profit from the revenues of the vacant see, as Alexander III did from St Andrews in the early 1270s. When the king's licence to elect was given, it often came in conjunction with the nomination of a favoured candidate. Disputes over elections in thirteenth-century Scotland were rare and even the Cheam case did not stem from the rejection of a royal candidate. The king's nominees were almost always elected without difficulty and the vast majority of bishops were either from the cathedral chapter itself, or had come from royal service. It was normal, for example, for the royal chancellor to receive a bishopric, and all five of the undisputed bishops of St Andrews between 1214 and 1286 had been major officers in the king's household prior to election. Even outside the Scottish ecclesiastical province, the kings showed an ability to exert their influence in elections. Alexander II secured his will in the election to Galloway in 1235, while his son acted to prevent a Manx cleric being chosen as bishop of the Isles in 1275.[24]

The leadership of the Scottish church was in the hands of royal

[23] *Scotichronicon*, v, 181; Anderson, *Early Sources*, 449–50; Duncan and Brown, 'Argyll and the western Isles', 207–10; Barrow, 'Badenoch and Strathspey', 1–16; Stringer, 'Reform Monasticism and Celtic Scotland', 163–5.
[24] Ash, 'The church in the reign of Alexander III', 41; Oram, 'In obedience and reverence: Whithorn and York', 83–100.

The Noble Patroness: Lady Dervorgilla Balliol

Dervorgilla Balliol was the most famous noblewoman of thirteenth-century Scotland. As the daughter of Alan of Galloway, she was descended from both a great native dynasty and Anglo-French nobility. Through her mother, Margaret, the sister and heiress of John, earl of Huntingdon, she would inherit a claim to the Scottish throne which, at her death, would pass to her son, the future King John. These parents also made Dervorgilla a great heiress, holding portions of Galloway and Huntingdon which she possessed jointly with her husband, John Balliol of Barnard Castle. In her epitaph she was remembered by another English chronicler as 'great in wealth and lands, but much greater in nobility of heart'.

Like many noblewomen Dervorgilla had an importance beyond her family connections and the lands which she held. She left a more lasting legacy in the religious houses which she founded as expressions of her personal piety. Throughout her life, and especially after her husband's death in 1269, Dervorgilla endowed a number of institutions with lands and money. She followed contemporary taste in providing for communities of friars at Wigtown, Dundee and Dumfries. Though these houses have long been demolished, a reminder of the Franciscans of Dumfries survives in the bridge over the Nith – Dervorgilla ordered it to be built, and assigned the tolls for crossing it to the friars. Her greatest foundations were made in memory of her husband. The abbey of *Dulcis Cordis*, Sweetheart, was founded in 1273 as the resting place for the heart of her 'lord and husband' and for the souls of Dervorgilla and her extended family, including the kings, earls of Huntingdon and lords of Galloway. Though the Cistercian community was dissolved in the Reformation, the red sandstone shell of the building remains. Only one of Dervorgilla's endowments survives. As a penance, John Balliol had promised to support a number of scholars at Oxford. On his death, Dervorgilla assigned more revenues from John's estates to the scholars and their house, and in 1282 she wrote 'with a mother's affection' to masters in the university organising the small community into a college with officers and statutes. The scholars of this Balliol College were enjoined to say masses for the souls of Dervorgilla and her family, and especially for 'our beloved husband', preserving his memory and interceding with his maker in perpetuity. Piety, love and family pride were closely entwined in the motives of this great noblewoman.[25]

[25] Huyshe, *Dervorgilla, Lady of Galloway and her Abbey of the Sweetheart*; Oram, 'Dervorgilla, the Balliols and Buittle', 165–81.

servants and nominees and the kings were active in preventing too much papal influence intruding into their kingdom. The lack of an archbishop as a formal leader of the Scottish clergy must have added to this atmosphere of royal patronage and direction. However, if the Scottish Church lacked a single leader, it did have a governing body. In 1225 the pope gave the Scottish clergy the right to hold provincial councils without an archbishop. Attended by bishops, abbots, archdeacons and other clergy, the council was headed by a bishop elected as 'conservator of the statutes'. It is unclear how frequently councils were held between 1214 and 1286, and although Alexander II attended the council of 1242, they were not subject to royal influence. They assembled for specific purposes, usually linked to ecclesiastical disputes, but the importance of the council within Scotland was as the mouthpiece of the clergy. In the 1240s, under the leadership of Bishop Bernham, statutes on a wide range of issues were codified, amounting to a statement of the laws and liberties of the church. Such liberties were to be defended against lay encroachment by the king as well as his subjects, a role perhaps demonstrated in the late 1260s. A statute that forbade attempts to compel clerics to remove punishments from those guilty of interfering with church property may have related to a dispute between Alexander III and Bishop Gamelin of St Andrews over the latter's excommunication of the king's servant John Denmuir. Though such disputes were apparently rare, royal officials were again accused of harming the rights of the clergy in Moray during the early 1280s.[26] Nevertheless, the king was usually regarded as a protector not a predator. The importance of the monarchy for the security of the church is suggested by the experience of Alexander III's minority. Even before the start of major disruption, the clergy were complaining about the depredations of both government and magnates to the pope and the English king. The years from 1251 saw other attacks on churchmen. Robert Kenleith, abbot of Dunfermline, was removed as chancellor and then hounded from his abbey and order, while the dispute over the bishopric of St Andrews led to the seizure of the lands of the bishop and rival claims being presented to the papal curia. The successful candidate, master Gamelin, remained outside the kingdom until late 1258. However, the church was not simply a victim of lay persecution without the king: clergy took active parts in the disputes of the minority, for example, and both Kenleith and Gamelin were leading players whose opponents were clerics connected to rival factions. To take another example, at St Andrews the cathedral priory was associated with Alan Durward and his allies, while

---

[26] Watt, 'The provincial council of the Scottish Church, 1215–1472', 140–55; Duncan, *Making of the kingdom*, 293; *Scotichronicon*, v, 361; *C.P.L.*, i, 481.

their local rivals, the canons of the church of St Mary on the Rock, outside the cathedral, were linked to Durward's enemies. As with secular politics, the absence of the king meant that means of balancing or settling rival interests were reduced. Internal tensions within the church were always present and could even be violent: in 1268 the monks of Melrose were excommunicated following an attack on the houses and lands of the bishop of St Andrews in the borders in which a clerk of the bishop was killed. Like secular society, the church was never just a single community, but was made up of institutions with interests that sometimes clashed. As the disputed elections for St Andrews and Glasgow showed, leadership of these institutions was also a matter of competition within clerical elites made up of ambitious individuals.[27]

These bishops and abbots were figures of political importance and power. It was hardly exceptional that when Henry III excluded his enemies from power in Scotland in 1255, the list included six clerics, headed by bishops Gamelin of St Andrews, William of Glasgow and Clement of Dunblane. In less disturbed times bishops and abbots were regularly counted on the royal council or employed on the king's diplomatic missions. Bishops like David Bernham and Clement of Dunblane combined these duties with their responsibilities in their dioceses and provincial council. If anything, however, the reign of Alexander III witnessed an increase in the political activities of the leaders of the church, particularly those of the bishops of St Andrews. Gamelin, whose election to the see was engineered by his Comyn allies and secured by his ability to win or purchase papal backing, was succeeded in 1271 by his long-term associate William Wishart, and then by another politically-minded cleric, William Fraser, in 1279. All three were churchmen who took orders as a route to power as much as a spiritual calling. Gamelin, a bastard of noble parents, and Wishart and Fraser, from relatively minor noble families, attained rank and authority through church office. Wishart's possession of twenty-two different benefices before he became a bishop, and his swift move from the diocese of Glasgow to the richer see of St Andrews when the latter fell vacant, revealed him to many as the model of a greedy and ambitious cleric. His rise was sponsored by the crown, as was Fraser's, and both followed Gamelin's route from royal chancellor to bishop of the senior Scottish see. King Alexander was not their only backer. All three rose with help from kin and allies. Fraser maintained close links with his brothers, themselves rising stars in the king's entourage, while Wishart's notoriety was increased by his promotion of his family in the Scottish

[27] Watt, 'The minority of Alexander III', 8–9; Ash, 'The church in the reign of Alexander III', 37–9; *Scotichronicon*, v, 371.

church, including the election of his nephew (some said his son), Robert, to the bishopric of Glasgow which William had vacated.[28]

These bishops of St Andrews were skilled in royal and church government and politics. Their influence in both was exercised in alliance with magnates like the Comyns, and with the king. Whilst they were relatively inactive in the reform of their diocesan clergy, they guarded their rights and those of the church jealously. Gamelin's famous clash with the king was caused by his support of his cathedral canons against a local Fife knight, John Denmuir, and the bishop withstood considerable royal pressure on their behalf. If Gamelin and his successors were not great reformers, they were effective leaders of the Scottish church and its interests, even against the king. In claiming this leadership, they followed earlier bishops of St Andrews who had exploited the growing cult of St Andrew in Scotland and retained the title of 'bishop of the Scots'. When William Fraser used a seal that bore the image of St Andrew, he was identifying his office with both the saint and with the whole Scottish church. The seal symbolised not just the importance of the bishops of St Andrews but the vital link between Scotland and its church.[29]

Under the leadership of Gamelin, Wishart and Fraser, the sanctity of the Scottish Church may not have increased, but its material power and ideological presence undoubtedly did so. This significance was demonstrated on the death of the king in 1286. Two of the six guardians chosen to govern the realm were bishops: William Fraser of St Andrews and Robert Wishart of Glasgow. The seal used to authorise the acts of these guardians carried the image of St Andrew. The symbol of the Scottish church was employed in the absence of the king to depict the realm and its community. The choice was natural. Alongside the kings and their realm, the Scottish ecclesiastical province gave Scotland a clear status as a distinct and defined land within Christendom. The leaders of the church were a group experienced in articulating and defending their rights as a separate community and a sense of the importance of these struggles. They shared the kings' interests in the strengthening of lordship and identity in the lands which made up the realm, and it was through clerical writers, in royal documents or historical writings, that the idea of Scotland as a single royal-led polity was expressed most clearly. Church and monarchy were the institutions that represented Scotland. It was no accident that the later thirteenth century marked a high point of the wealth and status of both within the kingdom.

[28] Stones, *Anglo-Scottish Relations*, no. 10. For full accounts of the careers of the bishops of St Andrews, see Watt, *A Biographical Dictionary of Scottish Graduates*, 203–6, 209–14, 590–4.

[29] Ash, 'The church in the reign of Alexander III', 47.

CHAPTER 7

Scotland and the Anglo-French World

THE ENDS OF THE EARTH

If the identity of the Scots and the boundaries of Scotland were fully fixed only during the thirteenth century, the existence of both land and people were known and recognised well beyond the British Isles. The terms of recognition may not always have been flattering. In Jean de Joinville's *Vie de Saint Louis*, Louis IX of France expressed the strange remoteness of this northern land to continentals when he reportedly said to his son that he 'would rather have a Scot come from Scotland to govern the people of this kingdom well and justly than that you should govern them ill'. For continental merchants, beyond the Scottish Sea meant a place of no return, while poets described Scotland as a country of moors, mountains and marshes, a setting for chivalric romance. These authors regarded the inhabitants as something less than fully civilised. A thirteenth-century French romance, *Sone de Nausay*, includes its French hero's visit to the Scottish court. The Scots are described as drinking beer to excess, stewing their meat into rags and as having strange sartorial habits which included wearing distinctive hats and short tunics, and habitually carrying their shoes on a string round their necks. Such details, while not implausible, fall into the category of travellers' tales and pander to the medieval appetite for racial stereotyping. However critical continental observers might be of Scottish custom, they showed an awareness of the Scots as a separate people.[1]

By the mid-thirteenth century this awareness had been increased and defined by the recognition of changes which had occurred within Scotland. The Kings of Scots exercised increasingly effective lordship over a realm which extended over northern Britain and into the Western

---

[1] Rickard, *Britain in Medieval French Literature*, 206–10.

Isles. The papacy recognised a Scottish ecclesiastical province with its own rights and liberties. These provided definitions of Scotland as a separate community in terms which were easily understood across western Europe. Ironically, this status was a product of the external influences which had been at work on Scotland during the century before 1214. The process of internal change during this period had also 'Europeanised' Scotland, linking the kingdom and its inhabitants to the values and populations of the core regions of Europe. We have seen the impact of this on the Scottish church in the thirteenth century. Secular elites also recognised themselves as members of a wider aristocratic world with a common culture that had its origins in the provinces of northern France. As across Europe, knighthood was recognised by Scottish nobles as the means of entry into the chivalric class. The debate over the knighting of the young Alexander III in 1249 indicated the significance of the act, and Scottish kings probably guarded the right to knight their own leading subjects. The bestowing of knighthood by Alexander II on his cousin John, earl of Huntingdon in 1227 and by Alexander III on David, earl of Atholl, and on Colban and Donald, the heirs to Fife and Mar, provided ceremonial expressions of royal authority and formed bonds of knightly obligation between kings and nobles. The seals of the kings, their vassals of Anglo-French descent, the comital dynasties of Gaelic origin, even Hebridean magnates all bore the image of the mounted knight as a symbol of their membership of the aristocratic elite. Like the clergy, Scotland's secular nobles identified themselves as part of a class which stretched well beyond their king's realm.[2]

Though the interchange of values, ideas and peoples had its greatest impact before 1214, it remained a vital element in Scotland's existence and character in subsequent decades. If this later period saw the strengthening of allegiances and identities in the royal heartlands of Scotland, these did not reduce the importance of links between the kingdom's inhabitants and surrounding societies. For example, in coastal burghs like Berwick, significant settlement from the Low Countries and eastern England encouraged economic connections with these regions. The descendants of these settlers were Scots but the trading links remained and increased. Flanders developed as the market for Scottish wool. The demands of the Flemish cloth-making industry drove the development of large-scale sheep farming in southern and eastern Scotland as it did in England. The wool trade brought increased prosperity for secular and ecclesiastical landowners and for merchants. Though St Omer was initially the favoured

---

[2] Bartlett, *The Making of Europe*, 24–59; McDonald, 'Images of Hebridean lordship', 129–43; Anderson, *Early Sources*, ii, 462; *Scotichronicon*, v, 290–3, 348–9, 380–1.

market, by the later thirteenth century larger centres, like Arras and Bruges, had taken over. In Bruges by the 1280s, Scottish wool was regarded as being of equal value to English fleeces, and superior to Welsh or Irish fleeces. The importance of the Scottish wool supply led to the establishment of a permanent community of Flemish merchants in Berwick, with their own building, the Red Hall, to safeguard their cities' interest in the greatest Scottish trading burgh.[3]

Flanders was not the only regular trading partner for Scottish merchants. The raw products that Scotland produced – wool and hides, tallow and cheese – were exported to towns from northern Germany to western France. In exchange for these animal products, merchants sought luxury or finished goods. In particular, the reputation of the Scots as beer-drinkers is undermined by evidence for the wine trade, with merchants buying the vintages of Gascony and the Loire for the home market. This market included Alexander III, whose financial accounts are full of references to the purchase of both red and white wine, and who died owing money to a Bordeaux vintner. More mundane but possibly more important is the evidence for the importation of corn, barley, beans and other foodstuffs from eastern English ports like Lynn and Yarmouth to Scotland. This suggests that the Scots, like the Welsh and Irish, still depended on English exports to supply grain and pulses, while Scottish livestock passed in the other direction. The importance of such trade to the Scots is certainly suggested by Henry III's imposition of an embargo on Scottish merchants during the political crisis of 1244.[4]

The Scottish economy was thus bound up with patterns of exchange that stretched across north-western Europe. Its mercantile class was well-used to dealing with traders, buyers and suppliers from many cities and lands. A similar ease of movement and contact can be found amongst the clerical elite. While the members of this group might seek to prevent the appointment of non-Scots to leading positions in the Scottish church, their actions did not represent the creation of a 'national' church. The Scottish clergy were members of an order whose ultimate allegiance to God worked through an ecclesiastical hierarchy that transcended secular lordships and realms. The presence of numerous Scots at the papal curia in Rome or Avignon, the attendance of a Scottish contingent at the church council at Lyons in 1274, and the need for Cistercians and for friars to attend the general chapter of their orders all integrated Scottish churchmen into the wider body of clergy. At a more individual level,

---

[3] Stevenson, 'The Flemish dimension of the Auld Alliance', 28–42.

[4] Stevenson, Documents, i, 71–4; C.D.S., i, nos 858, 907, 934–5, 937, 1,044, 1,768; E.R., i, 8, 11–12, 15, 25, 28; Davies, Domination and Conquest, 7–10.

aspiring Scottish clerics sought a route to advancement which took them beyond their homeland. During the thirteenth century, ecclesiastical preferment was increasingly linked to the acquisition of university training. Between 1200 and 1340 perhaps 600 Scots became Masters of Arts, and amongst this small group were the leaders of the church. For example, the powerful episcopate of the 1270s and 1280s, the Wisharts, William Fraser and their colleagues, were all graduates. To receive this schooling, Scots needed to travel abroad. Most went to Oxford or Paris, and significant group attended the great centre for canon law at Bologna. Some taught at universities, like Matthew de Scotia or John Duns Scotus at Paris, or the future bishop of Aberdeen, Peter Ramsay, at Oxford. All received a training which gave them access to contemporary intellectual developments and emphasised their membership of a Christian community beyond their temporal allegiances.[5] This was not exclusive to trained clergy. During the two centuries before 1214 the desire for wider access to a spiritual life had found one outlet in pilgrimage, a journey to a place of religious significance as an act of penance or devotion. Like their fellow Christians, many Scots enthusiastically took up the pilgrim's staff and, by the mid-thirteenth century, were travelling inside and outside Scotland in search of spiritual favour. The greatest centres of pilgrimage in the west – Santiago de Compostella in northern Spain, and Rome – attracted Scottish pilgrims, though it is likely that the most popular destination beyond their homeland was the shrine of St Thomas Becket at Canterbury. Alexander III himself visited Canterbury in 1278 while another Scot, William of Perth, was murdered at Rochester whilst en route to the shrine. William's own tomb in Rochester Cathedral became a site of pilgrimage and he was canonised in 1256. Besides these exceptional examples, many other Scots may have trudged the pilgrim roads of western Europe.[6]

For the military aristocracy, the ultimate expression of the pilgrimage was the armed expedition against the enemies of the faith. Such crusades still enjoyed royal patrons but, unlike Louis IX of France and Edward I of England, neither Alexander II nor his son showed a personal interest in crusading activity. Alexander III even supported the withholding of ecclesiastical taxation from English crusaders. However, a number of Scottish magnates did answer appeals to wage war to defend or extend Christendom in Africa or the Middle East. The earl of Dunbar joined King Louis' first crusade in 1248, and a number of lords, including the

[5] Ash, 'The church', 43, 45; Watt, 'Scottish university men of the thirteenth and fourteenth centuries', 1–18.
[6] P. Yeoman, *Pilgrimage in Medieval Scotland*, 110–20.

earls of Atholl and Carrick and Robert Bruce and his son, were in the expeditions that set out from France and England in 1270–1. The limited involvement of Scots can be explained by the costs and risks of these ventures. Dunbar sold property and his horse stud to finance his crusade and died while waiting to embark at Marseilles. Earl David of Atholl died from the plague which killed Louis IX at Tunis in 1270, while Adam of Carrick succumbed the next year at Acre. Not surprisingly, many nobles preferred to support the Holy Land by granting estates to the military orders, the Hospitallers and Templars, which had been established to combine religious and chivalric values. As across Europe, the Templars were the richer order in Scotland, but their chief house in Scotland, at Balantrodoch (later Temple) in Lothian, was not a military base but an administrative centre. The presence of the orders in Scotland provided a real link to events in the east, and Templar officials brought news of events there to this opposite corner of the Christian world.[7] For those Scots who funded the military orders and for those who took part, interest in crusading was not simply about personal piety – it was another connection with a wider world. In 1273 Robert Bruce and his retinue of Annandale knights paused on their return from Palestine at the great Cistercian abbey of Clairvaux in Burgundy. Bruce granted the monks lands in Annandale to free his family from the curse of the Irish Cistercian, St Malachy. This gift to the community which St Bernard had ruled, from a lord of Norman descent who was returning from the Holy Land, presented Robert and his men not as figures from the fringes, but as members of a noble elite which spanned western Europe.[8] Crusading appealed as a means of playing an active role in this elite. The attraction was not limited to lords of Frankish pedigree like Bruce: Gaelic lords and bards were also recorded on expeditions to Rome and Palestine in the thirteenth century, journeying to the centres of the Latin Christian world to which they belonged.

In many European lands, Scots were known and recognised as merchants, scholars, pilgrims, crusaders and travellers and, while not as widely travelled as some of their subjects, the kings of Scots had their own connections with the princely houses of the west. The marriages of the royal house were a key element in these connections. Alexander II and his son both took English princesses as their first wives and found their second among the great noble houses of northern France, the kin and vassals of

[7] Macquarrie, *Scotland and the Crusades*, 47–65; Cowan, Mackay and Macquarrie (eds), *The Knights of St John of Jerusalem in Scotland*, xviii–xxx; *Scotichronicon*, v, 376–7, 382–3.
[8] Macquarrie, 'Charters of the Bruces of Annandale', 72–9.

the French kings. The marriages of their close relatives extended and rein-
forced these ties. Alexander II's aunts married the counts of Brittany and
Holland and though plans to marry his sisters to Henry III and Richard of
Cornwall, Henry's brother, failed, alliances were formed instead with
English magnate dynasties, the Bigods, de Burghs and Marshals. The marriages that Alexander III negotiated for his children suggest an ambitious
approach. In 1281 his daughter, Margaret, married King Eric II of
Norway (Hakon IV's grandson) in a match designed to cement the peace
between the two kingdoms and to secure a throne for the Scottish princess.
The marriage of Alexander III's son, Lord Alexander, to Margaret,
daughter of Guy de Dampierre count of Flanders, linked the royal house
of Scotland to a rich and prestigious princely dynasty. Such marriages
would prove expensive and have effects very different from those intended
by Alexander III, but in the early 1280s they confirmed the Scottish
dynasty's place amongst the ruling houses of Europe.[9] Scotland's kings
and queens were proud of their connections. The visits to their courts by
kinsmen – like that of Enguerrand de Couci in 1272 or of Edward and
Edmund of England in 1267 and 1268 – and the journeys of Alexander III
and Queen Margaret to the court of her father, Henry III, and brother,
Edward I, were intended both for business and 'for the sake of solace and
recreation'. Family ties had political importance. In 1258 the regency
council for Alexander III included his French mother, Queen Marie, and
her second husband, John of Acre, the son of the titular king of Jerusalem.
The Scottish kings were part of a world of dynasties and courts which
made European politics the business of extended family networks.[10]

THE KINGS OF SCOTS AND THE PLANTAGENET DOMINIONS

The horizons of this world do not alter the fact that the Scottish king's
closest relationships were with the Plantagenet rulers of England. The
family ties between the two houses were only the tip of the iceberg.
Geography and recent history meant that there were manifold points
of contact and intercourse between the two realms. Above all, the noble
families of Scotland and the Plantagenet dominions were bound together
not just by common cultural values, but by direct relationships and interests, both old and new. The Comyns, Bruces, Stewarts and many others
had English or Anglo-French origins and retained family ties with

[9] Anderson, *Early Sources*, ii, 246, 249, 444–5, 570, 679–80; Stones and Simpson,
Edward I and the Throne of Scotland, ii, 188–90.
[10] *Scotichronicon*, v, 354–5, 366–7, 386–7; Stones, *Anglo-Scottish Relations*, no. 11.

Scotland and the House of Couci

At Pentecost (15 May) 1239 at Roxburgh, Alexander II of Scotland married the 'beautiful maiden' Marie, daughter of Enguerrand de Couci, 'a noble baron of the realm of France'. Alexander's new father-in-law was no ordinary noble. Enguerrand (III) the Great, *sieur de Couci* was one of the leading nobles in northern France. Through his mother he was a kinsman of Louis IX of France, while his second wife (and perhaps Marie's mother) was a cousin of Henry III of England. In his own right, Enguerrand was the greatest baron of Picardy, the heir of a line whose power and prestige stretched back to the eleventh century, and the builder of a fortress at Couci, the size and sophistication of which made it the envy of many princes and the model for a number of Scottish castles. The fears of the English concerning the marriage may have been less about an alliance between Alexander and the French king than about his connection with the lords of Couci. In 1244 it was not King Louis, but the Scottish queen's family who offered Alexander a force of knights for the army he was raising against Henry III.

By then Enguerrand the Great was dead, killed in 1242 by falling from his horse onto his sword, but the link with Scotland survived his end and the death of his son-in-law in 1249. The new king, Alexander III, was well aware of his mother's kin. Queen Marie left Scotland in 1251 but returned to her son's court on numerous occasions between 1257 and her death in 1285. Marie was not Alexander's only link with the house of Couci. In 1272 the infamous Enguerrand (IV) de Couci paid a visit to his sister and nephew, returning to France with 'a well-filled purse'. Alexander III also showed generosity to his cousin, Enguerrand de Guines. The young French noble came to Scotland to receive a Scottish heiress, Christine Lindsay, as his bride and inherited estates across southern Scotland. Alexander III's family ties may even have influenced his second marriage: Yolanda, daughter of Robert (IV), count of Dreux, was a kinswoman of Queen Marie. The Scottish king's choice of bride and his main-tenance of family ties with his continental cousins marked Alexander's court as a distant, but not unimportant centre, of the Francophone aristocratic world of the thirteenth-century west.

England. These ancestral connections were renewed and extended by marriage. Alexander II was related by marriage to the English magnate houses of Warenne, Chester, Ros, Vesci, Marshal, Bigod, de Burgh and more, while Robert Bruce's marriage to the sister of Richard de Clare, earl of Gloucester, and Malise, earl of Strathearn's match with Muriel Muschamp, daughter of the lord of Wooler, were only two of a host of such connections. The significance of these alliances went beyond personal bonds. Land and lordship were often also transmitted through marriage. The Bruces of Annandale had held estates in both England and Scotland since the 1120s. These were extended by the inheritance of Robert Bruce's mother, Isabella, sister of John, earl of Huntingdon. From 1237 John's estates from the English Midlands to north-east Scotland were shared between three heiresses and families, the Bruces, the English family of Hastings and the house of Galloway. This last family had already ended in the male line with the death of Alan of Galloway in 1234. His Scottish lordships and English estates were partitioned between his daughters and their husbands. Shares of this inheritance made the Balliols of Barnard Castle in County Durham major Scottish magnates, and added to the lands of Roger de Quincy, earl of Winchester in both realms. Winchester's death in turn provided his heirs, one of whom was Alexander Comyn, earl of Buchan, with lands that spanned the border.[11]

The fates of the Huntingdon, Galloway and de Quincy estates were the greatest examples of the way in which landholdings could be built up and broken down in thirteenth-century Britain without distinction being made between England and Scotland. The two royal lordships formed a single land market. The vassals of both kings could hold and acquire lands throughout the British Isles. As a result of marrying heiresses David, earl of Atholl, became lord of Chilham in Kent, and Gilbert Umfraville, lord of Redesdale in Northumberland, became earl of Angus. John de Vesci was lord of Sprouston in Scotland, Alnwick in England and Kildare in Ireland. The scale of these cross-border landholding connections is striking. By the later thirteenth century, nine out of thirteen Scottish earldoms were held by lords with some English estates, while seven of the English comital families possessed Scottish lands at some point between 1200 and 1290. These cross-border links were even more marked in northern England. The Bruces, Balliols, de Vesci and Umfravilles were part of an extensive network of links between this region and Scotland. In the three border counties of England, fourteen out of twenty-seven baronies were held by families with some Scottish estates. Below the barons, knightly and gentry families in these counties also had ties of kin and land that spanned the border, while lesser families from elsewhere could acquire lands in the two realms through service to a great cross-border magnate house like the de Quincys.[12]

<hr>

[11] Stringer, *Earl David of Huntingdon*, 178–89; Barrow, *The Anglo-Norman Era*, 12–19; Oram, 'Devorgilla, the Balliols and Buittle', 165–74; Simpson, 'The *familia* of Roger de Quincy', 102–4; Stell, 'The Balliol Family and the Great Cause of 1291–2', 150–65.
[12] Stringer, *Earl David of Huntingdon*, 190–2, 198–201; Stringer, 'Identities in thirteenth-century England', 28–66; Stringer, 'Nobility and identity in medieval Britain and Ireland', 199–239.

The border between the kingdoms of Scotland and England was a recognised division between two royal lordships and legal authorities, but it
was not a frontier between separate aristocracies. In other circumstances
rulers could regard such overlapping interests as a threat to their security. After the kings of France had taken Normandy from the Plantagenets
in 1204, both rulers encouraged their vassals to sever the links of landholding between England and Normandy, breaking connections that had
existed since the Norman conquest. The two kings in Britain did not see
a similar need to monopolise the allegiance of their great vassals. There
were isolated examples of mistrust in Alexander III's treatment of John
Cheam, bishop of Glasgow and in his purchase, at considerable cost, of
the lands of Ratho and Bathgate from Henry de Bohun. However, such
acts were a drop in the ocean. They were countered by actions like
Alexander's restoration of William Ferrers to the office of constable,
earlier granted by the king to the earl of Buchan. There was no discrimination against the large group of magnates with interests in both realms,
and the Scottish kings' officers and councillors included many such men.
Any such discrimination would have been damaging to his realm and
unnatural to rulers who were themselves part of this cross-border elite.
As superior lords of the earldom of Huntingdon, lords of Tynedale and,
later, of lands round Penrith, the kings of Scots were themselves English
barons, obliged to perform homage and service to the kings of England.
Alexander III and his father probably saw cross-border landholding as
being to their direct and indirect advantage. The possession of English
fiefs by them and their vassals was a source of additional wealth and prestige. The practice ensured that the Scottish kings had friends and influence within the neighbouring realm. Far from undermining the Scottish
kings' rights as rulers of their realm, lords with Anglo-Scottish holdings
had proved to be valuable supporters of royal authority within Scotland
during the preceding century. In relations with England these families
normally possessed an interest in keeping the peace. A major conflict
between the two kings and realms would have the character of a civil war,
like that of 1215–17. Avoidance of the kind of war which severed the links
between England and Normandy was the best means of preserving
landed interests which crossed the border.[13]

The absence of open conflicts between the kingdoms after 1217 meant
that cross-border interests could be maintained. During this period, and
especially between 1260 and 1286, duties to different kings could be performed without difficulty. In the 1260s the Bruces, Balliols, Umfravilles

---

[13] *A.P.S.*, i, 110; *Scotichronicon*, v, 380–1; *C.D.S.*, i, nos 368, 1,370, 1,409, 2,487;
Stringer, *Earl David of Huntingdon*, 107–10.

and others raised Scottish retinues to aid Henry III against his English enemies with King Alexander's full blessing. A decade later, John de Vesci of Alnwick was one of the leaders of Alexander's expedition to Man. The councils as well as the armies of the two kings contained men with ties of allegiance to both realms. On private business and in royal service, nobles could move easily between kingdoms. Their sense of identity was equally flexible. The attitudes and actions of cross-border lords show a recognition of different responsibilities and customs, in particular the more limited demands placed by Scotland's kings on their vassals, but in general they had no difficulty functioning as men of both royal lords. The relative pull of their allegiances depended on family traditions, the concentration of their interests and other factors. The acquisition of English lands did not reduce the identification of the earls of Mar and Buchan with Scotland, while the de Bohuns and Hastings thought of themselves as English despite having inheritances in the northern realm. Allegiances did not need to be defined exclusively. The Bruces of Annandale were hardly exceptional in being full participants in the aristocratic society of both kingdoms. Their neighbours, the Balliols, were even more cosmopolitan, holding their ancestral lands at Bailleul-en-Vimeu in Picardy and owing allegiance to three kings. While magnates had a sense of being Scots or English and of being part of a wider community, loyalties to a realm or nation were not necessarily exclusive or all-embracing. Nor were they the only level of identity. For a magnate like Malise, earl of Strathearn, his responsibilities as a landowner in Northumberland formed just one more layer to add to his roles as one of the Scottish king's chief vassals and the head of an ancient kindred and province. The Bruces and Balliols, who added Gaelic provinces to their estates during the thirteenth century, showed an equal ability to combine differing identities and allegiances.[14]

The implications of these extensive ties between the kings and nobilities of the English and Scottish realms went beyond this aristocratic level. They meant that Scotland's dealings with other lands in the British Isles cannot be understood in terms of external relations between separate realms and communities. Oaths of fealty and bonds of kinship and landholding made Scotland's secular elite part of a political world which involved not just England but extended through most of the British Isles and onto the continent. At the head of this network stood the kings of England, who in the thirteenth century were also lords of Ireland, superior lord of Wales and dukes of Aquitaine in south-west France. The kings

[14] C.D.S., i, nos 1,983, 2,283, 2,285, 2,359, 2,429; Anderson, Early Sources, ii, 644, 672; Scotichronicon, v, 355; Stell, 'The Balliol family', 154.

of Scots and many of their barons shared ties of allegiance to this royal lord with many other princes and barons in the west. These ties combined with the inevitable contacts between neighbouring lands to involve Scotland in the policies and problems of the Plantagenet kings.

Though open war between English and Scottish kings only occurred in 1215–17, their relationship was not free from tensions. These tensions were often related to links of landholding and lordship between the kingdoms. The claim that Alexander II inherited to the three English border counties continued as a major issue up to 1237. Though both King John of England in the 1200s and the minority government of Henry III in the 1220s used the claim as a diplomatic carrot to ensure the Scottish king's friendship, failure to deliver the new fief to the Scottish king led to war between 1215 and 1217 and major friction in the mid-1230s. Alexander II's links with England meant that in these disputes he could not be treated as a foreign ruler without allies amongst the English king's other vassals. Between 1215 and 1217 Alexander exploited his family's extensive connections within northern England and was accepted as leader of the baronial opposition in the region. In the 1230s he also found support amongst Henry III's other disgruntled vassals. Alexander formed an alliance with the greatest English magnate in Wales and Ireland, Richard Marshal, earl of Pembroke, and with Llywelyn ap Iorwerth, prince of Gwynedd, which must have caused Henry deep anxieties. The treaty of York in 1237 may have settled Alexander II's territorial claims and removed the grounds for regular tensions. It did not end issues of a more general sort which arose from the position of the Scottish king and his vassals relative to the English realm.[15]

Central to these issues was the precise relationship between the two kings. The terms of the relationship remained fluid and complex throughout the reigns of Alexander II and his son. Though the status of the king of Scots in both realms was a question of law, of his rights and duties as a royal lord and vassal, the nature of these remained a matter of debate. Statute and precedent were affected, even driven, by political circumstances, most obviously in the minority of Alexander III and its aftermath. While not set in stone, relations between the two rulers and their chief vassals followed paths which suggest an understanding of accepted patterns of behaviour. Most obviously, between the minority of Henry III and the death of Alexander III, the kings of England did not press their claims to be superior lords of Scotland and receive homage from the kings of Scots for their kingdom. This claim was certainly not

[15] Anderson, *Early Sources*, ii, 498–9; Anderson, *English Chroniclers*, 343–5; Stone, *Anglo-Scottish Relations*, no. 7.

forgotten. It was raised on two occasions: by Henry III in 1251, following the marriage of his daughter to the young Alexander III, and by Edward I to the adult Alexander in 1278. Both times Alexander refused to perform homage for his kingdom, and his refusal was accepted by the English king 'for the time' and 'reserving the right and claim . . . when they wish to discuss the matter'. For the Plantagenets, the question remained open. Simply raising the issue excited ill-informed English chroniclers to claim that Alexander had submitted to Edward in 1278. In practice, Alexander and his father were able to defend their right to hold Scotland from God alone without serious challenge. Even during Alexander's minority, King Henry showed respect for this position. His dismissal of the Scottish king's councillors and forceful intervention in Scottish politics in 1255 were both accompanied by promises that his acts did not reduce the Scottish king's rights or form precedents for future actions. Such statements were necessary to maintain Scottish support, but they do not indicate any determination to subordinate the Scottish realm to his lordship.[16]

Yet, as has been seen, the Scottish kings were vassals of the kings of England for their English lands. The oath of fealty in respect of these was sworn by Alexander II and his son on a number of occasions. Though it directly concerned their duties as English barons, this liege homage had wider significance. By its terms the Scottish king promised to be faithful to the king of England and keep his councils secret; in personal terms he was a 'liegeman . . . against all men' of his lord. This lord-man relationship gave the English king advantages in his relations with his royal vassal. Amongst them was the exercise of lordship which was based not on formal and institutional powers, but on a loose, personal superiority implied by the oath of fealty. This position was undoubtedly exploited by Henry III from 1251. The Christmas marriage of Henry's daughter to Alexander III also saw the Scottish king receive knighthood at Henry's hands and accept the latter's dismissal of his officers. These displays of patronage were not the exercise of formal authority but symbolised the Scottish king's 'reverence and honour' for Henry, based on the personal prestige of the Plantagenet king.[17]

The circumstances of Alexander's minority greatly increased the significance of such personal lordship. However, even when the kings of Scots were adults, the performance of homage and their visits to the

[16] Anderson, *English Chroniclers*, 363–8; Stone, *Anglo-Scottish Relations*, no. 12.
[17] *Chron. Fordun*, i, 295–6; *C.D.S.*, i, no 1,848; Anderson, *English Chroniclers*, 363–8; Stone, *Anglo-Scottish Relations*, no. 12. The importance of such informal lordship is discussed in Davies, *The First English Empire: Power and Identities in the British Isles*, ch. 1, especially 23–5.

English court may have suggested a dependent status, rather than full equality between rulers. This impression was certainly fostered by the English government outside the British Isles and, in particular, at the papal curia. During the tensions between Alexander II and Henry III in the mid-1230s, Pope Gregory IX wrote to the Scottish king urging him, as Henry's vassal, to keep the peace. Gregory's remark that Alexander's barons would be obliged to aid Henry implies that the pope regarded a war between the English and Scottish kings as rebellion by the latter, a view undoubtedly fostered by Henry's agents. These clerics argued a similar line on the question of the Scottish king's coronation. Alexander sought the full rite of coronation in the early 1220s, a decade later, and it was requested again in the late 1240s, probably for his son. On this last occasion, the English claimed that, as their liegeman, the king of Scots should be neither crowned nor anointed without their consent. This was too forceful a demand for the pope but, nevertheless, they continued to withhold coronation and the full royal status it conferred from the Scottish kings.[18] It was hard for Alexander II and his son to deny that they were liegemen of Henry III and Edward. This undoubtedly affected their status. The terms of their homage had implications for their dealings with other princes, since, as vassals, they were obliged to give aid and council to their lord against his enemies. English fears that Alexander II's marriage to Marie de Couci would lead to his alliance with Louis IX of France were one of the causes of the political confrontation of 1244. The settlement of this crisis at Newcastle included Alexander's promise to 'preserve good faith' to his liege lord, Henry III, and 'never enter into any treaty' with his enemies, nor to make or incite war against Henry's domains. The agreement stated the limits which his duties as a vassal placed on Alexander's wider activities. Such terms were not unique. Henry III accepted similar terms in the treaty of Paris with Louis IX. As dukes of Aquitaine, Henry and Edward excepted their fealty to the French kings from alliances with other princes.[19]

Given this wider context of overlapping obligations, Scottish kings were unlikely to see their duties to the king of England as limiting their ability to rule their own realm. English efforts to impose such limitations on Scottish royal government were rare. In 1244 it was argued that, as a liegeman of Henry III, Alexander II could not disinherit or exile Walter Bisset without his lord's consent. Alexander rejected this claim but, after Alexander's death, Henry was able to exert influence on Scottish politics,

---

[18] *Cal. Papal Reg.*, i, 83; *C.D.S.*, i, nos. 1,181, 1,266, 1,277, 1,798; Stone, *Anglo-Scottish Relations*, no. 6.

[19] Anderson, *English Chroniclers*, 351–8; Duncan, *Kingship of the Scots*, 121–2; Vale, *The Origins of the Hundred Years War* 48–63.

albeit in terms which avoided any reference to his superior lordship. In September 1255 Henry named Alexander III's councillors, excluding those he considered unfit, and the English king subsequently intervened as Alexander's 'principal advisor' to ensure that Ewen MacDougall was not permanently deprived of his Scottish lands. During the minority, Henry also sought to exploit the links between the landholding classes of the two realms. Between 1251 and 1255, two Anglo-Scottish barons, John Balliol and Robert Ros, were the nominal heads of the minority council. Though their English lands did not make them Henry's agents, they were vulnerable to pressure. The failure of Ros and Balliol to serve Henry's interests led to the English king plundering their estates and demanding huge fines from them in 1255. Both Balliol and Ros were noticeably absent from future opposition to Henry from Scotland. The possession of substantial holdings in England left lords open to leverage from the Plantagenet king.[20]

The events of the 1250s were an exceptional internal crisis for Scotland before 1286. Henry's interventions did not aim at the formal alteration of the relationship between the two realms, and though Alexander III's chief vassals showed a worrying tendency to seek the English king's political aid against each other, there were clear limits to what some Scots would accept. The settlement of 1255 produced a backlash. The seizure of Alexander III by the Comyns and their allies in late 1257 was a direct challenge to Henry's settlement and was justified as the defence of Scottish king and kingdom. Such claims were possibly behind the identification of the new council as a 'native party' by the English chronicler Matthew Paris. Certainly the leaders of the coup did not hold major English estates. Though these lords had themselves sought Henry's aid in 1251, they regarded the king of Scots as the sole legitimate source of royal authority in his kingdom. In normal circumstances, this view was probably natural for all members of the Scottish political class regardless of interests beyond the kingdom. Crises like 1244 did not alter this view, and in the 1260s royal lordship was resumed when Alexander III assumed control. While the English kings liked to emphasise the obligations which stemmed from their neighbours' homage, in practice they were dealing with the rulers of a separate realm. Alexander II gave financial aid to the English government in the 1220s, but his help was freely given by an ally, not owed by a vassal.[21]

The developing frontier between the two realms around the Irish Sea

[20] Stone, *Anglo-Scottish Relations*, no. 10; Anderson, *English Chroniclers*, 370–1, 374; *C.D.S.*, i, nos. 2,014, 3,111.

[21] Anderson, *Early Sources*, ii, 588–90; Anderson, *English Chroniclers*, 376; *Chron. Fordun*, 297–8; *C.D.S.*, i, nos 909, 1,086.

provided the most striking example of Scotland's practical equality. The extension of the Scottish kings' lordship over Galloway and Argyll, and the annexation of the earldom of Ulster by Henry III brought the two crowns to opposite shores of the North Channel by the late 1240s. The kings had a shared interest in this region in limiting the power and alliances of Gaelic lords in Ulster and the Isles but they also had their own agendas. The English kings were traditional protectors of the rulers of Man and allies of the kings of Norway. During the minority of Alexander III, Henry intervened to safeguard the interests of both these men. He co-operated with Hakon IV in the Isles, aiding the Norwegian king's adherents and opposing his enemies. The events of the 1260s, when Alexander forced the submission of the Islesmen, annexed Man and ended Norse lordship in the region, were an indirect blow to the English king. The latter's ineffectual response was a consequence of the political crisis he was facing in England, but Alexander's success showed that, like Henry in the previous decade, he could exploit his neighbour's temporary weakness.[22]

This crisis in Henry III's kingship lasted for nearly a decade from 1258. It illustrated the links between Scottish politics and those of neighbouring political societies. The sudden removal of Henry's influence from Scotland and his inability to support his allies in the west were part of a general weakening of Plantagenet lordship in the British Isles. The crisis also aided the success of Llywelyn ap Gruffydd, prince of Gwynedd in building, and then extracting English recognition for, a native Welsh monarchy. Like the treaty of Perth in 1266, the treaty of Montgomery the following year, which saw Henry accord Llywelyn the title of prince of Wales, was a partial product of the English king's weakness. Scots had recognised Llywelyn's title nearly a decade earlier, in the alliance of March 1258 between the prince and the magnates who had seized Alexander III. The alliance was based on shared opposition to Henry, who had raised armies against both parties. However, while effective in the short-term, this agreement represented no long-term coalition of interests. The events of 1258 were an exceptional experience for the Scots. For Llywelyn, fresh defiance of Henry was only the latest move in the house of Gwynedd's efforts to establish its authority over native Wales, begun in the 1200s by his grandfather, Llywelyn ap Iorwerth. Even after 1267, Llywelyn ap Gruffydd would remain in an uncertain position: his lordship over the other Welsh princes lacked the established

[22] McDonald, *Kingdom of the Isles*, 98–100; Duffy, 'The Bruce brothers', 63; Duncan and Brown, 'Argyll and the western Isles', 207–10; R. Frame, 'Henry III and Ireland: The shaping of a peripheral lordship', in Frame, *Ireland and Britain*, 31–58, 46–7; Brown, 'Henry the Peaceable: Henry III, Alexander III and royal lordship in the British Isles, 1249–1272', 43–66.

tradition of unitary monarchy which existed in Scotland, and his princi-
pality was held from the English crown. Though his predecessors had
sought equality with the kings of Scots, their authority remained more
limited in theory and practice.[23]

A comparison of these monarchies highlights the place of Scotland in
the British Isles. Unlike Wales and Ireland, the Scottish kingdom was
generally recognised as being outside the formal authority of the kings of
England. The stability of its internal political hierarchy and of its relations with the English crown contrasted with that of Gwynedd. Even
whilst disregarding Henry's protection of the rulers of Man, Alexander
III maintained his personal and political friendship with his father-in-law.
Neither Alexander nor his English relatives showed any sustained interest in altering the relationship between their realms before 1286. The
kings of England seemed satisfied with a status quo which meant the
north was by the far the most stable borderland of their widespread
dominions, causing them far less difficulty than Ireland, Wales or
Gascony. Throughout the 1250s interference within Scotland was a much
lower priority for Henry than the defence of his rights in either Wales or
Gascony. The king's single day spent in Scotland contrasted with his frequent campaigns in Wales and lengthy visits to the continent. After the
events of 1258, whereas Llywelyn was forced to fight a military and political campaign through the 1260s to attain his ends, Henry quickly
accepted the new council in Scotland. Subsequent disputes, over
Alexander's English estates or even the border between the two kingdoms, did not disturb the good relations between the kings.[24]

Such good relations involved more than just the two royal families. The
connections of land and family between the two kingdoms were not accidental. They were, instead, both a cause and product of Scotland's participation in a wider Anglo-French cultural and social world. Scottish nobles
of English or Gaelic descent were recognised as part of a wider aristocratic
society with common status and interests. By contrast, native Welsh lords,
still less Gaelic Irish kings, remained outsiders with limited connections
to their English neighbours. In the eyes of the latter, they belonged to a
different and inferior society. Though the Scots too could be disparaged
as violent and barbaric by English writers, the range of ties between the
elites of both kingdoms created, in practice, a different atmosphere. In

[23] Smith, *Llywelyn ap Gruffydd*, esp. 110–11, 274–9; *Littere Wallie*, no. 317; R. Frame,
'Overlordship and reaction, c. 1200–1450', in Frame, *Britain and Ireland*, 171–90, 177.
[24] Henry visited Roxburgh on 20 September 1255. He led or planned to lead campaigns
to Wales in 1245, 1257 and 1258, and was in France from June 1253 until December
1254, and again in 1259–60.

normal circumstances the king of Scots and his magnates would identify with the English crown and its marchers and not with the native communities of the British Isles. The activities of these Scottish lords in Moray, Sutherland and the Isles had clear parallels with the extension of English lordship in Wales and Ireland. Despite the events of 1258, there were no signs of Scottish sympathy for Llywelyn when Edward I launched his war against the prince in 1276–7, forcing him to surrender the gains of 1267. Nor did the Scots show obvious misgivings when Edward destroyed the house of Gwynedd, uprooted the symbols of their authority and brought native Wales under his direct rule in the early 1280s. Instead, Scottish magnates took part in these events by providing knights for Edward's armies. They did so as vassals of the king for their English estates, but there is no reason to believe that they did so unwillingly.[25]

Within a generation Scots would look back on the Welsh wars with a very different eye. They recognised that the fate of the Welsh princes and of native Wales had been an ominous portent for them, showing the way in which relationships within the British Isles could be altered violently.[26] The stability of their own kingdom's relations with England proved to be an illusion. It depended on the continued readiness of the kings of England to be satisfied with an informal and limited approach to their claims of superiority over Scotland's rulers. The maintenance of such an approach was not favoured by wider developments. The thirteenth century witnessed a tendency to tighten and define relationships in increasingly restrictive and legalistic terms: Edward I's treatment of the Welsh was a classic example of the exploitation of loose overlordship to impose a demanding and novel structure of authority on a dependent community. A combination of legal proceedings, bureaucratic interference and military force against declared traitors and rebels was deployed to establish a new kind of English lordship and ultimately bring the Welsh under the king's direct control. If the Scots saw themselves as very different from the native Welsh in status and identity, the French kingdom provided parallel examples. A powerful French monarchy capable of exercising authority over a realm which stretched from the Mediterranean to the Channel was only a product of the century before the 1280s. Like Scotland, France was a term which was originally applied to one province, the area round Paris,

---

[25] *C.D.S.*, ii, nos 83, 215–16, 219; Gillingham, *The English in the Twelfth Century: Imperialism, National Identity and Political Values*; Clanchy, *England and its Rulers 1066–1272*, 241–67.

[26] The fourteenth-century chronicle of John of Fordun included an account of Edward's conquest of Wales 'lest any foreign nation which may read the said history should, unchastened by the example of the Welsh, unwarily fall under the dominion of most wretched thraldom to the English' (*Chron. Fordun*, ii, 304).

but which expanded with royal authority. By the 1280s, the kings of France
were not only the rulers of a massively enlarged royal demesne, but they
had formed a political hierarchy and regnal identity which emphasised
their authority throughout their realm. The Capetian kings had established their rights as liege lords with powers to intervene in the running of
great principalities, like Flanders, Brittany and Aquitaine, the latter the
remaining lands of the Plantagenets on the continent. Royal rights had
grown from negligible origins to be a defined legal authority: the royal
parlement in Paris could hear appeals from princely courts, and royal officials could enter the princes' lands to enforce its judgements.[27]

With some justice, the kings of Scots may have associated themselves
with the Capetians. Their achievements in Scotland matched, on a
smaller scale, those of the French kings. However, though developments
to the 1280s support this parallel, Scotland's future would prove to be
closer to the experiences of the principalities. In wealth and population,
Gascony, Flanders and Brittany were Scotland's equals or superiors. Like
the Scots, Bretons, Flemings and Gascons were recognised as separate
peoples, distinguishable from the French by language, law, custom and
political history. Their rulers, though dukes and counts, had built up the
strength of central authority and common allegiance within their principalities. These princes were not simply vassals. The dukes of Gascony
had only acknowledged their feudal obligations to the king of France in
1259 in the treaty of Paris between Henry III and Louis IX. The status
of Brittany would not be formally settled until 1297. The fate of Flanders
was most significant: the thirteenth century had seen the counts of
Flanders reduced from being among the greatest princes of the west to
dependence on the French crown, and this was achieved through royal
exploitation of, and interference in, succession disputes and internal
rivalries.[28]

Capetian ambitions and the reactions to them of princes and communities in Flanders and Gascony would be of great significance to the
Scots in the decades after 1280, even though they may have seemed to
be of little direct importance during the lifetime of Alexander III.
Unlike Guy, count of Flanders or Edward I as duke of Gascony,

---

[27] Smith, *Llywelyn ap Gruffydd*, 338–581; Davies, *Domination and Conquest*, 109–28;
Carr, 'The last days of Gwynedd', 7–22; Smith, 'England and Wales: The conflict of
Laws', 189–205; Hallam and Everard, *Capetian France 987–1328*, 231–420; Wood,
'*Regnum Francie*: a problem in Capetian administrative usage', 117–44.
[28] For information about the political development of these principalities and their
relations with the Capetian monarchy, see Vale, *Origins of the Hundred Years War*, chs
3–5; Nicholas, *Medieval Flanders*, 150–86; Everard, *Brittany and the Angevins*, 34, 35,
176–81; Gaillou and Jones, *The Bretons*, 193–220.

Alexander held a royal title and had defended the freedom of his kingdom from claims of superior lordship. Moreover, while the Bretons and Welsh had failed to win recognition as separate ecclesiastical provinces and were exposed to interference by French or English archbishops, the Scottish church enjoyed papal protection.[29] Yet, the status of realm and church were not guarantees of stability. In an age of expanding, even predatory, governments, established communities – the Welsh, the Manxmen, even the Flemings – could be threatened with absorption into a larger political unit. The success of the kings of Scots in forming their realm did not ensure its future security or its survival as a distinct political society. It may have seemed unclear to many outside observers in the thirteenth century whether the Scottish realm was a fully separate society. After all, its kings and many of its leading nobles were vassals of the English kings and attended his court. The subtleties of these relationships, clear to the Scottish king, may have been less so to outsiders. The papacy, for example, had to balance the forceful assertions of the rights and identity of the Scottish church against English claims that the Scots king was the vassal of their royal master. The English kings themselves seem to have accepted a relationship with their neighbour that expressed their vague superiority in a way that avoided conflict. However, such a recognition of the mutual advantages provided by good relations was not a permanent acceptance of the status quo. By raising their claim to be superior lords of Scotland, both Henry and Edward were reserving discussion of the issue for the future, when need or opportunity presented itself.

This future was swift in coming. Within a few years of Edward's request for homage from Alexander III in 1278, the Scottish royal house had suffered its dynastic catastrophe. The extinction of the direct royal line could not have been foreseen. It would have put massive strains on any medieval realm, but its consequences for Scotland were, perhaps, especially severe. The end of the line of kings which had ruled unbroken since the 1090s removed the force which had done most to form the kingdom as it existed under Alexander III. The absence of a clear focus of royal lordship would expose the flaws in their achievement. Amongst these flaws the ability of the kings of England to claim and exercise influence over the status of Scotland and the activities of its nobility would quickly emerge as the most serious threat to the survival of the realm. The lack of royal leadership would test the will and ability of the Scots to maintain a sense of common allegiance and identity in the face of internal and external pressures. In March 1286 Thomas the Rhymer, the poet

---

[29] Everard, *Brittany and the Angevins*, 13–14, 68–75; Davies, *Age of Conquest*, 188–94.

from Earlston, prophesised that King Alexander would die on the follow-ing day. He said, 'a strong wind will be heard in Scotland, the like of which has not been known since times long ago . . . it will humble what is lofty and cast to the ground what is unbending'. What would stand and fall in the coming gale could not have been foretold.[30]

[30] *Scotichronicon*, v, 428–9.

PART TWO

War and the Reshaping of Scotland (1286–1371)

CHAPTER 8

The Crisis of Kingship (1286–96)

THE END OF THE LINE

On 29 March 1286 the funeral of Alexander III was held at Dunfermline Abbey. As in 1214 and 1249 the prelates and magnates gathered on the news of their king's death. This time, however, there would be no inauguration of a new king to balance the burial of the old. Alexander's sudden death had brought to an end the male line of the royal dynasty that had ruled Scotland for two centuries. His funeral was the setting for the first of a series of councils during the spring of 1286. At these meetings the Scottish political class gathered to seek ways of filling the political vacuum left at the heart of the kingdom by Alexander's death. This issue of the succession would turn from a short-term crisis into a drawn-out military and political struggle, and the next three generations of Scots would face the issues raised by this sustained crisis. At the centre of this would be the search for the kind of widely-accepted royal lordship exercised by Alexander III and his forebears, but the course of the struggle would transform the structure and character of the thirteenth-century kingdom and threaten its survival.

The threat to the survival of the Scottish realm would come from the kings of England. In 1286, however, the involvement of the English crown in Scottish affairs seemed natural and inevitable. As a powerful neighbour, as a kinsman of the Scottish royal house and as lord of Alexander and many of his magnates for their English lands, King Edward I was recognised as having a part to play in Scotland. From the funeral, the Scottish leaders sent two friars to Edward asking him for a sign of his goodwill towards them. During the summer more prestigious envoys sought Edward's aid. In May William Fraser, bishop of St Andrews, went south but probably failed to see Edward before he sailed for France. A further embassy finally reached the king at Saintes in his duchy of Aquitaine. The Scots reportedly asked for Edward's 'counsel and protection', perhaps inviting him to take the informal role played by his father in the 1250s. But Edward was not like his father. In his reply to the envoys, he may have linked any such protection with the recognition of more defined authority over the Scottish realm. Such a legalistic and high-handed approach would have been in character, but in 1286 neither party pressed the issue. Edward's attention was fixed on the more immediate concerns of Aquitaine which would preoccupy him until 1289, and the Scots returned home without the prospect of his assistance.[1]

The desire for this assistance was a measure of the problems facing the Scottish leaders in 1286. The assemblies held at Scone on 2 April and again on 29 April failed even to recognise an heir. In 1284 the magnates had sworn to accept Alexander's granddaughter, Margaret of Norway, as heir should the king die without producing further offspring. However, in April 1286 it was believed that the queen, Yolanda of Dreux, was carrying the dead king's child. This uncertainty inevitably produced delay and debate. After two meetings during April it was agreed to shelve the issue of the succession until later in the year. In the absence of even a nominal royal head, it was vital to find a basis for government and collective action. Probably under the leadership of bishops Fraser of St Andrews and Robert Wishart of Glasgow, it was agreed that an oath of fealty should be taken to the heir 'who ought to inherit' and that official business be authorised by a seal 'appointed for the government of the kingdom', bearing both the royal arms and an image of St Andrew. During the later 1280s, the term 'commune' or 'community' was used in official documents, signifying the involvement of a wide landed and political class in the running of the realm in the absence of its legitimate head. In late April 1286 the authority of this 'commune' was used to sanction the election of six guardians of the peace to head the royal government. The choice of guardians reflected contemporary concepts of representation: the church was represented by bishops Fraser and Wishart; the earls by the veteran Alexander Comyn of Buchan and young Duncan of Fife; and the barons by John Comyn of Badenoch and James Steward. However, the prime concerns of the Scottish elite were not social but political. Despite the oath and the guardians, eyes were already turning to the descendants of King David I's line within Scotland. Robert Bruce, veteran lord of Annandale, and his cousin, Lady Dervorgilla Balliol, were

[1] Stevenson (ed.), *Documents Illustrative of the History of Scotland*, i, no. 3; *Scotichronicon*, vi, 8–11; Barrow, *Robert Bruce and the Community of the Realm of Scotland*, 15–16; Duncan, 'The community of the realm of Scotland and Robert Bruce', 184–201, 187; Duncan, *Kingship of the Scots*, 175–8.

grandchildren of Earl David of Huntingdon. Whether the issue was raised in the April meetings or not, their descent was well known and rivalry between the Bruce and Balliol families may have added to the uncertainties. Though neither Bruce nor Dervorgilla's son, John Balliol, were named as guardians, amongst those chosen were figures whose sympathies with one or other of these men would become clear. Moreover, as members of a competitive elite, the succession was only one potential source of rivalry. For example, only the previous year King Alexander had forced the Steward's uncle, Walter Balloch to resign a share of his earldom of Menteith to William Comyn, the brother of the lord of Badenoch. The appointment of Earl Duncan may also have ruffled feathers. Though he held the senior earldom in Scotland, Duncan had only secured his province in 1284 after a long minority. His ambition to recover his rights and influence would cause difficulties for his neighbours.[2]

As the 1250s had shown, government by an aristocratic council was vulnerable to the pull of private interests against the duties of office, and the guardians inevitably lacked the authority and legitimacy of an adult king. These flaws were illustrated in the autumn and winter of 1286–7. In late September the guardian James Steward met with Robert Bruce and his son, the earl of Carrick, at the latter's castle of Turnberry. Together with other magnates, they concluded a band promising to aid Richard de Burgh earl of Ulster. This agreement related to shared anxieties about instability in the Isles and Ireland, but the meeting at Turnberry also had significance for Scottish politics. The gathering of the Bruces with Stewart and his uncle, Walter, earl of Menteith, the earl of Dunbar and Angus of Islay was a roll-call of families, largely from the west, most of whom would later support the Bruce claim to the throne. In the coming years these houses and their adherents would act in conjunction, and in 1286 Robert Bruce may have been seeking their support in any future need.[3]

Such an alignment of lords in uncertain circumstances was natural and probably not unique. However, the hope of support may have encouraged Robert Bruce to take forceful action. His moves were prompted by news from elsewhere. In late November the envoys returned from Edward I without any promise of aid and, about the same time, it was made known that Queen Yolanda would not have a child. Margaret of Norway was now the only descendant of King Alexander. Despite the oath of 1284, Bruce may have calculated that there would be widespread reluctance to accept

[2] *Scotichronicon*, vi, 4–9; Duncan, 'The community of the realm', 185–7; Barrow, 'A kingdom in Crisis', 120–41; Reid, 'The kingless kingdom: The Scottish Guardianship of 1286–1306', 105–29; Young, *Robert the Bruce's Rivals: The Comyns*, 90–5.
[3] Stevenson, *Documents*, i, no. 12.

a foreign girl as queen. Seeking to exploit this situation, he took the field 'in force of arms and with banners displayed'. With his son, Carrick, Robert captured the royal castles at Wigtown and Dumfries and Lady Dervorgilla's stronghold at Buittle. The Bruces' targets were the Balliols and the local royal officials, William Sinclair and John Comyn, the son of the earl of Buchan. The Bruces wreaked considerable damage in the south-west and the fear that the violence would extend through the south led to castles being garrisoned and the host raised by order of the guardians. At this crisis, however, the Bruces failed to win wider support. In particular James Steward adhered to his public duties as guardian, not his private relationship with Bruce. In their desire to seize the initiative, the Bruces had overestimated the readiness for action amongst their peers. However, the workings of factional tension had been displayed. Robert had sought to neutralise his political rivals in the south-west, especially the Balliols and Comyns, with the aim of securing a regional base, weakening his opponents and furthering his claims to power and, ultimately, kingship. As such, it was the first move in a violent competition between identifiable aristocratic groupings which would still be at full strength twenty years later when Robert Bruce's grandson would pre-empt his seizure of the throne by waging war against his enemies in the south-west. In 1286 the guardians stood together against the challenge of the Bruces but their retribution was limited. The Bruces' 'war' ended in a settlement which saw them hand back the castles they had taken and swear fealty to Margaret of Norway.[4]

If the acceptance of Margaret as lady of Scotland and future queen had not been straightforward, nor were the consequences of this decision. The Scots' access to their lady depended on the attitude of her father, King Eric II of Norway. Though Eric was keen for his daughter's rights to be recognised, he was unwilling to send her into an uncertain situation. His attitude towards the guardians was not softened by their failure to pay the money still owed for the dowry of his dead wife, King Alexander's daughter. Between 1287 and 1290, Margaret remained in Norway and the guardians were forced to rule on behalf of this distant and uninspiring figure. By 1289 the cracks in their authority were showing. While the guardians could maintain the routine of royal administration, raising rents, paying fees and auditing sheriffs' accounts, they lacked the stature of a king in the vital job of managing flashpoints and rivalries within the nobility. Instead, they were often drawn into these incidents. For example, when William the Bold, lord of Douglas, abducted the English

---

[4] *E.R.*, i, 38, 40, 46; *Documents and Records*, ed. Palgrave, i, 42–3; Young, *Robert the Bruce's Rivals: The Comyns*, 94–5; Oram, 'Bruce, Balliol and the lordship of Galloway', 29–47.

widow Eleanor de Ferrers at Tranent in 1288, the slowness of the Scots in responding to the English government's complaints was probably connected to Douglas's links to James Steward. Much more serious was the murder of one of the guardians, Duncan, earl of Fife, near Brechin in September 1289. Duncan, who was branded as 'cruel and greedy', had probably made enemies by using his office to extend his private lordship. The man behind the killing, Hugh Abernethy, was no bandit. He was a kinsman and neighbour of Duncan, an influential baron, a former sheriff and councillor of Alexander III with political ties to the Comyns. Hugh may have hoped that his allies would protect him, but he was pursued and imprisoned. Despite this swift justice, Fife's murder was a dramatic indication of the limits of the guardians' authority. The division of the earl's holdings, which saw Bishop Fraser take custody of his earldom, while the Comyns and Stewarts took over the dead man's offices, was driven less by concern for continued government than the desire to benefit from the violent removal of a colleague. Rivalries between the guardians and other magnates also created tensions in the north-east where John of Strathbogie, earl of Atholl seems to have renewed his father's hostility towards the Comyns of Badenoch. Alexander III had been able to resolve this rivalry, but with two Comyns as guardians, Atholl could hardly look to government to settle his grievances. Instead, he found a magnate ally in the shape of Donald, earl of Mar, and in 1289–90 there were clashes between these parties in Moray. In Man and the Isles too, there were signs of long-standing rivalries and antagonisms breaking out after the king's death. Though issues about the succession and government were not directly behind these difficulties, such feuding drew in the guardians and others. In particular, hostility towards the Comyns and their kin in the north-east and the Isles would enable the Bruces to make allies of Mar, Atholl and Clan Donald. The formation of political groupings connected, however loosely, to the interests of the Bruces or those of Balliol and the Comyns was probably underway by 1290. The failure to replace as guardians either Fife or the elderly Alexander earl of Buchan, who also died in 1289, may have been due to this factionalisation.[5]

The way out of these internal tensions lay outside the kingdom. There was still agreement in seeing Margaret of Norway as the future of royal government and desiring her presence in Scotland. The key to overcoming the reluctance of King Eric to despatch his daughter was Edward I of England. The rulers of England and Norway had traditionally been allies, and Eric regarded Edward as a friend who could protect his daughter's

[5] Stevenson, *Documents*, i, nos 22, 23, 28–38, 42, 49, 56, 104, 107; *E.R.*, i, 35–46; Stones, *Anglo-Scottish Relations*, no. 14; *Foedera*, i, 739; *Chron. Lanercost*, 59; *Scotichronicon*, vi, 32–3.

rights and safety. The English king's role would be founded on the marriage of his son, Lord Edward, to Margaret. Whether this match had been first suggested by Eric, Edward, the guardians or even Alexander III, it became the focus of renewed activity in early 1289. Scottish envoys travelled to Norway and to Edward in Gascony, a Norwegian embassy met with the English king at Condom, and on 10 May Edward sent a mission to Rome to obtain papal dispensation for the marriage of the cousins. Formal discussions began after Edward's return to England in August. The Scottish envoys were three guardians – Fraser, Wishart and John Comyn – and Robert Bruce, included as a possible threat to Margaret. On 6 November at Salisbury the Scots agreed to a treaty with the English and Norwegians. This marked only a preliminary deal, designed to ensure Margaret would be sent to either England or Scotland. It did not mention the planned wedding, though Edward and Eric retained control of Margaret's marriage. Instead the treaty focused on the state of Scotland: Margaret would only be sent to the kingdom if it was secure; reports on Scottish conditions would be sent to both kings; and inadequate guardians or officials could be removed by Edward, who would also arbitrate in any dispute between Scotland and Norway. On the same day Edward wrote to the Scots asking them to be 'obedient and supportive' to the guardians and informing them that he would send councillors to inform him of 'the state of the realm'. In the aftermath of Fife's murder, it is probable that the guardians actively sought Edward's support. Like his father in the 1250s, Edward was approached as a means of guaranteeing political stability in a Scottish realm which lacked a royal head.[6] However, this was not the 1250s. What was now at stake was not simply the short-term problems of a royal minority but the prospect of rule by a Norwegian queen and, more importantly, by the heir to the English throne. The marriage would effectively make the Scottish kingdom part of the Plantagenet dominions. When Scottish prelates and lords assembled at Birgham on the Tweed in March 1290 to confirm the treaty of Salisbury, they were aware of the implications of this. The succession of a Plantagenet king of Scots was not a complete leap into the unknown for a group with extensive ties of blood, land and service to that dynasty and its territories. Though the marriage would give Edward I a strong say in the running of Scotland in coming years and would probably result in the younger Edward ruling over both realms, such a union did not mean the

[6] *C.D.S.*, ii, nos 386–92; Stevenson, *Documents*, no. 75; *Foedera*, i, 719; M. Prestwich, 'Edward I and the Maid of Norway', 157–73, 165–7; Helle, 'Norwegian foreign policy and the Maid of Norway', 142–56, 149–51; Duncan, 'Community of the realm', 189; Duncan, *Kingship of the Scots*, 179–83. The dispensation for the marriage between the two cousins was granted by Pope Nicholas IV on 16 November.

end of Scotland's existence as a separate community. As dukes of Aquitaine and lords of Ireland, the Plantagenets were rulers of other realms and principalities which functioned as distinct units with their own governmental institutions, laws and customs. During the summer of 1290 the Scots sought Edward's recognition of their rights. On 18 July an agreement was reached, again at Birgham, between the Scots and Edward's envoys. Though its significance as a constitutional arrangement between the Scots and their prospective English ruler was never realised, the treaty of Birgham revealed much about Scottish political attitudes. It sought to define the issues which the political elite saw as being central to its identity and existence. The defence of these issues would be at the heart of the coming conflict.

By the terms of Birgham, 'the realm of Scotland shall remain separated and divided and free in itself, without subjection to the realm of England'. The English king promised to preserve 'the rights, laws, liberties and customs of the realm of Scotland', 'both of Holy Church and laity'. Elections to Scottish bishoprics and abbacies would take place within Scotland, as would the performance of homage by tenants-in-chief. Similarly, offences and breaches of the law committed in Scotland would be dealt with in Scottish courts, the highest of which – here termed parliament – would also meet inside the kingdom. The actions of a Plantagenet king of Scots were also defined. He would maintain a separate Scottish government, with a chancellor, chamberlain and other officers. In handling the marriage and guardianship of young Scottish nobles, the king would behave with fairness; and in demands placed on the Scots, for financial support or military service, the king should follow customary practice, making requests only 'to meet the common needs of the realm'. These terms were framed by the elite, the group directly concerned with issues of homage, of military service and payments, and of attendance at council. The magnates sought to preserve their status and relative freedom from royal interference and exactions; the clergy tried to preserve the access of their compatriots to the principal offices of the Scottish church against the promotion of English clerics. By articulating such concerns, however, this group showed a sense of community which existed alongside the issues that divided individual lords. The activities of the leaders of Scottish political society during the decades from 1290 would be shaped by the – often conflicting – pull of communal and factional interests. The stance taken at Birgham was much more than the defence of a narrow class interest. The alteration of law and custom by the crown and the transfer of the judicial and political process beyond the realm would have affected not just the elite, but the whole of Scottish society. It would spell the total absorption of Scottish church, realm and people into a Plantagenet state which, in both England and Ireland, made greater financial and physical demands on its subjects in pursuit of ambitions which went well beyond 'the common needs' of its parts.[7]

It was the group within Scotland with the closest knowledge of English government that sought guarantees for their rights. Their anxieties were not eased by the reservation of Edward's claim to be superior lord of the Scottish realm and, though Edward confirmed the treaty on 28 August, he showed a readiness, from the earlier agreement at Salisbury onwards, to press his role in Scotland to the full. While interference by an English official in Roxburghshire was met with a robust response from the guardians, during the summer of 1290 Edward was actively involved in the lands most recently brought into the Scottish realm. In June 1290 the Isle of Man was taken into Edward's protection, and an agent was appointed to bring the Hebrideans, who were enduring 'war and disorder', into the English king's peace. Edward may have been acting to ensure the stability of the Isles and Irish Sea, areas that impinged on his own concerns, but his intervention in Man re-established the English influence on the island which had been lost in the 1260s. The sense that Edward was exploiting his position was increased by the appointment of the abrasive Bishop Anthony Bek as lieutenant for his son and Margaret with powers to 'set the realm of Scotland in order'. Edward also pressed for a promise from the guardians that the royal castles would be handed to him in the name of the royal couple. Both these issues had been accepted by the Scots as part of the deal, but Edward was clearly losing no time in forming a concrete basis for his exercise of power in Scotland. However, Edward continued to fulfil his obligations by working for Margaret's arrival. During 1289–90 he retained King Eric's goodwill with generous loans, amongst them one of nearly £2,000 to cover the money he was owed by the Scots for his dowry. Edward had promised the Scots that Margaret would reach the British Isles by 1 November 1290 and, despite delays, he kept his word. During September, Margaret and her escort left Norway and reached her father's lands in Orkney. English envoys led by Bishop Bek and Earl Warenne travelled north to meet the Norwegians. They stopped at Perth to meet with the 'nobles of Scotland' and inform them of Edward's confirmation of Birgham. The stage seemed set for the marriage of two children which would bring Scotland peacefully into the collection of lands ruled by the Plantagenet family.[8]

[7] Stevenson, *Documents*, i, no. 92; Barrow, 'Kingdom in crisis', 131–3, 137–41; Duncan, *Kingship of the Scots*, 187–94.

[8] Stevenson, *Documents*, i, nos 103, 107; *Foedera*, i, 787; W. Fraser, *The Red Book of Menteith*, 2 vols (Edinburgh, 1880), no. 136; Helle, 'Norwegian foreign policy and the Maid of Norway', 150; Duncan, *Kingship of the Scots*, 195–6.

The news which reached the gathering at Perth shattered all the carefully-laid plans of the previous year: Margaret of Norway had died in Orkney in late September. A confused account of this 'disturbed' the kingdom, igniting an immediate competition for the throne which was fuelled by existing magnate rivalries. By early October Robert Bruce, who had not been at the Perth meeting, arrived with a large following, to be joined by Mar, Atholl and other lords with their retinues. They probably aimed to force recognition of Robert as rightful heir and even install him as king at nearby Scone. If so, their efforts were blocked, partly by the efforts of Bishop Fraser and John Comyn but also by the presence of the English envoys. Comyn and Warenne were Balliol's brothers-in-law, and with Fraser and Bek would support John Balliol's right to the throne. Together they prevented a Bruce coup which would have antagonised many Scots. Undoubtedly, these Balliol supporters were also mustering their adherents. A 'dread of civil war' descended on the kingdom and fighting between the two parties may well have occurred in the north. Though the guardians met at Edinburgh on 15 October, they were also divided between the rival candidates. On 7 October Fraser had written to Edward I indicating John Balliol as the likely king of Scots. By contrast with Bruce, Balliol remained in England but his ambitions were equally clear. As 'heir of the realm of Scotland', John promised Bishop Bek lands from the holdings of the Scottish crown. Fear of John's influence within England and the strength of his Scottish backers prompted a response from the Bruce party, and they produced an extraordinary document known as 'the appeals of the seven earls'. This was an attack on Bishop Fraser and John Comyn, 'acting and holding yourselves as guardians . . . with the part of the community of the realm supporting you'. This group was accused of planning to make John Balliol king against the rights of the seven earls and the 'community of the realm' to make and enthrone the king. This recalled the special role played by the earls in the inauguration ceremony but it also employed communal language and attacked their enemies' claim to enjoy the sanction of the community. The appeal was a work of propaganda which supported Bruce's rights to be 'legitimate heir'. The recipient of the document was King Edward, who was asked for his protection of the rights, lands and men of Bruce and his allies.[9]

By early 1291 both claimants and parties were looking to the English king for his assistance. In October 1290 Bishop Fraser even asked Edward

---

[9] Fraser, *Mentoith*, i, no. 136; *C.D.S.*, ii, no. 459; Stevenson, *Documents*, i, no. 125; Stones, *Anglo-Scottish Relations*, no. 14; *Documents and Records* ed. Palgrave, 14–21; Duncan, *Kingship of the Scots*, 197–8, 200–01. Robert Bruce also had allies amongst Edward's chief subjects, most notably his former brother-in-law, Gilbert de Clare, earl of Gloucester.

to come to the marches 'for the consolation of the Scottish people' and to prevent 'the shedding of blood'. Edward was ready to respond. The death of Margaret had robbed him of the opportunity to bring Scotland under his family's rule and the English king would not miss a second chance to establish formal authority over the neighbouring realm. When Edward came north in April 1291 he had his own agenda. Royal officials were already putting together a legal case to support Edward's claim to be over-lord of Scotland. He also summoned an impressive retinue of knights, barons and foot soldiers and had a fleet assembled in northern ports – though such preparations would serve to cow warring factions, the presence of a military retinue might have a more general purpose. In early May the Scots gathered at Upsettlington to meet Edward who was across the Tweed at Norham. Up until then the concerns of the Scottish lords had been with the competition for the throne and the threat of civil war, and Edward's involvement was recognised as the obvious – perhaps the only – means out of this crisis. Only on 10 May, when a parliament of the two kingdoms met at Norham, did the Scots leaders discover Edward's price. Edward offered to judge the succession and guarantee Scotland's peace and security, but as superior lord of the kingdom. The Scots had sought Edward's protection and his arbitration of the succession dispute, not his assertion of sovereignty over them. Bishop Wishart rejected the king's demand, but in return Edward threatened to use military force against the Scots, who were given until 1 June to respond.

The prelates and magnates of Scotland had gone to Norham aware of Edward's character and claims. They may have been ready to fend off a renewal of these claims to be superior lord of Scotland, but they did not expect a naked demand for submission. Recognition of Edward's rights would have cut through the customs, structures and integrity of their kingdom, the communal and individual status and rights which they had sought to protect at Birgham. Opposition to the demand was probably widespread, but the options of the Scots were limited. In early June they begged Edward to arbitrate between the claimants as a friend, not to judge the case as a lord. Concerning Edward's demands for overlordship, the Scots replied that only their king could answer on the status of his realm. Edward was ready for this response. The absence of a Scottish king strengthened, not weakened, Edward's hand, and he exploited the divisions created by the succession dispute. During May, with Edward's encouragement, a series of claimants raised their rights, among them John Hastings of Abergavenny, Floris, count of Holland, and Edward himself. Instead of an adjudication between Bruce and Balliol, there was now a complex legal case which would be slow to untangle. To receive an answer concerning his rights as overlord, Edward turned to these claimants. If

they, as potential kings, recognised Edward as overlord, their future subjects could only follow suit. On 5 June Bruce, Hastings and Count Floris
accepted Edward's claim. Balliol held out longer, encouraged by John
Comyn and by the belief that he possessed 'the best right', but on 11 June
he also submitted, fearing he would be left out of the succession. The claimants acknowledged Edward's lordship, and custody of Scotland was
handed to Edward while the case, known as 'the Great Cause', was settled.
The Scots had won some promises from Edward. He would keep the laws
and customs of Scotland whilst he judged the case, deal with the cause
quickly and return the realm at once to the successful claimant. His future
lordship would be limited to the act of homage and the services associated
with that obligation. Such concessions were of minor concern to Edward.
He had achieved his goal of imposing lordship on the kingdom of Scots.
This revolutionary change in the status of a neighbouring realm had been
effected without physical force, but Edward took pains to play down his
use of threats in the official version of events. The king had overridden the
opposition of leading Scots and exploited their divisions to establish what
he took to be his right.[10]

Edward followed events at Norham by establishing a court of 104 auditors to hear and judge claims to the throne of Scotland. However, the
twists of the case led to the adjournment of the court from November
1291 until the following August. In the meantime, Edward acted as
'superior and direct lord of Scotland' and during June he received oaths
of fealty from tenants-in-chief. His rule was hardly disruptive. The four
guardians remained in office with Bishop Bek and an English baron as
their colleagues. Sheriffs also retained their offices, but royal castles were
handed to English constables. In his dealings with the magnates of
Scotland, Edward was on his best behaviour. He granted wardships, paid
fees and gave gifts of deer from royal forests to the leading lords of the
realm. Many of these were familiar with the king and used to his rule, and
Edward may have hoped to use this familiarity and powers of patronage
to cement his position. In August 1291 Wishart, the Steward, Dunbar and
others were offered new Scottish lands should the kingdom fall to
Edward. Though these grants were cancelled, Edward was clearly explor-
ing the loyalties and interests of the Scottish nobility whilst he ran their
realm.[11]

[10] C.D.S., ii, no. 470; Duncan, 'The process of Norham, 1291', 207–30; Prestwich,
Edward I, 362–6.
[11] Duncan, 'Process of Norham', 222–7; Watson, Under the Hammer: Edward I and
Scotland, 16–17; Young, 'The Comyns and Anglo-Scottish Relations', 213–24; Rotuli
Scotiae, i, 3.

The Great Cause

The judgement between the claimants to the Scottish throne required proceedings of sufficient complexity to satisfy the burgeoning legal establishment of the late thirteenth century. Edward sought advice from legal experts from Oxford and Cambridge universities and from the masters of the University of Paris, whose opinions added greatly to the complexity of the case. Though each of the candidates put forward their separate claims in writing, the fact that the court of auditors included forty nominees each of Bruce and Balliol marked them out as the principal competitors. Balliol's case rested on two elements: first that Scotland was a realm and, as such, the king's rights and lands must be inherited without partition; and second that, as grandson of Earl David of Huntingdon's eldest daughter, Margaret, John was heir by primogeniture. The argument put forward by Bruce's lawyers was less straightforward. Precedents were produced showing that a living son could inherit over the child of an elder deceased son. As the son of Earl David's second daughter, Isabella, Robert was closer in degree to the royal line than Balliol. Bruce also argued that he had been designated heir by Alexander II which, if true, must have occurred between 1237 and 1241.

These competing claims were not the only lines of argument. John Hastings, grandson of the youngest of Earl David's daughters, recognised that he would not secure the kingship. Instead he argued that, as the Scottish realm was now acknowledged as a fief of the English king, it should be treated as other great English fiefs and divided between co-heirs. Most dramatically, Count Floris of Holland claimed that Earl David had resigned his rights to the throne to his sister, Ada, countess of Holland. Proceedings were suspended to allow Floris to prove his case. During the summer of 1292 it became clear that Balliol's position was strongest. Bruce, well-nicknamed 'the Competitor', sought to align with Hastings and Count Floris. He joined Hastings' argument for partition of the royal estate and entered an agreement with the count by which if either secured the throne, the other would receive a third of the royal demesne. Such efforts suggest the flexibility of Robert's approach but they failed in the face of the greater coherence of Balliol's claims. In early November the precedence of the senior line was recognised by the court. The final judgement in favour of John Balliol was given on 17 November. Though obscured by later crises, by rejecting claims for partition of the crown and its lands, this judgement preserved the Scottish realm as a unified kingdom.[12]

---

[12] Stones and Simpson, *Edward I and the Throne of Scotland*; Duncan, *The Kingship of the Scots*, chs 12–13.

THE REIGN OF KING JOHN

If Edward's rule of Scotland in 1291–2 was not disinterested, he did not forget his duties as the judge of the succession dispute. On 17 November 1292 he gave judgement in favour of John Balliol. Two weeks later, on St Andrew's Day, John was crowned king of Scots at Scone. Six and half years after Alexander III's death, Scotland was restored to the rule of a king. However, King John's position was very different to that of his fore-runners: he was king not by unquestioned right, but by judgement of a court and the events leading up to that judgement made him both a vassal king and a factional king. The implications of this were quickly brought home. From Scone, John travelled to Newcastle to spend Christmas at King Edward's court. On 26 December the new king of Scots knelt before the king of England saying, 'Lord Edward, lord superior of the realm of Scotland, I, John Balliol, king of Scots, become your liegeman for the whole realm of Scotland'. A week later John released Edward from all the promises he had made between 1286 and 1292, and specifically from the terms of the treaty of Birgham. Though Edward returned Man to John and remitted sums of money owed to him by a number of Scots, these were small marks of benevolence compared with the right to act as lord of Scotland which John had given him. Edward could now act as supreme judge in appeals from the Scottish king's court and, even before John's homage, his court was hearing the first such case.[13]

The oath which was sworn by John had altered the status of the king of Scots both inside and outside his realm. Even without his homage, however, John would have faced a difficult situation. Since 1290 his claim to the throne had been actively supported by a powerful faction, but there was another party opposed to him. John needed to secure the allegiance of all his subjects and to cement his authority. As part of this, on his return from Newcastle he called a parliament to meet at Scone in February 1293. Most magnates had accepted John as king and attended, but there remained irreconcilables. The elder Bruce resigned his Scottish lands to his son to avoid having to swear fealty to his enemy. The younger Bruce, now lord of Annandale, passed the earldom of Carrick to his own son. This third Robert Bruce began his career as earl by refusing to attend parliament and swear homage and, though he would do so in August, he

---

[13] Barrow, *Robert Bruce*, 50–3; Stones, *Anglo-Scottish Relations*, no. 20; *Rotuli Scotiae*, i, 16–17. Edward also exercised leverage on John during this period by charging him with a relief of £3,000 to inherit the lands of his mother, Dervorgilla, who had died in 1290. The repayment of this debt was set by the English king for both her English and Scottish lands as another demonstration of overlordship (Oram, 'Bruce, Balliol and Galloway', 32).

The Origins of the Scottish Parliament

On 8 February 1293, at Scone, a parliament assembled before King John. This meeting provides the first formal record of a parliament summoned by a Scottish king. No unequivocal evidence exists for such meetings under Alexander III and his forebears, and these kings dealt with major issues of justice and law in meetings of varying size, ranging from a few key advisors to large councils. Though assemblies of large numbers of the king's leading vassals were probably held with regularity and, like the gathering at Scone in 1284 which determined the royal succession, were understood as a means of obtaining consent for the king's actions, there was no indication that such meetings were developing specific functions and a set composition. In the absence of major political tensions or demands, such a development was unnecessary.

The impetus for change came from the onset of crisis and from the influence of England, where previous decades had witnessed the rapid development of parliament as a specific forum. In the 1250s English official accounts regarded major assemblies in Scotland as parliaments, and in 1289–91 they referred to meetings of the Scottish community in the same way. That the treaty of Birgham specifically defended separate meetings of parliament in the Scottish realm reflected, at least, a desire to avoid being summoned to English assemblies. It also showed a developed understanding of the institution, natural amongst a political class conversant with English practices. Ironically, however, it was Edward I who introduced this model directly. As lord of Scotland whilst the Great Cause was decided, Edward called parliaments, the first of which met at Berwick in August 1291.

John's reign marked the beginning of the Scottish parliament as a meeting of the kingdom's political class called by the king of Scots. The meeting at Scone was concerned with the exercise of royal justice after the interregnum and with the collection of homages for the new king, both essential tasks following a disputed succession. The use of parliaments to respond to the demands of Edward I and his courts represents their value as a source of collective consent for Balliol. In 1295 and 1296 the king and community initiated and confirmed the negotiations with France in formal parliaments involving nobles, prelates and representatives of the burghs. In three years John held perhaps eight meetings, giving the body a place in government which survived the collapse of his own kingship. When Robert Bruce sought a forum to legitimise his own rule and stress communal support for his rights, he would turn to parliament.[14]

---

[14] Duncan, 'The early parliaments of Scotland', 36–58.

and his father barely concealed their hostility towards John. Others, like Angus of Islay and William Douglas, shared this attitude, but most of the Bruces' allies readily recognised their new king.[15]

However, the partisan divisions of 1286–92 continued to shape Scottish politics. Divisions had been fuelled by the interests and rivalries of magnates at a local and regional level. John's allies expected their king to reward them for their support. These allies were a powerful group which included Bishop Fraser, the Comyns of Buchan and Badenoch, and many of the baronial families who acted as royal sheriffs. John recognised the importance of maintaining their support and there was a partisan feel to the royal council and the king's patronage. John Comyn, earl of Buchan and William, earl of Ross were granted or leased thanages which extended their provinces. Ross was also responsible for one of the new sheriffdoms created by the king in February. These three new sheriffdoms covering the Isles and Argyll may have appeared as an extension of royal government, but the creation of Ross as sheriff of Skye with authority over the northern Hebrides, and of Alexander MacDougall as sheriff of Lorn with powers in Argyll and Mull represented the king giving blanket support to his friends in the west and north. This was nothing new in itself, but in the 1290s it prompted renewed warfare and confirmed the alienation of Angus of Islay and others from the crown. Angus was among a group of Islesmen who took their grievances to the English king.[16]

The third western sheriff was James Steward, whose authority was largely limited to his family's lands in Kintyre, Bute and Arran. Though associated with the Bruce party, Steward had never joined in that family's more forceful activities before 1292 and had entered the new king's allegiance. However, shortly after Steward's appointment as sheriff, Edward I wrote to King John asking him to stop his officials harassing James's men in Ayrshire. Elsewhere too, John's accession was marked by the settling of scores. Since the murder of Earl Duncan in 1289, the earldom of Fife had been run by its neighbour, Bishop Fraser. In the summer of 1292, Macduff, uncle of the murdered earl, complained to Edward, who was then ruling Scotland, that Fraser had denied him possession of his lands in the earldom. Edward ordered Fraser to examine the case and Macduff recovered his estates. However, the bishop was one of King John's closest advisors and, at the king's parliament, Macduff was first called to prove his right and then arrested and imprisoned.[17]

[15] *A.P.S.*, i, 91–2; Stones, *Anglo-Scottish Relations*, no. 18. The eldest Robert Bruce, the claimant to the throne in 1290–2, died at an advanced age in 1295.

[16] *A.P.S.*, i, 91; *C.D.S.*, ii, nos 1,541, 1,631, 1,737; Young, *Robert the Bruce's Rivals: The Comyns*, 122–8; Barrow, *Robert Bruce*, 55–6.

[17] *Rotuli Scotiae*, i, 8, 12, 17–20; *A.P.S.*, i, 89–91.

The support which John gave to his friends made sense within a Scottish context but, as king, he was now subject to a higher authority. Relatively few cases were appealed to Edward's court from Scotland but, more than any other issue, the Macduff case exposed the limitations of John's kingship. On his release from custody, Macduff once again complained to Edward, now John's superior lord, and the case became a test of this lordship. John was summoned to the English king's court in late September 1293. John was used to such summonses as an English baron but it was unprecedented for a Scottish king to be treated in this fashion. He arrived at Westminster to argue that Edward's court had no right to judge the case and he refused to answer concerning his realm without the advice of his 'chief men'. Edward ignored this denial and threatened to charge John with contempt of court and confiscate his three chief castles. In the face of this pressure, John capitulated. He formally recognised Edward's authority and promised to return when the case was brought before parliament the following summer. Edward pursued his advantage by appointing his own official to take custody of the earldom of Fife as the young earl was his ward. It was a physical demonstration of the King of England's pre-eminence inside the Scottish realm.[18]

Edward's personal pre-eminence over John was also clear. The Scottish king duly turned up for the meeting of parliament at Westminster in June 1294, but the suit of Macduff was not considered, and was instead postponed until 1295. It was forced off the agenda by news from France. Just as Edward was imposing ever-tighter lordship on the Scottish realm, so King Philip IV of France was encroaching on Edward's position as duke of Aquitaine. In a move which caught Edward by complete surprise, Philip called him to court to answer charges relating to his duchy. When he failed to appear, Edward was deprived of Aquitaine. The news of this reached Edward's court in June and was treated as a declaration of war. Any similarity between his own position and that of the king of Scots was less important to Edward than John's presence in parliament as he planned his response. Edward included the Scottish kingdom and its resources in these plans and John promised his support. On 29 June a formal summons was issued to the king of Scots, ten Scottish earls and sixteen barons to raise their knights and join Edward's army at Portsmouth in early September. The agreement of its king to provide military service seemed to confirm the subjection of the Scottish realm to its overlord. It may have had the opposite effect. While the question of appeals to Edward's court involved fundamental issues of

---

[18]   *Rotuli Scotiae*, i, 19, 20; Stevenson, *Documents*, i, nos 317, 319, 320; Stones, *Anglo-Scottish Relations*, no. 21; Barrow, *Robert Bruce*, 58–9; Prestwich, *Edward I*, 371–3.

royal jurisdiction, so far it had had a limited impact on the wider nobility. By summoning twenty-six magnates to make a personal contribution to a continental war, Edward was directly involving these lords in expensive obligations to support his rights as duke of Aquitaine. Though a significant number of these magnates owed similar services as English barons, the Scottish nobility had specifically sought to avoid such duties in the treaty of Birgham only four years before. Edward's demand encouraged many of these magnates to seek ways to escape the grip of Plantagenet kingship.[19]

They were probably aware that they could place only limited reliance on the leadership of King John. Over the issue of appeals and the war with France, John had conceded crucial ground to Edward. Though he had inherited a difficult situation, his own handling of affairs had swiftly given Edward the chance to spell out his superiority. In Scotland John was ready to listen to plans to defend his rights and the rights of his realm but, when confronted by Edward, his resistance was easily overcome. John was unable to use his connections with the councillors of Edward, like Bishop Bek, to soften the English king's demands, and these contacts may even have fuelled distrust of John by his Scottish subjects. After the disasters of 1296 John would complain of the 'malice, deceit, treason and treachery' of the Scots and refer to a plot to poison him. However exaggerated these sentiments were, John had clearly failed to win the full support of his opponents, while even his backers would show doubts about the king and his qualities.[20]

From late 1294 there were signs that, with or without John's active leadership, some Scots were working to undermine Edward's lordship. The wider situation favoured such efforts. Edward's plans to raise and lead an army to France were forestalled by a major uprising in Wales which broke out under Madog ap Llywelyn in September. It was sparked by demands for men and money for the French war. While Edward struggled to contain the Welsh, the Scots sought absolution from the pope for promises made under duress, a clear reference to the English king's demands from May 1291 onwards. There was now hope that the tide could be reversed. Faced by a war in Wales which lasted until the spring and the loss of much of Gascony, Edward's position may have seemed similar to that of his father in 1258. In that year a Scottish party had defied King Henry with impunity and effectively removed his influence over Scottish affairs. During the spring and summer of 1295 many

---

[19] Prestwich, *Edward I*, 372–3, 376–81; Barrow, *Robert Bruce*, 62–3; *Foedera*, i, 804;
Vale, *Origins of the Hundred Years War*, 183–200.
[20] Stones, *Anglo-Scottish Relations*, no. 27.

Scottish leaders may have hoped for a similar outcome. In May John had failed to appear to answer the Macduff case and, possibly in response, Earl Warenne and Bishop Bek came north in July. Though the envoys may have sought to exploit their friendship with the Scottish king, the attitude of other Scots towards the English realm was increasingly hostile and they refused to receive them. They had established friendly contact with King Philip of France and, two days after John met Bek, the Scottish parliament met at Stirling and agreed to negotiate a formal alliance with the French king. On 23 October Philip confirmed a military alliance with the king of Scots to be sealed by a marriage between John's young son, Edward, and Philip's niece.[21]

Despite this marriage and the Balliol family's ancestral connection with France, chroniclers regarded the alliance as the work not of the Scottish king, but of his chief vassals. Writers referred to the establishment of twelve peers or guardians 'to defend the freedom of the kingdom' and it is possible that a formal or informal council was directing royal government in John's name. As in 1290 and 1291 prelates and magnates were conceivably articulating and defending their rights as the group that best represented the kingdom. However, as in those years, there were limits to communal activity. As the prospect of confrontation with Edward grew, it became clear that certain magnates were detached from the aims of these guardians. Unsurprisingly, the Bruces were not prepared to defend Balliol's rights but others had doubts about defying the king of England. In October 1295, in reaction to John's refusal to answer Macduff's case, Edward had ordered the seizure of English lands belonging to the Scottish king and his subjects who remained in Scotland. The loss of their English holdings caused many Scottish magnates anxiety and persuaded some to affirm their loyalty to King Edward. The Bruces may already have been forfeited in Scotland and wider threats to cross-border landholding in the event of Anglo-Scottish war were all too clear. During late 1295 the flaws caused by factional rivalries and by allegiances to Edward existed beneath preparations to defend the integrity of the Scottish realm.[22]

By March 1296 it was clear that any such defence would be against Edward in person at the head of a large army. For Edward, war was justified as the conclusion of a legal process. John had failed to attend his lord's court in the Macduff case and Edward came north to enforce judge-

[21] Prestwich, *Edward I*, 219–25; Davies, *Age of Conquest*, 382–3; C.D.S., ii, nos 719, 720, 872; A.P.S., i, 95; *Chron. Lanercost*, 115–16.
[22] *Chron Fordun*, ii, 321; Barrow, *Robert Bruce*, 63–4; Young, *Robert the Bruce's Rivals: The Comyns*, 139–40; C.D.S., ii, nos 718, 723.

ment against a defaulter. This legalistic approach was characteristic of the king but almost certainly overlay his fear that the Scots were in alliance with his French enemies. A final summons was issued to John to meet Edward at Newcastle in early March. It was ignored and both sides mustered their armies and supporters, with the Bruces and the earl of Dunbar adhering to Edward. Leadership of the Scots seems to have been in the hands of a group of earls and barons who sought to forestall Edward by raiding northern England. Their tactic failed. On 30 March, while the Scots retreated over the border, Edward led his army to Berwick and stormed the town 'without tarrying'. The richest and largest of Scotland's burghs was put to the sword, thousands of its population reportedly perishing in the sack. The Scots' reply to this display of Edward's attitude to his 'rebels' was a second raid and a formal defiance of the English king in which John renounced his homage. Neither act caused Edward to pause. In the last week of April he sent Earl Warenne to secure Dunbar castle. On 27 April the earl met and routed a sizeable Scottish army, killing many footmen and capturing the earls of Ross, Menteith and Atholl.

The battle of Dunbar ended organised resistance to Edward. What followed was a royal progress rather than a campaign. In a march through the royal heartlands of Scotland Edward took possession of Roxburgh and Jedburgh in May, Edinburgh, Stirling and Perth in June, and Forfar, Aberdeen and Elgin in July. Of the Scottish king's castles, only Edinburgh and Linlithgow put up any resistance and, as Edward moved northwards, Scottish nobles hastened to make peace with him. They sought to preserve their lands and status but also to protect their tenants and neighbours from retribution. Such skills of submission would be well-practised by such men in coming years. In 1296 the lords who made peace were not encouraged to resist by their own king. John had not provided active leadership in the campaign and though he was still accompanied by a significant group, including the Comyns, he sought a settlement. His efforts to negotiate personal terms were rejected by Edward who demanded total surrender. John was forced to admit his rebellion, renounce the French alliance and resign his kingdom, suffering the humiliation of being stripped of his royal insignia and the surcoat bearing the arms of Scotland.[23]

Though the Scots had been defeated in war, the real story of 1296 was one of political failure. From their king down, the leading Scots had been unwilling to resist Edward after Dunbar. Moreover, from the outset of

[23] Stevenson, *Documents*, ii, no. 152; *Chron. Lanercost*, 115, 124–5, 128–9, 138–45; *Chron. Fordun*, ii, 317–21; Barrow, *Robert Bruce*, 69–74.

The Bruces of Annandale

While the victory of John Balliol in the Great Cause might have seemed to settle the issue of the throne, it is clear that the Bruces thought otherwise. The rivalry between the families of Bruce and Balliol which began long before 1290 was not ended by the judgement of the case. On 7 November 1292 Robert Bruce (V) or 'the Competitor', anticipating his defeat, resigned his right to the realm of Scotland to his son. Aged about seventy, the elder Bruce was keen to pass on the family's claim to the kingship to a new generation. His death in 1295 deprived the Bruce family of an indefatigable presence during the opening years of warfare. The new head of the family was Robert Bruce (VI). Overshadowed in all accounts by both his father and his son, Robert (VI) received the lordship of Annandale in 1292 but resigned the earldom of Carrick to his eldest son, perhaps because of the death of Countess Marjory. His failure to renew the Bruce claim in 1296 and his adherence to Edward I thereafter meant that he remained a minimal presence in Scotland until his death in 1304. It would be his children, five sons and five daughters, under the leadership of Robert (VII) who would turn the name of Bruce from a baronial to a royal dynasty.[24]

the campaign, the English king had exploited the support of influential Scots where his own armies had not penetrated. The Bruces were appointed to secure the allegiance of their own lands in Annandale and Carrick, and Alexander of Islay was asked to take possession of Kintyre. Even amongst those Scots who supported King John, resistance was hampered by mistrust. The Bruces' former allies, Mar and Atholl, were accused of holding their forces back from the fight at Dunbar, and the activities of James Steward after the battle suggest that the loyalties of such men to King John were brittle. James had submitted to Edward at Roxburgh in May. At once, he and his large connection took up positions in the new regime. Steward received the surrender of Dumbarton and Kirkintilloch castles and their keepers, while his cousin, Alexander, earl of Menteith, was appointed to lead the campaign against the MacDougalls of Lorn. By October, and with Edward's blessing, James had married the sister of Richard, earl of Ulster and received lands in Ireland. Like many others, Steward was bowing to the circumstances of 1296. He was also making a political choice. To James, like the Bruces, the patronage and lordship offered by Edward seemed preferable to a prolonged defence of Balliol's kingship. These Scots may have been pre-

---

[24] Duncan, 'The Bruces of Annandale', 89–102.

pared to accept the English king's rule in return for his recognition and protection of their positions and liberties as individuals and members of an aristocratic community.[25]

Such a view would quickly prove to be unrealistic. Even in May there could be few illusions left about Edward's intentions for the Scottish realm. After Dunbar the king had famously responded to the request of Robert Bruce (the son of the 1291 claimant) that he be awarded the Scottish realm, with the words, 'Have we nothing else to do but win kingdoms for you?' Though he took no Scottish title and made no statement about the status of the kingdom, Edward was clearly now the direct ruler of Scotland. His rights were given formal recognition in late August when oaths of fealty from over 1,600 Scots to Edward were recorded on the Ragman Roll. This record was made in Edward's parliament at Berwick, which was to be resettled with English burgesses and made into the centre of Edwardian government in Scotland. Unlike Edward's administration of 1291, this new regime was colonial in character. Earl Warenne was to be lieutenant, and both the central officials and the vast majority of sheriffs were Englishmen, their control backed by the presence of garrisons in castles from Inverness and Urquhart to Wigtown and Dumfries. Edward took no royal title for Scotland because, in his eyes, no such title now existed. The unmaking of Scottish kingship was symbolised by the stripping of Balliol and by the despatch of the records and regalia of the crown, the Holy Rood of St Margaret and the Stone of Destiny, to England during the summer.[26]

This was the language of conquest which Edward had also employed in the destruction of the house of Gwynedd and princely power in Wales. The same combination of ruthlessly-pressed legal powers and the resort to physical force had been used to crush opposition to Edward's claims to authority. The similarities make it seem likely that the establishment of his direct lordship in Scotland had been in Edward's mind since the death of Margaret of Norway. The way in which he pursued his rights as overlord suggests, at the very least, a determination to reduce the Scottish realm to a mere fief within his dominions. The reaction of the Scottish leaders between 1294 and 1296 was the natural response to unprecedented direction and interference in their affairs by the English king. However, this response and the earlier statements of the collective rights and liberties of the Scottish community were undermined by divisions within that community. Edward exploited these divisions but did not create them. Instead they were the product of aristocratic rivalries,

[25] C.D.S., ii, no. 737; Rotuli Scotiae, i, 22, 23, 29, 30; Stevenson, Documents, ii, no. 401.
[26] C.D.S., ii, no. 823; Barrow, Robert Bruce, 75–9; Watson, Under the Hammer, 30–3.

fuelled by a competition for the kingship which Edward's judgement had not fully ended. In the coming years the royal title and rights, which Edward had sought to expunge, would remain both a source of division for Scots and the focus of their claim to be a separate realm.

CHAPTER 9

The Scottish Wars (1297–1314)

THE WAR OF THE GUARDIANS (1297–1305)

Edward I returned south from Berwick in the autumn of 1296 confident that Scotland had been brought under his direct lordship. The king was impatient to return to his greatest concern. The campaign against Scotland had diverted Edward from waging war on the continent against the Scots' ally, King Philip of France. Over the winter Edward prepared a decisive blow. Armies would be sent to both Gascony and Flanders and Philip's north-east frontier would be threatened by an extensive, and expensive, coalition of Edward's allies. These ambitions demanded the mobilisation of resources from across Edward's dominions. Like England, Wales and Ireland, Scotland was expected to contribute money and manpower in pursuit of Edward's continental interests. In England these demands would produce the greatest crisis of Edward's reign. In Scotland they would spark lasting resistance to his rule.[1]

Little concession was made for the recent change in Scotland's status. In Edward's eyes, the war of 1296 had ended resistance to his demands for military service from Scottish lords. He now expected these men, who had submitted to his authority, to join his armies with their vassals. Some were already in England in early 1297 and agreed to serve on the continent while others remained in captivity. Those magnates in Scotland were mostly those, like James Stewart or Robert Bruce, earl of Carrick, whom Edward regarded as his supporters. Though Edward did not extend his demands for a land tax to Scotland, where it would have been without precedent, he clearly expected his officials to extract significant revenues from his new dominion. In May 1297 the treasurer of Scotland, the efficient Hugh Cressingham, was able to send over £5,000 to the

---

[1] Prestwich, *Edward I*, 385–90; Vale, *Origins of the Hundred Years War*, 206.

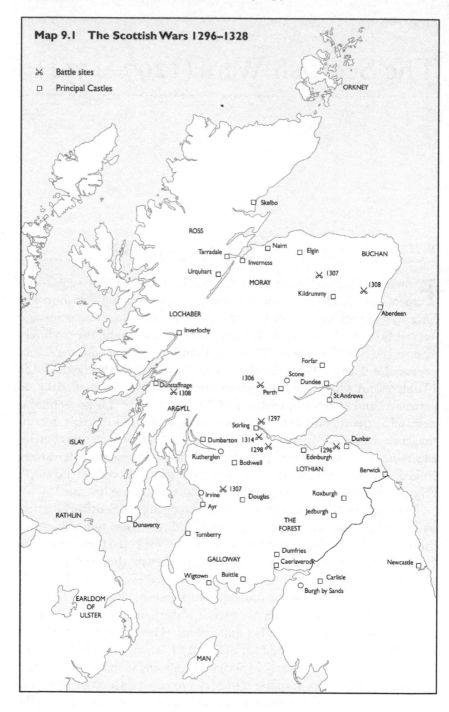

Map 9.1 The Scottish Wars 1296–1328

Battle sites

Principal Castles

English exchequer, drawing funds from crown revenues, confiscated estates and the seizure or control of wool exports.[2]

Like their king, English officials in Scotland were lulled into a false sense of security by the events of the preceding year. While fighting between the magnates of the Isles continued into the spring despite their efforts, in the southern and eastern sheriffdoms these officials had taken over an administrative system which, in their eyes, was a less-developed version of English government, and they had made it turn a profit. To Scots in these sheriffdoms, and in earldoms and lordships, the situation appeared in a different light. Though few of these men and women had suffered direct loss in the war of 1296, all were affected by the resulting changes to the framework of political life. Their king had been removed by force and many of their natural leaders, earls and barons, were also absent. During August large numbers of this wider group had been made to transfer their allegiance from their traditional lord, the king of Scots, to the ruler of another realm. The Scots named on the Ragman Roll and their peers and neighbours were not a formless mass beneath the king and his barons. The knights and freeholders, tenants of crown and magnates, the burgesses and lesser clergy belonged to wider structures, communities and affinities, and they had their own sense of rights and customs, and their own roles and duties. As individuals and groups, these Scots were now forced to confront major threats to their positions. Sheriffs and constables, who before 1296 had been local men, were now largely English administrators backed by garrisons of paid soldiers. This was rule by 'aliens', foreigners with no sense of the traditions and limits of Scottish government, guaranteed to excite fears of arbitrary and grasping rule in the locality. These sheriffs and garrisons were also agents of a king who had trampled on the rights of their king and the liberties of their realm. Such tensions were compounded by demands of this government, real or feared, on this vital group of Scots. Burgesses and landowners were anxious about plans to seize wool for sale by the crown. Clergy feared that their benefices would be filled by English nominees. Rumours spread that 'le menzane de Escoce', the middle folk, squires, burgesses and freeholders, 'would be seized and sent beyond the sea in his [Edward's] war to their great damage and destruction'. By spring 1297 many Scots of middle rank saw English rule as a direct threat to their security and safety. In the face of these threats they were prepared to take up arms.[3]

---

[2] C.D.S., ii, nos 742, 884–5, 888–9, 940, 942; Rot. Scot., i, 40; Prestwich, Edward I, 476; Watson, Under the Hammer, 30–7.

[3] Stevenson, Documents, ii, no. 452; Barrow, Robert Bruce, 80–3; Duncan, The Nation of Scots and the Declaration of Arbroath; Duncan, 'Community of the realm', 193.

By May there were clashes between English officials and local Scots in a number of different regions. 'The Scots massacred all the English they could find' and expelled English clergy from their churches. Such actions are reminiscent of other closely-contemporary uprisings elsewhere in Europe. The Sicilian Vespers of 1282 and the Matins of Bruges in 1302 may have had urban origins, but they were also revolts against foreigners (in these cases the French) whose rule was associated with excessive demands for money and manpower. In Flanders and Sicily, identifiable aliens were killed and driven out by groups of locals led by knights and townsmen. The Scottish revolt of 1297 would find similar leadership. In Clydesdale the leaders of the rising were William Douglas, a turbulent local lord, and a man of lesser standing, William Wallace. While Douglas's birth and lands placed him at the forefront of local events, Wallace was from the wider body of men involved in the rising. His killing of the English sheriff of Lanark had ignited warfare against English forces in the south-west and made Wallace the leader of a rising of lesser landowners and their kin from the locality.[4] It was natural for these men to seek magnate leadership. Douglas, Wallace and many of their followers were part of the extensive connection of James Stewart and may have encouraged him to provide the protection and leadership of a lord for his men. For Stewart, failure to support his tenants and neighbours would risk the loss of influence over them. Moreover, he had his own grievances. Both Stewart and his neighbour, Robert Bruce, earl of Carrick, had seen control of the south-west taken from them and handed to an English lord, Henry Percy. The loss of this influence encouraged Stewart to give support – first indirect and then active – to Douglas, Wallace and their adherents. Carrick was slower to show his hand. Though his father stood firm in English allegiance, Earl Robert was suspect. He was made to swear a public oath of fealty to Edward in May and then led an attack on Douglas's lands. However, under cover of these moves, Bruce prepared to join the Steward. Despite the refusal of his father's tenants in Annandale to support him, the earl rode to Carrick. The Steward, the earl and Bishop Wishart took up arms to defend 'the commune of our land', the rights and customs of themselves and their people. As well as this cause, however, these magnates were also linked by their sympathy for the claims of the Bruce family for the throne. Following the defeat of Balliol and his removal from the realm, lords from the opposite party were claiming to champion 'the old kingdom'.[5]

---

[4] *Chronicle of Walter of Guisborough*, ed. H. Rothwell, 294–5; *Chron. Fordun*, ii, 321–2; Fisher, *William Wallace*, 30–70. For discussions of the Sicilian Vespers and the Matins of Bruges, see Dunbabin, *Charles I of Anjou*, 102–11; Nicholas, *Medieval Flanders*, 186–94.
[5] *Chron. Guisborough*, 295–7, 299; Stevenson, *Documents*, nos 452, 457; *Chron. Lanercost*, 163–4; *Rot. Scot.*, i, 34–5.

After the previous year, it would not be surprising if the confidence of the Scottish magnates was low. Spirits would not have been lifted by the speed of the English response. A force of knights and foot under Percy quickly confronted the Scots lords at Irvine, while a larger army was assembled at Roxburgh. Bruce, Steward and Wishart opted to negotiate. In early July the magnates agreed to terms allowing their people to disperse and giving guarantees about their subsequent treatment. Bruce and Steward were permitted to depart on promises that they would renew their homage to Edward when the king confirmed the agreement. Others were treated less leniently. The two magnates 'put the blame on William Douglas and the bishop of Glasgow'. The bishop was imprisoned and Douglas was treated as an irreconcilable and sent in chains, first to Berwick and then to London, while his lands passed to the English crown. It was a warning to the Scottish lords that defeat carried a high price.[6]

This easy success led English officials to believe that their 'enemies are dispersed and dismayed' and to demobilise their field forces. Treasurer Cressingham was less confident. In late July he complained that since the Irvine talks 'matters have gone to sleep' and that the English administration had ceased to function beyond Roxburgh and Berwick. While English efforts were directed against the great lords who opposed them at Irvine, other challenges to their rule were gathering momentum. In the south, Wallace remained at large and, after the submission of the magnates, was the focus for continued warfare. He gathered a 'great company' in the natural fastness of Selkirk Forest and led it in campaigns in Roxburghshire and Clydesdale. During May other risings ignited further north. In Fife the leader was Macduff, the head of the kindred of the earls. Like Bruce, Macduff had not fought for King John in 1296 but was now ready to defend not the exiled king, but the realm and his province against alien rule.[7]

The greatest threat to the English government developed in Moray. The rising was centred on the coastal sheriffdoms of the province which would prove to be a heartland of resistance to the English and its leader was from a family with a prominent part to play in this conflict. Andrew Murray was the heir to a great baronial house who could call on the men and use the castles of his father in the districts round Inverness. However, vital support for the rising was provided by the burgesses of Inverness who probably resented the presence of an English garrison in their burgh. In late May Andrew and the burgesses began a series of attacks against English officials and castles in the north. In contrast to events further

---

[6] *Chron. Guisborough*, 298–9; Stevenson, *Documents*, nos 452, 453, 454, 457, 467, 475; Palgrave, *Documents*, 197–200.

[7] Stevenson, *Documents*, nos 453, 455, 458, 462, 465; *Rot. Scot.*, i, 42; Barrow, *Robert Bruce*, 85.

south, no English army came to the region. Instead the government exhorted Scottish magnates to suppress the rebels. The Earl of Strathearn captured Macduff, while Gartnait, heir to the earldom of Mar, and Henry Cheyne, bishop of Aberdeen, were asked to aid English sheriffs in Moray. In early June a group of lords, including the heads of the Comyn family, was given permission to return from England. Edward hoped that John Comyn, earl of Buchan and John Comyn of Badenoch would add their extensive resources in the north to defeat Andrew Murray. In July Buchan marched with the bishop and Gartnait and confronted Andrew with a 'great host of felons' on the river Spey. They blamed their failure to attack on rough ground but, in reality, their reluctance had other causes. By August most northern magnates had broken contact with the English government.[8]

As one English chronicler recorded, 'although the magnates were with our king in body, their hearts were far away from him'. Comyn of Badenoch and the Steward remained with the English while Buchan, Carrick and others retired to their lands. Their ambivalence was natural. They were restrained from open support of the rising by the presence of close kinsmen with King Edward's army and by fear of suffering the fate of William Douglas. However, as the northern lords showed, there was no desire to confront fellow Scots in battle on Edward's behalf and, with or without their encouragement, 'the retinues of the magnates', the 'footfollowers' of sheriffdoms, earldoms and lordships, joined Wallace and Murray. The inaction of the great nobles worked in favour of the rebels. August was the critical month. In both the north and south-west the rebels secured their positions and moved beyond their original recruiting grounds. Their rapid successes demonstrated for the first time the inability of scattered English garrisons to defend themselves without support. This lack of support was due not just to the Scottish magnates, but to a failure of English leadership. The lieutenant, Earl Warenne, was reluctant to take up his post and, from July, the attention of the English government was consumed by the clash between King Edward and his lords over their service in his French campaign.[9]

It was not until early September that a sizeable English army moved north from Berwick. By then Wallace and Murray had joined forces. They took up position around the rocky outcrop of Abbey Craig to the north of the Forth at Stirling. The bridge at Stirling and the castle which

[8]   *Rot. Scot.*, i, 41–2; Stevenson, *Documents*, nos 457–60; *C.D.S.*, ii, nos 922–3; Watson, *Under the Hammer*, 46–7; *Chron. Guisborough*, 297–8; Barron, *The Scottish Wars of Independence*, 32–59.
[9]   *Chron. Guisborough*, 299. For the English crisis see Prestwich, *Edward I*, 412–35.

loomed over it were the strategic heart of Scotland. This was the lowest crossing of the river Forth whose waters formed the greatest natural barrier in Scotland east of the mountains. In 1297 the castle remained in English hands and Warenne brought his army under its walls and faced the rebels. Initially he sought a repeat of the capitulation at Irvine but the Scots now had different leaders. Wallace ended the talks with the words 'we are not here for the good of peace, but are ready to fight to defend ourselves and free our kingdom'. Encouraged by Cressingham, Warenne ordered a direct attack and the English army began to file across the narrow bridge and form up on the north bank. Seeing their enemies divided by the river, Wallace and Murray led an attack on the isolated vanguard and cut it to pieces, killing Cressingham in a savage fight. Warenne and the rest of his army fled, while Steward and his neighbour, the earl of Lennox, who had been in the English force, changed sides and led the pursuit. In the weeks which followed, English garrisons across central and southern Scotland surrendered leaving only Edinburgh, Roxburgh and Berwick in their hands. In November these were besieged and Wallace led a foray into northern England, taking plunder and blackmail from the enemy.[10]

If the military results of Stirling Bridge were clear, its political consequences were less certain. The kingdom had been recovered from the English by an army of lesser men acting without the leadership of the greatest Scottish magnates. A month after the battle, Murray and Wallace were claiming the leadership as 'commanders of the army of the kingdom of Scotland', and when Murray died in November, Wallace was left in a position of primacy. Wallace certainly had aristocratic support, from the Steward, Lennox and Strathearn amongst others, but it was not universal, and it was said that 'by force and by dint of his prowess [he] brought all the magnates of Scotland under his sway whether they would or not'. Some reluctance to accept the leadership of a squire is not surprising, but during the winter Wallace was knighted and named guardian of the realm. The office used between 1286 and 1292 was revived but, rather than a committee of prelates and magnates, it was now held by a single warleader. Wallace's authority was legitimised by reference to the community of the realm and was exercised in the name of King John. Despite his defeat, dispossession and imprisonment, the king would prove a valuable symbol of the status and unity of the realm, while any discussion of alternative rulers would have opened deep divisions. However, such divisions

---

[10] *Chron. Guisborough*, 299–306; *Chron. Lanercost*, 163–5; *Chron. Fordun*, ii, 322; Watson, *Under the Hammer*, 48–9; McNamee, 'William Wallace's invasion of Northern England, 1297', 40–58.

lingered from previous years. Wallace had emerged from the lands of the Steward and Bishop Wishart and, despite the bishop's continued imprisonment, these connections persisted. When a new bishop of St Andrews was elected following the death of William Fraser in France during the summer, old suspicions flared up. The election was held at St Andrews in early November and Wallace reportedly imposed William Lamberton on the chapter. Lamberton was a clerk from Wishart's cathedral and his promotion probably angered the Comyns. The earl of Buchan's brother, the provost of St Mary's church at St Andrews, disputed the form of the election and took his complaints to the papal curia. Fraser's death and Lamberton's election deprived the Comyns of a powerful ally in the church and may have fuelled their mistrust of Wallace as a possible threat to their lordship and influence in the realm.[11]

Yet, despite tensions amongst the Scottish leadership and stories of plots against the guardian, the magnates, clergy and others who opposed Edward's rule accepted Wallace as the best hope for the defence of the kingdom. In early 1298 this group was strengthened by the return of the earls of Atholl and Menteith and John Comyn, son of the lord of Badenoch, who had deserted Edward's army in Flanders. They had returned via France and had added their voices to Scottish efforts to renew the alliance with King Philip. However, the guardian concentrated on military preparations. Later accounts spoke of Wallace's efforts to enforce the obligation to serve in the common army, hanging those who refused. The winter campaign in England allowed him to keep his own power-base, 'the army of the kingdom' supplied and in the field. These actions anticipated major warfare. During the winter English forces had relieved their garrisons in south-east Scotland, but when King Edward returned from Flanders in March 1298 preparations were begun for a massive expedition. In early July the king crossed the border with an army of 3,000 cavalry, 15,000 English foot and 10,000 Welshmen, a force designed to cow or crush resistance. The problems of an army of this scale were, however, revealed during the march through Lothian. Too large to live off the land, it depended on supplies brought by sea. When these were delayed, the discipline of the army began to break down. At Linlithgow, the Welsh mutinied and Edward considered retreat, but news arrived that the Scottish army was nearby at Falkirk. Wallace was offering battle when a more cautious strategy might have forced Edward to break up his army.

[11] Stevenson, *Documents illustrative of Sir William Wallace, his life and times*, 159, 191–2; *Chron. Guisborough*, 306; *Chron. Fordun*, ii, 321–2; Barrow, *Robert Bruce*, 90–1; Young, *Robert the Bruce's Rivals: The Comyns*, 167–9; Watt, *Scottish Graduates*, 206, 319; Palgrave, *Documents*, 331–2; Reid, 'The kingless kingdom', 105–29.

However, the guardian's position depended on holding the magnates and his own army together, and a victory was the best means to achieve this. He had prepared a strong position on the road to Stirling and awaited the enemy. The resulting battle on 22 July was a bloody defeat. The Scottish horse fled at the outset of the battle, leaving the schiltroms of close-packed spearmen to be slowly broken down by archery and repeated attacks by the English cavalry and foot. By nightfall, thousands of Scottish foot had been killed and 'the army of the kingdom' destroyed.[12]

As in 1296 the defeat was blamed on political division. The Comyns and other lords were said to have deserted the field treacherously. Their flight in the face of Edward's massive force can be explained without reference to personal animosities. However, it is striking that the only nobles killed on the field – the Steward's brother and Macduff of Fife, who had fought on foot alongside their adherents – were no friends of the Comyn family. However, though the defeat was much bloodier, Falkirk brought no fresh collapse of resistance like that which had followed Dunbar. After his victory, Edward's army took Stirling, but the battle had not eased the king's supply problems. The infantry was sent south to Carlisle while the king and the cavalry rode through Clydesdale to Ayr, seeking the submission of the districts most closely associated with Wallace. Edward was to be disappointed: he reached Ayr to find the castle burned and, denied this base, he led his men back through the borders, leaving much of Scotland in open defiance of him.[13]

The destruction of Ayr Castle was the work of Robert Bruce, earl of Carrick, and it was symbolic of a new attitude amongst the Scottish magnates. The earl's readiness to defend his 'country' and defy the king contrasted with his behaviour at Irvine. His decision to destroy the castle and retreat into the hills of his earldom was a style of warfare adopted by other lords in the coming years. Falkirk would teach the Scots to avoid pitched battle. It also brought a change of leadership. The destruction of his army spelled the end of Wallace's primacy. He had escaped the field but resigned his guardianship soon afterwards, and in the autumn, probably in a gathering of magnates and their adherents, new guardians were chosen. The choice of Robert Bruce, earl of Carrick and John Comyn,

---

[12] *Scotichronicon*, vi, 86–9; Watson, *Under the Hammer*, 61–7; Barrow, *Robert Bruce*, 99–103.

[13] It is the Scottish historical tradition which stresses the divisions in Wallace's army, blaming both the Comyns and, interestingly, Robert Bruce, earl of Carrick, who is said to have fought in Edward's army. Given the more contemporary English reference to him burning Ayr a few weeks later, Carrick had probably remained in his earldom, though his father, also Robert Bruce, may have been with Edward (*Chron. Guisborough*, 328–9).

William Wallace

William Wallace remains the best-known individual in medieval Scottish history, the only man of the wars whose name has a real resonance in the twenty-first century. For historians, however, Wallace has always been a perplexing figure. His role in 1297–8 was vital to the maintenance of the Scottish kingdom, but while his brief guardianship, his advocacy for the Scottish cause at the French and papal courts and his leadership of an armed band in the last resistance to Edward I between 1303 and 1305 are known, much else about Wallace remains a mystery. His origins and life up to his sudden rise in 1297 are obscure while, even more importantly, his influence on the attitudes of his contemporaries and of later Scots is hard to chart.

While contemporary English chronicles regard him as a brigand raised unnaturally to knighthood and gentility, turned from a raven to a swan as one put it, later medieval Scottish narratives stressed his heroic qualities, declared his knightly pedigree and developed his role as Bruce's precursor. But for these writers and their successors, Bruce, not Wallace, was the principal defender of Scottish freedoms. This perspective was altered by the composition of an epic poem, *Wallace*, by a southern minstrel known as Blind Hary in the 1470s. *Wallace*, composed 170 years after the events it described, provides the earliest written account of its hero's exploits, even if the poem was based on a corpus of tales which portrayed William as a folk hero. It was via the poem that William's reputation grew. First printed in 1508, during the next three centuries it was produced in a series of editions and translations and was one of the most widely-owned books in Scotland. Its popularity established Wallace as the archetypal patriotic freedom-fighter and spawned nineteenth-century monuments – the tower near Stirling and a statue near Dryburgh – giving William a popular profile revived recently in cinematic form.

What is also striking is that, since the 1470s, Wallace has been used as a model by Scots of almost all political colours, including many who regarded the 'brigand' as an early champion of the British constitution! The current view, which claims William as a threat, alive or dead, to kings and nobles who lacked his devotion to the cause, should also be regarded with caution. His limited role in 'official' accounts of the wars may reflect not an effort to limit his achievement, but a perception that this achievement was itself limited. Wallace was an exceptional figure but, before Hary, it is striking that the best evidence for his importance comes from the implacable hostility of Edward I towards a man who could not and would not negotiate his submission.[14]

[14] Fisher, *William Wallace*; Fraser, "'A swan from a raven", William Wallace, Brucean propaganda, and *Gesta Annalia II*', 1–22; Cowan, 'Identity, freedom and the Declaration of Arbroath', 59–61; *Hary's Wallace*, ed. M. P. McDiarmid.

son of the lord of Badenoch, was not simply a return to the natural leaders of the community. Though from magnate families, Bruce and Comyn represented a new generation of leaders, young men who were still heirs to their fathers. The return to the joint leadership of the 1280s had less to do with constitutional principle than with the pragmatic recognition of factional rivalries and the need to share power between two competing parties. Bruce and Comyn would add a personal antagonism to these rivalries with significant consequences for the Scottish realm.[15]

Shared leadership had other advantages. The military and political circumstances which prevailed from the summer of 1298 forced a decentralised approach on the Scots. English garrisons in Stirling, Edinburgh, Roxburgh, Lochmaben and Berwick formed centres for the administration of south-east Scotland and the borders, and restricted contact between the north and the south-west, the areas most securely in the Scottish king's allegiance. In these areas the guardians relied for government on local leaders, some of them knights and barons, but mostly other magnates. In the north-east, for example, Buchan continued as justiciar while Atholl, an ally of Bruce, was sheriff of Aberdeen. Such appointments recognised existing influence and increased the effectiveness of a local government of which the primary role was to raise men and supplies for the war. Local and regional concerns figured large in the waging of this war. Magnates had a special concern for the defence of their own lands and people, while action against English garrisons was often led by local men. The long siege of Stirling, which starved the castle into submission during 1299, was the work of Stirlingshire men led by Thomas Morham and Gilbert Malherbe.[16]

However, the Scottish leaders could operate together. In August 1299, 'the great lords of Scotland', a group including Carrick and Comyn, the Steward and Bishop Lamberton and the earls of Buchan, Menteith and Atholl, gathered with their followers at Peebles. The meeting had a political significance and ended with Lamberton's appointment as a third guardian, but its purpose was to attack Roxburgh from the Forest. However, the meeting broke up as a result of political dissensions and the news of an attack by lords in English allegiance on 'the Scottish people'. While John Comyn and Buchan hastened northwards to protect their lands and followers, the Steward and his cousin, Menteith, fell back to Clydesdale, and Carrick passed south-westwards through Annandale and Galloway. Though it was reported that 'each great lord has left part of his people'

[15] Reid, 'The kingless kingdom', 109–10.
[16] Young, *Robert the Bruce's Rivals: The Comyns*, 174; Watson, *Under the Hammer*, 69–80; Barrow, *Robert Bruce*, 105–6.

in the force which remained to harry the English from the Forest, the episode illustrated the regional concerns of the magnates and the dependence of the war on their resources. The three guardians, Bruce, Comyn and Lamberton, again came together in late 1299. They were in the Torwood, south of Stirling, preparing to meet Edward's attempt to relieve the castle. In the event, Edward was unable to persuade his mistrustful subjects to join a winter campaign and Stirling surrendered to its besiegers in December. The capture of this key fortress demonstrated the effectiveness of the Scots' localised approach to warfare. The following summer, when the king did lead an army into Galloway, taking Caerlaverock in a famous siege and reaching the Cree, the guardians succeeded in keeping a force in the field. Though this host was scattered by Edward's army on the banks of the Cree, the Scots eluded pursuit by taking to the moors and hills of Galloway. The control and use of such upland country allowed the Scots to harass Edward's forces in southern Scotland. The Scottish leadership made considerable efforts to secure Galloway, while two major English expeditions attempted to establish control of the province. Similarly, Selkirk Forest (the Forest, as it was known), was another vital region of rough terrain. Long the haunt of robbers, it had been used by Wallace as his stronghold and recruiting ground in 1297 and, from 1299, the guardians sought to maintain a force in the Forest, drawing on the 'foresters' in their attacks on the surrounding lands in both England and Scotland.[17]

Between 1299 and 1301 the strategy of the Scottish leaders proved relatively effective in frustrating Edward's efforts. However, for these leaders, the struggle was not simply to resist the English king. Though they supported a 'Scottish cause' based on resistance to Edward's rule, which trampled on their rights as the community of the realm, threatened their individual status and lordship and placed them under 'alien' governors, this was not their sole concern. As the meeting of August 1299 showed, the Scottish leadership was a coalition of magnates, concerned with the defence of regional interests, lands and followers. The Peebles council revealed more direct divisions. A dispute erupted over the lands of William Wallace between his brother, Malcolm, and David Graham, who drew weapons on each other. These two knights were linked to different guardians, Wallace to Carrick and Graham to Comyn, and their quarrel exposed the animosity between these leaders. Comyn seized Bruce by the throat while his cousin, Buchan, 'turned on the bishop of St Andrews'. Such factional rivalries were not simply a distraction to the

---

[17] *National Manuscripts of Scotland*, ii, no. 8; *A.P.S.*, i, 454; Barrow, *Robert Bruce*, 106–14; Watson, *Under the Hammer*, 101–5; Prestwich, *Edward I*, 487–9.

proper business of defending the realm, they represented the continuation of the deep-seated antagonisms which had dominated Scottish politics since 1286. Lesser nobles like Wallace and Graham, as well as the magnates, stood in opposite camps. At issue was the leadership of Scotland. For Bruce, and, in more limited ways, for Steward, Atholl and others, the domination of the Scottish party by the Comyns posed a threat to their rights and influence. For the Comyns, Bruce's ambitions were suspect. Buchan accused his rivals of 'treason and lese-majestie', reflecting suspicions that Bruce would never work happily for the return of King John and the dominance of his adherents. The appointment of Bishop Lamberton as chief guardian at Peebles was a settlement which benefited Bruce and his allies, but merely papered over the cracks. By May 1300 this unity was again threatened. Carrick had resigned office, probably to defend his earldom, and Comyn now refused to work with Lamberton, perhaps with the aim of ousting him as guardian. The bishop was supported by the Steward and Atholl, both Comyn's enemies, and the latter settled for the replacement of Carrick by an ally of his family, Ingeram Umfraville.[18]

From early 1301, these shifts of power within the aristocratic coalition were subjected to a new influence: after a gap of five years, King John took a role in the leadership of his realm. In 1299, as the result of pressure from Pope Boniface VII and King Philip of France, Edward I had released John into the hands of the pope. Two years later John, king of Scots was placed under the French king's protection on his own estates in Picardy. The recognition of John's rights and the diplomatic support of Philip IV and Pope Boniface had been achieved by repeated Scottish embassies and caused Edward increasing anxiety. Hopes of external diplomatic and military support formed a vital part of the strategy adopted by the Scottish leadership. However, the possibility of John's re-emergence as an active leader also had an impact on the men who fought in John's name. The Scottish king now appointed his own guardian, John Soules, a knight from a great baronial house who had attended him in France. Neither Bruce nor Comyn may have been overjoyed with this development, but Comyn continued to work with a leader who was much more an agent of King John than any of the guardians since 1297.[19]

While diplomatic efforts continued under Lamberton's leadership, the Scots leaders faced a new English campaign during the autumn and winter of 1301. Edward's ambitious plan involved two armies operating

---

[18] *National Manuscripts of Scotland*, ii, no. 8; Sayles, 'The guardians of Scotland and a parliament at Rutherglen in 1300', 245–50.

[19] Reid, 'The kingless kingdom', 111–13; Barrow, *Robert Bruce*, 114–16.

Baldred Bisset and the Debates at the Curia

The efforts of the guardians and leaders of King John's cause were not limited to warfare: diplomatic activity had equal significance. By securing recognition and help from Pope Boniface and King Philip, the Scots hoped to force Edward I to negotiate. From 1298 the pope showed a willingness to champion the Scottish cause. The chance to appear as an authority able to exercise super-iority over warring Christian princes clearly appealed to Boniface, and in 1299 he issued the bull, *Scimus Fili*, ordering Edward to desist from attacks and to enter negotiations. Edward's response to this reached the curia in summer 1301, and the new guardian, John Soules, sent envoys to put the Scottish case to Boniface directly. The advocates included Baldred Bisset, a clerk of St Andrews diocese who had spent time at the great legal centre of Bologna. Bisset was named as 'chief spokesman of the Scots' at the curia and would be remembered as the architect of the Scottish case before Boniface.

The arguments put forward by Edward consisted of two elements. A letter in the name of his nobility rejected *Scimus Fili*, claiming that for Edward to obey its terms would be 'in prejudice of the liberties, customs and laws of their fore-fathers'. A second answer was a justification of the English king's actions with regard to Scotland, and it cited historical precedents, from the twelfth century and from an older, mythical tradition, which regarded Scotland (Albany) as a portion of Britain subject to the rulers of the southern part of the island. The answer to these arguments was preserved in later Scottish chronicles and was ascribed to Baldred Bisset. Two texts survive from around this time, referred to as the *Instructiones* and the *Processus*, and advance a coherent position. Edward's arguments about the distant past are dismissed as 'unproven fictions' and, to answer them, stress is placed on the existence of a Scottish kingdom with its own liberties since time immemorial. In terms of more recent proofs, the bull *Cum Universi*, the 1278 statement of Alexander III, and the treaty of Birgham were cited to refute the opposing argument. The Scots clearly pos-sessed the means to compete effectively with Edward's advocates, and Boniface's continued sympathy was displayed in his decision to release the Scottish king to French protection during summer 1301. In the event, however, the possibility of greater assistance failed in the following twelve months leaving the Scots isolated before King Edward.[20]

---

[20] Goldstein, *The Matter of Scotland: Historical Narrative in Medieval Scotland*, 66–78; Barrow, *Robert Bruce*, 116–18; Goldstein, 'The Scottish mission to Pope Boniface VIII: A study of the Context of the *Instructiones* and *Processus* of 1301', 1–15; Watt, *Scottish Graduates*, 50.

in southern Scotland. The king advanced through Tweeddale into the Forest and then to Clydesdale where Bothwell Castle was taken in September. Meanwhile his son, Edward, prince of Wales, marched through Galloway and Carrick, reaching Ayr in August to link up with men and supplies sent from Ireland. The Scots, led by Soules and Buchan, harried both armies and prevented them from joining up in northern Ayrshire. Despite this, Edward had made a deep impression on the south-west and wintered at Linlithgow. Though he had not achieved a military breakthrough, he had put his enemies on the defensive. In the face of papal and French hostility, the mistrust and criticism of his own subjects, and the stubborn resistance of his Scottish opponents, Edward's will maintained a massive war effort. The costs of raising and supplying garrisons and armies were enormous, and the attempts of Edward's officials to meet his demands were impressive. However, despite these efforts, in early 1302 the war remained to be won.[21]

For Edward, the key to victory did not simply lie in defeating the Scots in the field, taking their castles or devastating their lands. Nor was it found in the wholesale dispossession of the landed class, as had happened in Wales – this would merely have fixed men in their opposition to him and concerned his own supporters. Instead, the goal of his warfare was to win or force Scottish acceptance of his rule. Edward was usually ready to accept the submission of his Scottish enemies and restore them to their lands in both England and Scotland. His officials were empowered to receive the homage of magnates, knights and of the 'middle folk', who were the backbone of local communities. Throughout the war the king maintained significant Scottish support. Some, like the earl of Angus or the elder Robert Bruce, consistently supported Edward, following ties of lordship and service. The earl of Dunbar gave equally constant support, motivated by the vulnerability of his lands to English control but also by his antipathy towards Balliol. The attitudes of King John's cousin and chamberlain, Alexander Balliol of Cavers, and of the earl of Buchan's brother, Alexander Comyn, went against family ties. Both served Edward consistently from 1297 and showed genuine adherence to the king's interests. Dunbar and Balliol also acted as leaders of local communities in the south-east which adhered to the king. Their actions show that it was possible for Scots – nobles, but also middle folk – to take a variety of stances in the difficult circumstances of 1297 to 1304. Desire to serve the winner may have loomed large in the minds of those who aided Edward, but it was not the only motive. In Galloway the king could exploit the traditional

---

[21] *Chron. Lanercost*, 171–2; Watson, *Under the Hammer*, 120–33; Prestwich, *Edward I*, 493–4.

antipathy of the Gallovidians for the Scottish kings, and Edward had allies amongst the captains of the strategically-vital province.[22]

The aim of warfare was to make men switch allegiance. Many had the choice forced on them. Simon Fraser, the leading lord in the Forest, was caught between two camps. After serving Edward loyally for two years, Simon was captured by the Scots in 1299. He only changed sides after two years in custody and became a leading opponent of Edward. Earl William of Ross faced a similar fate. He refused allegiance to Edward in 1296 and was imprisoned by the king for seven years. The need to recover and defend his battered lands in the north finally induced Ross to pay Edward homage in 1303. The king's campaign of 1301–2 was designed to force Scots, especially in the west, into his allegiance. In the Isles, the MacDonalds assured the king of their loyalty, while their enemies, the MacDougalls of Argyll, entered negotiations which led to their submission. Round the Clyde, the Campbells and the earl of Lennox also made peace over the winter. Their submissions were followed by that of Robert Bruce, earl of Carrick. In September 1301 Bruce's castle at Turnberry had been taken by the English and, though the men of Carrick fought on through the winter, their earl felt trapped between the adherents of King Edward and King John. The final straw came in early 1302 with the conclusion of a truce between the two sides which raised the possibility of John's return and the occupation of disputed lands by the French. These prospects persuaded Robert to enter Edward's allegiance, receiving guarantees about his lands and rights. The acceptance of the king's lordship did not remove Bruce from influence in Scotland. As a leading magnate in Edward's service, Bruce provided leadership and protection to Scots in the same party, especially amongst the tenants and retainers of his friends in the guardians' camp like Atholl and the Steward. For him and others amongst Edward's Scottish adherents, allegiance to the English king sprang from short-term expediency, not the abandonment of claims and loyalties.[23]

In the coming months, many Scots would face the same choice. The hopes of fighting off Edward until King John returned or the French sent aid were dashed by the defeat of the latter by the Flemings in July 1302. The efforts of an impressive embassy, including Soules, the Steward, Buchan and Lamberton, to lobby the French king were in vain. In May 1303 a peace was agreed between Edward and Philip which left the Scots

[22] C.D.S., ii, nos 1,023, 1,025, 1,032, 1,049, 1,088, 1,109, 1,154, 1,226, 1,230, 1,244, 1,287; Barrow, Robert Bruce, 112.
[23] C.D.S., ii, nos 1,022, 1,034, 1,204, 1,238, 1,253–55, 1,275; Watson, Under the Hammer, 30, 83–6, 197; Stones, 'The submission of Robert Bruce to Edward I, c. 1301–2', 122–34.

isolated. Even before this the English king was preparing a major campaign against his Scottish enemies. Now he had a free hand. Though the
Scottish forces in the field, now under the leadership of John Comyn, had
won a striking victory over an English force at Roslin, south of
Edinburgh, in February 1303 and had captured Selkirk soon afterwards,
from the summer they would be outdone by the scale of Edward's army.
This host would be smaller than those raised in 1296, 1298 and 1301, but
it was far larger than the retinues of Comyn and the other Scottish
leaders. Edward could also call on his Scottish allies, raising 3,000 men
from Galloway and the south-west, many of them under Carrick's
command. By June the king's army was before Stirling. Instead of
wasting time besieging the fortress, Edward bypassed it by building a
bridge of boats across the Forth. His goal was Scotland north of the Forth
and the Tay, an area untouched by major war since 1297 and the
guardians' secure base. Despite the supply problems which continually
threatened to end the advance, Edward pressed on. After he took Brechin
on 15 August, resistance began to crumble. By early September, Edward
was on the borders of Buchan and a fortnight later he was in Badenoch.
These centres of Comyn power were probably key targets of the campaign. Cromarty, Urquhart and, probably, Inverness received English
garrisons, and the earl of Ross, the leading magnate in the region, was left
as Edward's lieutenant beyond the Spey.[24]

The leaders of the Scottish cause responded to the king's advance by
harrying his forces further south. William Wallace, once more in the forefront of the war, joined Simon Fraser in attacks from the Forest on the
marches and into England. Comyn raided the Lennox and skirmished
with Edward's forces at Linlithgow. This resistance was encouraged by
English supply problems. However, when Edward returned from the
north he swept these aside. He determined to winter, once again, in
Scotland, remaining at Dunfermline, while his son was based at Perth.
This decision, and the exertions of Edward's officials to feed the army
through the winter, was the key to the Scottish defeat. Though Comyn,
who was based in Atholl, continued to harry English forces in the Tay
valley during the winter, the prospect of facing Edward in the spring persuaded him to seek peace. In January 1304 he opened negotiations and the
following month Comyn and his close adherents submitted to Edward on
terms. His submission was probably preceded and followed by a rush of
similar arrangements and by March the earl of Menteith and his brother,

[24] *Chron. Fordun*, ii, 325–8; *C.D.S*, ii, no. 1,363; Barrow, *Robert Bruce*, 124–9; Watson,
Under the Hammer, 175–80; Haskell, 'Breaking the stalemate: The Scottish campaign of
Edward I, 1303–4', 223–42; Freeman, 'Wall-breakers and river-bridgers', 1–16;
Stevenson, *Documents*, no. 438.

John, and the earls of Strathearn and Atholl had all come to Edward's peace. They probably attended the king's parliament in March at St Andrews, and most served in the final act of the war, the siege of Stirling Castle, which was carried out with ruthless efficiency. After three months, Edward finally accepted the surrender of the castle on 24 July 1304. Major resistance to his rule was over.[25]

After seven years of war, the Scottish lords and people were once again under Edward's rule. The stubborn resistance of the guardians, lords and lesser folk had not been without its gains. The submissions of 1304 were different from the capitulation of 1296. Although the restoration of King John and the removal of Edward's direct lordship had not been achieved, concessions had been made by the English king. When John Comyn negotiated his surrender, he had asked for the restoration of the lands and rights of Edward's opponents throughout his dominions. He also asked the king to maintain the 'laws and customs' of the realm as they had been under King Alexander. These two issues were of central importance. Security of lands and laws had been sought by the nobility in the treaty of Birgham and, in the years of war, Edward had been petitioned by Scots in his allegiance to 'confirm and maintain' the laws of Alexander. Even in the absence of a king of Scots, the idea of the king's law had a value which was both real and symbolic. The law represented the continuation of a distinctive Scottish tradition of government and society and was identified as a source of stability and security in a time of troubles.[26]

Unlike in 1296, Edward recognised the need to respond to such demands as a means of maintaining the allegiance of the Scots. During the next eighteen months Edward would show a willingness to restore forfeited lands in England and Scotland to his former enemies, even dispossessing his supporters of their gains. He also consulted with the Scots about their future government. The results of this were published in September 1305 at a parliament at Westminster. This 'Ordinance for the good order of Scotland' sought to establish Edward's rule through a degree of participation with the Scots. Though the lieutenant would be Edward's nephew, John of Brittany, and the officers of state, chancellor, chamberlain and others were English administrators, the offices of justiciar in Galloway, Lothian, Scotia and beyond the Mounth (the Grampians) were each shared between an English and Scottish lord. More importantly, eighteen of the twenty-two sheriffs appointed were Scots, many of them from families with lands in their sheriffdom and traditions of holding the office. King Edward was counting on the local

---

[25] Watson, *Under the Hammer*, 181–94; Barrow, *Robert Bruce*, 127.
[26] Watson, 'Settling the stalemate: Edward I's peace in Scotland, 1303–1305', 127–43.

influence of such men to provide a focus for the allegiance of these communities and to prevent the friction at this level which had sparked the rising of 1297. Concerning the laws of the realm, Edward showed prejudice as well as pragmatism. 'King David's laws', the legislation of the crown which followed Anglo–French custom, would receive amendment and reform where necessary by the lieutenant and 'good people', overseen by Edward himself. However, 'the laws of the Scots and Brets', customary, kin-based law involving payments of compensation for crimes, were 'forbidden': they were among those practices 'displeasing to God'. As in Wales and Ireland, clear distinctions were being made between such native practices and Anglicised custom, with the latter being accorded a superior status. Edwardian government would undoubtedly have brought a different and less sympathetic eye to the variations of law, custom and language within Scotland.[27]

Despite this, the ordinance stands as a pragmatic attempt to form a basis for Edward's rule, the work of a king aware of the difficulties of the past war and of his own advancing age (Edward was sixty-six in 1305). He sought to avoid the causes of the earlier rebellion and to hold the political class to their allegiance but, characteristically, he was not prepared to wipe the slate completely clean. Sentences of exile were passed on a number of Scots leaders whom Edward regarded as having offended him in person and made late submissions. Several of these were offered favour or forgiveness in return for the capture of Wallace, who remained outside Edward's peace. By 1305 Edward regarded Wallace as an irreconcilable foe. The former guardian was taken by the keeper of Dumbarton, John Stewart of Menteith, who surrendered him to Edward for trial and execution in London in the weeks before the ordinance was issued. The treatment of Wallace matched the death of the Welsh prince, Dafydd ap Gruffydd, at Edward's hands twenty years before. Despite the talk of the 'good of the king and the people' in the ordinance, there was no doubt in the mind of the king or his new subjects that, like Wales, Scotland was once more a conquered land.

THE WAR OF THE BRUCE (1306–14)

Edward's ordinance did not settle Scotland. From the spring of 1304 to early 1306 an atmosphere of insecurity prevailed amongst the king's new subjects. Most leading Scots had accepted defeat in the face of Edward's sustained warfare and in the knowledge that no help would come from the

---

[27] Stones, *Anglo-Scottish Relations*, no. 33.

French king. They sought King Edward's peace and protection for their lands and followers, but such peace could not come easily after nearly nine years of warfare. Many parts of Scotland had suffered major dislocation. Some nobles, like the son of William Douglas, and numerous burgesses, freeholders and lesser men had lost lands and suffered poverty and dispossession. Individuals and bands had grown used to the bearing of arms and developed a hostility to English lordship. Many such must have remained outside the peace. In the south-west and in the north there were reports about such 'evil-doers', and some at least were retained by lords and employed in local feuds. For men like these and for lesser clergy, perhaps especially friars, the settlement and its legal safeguards were far removed from their own experiences and anxieties. The peace did not end the identification of the troubles with the rule of the English king. The worries of Edward's adherent Alexander Comyn of Buchan that 'the people of his country', his tenants and neighbours, would be hostile to him for his loyalties were an expression of continuing tensions.[28]

Further disturbances after 1305 were probably inevitable but the character and scale of fresh conflict was determined by the ambitions and rivalries of Scottish magnates and prelates. Through the preceding decades these had shaped the kingdom's politics, and they would now initiate a renewal of conflict. The presence of almost all the leading Scots in Edward's camp did not end their competition but, in a sense, increased it. At stake now was the restoration and distribution of forfeited lands and royal offices, all to be gained through Edward's hard-to-win favour. The flow of petitions to the king and the judgements of the king's officials continued steadily through 1304 and 1305. The settlement of Scotland by Edward involved not just decisions about administration and the recognition of Scottish customs, but the distribution of jobs and power amongst a factionalised political class.[29] The leaders of this class were quick to grasp this. On 11 June 1304, whilst in Edward's army besieging Stirling, Robert Bruce entered a band with Bishop Lamberton which promised mutual aid in 'future dangers . . . to resist and defeat their enemies'. The bishop, who had only submitted to Edward in May, and Earl Robert were probably not alone in planning for a political environment where their enemies still existed and could work against them in the king's counsels. The most obvious of these enemies was John Comyn. The deaths of their fathers since 1300 had left Comyn and Bruce as the heads of great baronial houses and of rival parties in the kingdom. John Comyn's negotiation of a general submission had probably won him King

[28] *C.D.S.*, ii, nos 1,617, 1,633, 1,735.
[29] Watson, *Under the Hammer*, 200–11.

Edward's respect. Though not in the forefront of further discussions, his influence on the king's actions is clear. The sheriffs chosen under the ordinance included many of the Comyns' friends, and John and his cousin, the earl of Buchan, were fully restored to their estates. Having recognised the impossibility of maintaining the rights of their Balliol cousins to the kingship in the circumstances of 1304, the Comyns accepted Edward's lordship. For Bruce, by contrast, the conditions of 1304–5 were increasingly difficult. While Comyn prospered from Edward's favour, Bruce seems to have been treated with suspicion. The influence he had held as Edward's chief Scottish adherent was lost. His actions as guardian of the young earl of Mar and his rights as earl of Carrick both came under scrutiny. By 1305 he had lost his posts as sheriff of Ayr and Lanark, being replaced in both by friends of the Comyns. Bruce was not alone: Earl John of Atholl held the office of lieutenant north of the Forth but found the exercise of his post hampered by the claims of his regional rivals, the Comyns. In the south-west Bruce retained many friends and also developed his links with the connection of the exiled James Stewart. Most importantly, Bruce was allied to both Bishop Lamberton and Bishop Robert Wishart of Glasgow. Wishart had returned to Scotland in late 1305 and it seems likely that over the winter he was encouraging the disaffected earl to rise against King Edward and pursue his inherited claim to the throne.[30]

By the spring of 1306, only six months after Edward's ordinance, Robert had risen in war. The hindsight of the chroniclers places Robert's royal ambitions at the heart of events in early 1306. However, while the crown was never absent from Bruce's planning, it is possible that the seizure of the throne sprang not from a deep-laid conspiracy, but was precipitated by a sudden crisis. At the centre of this crisis were the relations of Bruce with Comyn. In early February a meeting between the two magnates was arranged for the Franciscan friary at Dumfries. Rather than being a far-fetched proposal for Bruce to seize the throne and give Comyn his lands, a plan which the latter would never have accepted, the background to this meeting was probably in their local interests in Nithsdale and Annandale. The court of justiciary was sitting in the burgh at the time and one of the justiciars, Roger Kirkpatrick, was with Bruce. The two lords were probably present for the court and met 'to resolve certain matters touching them'. However, after speaking peacefully, Bruce suddenly 'charged Comyn with treachery to him', for accusing him to the king so that 'Bruce's circumstances had declined'. Comyn was not

---

[30] Watson, *Under the Hammer*, 215–16; Barrow, *Robert Bruce*, 138–46. For the Cambuskenneth Bond, see Barbour, *The Bruce*, 70–1n.

attacked for revealing a plot to seize the throne but for eclipsing his rival in Edward's eyes. Seven years before, the two men had come to blows in a sudden quarrel and now Bruce struck Comyn with his sword, his followers joining in to slay John and his uncle.[31]

The killing of Comyn before the high altar of a church was probably an act of sudden personal rage, but it would prove the defining political act of fourteenth-century Scotland. It precipitated Bruce into seizing the throne and making a forceful and permanent rejection of English lordship. The deed put Robert outside King Edward's peace and turned political rivals into determined enemies who sought his death for the slaying of their kinsman. If the act was unpremeditated, the speed of Robert's next moves were impressive. Starting by seizing Dumfries Castle from its garrison Bruce launched a rapid campaign across the south-west during the next month in a much more impressive repeat of his grandfather's rising of 1286. He took or besieged the royal castle at Ayr and the strongholds of Comyn and his allies at Dalswinton, Tibbers and Inverkip. Bruce's supporters also secured the castles of Rothesay and Dunaverty on Kintyre, though he was rebuffed by the men of Galloway and by the keeper of Dumbarton. Taken by surprise, King Edward's agents were slow to react. However, while Robert made determined military moves during this month, his political intentions may have been less certain. He remained in contact with the English council, whilst waiting until certain demands were answered. Though he promised 'to defend himself with the longest stick he had', during February he made no overt move for the throne. The influence of Wishart, Bruce's 'chief adviser', was probably now decisive. Robert visited Glasgow frequently and, at the beginning of March, the bishop absolved the earl for the killing of Comyn, made him swear to take the advice of the clergy and 'freed him to secure his heritage'.[32]

This heritage was the kingship of the Scots. By the last week of March Robert had left his own 'country' and was at Scone. He was made king wearing vestments supplied by Wishart. Isabella, countess of Buchan stood in for her nephew, the earl of Fife, in the ceremony. If this inauguration contained makeshift elements, a significant body of Scots gathered round King Robert's banner. Along with the heads of the Scottish church, Wishart and Lamberton, were the earls of Lennox, Atholl and Menteith, the young heir of the Steward and numerous barons and

---

[31] Barrow, *Robert Bruce*, 146–8; Young, *Robert the Bruce's Rivals: The Comyns*, 197–8. For a full account of the chronicle narratives, see Barbour, *The Bruce*, 78–81 and n.

[32] Our knowledge of Robert's moves in February comes from an English report (Stones, *Anglo-Scottish Relations*, no. 34).

knights. The core of these came from the followings of Bruce and his allies and it could hardly be disguised that a faction had seized power. Whether deep-laid or opportunistic, Robert's actions in early 1306 had altered the whole basis of Scottish opposition to Edward I.

Beyond Robert's network of friends, it was hard to justify his seizure of the kingship. It was usurpation and rebellion. Bruce and his adherents had broken their oaths of fealty to King Edward and had stolen the royal title from John Balliol, in whose name the earlier wars had been fought. These crimes were compounded by the sacrilegious slaying of John Comyn. Though Bishop Wishart proclaimed the war against the King of England to be 'in the service of God', for many Scots support of Bruce as king was illegal or, at best, highly dangerous and morally dubious. To widen his support, Robert chose not to slip back to his south-western strongholds but to stand his ground. During the spring he was active in Perthshire, Aberdeenshire and Angus where, despite the support of Atholl, the Hays and a number of new recruits, Bruce was vulnerable. The other major local magnate, Malise, earl of Strathearn, refused to support Bruce despite intimidation, as 'he did not wish to be as fragile as a glass' and break his oath to Edward at its first test. As an ally of the Comyns, Malise mistrusted Robert, probably believing that his brother-in-law, Buchan, in the north and King Edward from the south would defeat Bruce. Though the Comyns were slow to act, by June the king's men were in the field. An army under John Comyn's brother-in-law, Aymer de Valence, marched north and occupied Perth. Robert offered battle at Methven nearby but his army was routed by de Valence in a dawn attack on 19 June.[33]

The defeat scattered Bruce's party. The king, his family, Atholl and others fled west only to be routed near Loch Tay by their pursuers and defeated a third time by Comyn's cousin, John MacDougall of Lorn, at Dail Righ. Sending Queen Elizabeth and his daughter, Marjory, northwards with Atholl, Robert turned south-west, hoping to reach his friends in the Lennox and Cowal. Though he was joined by Earl Malcolm of Lennox, the region was no longer safe and Bruce was pursued by John Menteith from Dumbarton and by English forces. He took ship, first for Kintyre and then, with his enemies not far behind, into the Hebrides. Robert's family and friends were less fortunate. Queen Elizabeth, Marjory and Atholl were captured by the Earl of Ross at Tain, and Robert's brother, Neil, was captured when Kildrummy fell to the Prince

---

[33] Barrow, *Robert Bruce*, 150–61; Duncan, 'The War of the Scots, 1306–1323', 136–8; Neville, 'The political allegiance of the earls of Strathearn during the War of Independence', 133–53.

of Wales. With bishops Wishart and Lamberton already in custody, Bruce had lost most of those closest to him. For King Edward, who had once more led his army north, these captives were perjured rebels. No longer restrained by the need to set examples of clemency to the wider Scottish community, Edward was ruthless. Atholl, Neil Bruce, Simon Fraser and many others were executed, and though the ladies and the prelates were protected from such deaths, they were placed in harsh imprisonment. Efforts were also made to deprive the bishops of their sees. Only six months after Robert's inauguration, he had been hunted from the mainland. To English writers he was 'King Hobbe', the crowned fool, or the King of Summer who disappeared with the coming of Autumn.[34]

But Bruce had not disappeared. He and his remaining companions probably spent the winter in the Isles, amongst people known to the king. Robert moved between the lands of the MacDonalds of Islay, and those of the MacRuairis of Garmoran, kinsmen of his first wife, Isabella of Mar. These Hebridean magnates, Angus Og of Islay and Lady Christina of Garmoran, were enemies of Robert's foes, the MacDougalls and the earl of Ross. Their support of the king at this critical moment was of huge significance. Safe from immediate pursuit, Robert was free to make plans aided by the Islesmen. With their help, Bruce sent his brothers to recruit allies from the Irish of Ulster and, in the spring, Robert would return to the Scottish mainland with ships and men from the Isles. The king spent the winter not as a hunted and desperate man, but as a lord of the west, amongst his neighbours, building up his strength for a renewal of the war.[35]

This war would be waged from the west. Its risks were clear from the events of 1306 and became clearer when Bruce's brothers, Thomas and Alexander, with a force from Kintyre and Ireland, landed in Galloway in February 1307. They were quickly defeated by the local captains who had no love for the Islesmen or the men of Carrick. Thomas and Alexander were handed to Edward and were hanged and beheaded at Carlisle. Robert himself crossed from Kintyre to Arran and then Carrick. He avoided defeat by the garrisons of Ayr and Turnberry but found no great rush of support from his province. King Edward was still at Carlisle and, though his ailing health was well-known, many would not have favoured Robert's chances. Yet Robert knew his ground. To Edward's astonishment, from the hills of Carrick Bruce harassed and outran his pursuers, and in April he defeated a small force at Glen Trool. In early May he moved into north Ayrshire and used the support of local adherents like

[34] Duncan, 'The War of the Scots', 138; Barbour, *The Bruce*, 104–29; Barrow, *Robert Bruce*, 161–3.
[35] McDonald, *Kingdom of the Isles*, 171–4; Duffy, 'The Bruce brothers', 64–6, 72–4.

Robert Boyd, Alexander Lindsay and James Douglas to gather men. A major blow was struck at Loudon Hill on about 10 May, when Bruce faced and drove off a force of cavalry under de Valence.[36]

In purely military terms Robert had merely won some elbow room on his home ground. His enemies still dominated the larger region and quickly dispatched troops to reinforce Ayr. However, the battle's significance was beyond its scale and local consequences. For the first time in the wars the king of Scots had won a victory in the field. The defeat of Edward's lieutenant sowed seeds of doubt amongst his officials and exposed the fragility of his rule. Within a week reports warned of a '*mauvaise covine*' amongst Edward's Scottish adherents and claimed that Bruce had 'the goodwill of the people' and had 'destroyed Edward's power among the English and Scots'. They spoke of 'false preachers', men 'previously charged before the justice for advocating war', who now exhorted support for King Robert. The legacy of the previous war, in general disturbance and in the experiences of Scots in bearing arms against the English, would now rapidly work in Robert's favour. These preachers were already broadcasting and mythologising their king's success and prophesying the death and downfall of Edward. The first part of this prophecy was swiftly fulfilled: on 7 July King Edward died at Burgh-on-Sands near Carlisle.[37]

The death of Robert's enemy did not alter his strategy at once. The new king of England, Edward II, continued his father's planned campaign into the south-west during August, but understandably the new king's thoughts were elsewhere and by September Edward II was on the road south. Robert followed his departure with a raid on Galloway, the regional centre of hostility to his dynasty, while his adherents clashed with de Valence in Clydesdale. Now Bruce could look ahead. He probably calculated that there would be no major English host in Scotland for six months and determined to exploit this space to widen his lordship by launching a winter campaign. His target lay in the north. North-eastern Scotland, from the Mounth to the Great Glen, had been a secure base for the guardians in the previous war. Robert sought to establish his lordship in this region and in the process to defeat his long list of enemies in the north. William, earl of Ross, the MacDougalls of Argyll, John Comyn, earl of Buchan, and the new earl of Atholl, David of Strathbogie, were joined by many barons and the bishop of Aberdeen, Henry Cheyne, in their hostility to Bruce. The defeat of these lords before Edward II returned was vital for Robert's success. During the autumn of 1307 Robert moved

---

[36] Duncan, 'War of the Scots', 138–9; Barbour, *The Bruce*, 166–201, 282–309.
[37] *C.D.S.*, ii, no. 1,926; *Nat. MSS. Scot.*, ii, no. 13; Prestwich, *Edward I*, 510–11, 556–8.

northwards swiftly. Skirting Argyll, he captured Inverlochy Castle and secured access through the Great Glen to the north. Urquhart, Inverness and Nairn were captured quickly, giving Robert a base in the centre of the region. Negotiating a truce with Ross, Robert moved east but was struck down by illness. Recognising an opportunity, Buchan and Atholl marched against him at Slioch near Huntly. Robert's army under the command of his brother, Edward, was clearly outnumbered. It took refuge in a 'wooded bog' and skirmished with the earls before falling back. Defeat at this point would have been disastrous and it was not until March that Robert resumed his attacks. He negotiated a truce in the east and struck at Ross, forcing the earl to fall back into his province. Finally Robert turned back east. In May he confronted the army of the earl of Buchan and his allies at Inverurie. Once again ill, Robert rose from his litter to lead his men, driving the enemy from the field. In the next few weeks, Robert exploited his victory ruthlessly. Buchan was harried with fire and sword and left utterly devastated. During the summer Aberdeen was taken and Robert's lordship extended to the Mounth. His enemies had either been driven from the region, like Earl John of Buchan, or were ready to accept his kingship, like William of Ross.[38]

Despite its speed, the northern campaign was hard fought and hard won against a group of enemies with far greater resources than Robert. Bruce did enjoy crucial support from the bishop of Moray, David Murray, whose clergy preached the king's cause and whose extensive family connections supported him, but the critical advantage for Robert was that he was a king taking on a coalition of magnates. His own party adhered to his lordship, while his opponents worked poorly together, concerned to defend their separate lands rather than to combine and defeat the enemy. In this the killing of John Comyn may have borne Robert fruit, removing a determined and established leader, the lord of strategically-vital lands in Lochaber and Badenoch. The insecurity of northern lords about their own followers and reports of Bruce's recruiting suggest that his reputation and claims were undermining the authority of his enemies over their own men. However, it was military skill and not the collapse of his enemies' power which was decisive. The king moved swiftly between opponents, striking east and then west and preventing them joining forces. He also enjoyed significant help from the west. The ineffectiveness of Ross in 1307–8 was due not just to Robert, but to the activities of his enemies, the MacRuairis, in the west of his earldom. Similarly, when

---

[38] Barnes and Barrow, 'The movements of Robert Bruce between September 1307 and May 1308', 46–59; Barbour, *The Bruce*, 310–35; Barrow, *Robert Bruce*, 174–8; Duncan, 'War of the Scots', 142–4.

Robert left the north-east and launched a swift campaign against
Alexander and John MacDougall in the late summer of 1308, he was
probably assisted by his Hebridean allies and by the 'barons of Argyll',
the crown tenants in the province.[39]

Robert's rapid successes in 1307 and 1308 can be attributed in part to
the failure of his enemies and, in particular, to the death of Edward I. This
certainly demoralised the English crown's adherents and encouraged its
enemies. It also removed the driving force behind the English war effort.
Had Robert been faced by a royal-led expedition in 1308, his task would
have been harder. Instead, after 1307 political problems and a lack of personal interest meant that Edward II did not return to Scotland until 1310,
by which time Robert was in a strong position. The problems which
Edward faced owed much to the strains of the previous war and the legacy
of debt and distrust which his father's demands had built up. Moreover,
in 1307–8 Robert was not acting with knowledge of Edward's position and
his campaigns between October and May would have seen the defeat of
his enemies in the north before major help could have reached them.[40]

Edward II's failure to return to Scotland or to send sufficient help in
the year from June 1308 did allow Robert a crucial breathing-space. The
English king's growing confrontation with his barons during the year
meant Robert could confirm the new pattern of warfare with attacks on
Argyll and Galloway. Between 1298 and 1304 the guardians had essentially fought a defensive struggle. In both military and political terms they
had sought to defend the rights of their crowned but exiled king and the
interests of the established aristocratic community. By contrast, Robert
had seized the throne in defiance of law and custom and now pursued an
aggressive war directed, in the first instance, against those lords and families who had led the earlier struggle. The 'herschip of Buchan' made plain
the king's readiness to uproot the power of those magnates who did not
submit. Another contrast with the guardians was the cohesion of Bruce's
party. The king's following was built around a close-knit group of adherents, bound to his leadership. First amongst these was Robert's last surviving brother, Edward, who led an attack on Galloway in June 1308 while
Robert was in the north. From this point Edward Bruce would play a vital
role as his brother's lieutenant in the south-west. In a similar fashion,
James, son of William Douglas, rose through a combination of service to

[39] Barbour, The Bruce, 360–7; Barrow, Robert Bruce, 178–81. In 1308 Edward Bruce
was aided in Galloway by a force of Islesmen under Angus of Islay (Scotichronicon, vi,
244).
[40] Tuck, Crown and Nobility, 50–61; Maddicot, Thomas of Lancaster; Phillips, Aymer de
Valence Earl of Pembroke.

Robert and personal ambition. During 1307, with some assistance, he had driven the English from Douglasdale; by the end of the year he had moved east into the Forest, securing this vital district. James Douglas was no freelance: he served in Edward Bruce's army in Galloway and on the royal council, showing his close loyalty to King Robert. Robert was able to leave the war in the south to such men, relying on bonds of family and service, strengthened by the traditions of kingship.[41]

The survival of Robert's kingship also depended on his ability to widen his base of support within Scotland. This process was begun by warfare. From Carrick and Kintyre to Buchan and Ross, the provinces of the west and north had largely been brought to accept Robert's lordship. His successes had won the submission and support of lords like the earl of Ross, James Stewart and Bruce's own nephew, Thomas Randolph, who would become the king's chief lieutenant. By early 1309 Robert had something which could be claimed as the Scottish kingdom and he was keen to display his authority as its ruler. In March 1309 the king held a parliament at St Andrews. This surely had a different character to the councils of the guardians. A crowned king presided over an assembly of prelates, earls, barons and representatives of local communities claiming to be acting for the whole realm. This communal character was stressed by Robert. Letters survive from the lords and communities to the king of France, commending Robert as their 'lawful and true prince', and from the clergy of Scotland, announcing their fealty to him as king of Scots. This second document, known as 'the declaration of the clergy', was probably for Scottish consumption. It justified Robert's kingship, dismissing John Balliol's accession as the work of Satan and proclaiming Robert's 'right of blood'. However, the letter has a defensive feel. Oblique references to the submissions to Edward I in 1296 and 1304, dismissing them as obtained through 'force and violence', suggest a need to justify the breach of fealty to the English crown from King Robert down. The most forcefully argued claim for Robert's kingship was that 'he had restored the realm by the sword', the real basis for Robert's success but hardly a sure title. In truth the parliament was a gathering of the king's partisans and of recent, forced converts. Perhaps four bishops and three earls attended, and claims that the communities of Fife, Mar and Buchan were represented barely concealed the fact that the earls of these provinces were in English allegiance. Despite his successes, Robert continued to be opposed by many Scots.[42]

---

[41] For Douglas's early career see Duncan, 'War of the Scots', 139–41; Brown, *The Black Douglases: War and Lordship in Late Medieval Scotland*, 14–19.
[42] *A.P.S.*, i, 289, 459–60; Barrow, *Robert Bruce*, 183–6 and n.

Edward II still had adherents in outposts like Stirling, Perth, Dundee and Bothwell, while Lothian and the marches were largely in his allegiance. Robert had not even claimed the presence of these communities at his parliament and their leaders, like Patrick, earl of Dunbar and William Soules of Liddesdale, were active supporters of the English king. From 1309 this loyalty was tested by sustained attacks from Robert's men. The attacks took the form of mobile, plundering forays across enemy territory, driving off livestock and extracting payments of grain and cash as blackmail in return for truces. Their aim was to impoverish local communities and supply Robert's own forces, whilst demonstrating the inability of Edward's garrisons to protect his adherents. Such tactics would be central to Scottish warfare in coming decades. The attacks continued despite a truce which ran between July 1309 and March 1310, and it was the complaints of the men of Lothian and the advice of his Scottish lords that persuaded Edward to take the field. His efforts were hampered by the refusal of many English magnates to serve alongside Edward's hated favourite, Piers Gaveston, and after a brief march through Lothian, the king fell back to Berwick. The expedition showed Robert the English political divisions. Having retreated before Edward, Bruce now struck back. He began a sustained series of attacks on Lothian and the English marches which lasted into the summer of 1311. Robert and his lieutenants also began to pick off Edward II's last adherents beyond Lothian. In the south-west Edward Bruce completed the subjugation of Galloway, capturing Dumfries in February 1313. A month earlier, Perth, which had been blockaded since 1311, was stormed by King Robert who had the leading burgesses executed for their resistance. In May 1313 Robert exploited English divisions to capture the Isle of Man.[43]

This run of victories was the mark of Robert's confidence and his enemies' disarray. Lothian was now at his mercy. The local population claimed to have suffered losses worth £20,000 between 1310 and 1313 in money, corn and cattle. In December 1312 Robert was able to lead a force through the region to launch a surprise attack on Berwick. Though this failed, his capture of Linlithgow in September 1313 prompted a major political move. King Robert issued an ultimatum to those Scots in Edward's allegiance giving them a year to submit to him or face the permanent loss of their lands. In response to this and to their losses at the hands of Bruce and the local garrisons, 'the people of Scotland' appealed to Edward II for his help. For once, the King of England was in a position to promise significant support for his adherents and wrote at once praising their efforts against his 'enemies and rebels'. Free, at last, from major

[43] *Chron. Lanercost*, 194–5, 199–200; McNamee, *The Wars of the Bruces*, 45–59.

opposition at home, Edward announced plans to lead an army north at midsummer 1314.[44]

The implications of this unity and Edward's preparations were not lost on Robert. As in the winter of 1307–8, the Scottish king exploited this breathing-space to move against the key English garrisons. On 28 February 1314 James Douglas led a force into Teviotdale and took Roxburgh, scaling the walls at night with rope ladders. A fortnight later Thomas Randolph, encouraged by Douglas's success, repeated his tactics, climbing the rock at Edinburgh to take the castle. Robert ordered the destruction of both strongholds to prevent their recapture. Two major castles, which would have acted as bases for Edward's summer campaign, had been lost to him. At a third castle, Stirling, surprise was not attempted. Perhaps in late March, Edward Bruce laid siege to this vital fortress. Both besiegers and besieged recognised that their efforts would be overtaken by the events of the summer and agreed a local truce. If the garrison was not relieved by midsummer, it would surrender.[45]

The siege of Stirling was not the cause of Edward II's campaign but the truce made it the obvious goal for the king's army. This army was probably on the scale of those of his father. It assembled at Berwick in early June and marched to Edinburgh. In response, Robert gathered his own host near Stirling, a smaller army, but one that was experienced and used to the king's leadership. Robert was ready to fight or withdraw to the west. On 23 June Edward moved north from Falkirk through the great Torwood. Over the next two days (23–24 June) in a series of clashes, the English king's army was totally defeated, the final rout occurring on the plain lands near the Bannock Burn. Though Edward escaped by horse and then boat, the bulk of his army and many of his nobles were killed or captured.[46]

Bannockburn did not end the war against Edward. It would be four-teen years before an English king would recognise Robert's kingship. Though the battle added hugely to Bruce's prestige, it did not give him and his family a secure title to the Scottish throne. However, Bannockburn was the end of one war. It was a decisive defeat for Robert's Scottish enemies. The death in battle of John Comyn, the son of the lord slain in 1306, followed the demise of John, earl of Buchan and removed the last leader of the great house of Comyn in Scotland. Other enemies, like Ingeram Umfraville, Earl Patrick and William Soules, were captured

---

[44] C.D.S., iii, no. 337; Rot. Scot., i, 113–14; Tuck, Crown and Nobility, 66–8; Barbour, The Bruce, 376n, 402n, 518n.
[45] Barbour, The Bruce, 377–403; Chron. Fordun, ii, 339; Thomas Gray, Scalachronica, trans. H. Maxwell (Glasgow, 1907), 51–2; Duncan, 'War of the Scots', 149–50.
[46] Barrow, Robert Bruce, 203–32; Barbour, The Bruce, 410–519.

Bannockburn (23–24 June 1314)

The fight at 'Stirling', 'before the Bannok' or, as it has become best known, at Bannockburn has assumed a central place in accounts of the Scottish wars. The significance accorded the battle is natural and largely deserved. The events of 23 and 24 June 1314 marked a major shift in the military balance. For the first time Robert stood and faced an army led by his principal enemy, the English king. On 23 June one division of the Scottish king's army under Randolph met and repulsed the cavalry vanguard of Edward II's host on its way to relieve Stirling Castle. The action encouraged Edward to make his camp on the open ground, cut by steep-banked burns, between the rising ground and the Forth. Persuaded by this success and by the advice of Scottish defectors from Edward's camp, Robert decided not to withdraw westwards but to take the initiative. With first light the Scottish king's army moved down from the high ground of the New Park in three battles. Though they had been ready for a night attack, the English were wrong-footed by this attack. Trapped between the river, the burns and the Scots, they were unable to deploy their forces. Efforts to halt the advance with isolated attacks failed and Edward's army disintegrated, thousands dying in the rout.[47]

---

or quickly submitted after the battle. The men of Lothian and the marches followed these examples and Robert was quick to complete his triumph. In November, in a parliament at Cambuskenneth by the site of his recent victory, the king issued a statute forfeiting and disinheriting those Scottish lords who had died or remained outside his allegiance. The group of 'disinherited' was not small. Many were barons whose principal lands and interests were in England and who had consistently served the English crown. However, amongst the exiles were David, earl of Atholl, John MacDougall and others who had been driven from their lands and retained support and connections in Scotland. These men were now totally dependent on the king of England. Within Scotland, tensions and doubts remained amongst the lords who had only recently and after much fighting accepted Robert as king. However, for the rest of the king's life, these doubts would not be raised openly in Scotland. The warfare which would continue to dominate Scottish politics and society after 1314 would overwhelmingly take place outside the realm, in the dominions of King Edward.[48]

---

[47] Barbour, *The Bruce*, 440–508; Barrow, *Robert Bruce*, 209–32.
[48] For the statute of the Cambuskenneth Parliament of 1314, see *Regesta Regum Scottorum*, v, *The Acts of Robert I*, ed. Duncan, no. 41.

CHAPTER 10

Robert I

WAR AND CONSPIRACY (1314–23)

By late 1314 Robert Bruce had come a long way from the 'King Hobbe' of 1306. His stature and security had grown immensely and allowed him to demand fealty of all Scots on pain of forfeiture of their lands in his realm. Such gains had not lifted the shadow of his usurpation, his seizure of the throne in violation of previous oaths to both King John and Edward I. Though John had died in 1313, he left a son, Edward Balliol, who would not relinquish his title to the Scottish crown. The ground and balance of warfare had shifted since 1314 but Robert still faced the same challenges to his right to rule, from both his Scottish enemies and the English king. As earlier, success in war remained the chief means by which Robert could maintain his authority within Scotland and the only way he could win recognition for his title from European rulers. The needs and effects of his war shaped Robert's kingship in an environment very different from the decades before 1286. The king's actions and the events of his reign began the transformation of Scottish political society under the impact of war.

King Edward II of England, after the defeat of his army and his own narrow escape, returned home to face further humiliation at the hands of a coalition of lords led by his cousin, Thomas, earl of Lancaster, who forced Edward to accept their demands. In the coming years such divisions would hamper the English war effort. Despite these problems, the English king refused to abandon the claim to Scotland he had inherited from his father and to recognise Bruce's rights as king. He continued as Robert's declared enemy, offering shelter and support to disinherited Scots. In response, Robert intensified the war against Edward's dominions. By carrying the war beyond Scotland, Robert sought to force the English king to make peace and recognise his title and lordship. Yet the goals of the Bruce party after 1314 were not limited to the consolidation and completion of their gains in Scotland since 1307. For King Robert and his allies, the widening of the war presented them with opportunities to win greater lordship in other parts of the British Isles. The Bruces and many of those around them had been brought up with connections and horizons that stretched far beyond Scotland. Just as Edward I had force-fully redrawn political relationships within the British Isles since the 1270s, Robert's military success may have led him to believe he could extend the rule of his own family.[1]

The targets of King Robert's forces in the years after Bannockburn were not foreign lands to him. Ulster and the northern shires of England were regions that he and his forebears knew well and where they had been known as friends as well as enemies. The king's attacks on northern England were certainly no new departure in the war which depended on Robert's personal interests. The English marches had been subject to Scottish forays since 1296 as a means of bringing the war to the enemy. Such attacks plundered goods and livestock and burned crops and build-ings, denuding the lands closest to Scotland of the means to support cam-paigns across the border. From late 1314, Robert launched invasions of northern England that displayed a new impetus, range and ambition. In August 1314 Edward Bruce led a host which crossed the Tees into Yorkshire before returning north through Westmoreland. This route was copied and extended southwards in succeeding years, with armies led by King Robert and his lieutenants penetrating deep into Yorkshire and Lancashire on several occasions. The goals of these attacks went beyond plunder and destruction. Though animals were driven off and barns, mills, orchards and crops destroyed, the campaigns had wider aims. Greater profit was made from taking payments from northern towns, clergy and rural communities in return for protection from attack. Daily rates were charged for such truces and the total amount gained by the Scots from this tactic between 1315 and 1322 may have topped £20,000.[2]

This blackmail was demanded not only to raise funds and impoverish the enemy. It marked the extension of methods already used by Robert's partisans in Lothian before 1314. There this mixture of war and peace was used to disrupt the loyalties of the communities under attack, and in the English marches it led the men of Tynedale to do homage to Robert and provoked other northern knights into rebellion against King Edward. The Scottish king was far more than a raider. He granted lands to

[1] Tuck, *Crown and Nobility*, 70–2; Maddicott, *Thomas of Lancaster*, 160–84.
[2] McNamee, *Wars of the Bruces*, 72–122; Scammell, 'Robert I and the North of England', 385–403.

Scottish lords in Tynedale and Cumberland, posing as a lord in border districts which had been held by Scottish kings in the previous century. As in Lothian, the effect of such harrying could only be cemented by the capture of castles and towns. In 1315 a serious effort was made to take Carlisle, a city with which the Bruces had long-standing links, while in 1318 a number of border castles in Northumberland were captured. Robert's chief goal was Berwick, the last Scottish stronghold outside his lordship, which he besieged without success in early 1316 and late 1317. Whatever King Robert's ambitions in northern England, rule over the Scottish realm remained the aim of his war.[3]

In the aftermath of Bannockburn, wider ambitions did play their part. In spring 1315 a Scottish army of several thousand men crossed the North Channel to the coast of Ulster. The expedition had multiple aims. The English of Ireland had provided a constant flow of men and supplies for their lords' efforts to impose their rule on the Scots. The ports of the east coast, Dublin, Dundalk and Drogheda, were bases that threatened western Scotland. In February 1315 the Hebridean exile, John MacDougall of Lorn, had expelled Bruce's garrison from Man and planned to use the island as a base for a campaign in the Isles. The arrival of the Scottish army in Ireland countered this danger, but these strategic goals were linked to the pursuit of family ambitions. The leader of the army was Edward Bruce. The campaign which followed had the declared aim of making him king of Ireland. During 1315 the Scots began the long blockade of Carrickfergus, the chief castle of the earldom of Ulster, before marching deep into Leinster and returning north to defeat Earl Richard of Ulster at Conor in September. Edward had himself crowned king and sought to entrench his position in Ulster and win Gaelic Irish adherents. His actions represented a direct challenge to the existing lord of Ireland, Edward II, and the shockwaves of the Bruce expedition were felt throughout Ireland and penetrated into Wales. If, with hindsight, the fundamental insecurity of Edward Bruce's position was obvious, in the years from 1315 the Bruce brothers did not regard the war in Ireland as a diversion from the main theatre of conflict, and in early 1317 King Robert led an army to his brother's aid. The two kings marched almost the length of Ireland, fending off attacks, before returning to Ulster. However, without such support, Edward's position was weak. During most of 1317 and 1318 all he could do was maintain his position in Ulster, where Carrickfergus was eventually taken, having failed to win fixed support elsewhere. In autumn 1318, after being reinforced, Edward sought to

---

[3] R.R.S., v, ed. Duncan, no. 424; *Chron. Lanercost*, 212–15; McNamee, *Wars of the Bruces*, 78–9; Summerson, *Medieval Carlisle*, ii, 215–19.

invade Leinster once more. At Fochart, near Dundalk, on 14 October the Scots met an Anglo-Irish army. In the ensuing fight Bruce was deserted by his Irish allies and crushed. The king of Ireland and his leading captains were slain, their bodies beheaded and quartered by the relieved victors. By December even Carrickfergus had been lost to the resurgent English.[4]

The warfare waged by the Bruces and their adherents between Bannockburn and Fochart was intended not to break a stalemate or simply secure peace. It was not surprising that leaders who had won a string of successes since 1307 were ready to seize the opportunity to extend their lordship beyond Scotland against a weakened enemy. Fochart brought an abrupt end to this short period of aggressive confidence, though not to Bruce involvement in either Ireland or northern England. Even before the defeat, the ambitions of the Bruce brothers were placing strains on Robert's adherents and realm. Though the summer of 1315 had seen Robert besieging Carlisle while Edward ravaged Ulster, thereafter major campaigns in one region required a defensive stance in the other, suggesting a need to husband men and supplies. Such difficulties would have been greatly increased by the deaths of several thousand seasoned Scottish and Hebridean adherents of the Bruces at Fochart. Six weeks after the defeat, Robert held a parliament at Scone. At this meeting statutes were passed specifying the equipment and discipline of the 'king's army'. With the loss of many veterans from his western power-base, the king sought to ensure the means to defend his realm in an atmosphere of fresh anxiety.[5]

The death of Edward Bruce also deprived the king of his last adult kinsman and one of the close-knit group of adherents who were entrusted with the leadership of the Bruce cause. By 1318 Thomas Randolph and James Douglas had emerged as Robert's chief military lieutenants. While Randolph campaigned in Ireland and England, Douglas built a reputation as the merciless harrier of northern England and defender of the Scottish marches. It was characteristic of his kingship that Robert also delegated wide powers of lordship and government to these war leaders. From 1309 Robert gave Randolph powers in the north, first as lieutenant then as a great magnate. Edward Bruce held a similar place in the south-west, as earl of Carrick and lord of Galloway. While Douglas received no great lordships until 1320, after Edward's departure he was clearly promoted as

---

[1] Lydon, 'The Bruce invasion of Ireland', 71–88; Frame, 'The Bruces in Ireland', 3–37; Duncan, 'The Scots invasion of Ireland, 1315'; Duffy, 'The Bruce brothers'; McNamee, *Wars of the Bruces*, 166–205.

[5] *R.R.S.*, v, ed. Duncan, no. 139.

Robert's principal officer in the marches in war and government. By giving such powers to his trusted supporters, the king sought to ensure that their lordship bolstered his rule in lands that lacked natural loyalties to the Bruce dynasty.[6]

Just as Robert sought to consolidate his control of the realm he had won in war, so he also sought to formalise relations within his own following. His queen, Elizabeth, and daughter, Marjory, were amongst those released in exchange for English lords captured following Bannockburn. Their return allowed Robert to think about the future of his line. Before 1315 that future had been limited to Edward Bruce who had acted as his brother's deputy and would surely have taken the kingship if Robert had died. Edward was not a man to step aside, and before he sailed in pursuit of the kingship of Ireland, Edward wished his rights in Scotland to be recognised. In late April 1315 at Ayr, whilst his expedition mustered, an ordinance was issued which named 'the energetic and experienced' Edward as heir to Robert should the king fail to have sons of his own. Lady Marjory's rights were set aside, a judgement which also reflected anxieties about a female succession after the preceding decades and fears about possible rivalry between Edward and Marjory's new husband, Walter Stewart. Robert's choice of Walter as his son-in-law strengthened the close bonds between the Bruces and their long-standing allies. The Stewarts were now part of the royal dynasty. However, by December 1318, these dynastic plans were in tatters. Marjory had died in 1316 after giving birth to a son and, with Edward's death, this infant, Robert Stewart, was named as the new heir in a second tailzie. The prospect of a long minority was recognised and Randolph was named as sole guardian in such a situation, with Douglas as his replacement. Douglas and Walter Stewart had already acted as wardens of the kingdom when Robert went to Ireland. The future of the dynasty and the leadership of the realm rested in the hands of a tight group of Bruce partisans.[7]

Robert's rule did not depend on these lieutenants. The fruits of royal patronage, the composition of the king's council and host encompassed a much wider section of the nobility. Though, not surprisingly, the principal roles were taken by men in the Bruce camp before 1314, like Gilbert Hay, Robert Keith and John Menteith, more recent adherents such as Earl Patrick of Dunbar, Alexander Seton and Philip Mowbray were also active in Robert's service. For some of these new supporters, however, the realities of Bruce kingship were hard to swallow. They generally recovered their lands and rights, but full rehabilitation could be slow. Though Robert was

[6]   *R.R.S*, v, ed. Duncan, nos 24, 28, 35, 101, 389; Brown, *The Black Douglases*, 20–6.
[7]   *R.R.S.*, v, ed. Duncan, nos 58, 301; *Scotichronicon*, 383; Barbour, *The Bruce*, 580–1.

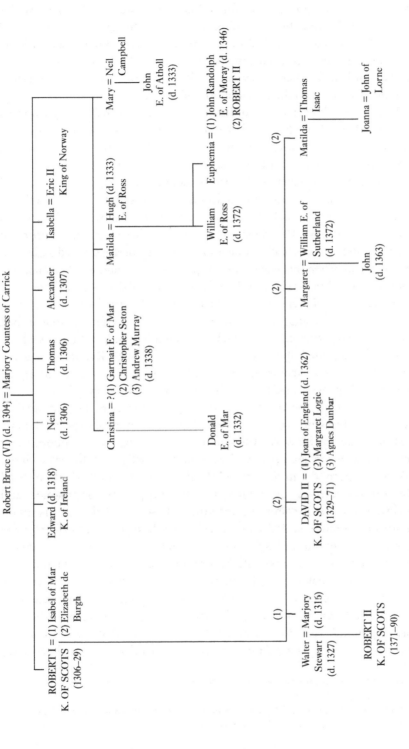

Robert Bruce (VI) (d. 1304), = Marjory Countess of Carrick

ROBERT I = (1) Isabel of Mar
K. OF SCOTS   (2) Elizabeth de
(1306–29)   Burgh

Edward (d. 1318)
K. of Ireland

Neil
(d. 1306)

Thomas
(d. 1306)

Alexander
(d. 1307)

Isabella = Eric II
King of Norway

Mary = Neil
Campbell

John
E. of Atholl
(d. 1333)

Christina = ?(1) Gartnait E. of Mar
(2) Christopher Seton
(3) Andrew Murray
(d. 1338)

Matilda = Hugh (d. 1333)
E. of Ross

Donald
E. of Mar
(d. 1332)

William
E. of Ross
(d. 1372)

Euphemia = (1) John Randolph
E. of Moray (d. 1346)
(2) ROBERT II

(1)

(2)

DAVID II = (1) Joan of England (d. 1362)
K. OF SCOTS   (2) Margaret Logie
(1329–71)   (3) Agnes Dunbar

(2)

Margaret = William E. of
Sutherland
(d. 1372)

(2)

Matilda = Thomas
Isaac

Walter = Marjory
Stewart   (d. 1316)
(d. 1327)

John
(d. 1363)

Joanna = John of
Lorne

ROBERT II
K. OF SCOTS
(1371–90)

Table 10.1. The Bruce Dynasty (1306–71)

clearly keen to retain new recruits to his peace, lords like William Soules and Ingeram Umfraville, whose families had fought hard for the realm and for the Balliol cause, now had to recognise the man who had seized King John's throne and favoured his own adherents. While the acceptance of Bruce's lordship by such men was a mark of the king's success, their lasting support depended on the continuation of that success.[8]

Even before Fochart, new difficulties emerged to shake King Robert's security. Though he had ridden out the sentence of excommunication passed on him for killing Comyn, Bruce was denied the recognition and sympathy of the papacy. In the late summer of 1317 envoys arrived from Pope John XXII instructing Robert to make a peace or truce with Edward II in the interests of Christendom. Robert recognised this move as a threat to his royal claims, which the envoys refused to acknowledge, and to his military ambitions. The most immediate of these was the capture of Berwick. Before a truce could be announced, Robert launched a siege of the town and, when this failed, was preparing to lay another when an intrepid friar arrived in his camp and read the papal bull declaring the two-year truce. Robert replied that he 'would have Berwick'. Finally, in spring 1318, the town was taken and garrisoned by the king's forces. James Douglas had said he would rather enter Berwick than paradise and, in the eyes of the papacy, he had made his choice. In June, along with Randolph and the king, Douglas was excommunicated and Scotland placed under an interdict. The Scots were absolved of their allegiance to the king.[9]

In themselves, the interdict and excommunication did not weaken Robert. English stories of clergy being killed for refusing to perform mass are unconvincing. However, the sentence on the king was compounded by news of Fochart in late 1318. At the December parliament, Robert ordered that 'conspirators' and 'inventors of tales and rumours' which aroused 'discord between the lord king and his people' be imprisoned and attainted. For the excommunicant king, whose only heir was his infant grandson, rumour and discord carried fresh fears. These fears were increased by news from England where, after the fall of Berwick, Edward II had struck a compromise with his opponents. During early 1319 Robert prepared for a major English attack, the first for five years. In May he received an offer from Edward which promised him life and peace if he recognised the direct lordship of the English king over Scotland. The offer was meant and treated as an insult. Robert replied that 'he did not care much for the king of England's peace', 'Scotland was his by hereditary

[8]   Penman, 'A fell coniuration agayn Robert the douchty king: the Soules conspiracy of 1318–20', 25–57, 36–8, 50–1.

[9]   *C.D.S.*, ii, nos 593–4; *R.R.S.*, v, ed. Duncan 140–5; Barrow, *Robert Bruce*, 246–7; Simpson, 'The Declaration of Arbroath revitalised', 11–33.

right and by right of battle' and 'he would acknowledge no earthly lord'. Neither his will nor his military skill had deserted Robert. During the summer Edward gathered an army which included five earls and in early September this force laid siege to Berwick. In response, Robert unleashed his lieutenants. Randolph and Douglas bypassed the English host and ranged through Northumberland and Yorkshire. On 12 September the Scots routed an army of local levies, led by the Archbishop of York at Myton-on-Swale. The threat they posed to Edward's kingdom and even to his queen and chancery at York broke the nerve and unity of the English army at Berwick. Led by Lancaster, whose lands were being harried, the host abandoned the siege and retreated. Robert and his men kept up the pressure and in December, with Berwick safe in his hands, the Scottish king agreed to a two-year truce with England.[10]

Though the military challenge had been warded off, other threats remained. In November 1319 the pope summoned four Scottish bishops to appear at the *curia* to answer for their actions and those of King Robert. Among them were the king's allies bishops Lamberton, Murray and William Sinclair of Dunkeld. The position of these prelates and a further pronouncement of excommunication against Robert prompted the king into action. In April 1320 letters were composed in the names of the king, of Bishop Lamberton and the clergy, and of the nobility and freeholders which presented the Bruce and Scottish case to Pope John. Although John neither recognised Robert as king nor lifted the sentences against him, and proceeded to excommunicate the bishops when they failed to appear before him, the pope's response to the letters was conciliatory, suggesting a more even-handed approach to the search for peace.[11]

The Letter of the Barons (6 April 1320)

The letter of the Scottish barons, better known as the Declaration of Arbroath, formed part of the Scottish approach to Pope John in early 1320. While the letters from king and clergy do not survive, this document was preserved in several versions and a number of manuscripts during the later middle ages. Its survival may not have been purely accidental. Instead it suggests that, from early on, the letter was recognised as having a significance beyond its immediate context which has led to its identification as the centrepiece of Scottish national ideology. This has accorded it a popular and hugely-inaccurate place as some form of declaration of Scottish independence. Though designed simply

---

[10] *R.R.S.*, v, ed. Duncan, 147, no. 139; Tuck, *Crown and Nobility*, 72–5; McNamee, *Wars of the Bruces*, 90–4; Barrow, *Robert Bruce*, 239–40; Barbour, *The Bruce*, 627–65.
[11] Simpson, 'The Declaration of Arbroath revitalised', 11–33.

The Letter of the Barons (6 April 1320) (*continued*)

to stave off papal censure, the ringing language and the coherence of its rhetoric do justify some of the claims made for the document.

The letter was issued in the names of eight earls, thirty-one named barons and 'the other barons and freeholders and whole community'. It laid out the case for the Scots and King Robert by dwelling on their rights as an ancient people ruled by an unbroken line of kings of native blood. Under these kings and under papal protection, the Scots had lived in peace until Edward I attacked them, causing immense damage to the people and to the church. The continuation of these attacks weakened Christendom in the face of 'the heathen' and was born of English avarice alone. Robert had delivered his people from this oppression and ruled by right, by the assent of his subjects and by 'divine providence'. Yet should he seek to make peace with England which threatened the rights of nobles and community, 'we would drive him out as our enemy and a subverter of his own right and ours ... For as long as one hundred of us remain alive, we will never ... be subjected to the lordship of the English. For we fight not for glory nor riches, nor honours, but for freedom alone.'

Such language is dramatic and inspiring but should be read in its context. This pledge of support and the conditions applied to Bruce's leadership had a specific purpose. The letter was designed to convince Pope John that Robert's intransigence was not the issue. Should Bruce bend to pressure, his subjects would remove him and continue their collective struggle. Kings of France and England had sought to deflect papal pressure by sending similar letters. In 1301 over 100 English lords had written to Boniface VIII stating that they would not allow Edward I to bow to the pope's demands that he abandon his claims in Scotland. The Bruces themselves had already used this approach. In the Irish Remonstrance of 1318 the claims of Edward Bruce were championed by the oppressed Irish in an approach to the pope. The letter of the barons was, like these documents, a piece of royal propaganda, presenting a case to the *curia*. It was almost certainly produced in the king's chancery and seals were attached, not in a great council, but individually over a number of weeks. Yet, despite this, as the strongest expression of the Scottish cause, perhaps even the most effective statement of the collective rights of a medieval people, the baron's letter deserves its place in the history of Scotland.[12]

---

[12] Barrow, 'The idea of freedom in late medieval Scotland', 26–32; Donaldson, 'The pope's reply to the Scottish barons in 1320', 119–20; Duncan, 'The making of the Declaration of Arbroath', 174–88; Simpson, 'The Declaration of Arbroath Revitalised', 11–33; Cowan, 'Identity, freedom and the Declaration of Arbroath', 38–44: Cowan, *'For Freedom Alone': The Declaration of Arbroath, 1320.*

The letters themselves were designed to present a united, communal front by the Scottish church and people in support of King Robert. The events of 1320 would reveal limits to this unity. The association of several lords with the letters to Pope John overlay deep distaste for Bruce's kingship which those letters championed. Such distaste was fuelled by a possible revival of the claims of the house of Balliol in the person of King John's son, Edward. In late 1318 Edward Balliol returned to England from his lands in France. The next year he served with the English king before Berwick and was retained in England alongside those Scots who had refused to enter Bruce's allegiance. His presence was highly significant. Inside Scotland were many nobles with ties of sympathy and kinship to Balliol and the Disinherited. These nobles had recognised Robert's kingship as a pragmatic means of retaining their lands in his realm and in the absence of an alternative source of royal lordship in Scotland. Edward Balliol now stood as an alternative and his presence in England was probably behind the conspiracy against his Bruce rival during the summer of 1320. The conspirators were linked together by their consistent opposition to Bruce before Bannockburn and by their kinship to the fallen house of Comyn. Their leaders were Agnes Comyn, countess of Strathearn, whose husband and brother had lost their earldoms in the wars against the Bruce party, and her nephew, William Soules. Soules had recovered his lands and office as royal butler and had even appeared on the king's council in May 1320, yet he was clearly unhappy with Robert's lordship. Though one account accused Soules of seeking the throne, most spoke of treason and conspiracy 'with other great men' to bring down the king. The restoration of a Balliol king would have been a cause more likely to attract the support of that family's former partisans. The price of this would probably have been acceptance of the English king as Balliol's overlord. This might have been unpalatable for many, but would have restored peace between the two realms on terms better than any offered since war began nearly a quarter of a century earlier. Soules and his accomplices would have secured influence and patronage from a grateful king and recovered lost estates in England. By 1320 some Scots may have seen Bruce as an obstacle to the secure re-establishment of a peaceful Scottish realm. In the summer of 1320 the conspirators began to muster their followers.[13]

King Robert struck first. Made aware of the plot, he rounded up Soules and the other conspirators, a group of perhaps a dozen nobles, and dispersed their retinues, while others led by the ex guardian, Ingeram

[13] Penman, 'Soules conspiracy', 38–46; Barbour, *The Bruce*, 698–703 and n; Fordun, ii, 341.

Umfraville, fled into England. Robert summoned a parliament to meet at Scone in August. The assembly imprisoned Soules and Countess Agnes, who confessed the plot, and sentenced to death four knights for the conspiracy and David, lord of Brechin for his failure to warn the king. Though others were acquitted of charges, the plans of the conspirators and their hopes of wider support were a reminder that, for all his successes, Robert remained a usurper in the eyes of some in his realm. However, the events of 1320 also revealed the strengths of Bruce's position. Two lords, Earl Patrick of Dunbar and Murdoch Menteith, had betrayed the plot to the king. Both were recent Bruce adherents who chose loyalty to the king in the crisis. Menteith was rewarded for his actions with an earldom, but such material motivations were probably bolstered by the recognition of Robert's strength and a desire to avoid a return to warfare waged within the Scottish realm. Though Robert would never be fully free from the factional rivalries which had divided the realm since the 1280s, the king had survived a series of challenges between 1318 and 1320 and retained the allegiance of most of his subjects.[14]

The forfeiture of his enemies at the so-called Black Parliament at Scone released Robert to act with a new confidence. In the spring of 1321 his envoys met English ambassadors for peace talks. These revealed the gap between the two sides. The Scots refused to negotiate on their master's full rights, and the English would not consider the abandonment of their king's claims to lordship over Scotland. Within months, however, English politics presented Robert with a chance to secure peace on his terms. The fragile truce between Edward II and his magnates was once more broken. By the end of 1321 war was raging between the king and his enemies. In the north, Edward's leading opponent, Thomas of Lancaster, sought new allies. He concluded a deal with King Robert. In return for an army led by the king or Randolph, the earl would reach a settlement with Bruce. Lancaster's move was probably a sign of his waning fortunes and cost him northern support. Though Randolph led a force into England, Lancaster could only retreat before the king's forces. He was seeking to reach the Scots when he was caught and defeated at Boroughbridge by a northern army under Andrew Harclay.[15]

The capture and execution of Lancaster crowned Edward's triumph and made the renewal of his war with Bruce inevitable. While Edward marshalled his forces, Robert, Randolph and Douglas harried the English marches. In August the English king marched north with nearly 20,000

[14] Penman, 'Soules conspiracy', 49–54.
[15] Maddicott, *Thomas of Lancaster*, 240–58, 301–17; *R.R.S.*, v, ed. Duncan, 150–2; *Foedera*, ii, 479.

men, ignoring Berwick and moving into Lothian. Far from guaranteeing success, the size of Edward's host led to its failure. Robert had stripped the south-east of herds and forage and then fallen back, and when Edward's supply fleet was delayed, his army was forced to retreat or starve. By early September the campaign was over. Though Edward remained in the north, his forces were disbanded. Robert seized his chance. He now crossed the border and harried Northumberland. In October the Scottish king led an army into Yorkshire, showing his mastery in war and seeking a decisive victory by capturing Edward. Whilst Edward escaped, he did so only after his remaining troops were routed at Byland. The 'chicken-hearted' king could tyrannise his own subjects but proved unable to defend his people against the Scots who now roamed through Yorkshire burning and looting. Northern England was desperate for peace and its leading protector, Andrew Harclay, made his own terms over the winter. This private peace was in open defiance of King Edward, whose response was to arrest and execute Harclay as a traitor. Despite this, Edward was forced to recognise the need to end the war. Though questions of lordship remained unanswered, in May 1323 a thirteen-year truce was agreed between the two kings.[16]

BRUCE KINGSHIP

Robert's task as king of Scots extended beyond meeting and fending off the challenges of war and disputed allegiance. He also needed to forge the structures of government and lordship which would cement the position of his dynasty. While the thirteenth-century monarchy provided a pattern for Bruce's kingship, Robert ruled a realm deeply affected by the impact and continuing needs of war. His success meant not a simple return to past relationships and rules, but a new personal and political balance. It was Robert, far more than Edward I, who had cut a swathe through the Scottish political establishment. The expulsion of the Balliols, Comyns, Strathbogies, Soules and a host of other barons severed bonds of lordship and family. Whole communities, in Atholl, in Badenoch, in Galloway, lost their natural heads. Between 1309 and 1320 such provinces and many lesser estates passed into Robert's hands through the forfeiture of their lords. These forfeited lands were not treated as additions to the possessions of the crown. Instead they were granted out to new owners. Moreover, from as early as 1309, Bruce showed a readiness to make permanent gifts of royal lands and rights to

[16] McNamee, *Wars of the Bruces*, 98–104.

his subjects. Hereditary custody of the sheriffships of Cromarty and Dumbarton was granted to the earls of Ross and Lennox, while lands from thirty of the royal thanages, the traditional centres of the king's revenues and residence, were given away. In the greatest acts of patronage, the crown's lands in the sheriffdoms of Elgin and Nairn were incorporated into Thomas Randolph's earldom of Moray, and lordship over the royal forests of Ettrick, Selkirk and Jedburgh was given to James Douglas. Even the lands Robert had held before 1306, Carrick, Annandale and Garioch, were granted out by the king amongst his close family.[17]

The hundreds of new grants of land made by King Robert were not blind generosity. Of magnate stock himself, Bruce understood aristocratic attitudes and interests and recognised the critical place of the nobility in his management of the kingdom. Land was the reward for service and adherence. Noble families like the Boyds and Lindsays in the south-west, or the Frasers, Keiths and Hays in the north-east received new estates from a king who remembered their support with gratitude. However, Robert was not simply concerned with the payment of political debts. His landed patronage represented a restructuring of the nobility, reforming the political class in his own image and interest. The promotion of men who had shown loyalty and ability in Bruce's cause strengthened King Robert's own position. The flow of lands to new owners in the aftermath of a Bruce victory bound these men and women to the defence of Robert's dynasty, creating special ties of land and loyalty between the king and much of the nobility. The return of the disinherited enemies of the Bruces was now a threat not just to the king, but to those who had benefited from his distribution of lands and rights.

As both royal officials and private lords, the nobility were the link between the crown and the localities. Robert's patronage aimed at the repair of connections disrupted by war and disinheritance. The king's most substantial grants were made in areas whose lords had been hostile to the Bruces, like Galloway and much of the north, or in the marches with England, where his rule was still challenged in war. In the north, Robert created Thomas Randolph as earl of Moray with a province formed from royal lands and the Comyn lordships of Badenoch and

---

[17] R.R.S., v, ed. Duncan, nos 78, 194, 389; R.M.S., i, app. 1, no. 38; Grant, 'Thanes and thanages', 65–6. Annandale was given to Thomas Randolph and Carrick to Edward Bruce, then Robert's son, David Bruce, and at the end of the reign to Edward's bastard, Alexander. Garioch was granted to Andrew Murray and his wife, Christina Bruce, the king's sister. For an excellent summary and interpretation of Robert's patronage and its effects, see Grant, *Independence and Nationhood*, 26–8. A much more detailed analysis is provided in Penman, 'The kingship of David II', 1–34.

Lochaber. Randolph was to bind these communities to King Robert's peace and balance the influence of the earls of Ross. Across the marches, Robert assigned lordships to a group of noblemen. Randolph was lord of Annandale, Douglas held Selkirk and Jed forests, and the king's bastard, Robert Bruce, was granted Liddesdale and Sprouston. For a ruler who faced far greater challenges to his rule than his predecessors before 1286, Robert needed to rely on his magnates as the upholders of his allegiance in threatened areas. His delegation of authority was marked by the grant of regality rights to Randolph, Douglas and others, exempting them from normal supervision by royal officials.[18]

By giving magnate status to his lieutenants, Douglas and Randolph, and to his bastard son, the king was creating a Bruce circle at the head of the nobility. Included in this group were not just the king's son-in-law and grandson, Walter and Robert Stewart, but his sisters' husbands. Andrew Murray, son of the leader of 1297, and Hugh, earl of Ross were from established northern houses who benefited from Robert's favour. This favour indicated the king's desire to draw in such families to his close circle and work with them where possible, avoiding unnecessary disruption to the structures of lordship for the sake of the stability and legitimacy of his regime. The same attitude was present in the king's relations with the old comital lines which stood at the head of the nobility. Despite upheavals, eight such families retained their earldoms at the end of Robert's reign and, as late as 1327, the king was ready to restore Earl Donald of Mar. His sense of the role played by the earls was also demonstrated by his indenture with Duncan of Fife in 1315 when the latter returned from England. Robert imposed harsh terms on Duncan but recognised the need for an earl of Fife who could inaugurate the king. Amidst political change, the king was keen to uphold the traditions of Scottish crown and nobility. This approach could not be universal. David Strathbogie was deprived of his earldom of Atholl for defecting before Bannockburn, and Angus was forfeited by the Umfravilles. Both were granted to Bruce adherents. John Campbell, the king's nephew, received Atholl, and John Stewart became earl of Angus. The strongest action was reserved for the earldom of Buchan. As the centre of Comyn lordship, Buchan was broken up, its lands partitioned and its title suppressed. The lordship of Galloway also lapsed after Edward Bruce's death. Though lands were granted to Bruce partisans in the province, no new lord was created. The lack of any magnate leadership may have contributed to the problems experienced in Galloway by the Bruce party in

[18] *R.R.S.*, v, ed. Duncan, no. 389; Brown, 'The development of Scottish border lordship', 1–22.

coming years and, as an exception, highlighted the general value of Robert's settlement.[19]

This redistribution of landed power went far beyond the twenty or so earls and great lords and their provinces. Major change also occurred amongst the lesser barons and royal tenants who provided leadership in the sheriffdoms of the east and south. In these sheriffdoms Robert granted out the minor estates of his magnate enemies, but also the holdings of their adherents, like Godfrey Ros in Ayrshire or the Mowats in the north-east. Even burgesses and freeholders suffered forfeiture in some areas. These forfeited lands were used to benefit a large group of Bruce partisans, amongst them local lords, such as Alexander Seton, Henry Sinclair and Robert Lauder in Lothian, who emerged as leading barons in their locality. Rewarded too were many lesser figures who had done vital service in the wars, like Douglas's tenant, Thomas Dicson, or William Francis, who had guided the attack on Edinburgh Castle. The king was ensuring that his committed adherents were given greater status and resources to lead his cause in their local communities.[20]

In the twenty years from 1309 Robert distributed lands and rights on a scale unparalleled in late medieval Scotland. His aim was to strengthen and extend the identification of the political class with the Bruce dynasty and its right to the throne. To achieve this the king gave away much in the way of powers and property. By creating massive regalities for Randolph and Douglas, and by adding to the lands and prestige of the Stewarts, Murrays and earls of Ross, Robert provided the material and ideological basis for the emergence of these houses as great regional magnates who would come to place limits on the reach and resources of the crown. Even during his own reign, the centres of Robert's kingship within Scotland became increasingly confined to the lands between the Forth and the Mounth, and round the Firth of Clyde. Though Berwick remained a key royal centre, Robert was an infrequent visitor to Lothian and the rest of the marches, as well as beyond the Mounth.[21] He was content to leave the management of these regions, which the thirteenth-century kings had supervised in person, to his magnates and officials. However, such delegation was the aim of Robert's patronage. The king could draw on the

[19]   R.R.S., v, ed. Duncan, nos 72, 405n; Young, 'The earls and earldom of Buchan in the thirteenth century', 198–9; Oram, 'Bruce, Balliol and the lordship of Galloway 29–47. Robert's reluctance to deprive existing comital houses was also evident in his readiness to allow Isabella Strathbogie, sister of Earl David and mistress of Edward Bruce, to hold the title of countess of Atholl (R.R.S., v, ed. Duncan, no. 372).
[20]   R.M.S., i, app. 2, nos 169, 181, 192, 253–8, 285 and passim.
[21]   For Robert's itinerary, see R.R.S., v, ed. Duncan, ch. 13; McNeill and MacQueen, Atlas of Scottish History, 167–70.

support of the men he had rewarded and there were few clashes of interest and ambition which disrupted the marches or the north. Instead
Robert's settlement prevented any one magnate from securing regional
dominance, allowing the crown to hold the political balance. The evidence shows that the king's court was able to settle the inevitable disputes
which arose from such regions, like that between the earl of Ross and
Andrew Murray, or between Douglas and Melrose Abbey.[22] His experiences must have made Bruce a pragmatist. A return to pre-war kingship
was not possible. The landed settlement solved his short-term need for
support and strengthened his hold within local communities now headed
by his men. Randolph and Douglas were only the most spectacular examples of this. Below them was a wider group equally anxious to rise in
Robert's service. His sheriffs, the key agents of local royal government,
were crucial to this. They came from varied backgrounds. Henry Balliol,
sheriff of Roxburgh, was a late convert to Bruce's party who came from a
local office-holding family, while Alexander Pilche in Inverness was from
a burgess background but had long-standing ties to Robert's cause.
Almost all the sheriffs, whether rising men or established officials, converts or loyalists, received new lands in their sheriffdoms from the king.
The royal household was also dominated by baronial adherents who had
benefited from Bruce patronage. However, the chamberlains, Alexander
Fraser and his successor, Reginald More, the justiciar of Lothian, Robert
Lauder, and other officers, like Malcolm Fleming and Alexander Seton,
were king's men through more than just material connections. From 1314
such men proved to be fixed in their allegiance to the dynasty and capable
of running a renewed and effective administration. There was far more to
the Bruce regime than Robert and his magnate kin and deputies.[23]

The king's generosity inevitably reduced the material resources of the
crown. In July 1326 in a parliament meeting at Cambuskenneth, Robert
sought financial assistance from the estates, arguing 'that the lands and
rents which used to belong to the crown had, by diverse donations and
transfers made on the occasion of war, been so diminished that he had not
the maintenance becoming his station'. The king justified his patronage
through the needs of war but his grants and alienations had clearly
impoverished his office by comparison with earlier kings. However,
Robert was not without income: financial records reveal the growing
value of rents and customs duties raised from the burghs which provided
nearly £3,000 for the crown at the end of the reign. Despite his patronage, the king could still draw on landed revenues. In 1325 he raised over

---

[22] *R.M.S.*, i, app. 2, nos 694, 702; *R.R.S.*, v, ed. Duncan, nos 166, 200–1.
[23] For the identity of Robert's sheriffs, see *E.R.*, i, 102–8.

£500 for work on Tarbert Castle from Atholl, Argyll and Islay, while royal lands were augmented by the king's temporary possession of church revenues, including incomes from the bishoprics of Aberdeen, Glasgow and St Andrews. However, during both war and relative peace Robert also copied his English opponents and resorted to *prise*, the seizure of goods from the king's subjects in return for promises of payment. Such practices were regarded as being to 'the intolerable burdening and grievance of the community' and the 1326 parliament extracted a promise that Robert would abandon *prise*. In return, the king received an annual subsidy. This tax, a tenth of lands and rents granted for his lifetime, marked the abandonment of the earlier practice of the crown 'living of its own'. Robert's patronage encouraged him and his successors to seek financial aid from their subjects in the manner of English kings.[24]

This approach to finance led to negotiations with the community in parliament. Robert followed established custom in seeking consent for taxation from his subjects and, after contemporary practice, called representatives from the burghs and free tenants to parliament to broaden the basis of this consent. As in England, Robert accepted that concessions could be asked in return for a grant of cash and also that such terms need not be honoured to the letter by the king. The wider attendance called to the 1326 parliament was not an indication of any wider royal dependence on the community. Despite holding regular meetings of the estates and the communal language of some Bruce propaganda, Robert did not regard his rule as any novel partnership between crown and community. From 1314 he called regular parliaments and secured communal consent for his legislation, financial demands and plans for the succession and guardianship. Scottish political experiences since 1280 may have encouraged Robert to secure such consent, and to lay detailed plans for an heir and a possible guardian. However, on all these issues, initiative and leadership came from the crown. Robert's achievements as the defender of the community were a source of strength and political advantage, not limitation. As he argued in 1326, Robert expected greater support from his subjects as 'in . . . both his person and his goods he had sustained many hardships for the recovery and protection of the liberties of them all'. In an assembly dominated by men used to his leadership and grateful for his patronage, any sense of shared interests was centred on Robert and his rights as king.[25]

Robert certainly admitted no new, general limits on these rights. Over fifty of his acts as king linked his rule to that of Alexander III 'our last predecessor'. It is hardly surprising that Robert refused to acknowledge

---

[24] *E.R.*, i, lxxix–ci, 52–100; *A.P.S.*, i, 475–6; Duncan, 'The early parliaments', 49, 55.
[25] *A.P.S.*, i, 475–6.

the rule and claim of the Balliols, but Bruce was also claiming for his kingship the full traditional powers of the old royal dynasty. For all his grants
of provincial lordship, Robert pursued the full territorial interests of
King Alexander, from his grants in Tynedale to his recovery of Man in
the 1320s. Even where direct lordship was delegated to magnates, Robert
did not relinquish his power to intervene. Just as Berwick was a royal base
in the south, so Robert built a manor house on the Clyde at Cardross and
enlarged Tarbert Castle in Kintyre to provide him with windows on
western isles and seas. Though greater now in extent, such overkingship
had long been part of Scottish royal practice. Neither did Robert admit a
loss of royal rights over the Scottish church. His willingness to confirm
and increase the benefactions of the crown to monastic houses sprang
partly from a desire to maintain the role of patron taken by his forebears.
Houses that had suffered in war, like Deer Abbey in Buchan or Melrose
in the marches, received fresh endowments from a ruler anxious to be
seen as the restorer of the church as well as of secular government. Such
anxieties occurred in the context of Robert's desire to ensure authority
over the church against the hostility of England and the papacy. As will
be discussed later, his direction of the church's ideological and material
resources was vital. As early as 1309 the king appointed clerical adherents
to administer the lands of the bishopric of Glasgow during Bishop
Wishart's captivity. After Wishart's death in 1316 the choice of his successor was a major test of Robert's ability to control episcopal elections.
His first candidate was rejected and it took six years before the second,
John Lindsay, was accepted by the papacy. Lindsay's consecration in 1323
was a mark of improving relations with Pope John, and future elections
passed off more smoothly. However, even when the king was in conflict
with the pope between 1318 and 1320, Robert seems to have been able to
maintain his influence on the church hierarchy without much difficulty.
Their relationship in this period was highlighted by the assembly at St
Andrews on 5 July 1318. Here, in the presence of King Robert, numerous nobles, seven bishops and fifteen abbots, William Lamberton, bishop
of St Andrews, dedicated his cathedral. The ceremony completed work
under way since the twelfth century and Robert reportedly marked the
occasion with an annuity of 100 marks to the church in thanks for
Bannockburn. These events maintained the alliance of crown and episcopate and this was reflected too in major gatherings of Scottish clergy
which met under his auspices on at least two occasions in the 1320s.[26]

[26] *E.R.*, i, 52–8, 123–36; Reid, 'Crown and community under Robert I', 203–22;
Barrow, *Robert Bruce*, 264–7, 319; *R.R.S.*, v, ed. Duncan, nos 48, 269; Watt, *Medieval
Church Councils in Scotland*, 111–13.

Robert's determination to retain the rights of the crown occurred in circumstances very different from those of the thirteenth-century kings. For all his success, Bruce was still the first of a new dynasty whose legitimacy, though not challenged openly in Scotland in the decade from 1320, was still subject to doubts. Such doubts heightened the significance and sensitivity of Robert's exercise of power. During the 1320s the king remained preoccupied with securing his achievements. Central to this was the question of the succession. In 1324 Queen Elizabeth gave birth to twin sons. Though one died in infancy, the survivor, David, was formally named as heir to the throne in the parliament of 1326. The prospect of a second Bruce king of Scots was renewed but the chance of Robert bequeathing his throne to an adult successor had receded. David was seven years younger than his nephew, the previous heir, Robert Stewart, and it was unlikely that he would reach adulthood before the death of King Robert who was in his fifties and had endured poor health. In the mid-1320s, however, the birth of the king's son added to the immediate sense of security. Contemporary verses spoke of 'fortunate David' who 'has heartened the doubters . . . Rejoice therefore, Scots and have no fear'.[27] David's father was at the height of his power – Robert enjoyed the support of a wide network of nobles, clerics and lesser men, ruling without apparent friction and able to use the needs of war to bolster his powers as king, whilst not seeing his lordship tested by defeat. However, for as long as the war against the claims of the English kings and disinherited Scots continued unsettled, Robert's achievement was not safe. Despite the truce of 1323, Edward II maintained a diplomatic campaign at the papal *curia* against Bruce's claims. Elsewhere, however, recognition was being won. Robert's position was aided by the outbreak of war between Edward and King Charles IV of France which led to a formal Franco-Scottish alliance being agreed at Corbeil in 1326.[28] Settlement in England was only achieved as a result of renewed political conflict within the Plantagenet dominions. In the summer of 1326 Edward II's hugely-unpopular regime collapsed under the attack of his exiled enemies led by his own queen, Isabella, and her lover, Roger Mortimer. In November Edward was captured and in January 1327 his enemies deposed him in favour of his son who was crowned Edward III. This instability was an invitation for Robert. In late 1326 his nephew Donald, earl of Mar arrived in Scotland. Mar had grown up in England and was a close friend of Edward II. He now sought his uncle's help for the captive king. Robert

[27] *Scotichronicon*, vii, 12–15.
[28] Macdougall, *An Antidote to the English: The Auld Alliance, 1295–1560* 25–7; McNamee, *Wars of the Bruces*, 239.

agreed but had his own agenda. At Easter 1327 Robert crossed to Ulster where he claimed the earldom of his father-in-law, Richard de Burgh, who had died the previous year. Bruce's presence threatened the new English regime and the English colony with a renewed Scottish presence in Ireland and, exploiting Anglo-Irish fears, Robert offered a separate peace between Scotland and the colony. Whilst the king spent four months in Ulster, the English government raised forces for an attack against Scotland. The campaign merely reaffirmed Scottish dominance. Whilst Robert remained in Ireland, an army led by Randolph, Douglas and Mar entered northern England and totally outmanoeuvred their enemies. Edward III was humiliated, whilst the campaign left his government bankrupt, both financially and politically, and fearful of Bruce's next move.[29]

The regency of Isabella and Mortimer was much more vulnerable to military pressure than Edward II had been. For the first time, an English government was ready to seek peace in language acceptable to Robert. In October 1327 terms were proposed and quickly accepted, and in the spring of 1328 the peace was ratified at Edinburgh and Northampton. By this treaty Edward III renounced his claim to lordship over Scotland and Robert Bruce was recognised as king of Scots, without any subjection, over all the dominions of Alexander III. In return the Scots would pay £20,000 for the peace. The treaty was cemented by a marriage between David Bruce and Edward III's sister, Joan, which took place in a lavish ceremony at Berwick in July 1328. Ominously, however, neither king was present. Edward III and many of his subjects regarded the treaty as a 'shameful peace' which surrendered the rights of the crown, and the Londoners refused to allow the stone of Scone to be returned to Scotland. Robert had secured recognition from an English government which was increasingly discredited and which ruled in the name of a teenage king, hostile to its actions. When Edward III seized power in 1330, imprisoning his mother and hanging Mortimer, it revealed the fragility of the treaty of Edinburgh-Northampton.[30]

By then King Robert was dead. His absence from his son's wedding was probably the result of the illness which rendered him increasingly bedridden and which later writers have suggested was leprosy. Though the king was able to travel by ship to Ulster in August 1328, returning via

[29] Nicholson, *Edward III and the Scots*, 15–41; McNamee, *Wars of the Bruces*, 240–5; Nicholson, 'A sequel to Edward Bruce's invasion of Ireland', 34; Frame, *English Lordship in Ireland, 1318–1361*, 139–42.
[30] Nicholson, *Edward III and the Scots*, 42–56; Stones, *Anglo-Scottish Relations*, nos 40–1; Stones, 'The Anglo-Scottish negotiations of 1327', 49–54; Stones, 'The English mission to Edinburgh in 1328', 97–118; Tuck, *Crown and Nobility*, 75–80.

Tarbert and Arran, his movements by land were more limited. His final journey took him from his ancestral castle of Turnberry to the shrine of St Ninian at Whithorn in early 1329. From there he returned to his house at Cardross where he died on 7 June. At the end of his life Robert showed the same combination of pragmatic flexibility and fixed ambition which had characterised his career as magnate and king. A determination to secure his rights as king of Scots had driven Robert's actions for three decades. For Robert the payment of £20,000 for a peace with a tottering minority regime made sense in the short-term. Even temporary recognition by the English king for his rights was a vital achievement, raising the status of his dynasty and office at home and in Europe. After a life at war, Robert died with his realm at peace.[31]

Since 1314 Robert I had done all one man could to safeguard his dynasty and regime, but also to secure Scotland as a separate realm. Bruce's achievements made him the decisive figure in the whole period of war and crisis between 1286 and the 1350s. Without his ability, without his ambition, Scotland's future would have been very different. Yet Robert's legacy was never simply that of a champion of his people. The Bruce was a partisan figure, hated as well as supported by his contemporaries in Scotland. His goals were personal and dynastic, stretching beyond the Scottish realm but centred on the kingship. These ambitions were disruptive and destructive, achievable only by the elimination of many leading Scots. Yet they also proved decisive. In pursuit of them, Bruce renewed the war in 1306, providing a focus of allegiance which, during the next two decades, harnessed traditional loyalties and wider sentiments to his private cause. This alignment was dependent, above all, on Robert's ability. In war his actions were characterised by controlled risk-taking, balancing sustained aggression with a good sense of the odds and objectives of his efforts. In politics he was equally clear-eyed, ready to buy allegiance and to stamp out opposition depending on the situation. Without Robert's personal skill and his ability to choose and use men with their own qualities, neither the Bruce cause nor the Scottish cause would have been restored in the long years after 1306.

Not even the Bruce's efforts could guarantee the future of his dynasty and kingdom after his death. Robert's success and its limitations would be demonstrated in the opening years of his son's reign. Initially things went well. Though David II was a child of five, the transition of power was smooth. As intended, the able and experienced Thomas Randolph, earl of Moray acted as guardian of the realm. Randolph retained the

---

[31] Nicholson, 'A sequel to Edward Bruce's invasion of Ireland', 36; *R.R.S.*, v, ed. Duncan, pp. 156–7; *Scotichronicon*, vii, 44–5.

services of the key figures in the old king's household and council and successfully completed the payment of the money owed for the treaty. The minority government felt sufficiently secure to delay the crowning of the new king for over two years. In November 1331 David II was made king of Scots at Scone with the full rite of coronation. The privilege, which had been sought by Scotland's rulers for over a century, was bestowed by Pope John in 1329. Edward III's renunciation of his rights to superior lordship over Scotland had removed any doubts about the status of Scotland's kings. Anointed with holy oil as a mark of sacred power, David II enjoyed the benefit of his father's efforts.[32]

However, any optimism at the coronation must have been tempered by an awareness of problems. Bishop Lamberton's death in 1328 had removed a valuable source of ecclesiastical leadership. His demise, followed by the loss of Robert's commanding presence, allowed the first cracks to develop within the Bruce party. The departure of James Douglas for Spain, bearing the old king's heart in war with the infidel, may have been designed to remove a lord who, though undoubtedly a valuable military leader, was also a difficult presence for Randolph. The guardian's relationship with young Robert Stewart may have shown signs of a similar rivalry. Without their king, the competitive instincts of these magnate houses would become more apparent. More worryingly, Bruce's death revealed the patchiness of his settlement. There remained lords and communities whose attachment to the dynasty was less certain and secure than the old king hoped. In only two decades Robert and his partisans could not expunge all established loyalties which did not conform to their view of the kingdom. In exile stood the Disinherited, claimants to Scottish lands and lordships whose families had been expelled by Bruce before 1314 or after the conspiracy of 1320. These nobles were ready to exploit new flaws amongst their enemies and renew old contacts within Scotland. Robert was aware of the danger posed by the connections of these lords in his realm and had excluded discussion of their claims from the terms of the 1328 treaty. It would be against the Disinherited and their backer, Edward III, that the achievement of King Robert in securing the allegiance of Scots for his dynasty would be tested in the coming years.[33]

---

[32] *Scotichronicon*, vii, 56–7; *Nat. MSS Scot.*, ii, no. 30.
[33] Nicholson, *Edward III and the Scots*, 57–74; Penman, 'The kingship of David II', 69–75; *Scotichronicon*, ix, 58–9.

CHAPTER 11

The War of the Three Kings (1332–57)

THE RETURN OF THE DISINHERITED (1332–41)

War returned to Scotland as a struggle for crown and kingdom between the rival dynasties and parties which had divided the realm for forty years. The opposing factions were the new Bruce establishment and those who had been expelled and disinherited to make way for it. In the early 1330s these Disinherited saw their opportunity and, like Robert Bruce in 1306, launched a war to win their rights. Now they, and not the Bruce party, had an adult leader. Edward Balliol was not prepared to accept his father's defeat and in 1331 travelled to England to provide the focus for a group of lords who sought to overturn Bruce's victory. Amongst this group were native Scots – David Strathbogie, claimant to Atholl and Badenoch, and the Mowbrays – whom Robert I had forfeited in 1320. There were also Anglo-Scottish families – the Umfravilles and Ferrars – who had lost their Scottish lands for remaining in the English camp. Finally, there were the husbands of Comyn heiresses: the Englishman Gilbert Talbot and the French lord, Henry Beaumont, whose wife, Alice Comyn, was heiress to Buchan. In their own eyes, these lords were not just adventurers bent on private gain. Instead, from Edward Balliol down, they were men and women seeking rights denied them by Robert's usurpation of King John's throne. In 1332 they began military preparations, even though Edward III of England refused his open support. The English king was wary of renewing a war which had been so disastrous in the preceding decades and denied the Disinherited land access to Scotland. Despite this, in July Balliol and his allies assembled a small army and fleet in the Humber estuary for a descent on the Scottish coast.[1]

---

[1] Nicholson, *Edward III and the Scots*, 57–79; Cameron and Ross, 'The treaty of Edinburgh and the Disinherited (1328–32); Ross, 'Men for all seasons, 2', 1–15, 8–9.

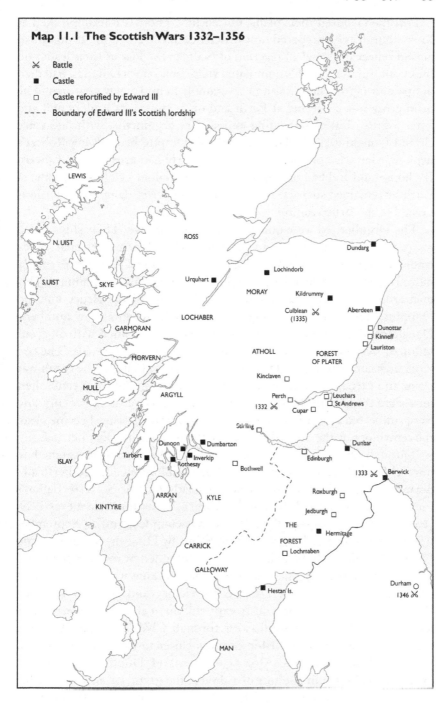

Map 11.1 The Scottish Wars 1332–1356

✗   Battle

■   Castle

☐   Castle refortified by Edward III

– – – –   Boundary of Edward III's Scottish lordship

LEWIS

N. UIST

ROSS

Dundarg ■

S.UIST

SKYE

Urquhart ■

Lochindorb ■

MORAY

Kildrummy ■

Culblean ✗
(1335)

Aberdeen ■

LOCHABER

GARMORAN

☐ Dunottar
☐ Kinneff
☐ Lauriston

MORVERN

ATHOLL

FOREST
OF PLATER

MULL

Kinclaven ☐

ARGYLL

Perth ■
1332 ✗

☐ Leuchars
☐ St Andrews

Cupar ☐

Stirling ☐

Dunoon ■

Dumbarton ■

Dunbar ■

Tarbert ■

Inverkip ■
Rothesay ■

Bothwell ☐

Edinburgh ☐

1333 ✗   Berwick ■

ISLAY

Roxburgh ☐

ARRAN

KYLE

Jedburgh ☐

KINTYRE

THE

Hermitage ■

CARRICK

FOREST

Lochmaben ☐

GALLOWAY

Durham ○
1346 ✗

Hestan Is. ■

MAN

Fortune favoured their plans. On 20 July Thomas Randolph died at Musselburgh as he prepared for the defence of the kingdom. Rumours of poison reflect the shocked reaction of Scots to the loss of their leader on the eve of war. Randolph's nominated successor, James Douglas, had died in Spain in 1330. There was now a scramble to find a new guardian. The main army was gathering at Perth and on 2 August its leaders met and 'after a great deal of wrangling and sundry arguments, with one voice elected Donald earl of Mar as guardian'. Despite being King Robert's nephew, Mar was not a comfortable choice. He had grown up in Edward II's household and had previously supported Balliol's claims. To some at Perth he remained suspect. At the moment of crisis, dangerous divisions existed in the Bruce camp.[2]

The Disinherited were quick to seize the initiative. Their ships sailed on 31 July and were already in the Forth when Mar was elected. They landed at Kinghorn on 6 August and, after routing a local force, swiftly moved against their enemies at Perth. Early on 11 August, Balliol and his men crossed the river Earn and faced the army of the Bruce king on Dupplin Moor. Despite having a considerable advantage in numbers, Donald of Mar faced problems. His council of war ended with an accusation of treason against him from Robert Bruce of Liddesdale. The two lords then competed to lead the opening attack on Balliol. The result was chaos and carnage. While the leaders were killed in the front rank, their men were trapped in the crush as they pressed towards the enemy, and were suffocated and cut down in hundreds. As the disaster became clear, the remainder of the army fled, leaving the field to the Disinherited.

Through the late summer of 1332, Balliol's victory threatened to unravel King Robert's achievement. The Disinherited entered Perth and during the next six weeks there was a steady flow of Scots to Balliol's camp, especially from Fife and Strathearn, areas that had never been centres of Bruce support. Balliol's rise was completed on 24 September when he was crowned king of Scots at Scone by Duncan, earl of Fife and Bishop Sinclair of Dunkeld in a ceremony attended by many prelates and lords from the region. The position of the new king was not unlike that of Robert Bruce in 1306. Despite his victory and signs of support, Balliol's position was dangerously exposed. Soon after his coronation he left Perth and marched south-west through Clydesdale and Ayrshire, seeking to establish his lordship in areas closer to English support and where he had family ties. Already, on news of Dupplin, the men of Galloway had risen in support of Edward, the grandson of Dervorgilla, acclaiming him as their 'special chieftain'. Balliol passed through the

[2] *Chron. Lanercost*, 268–9; *Scotichronicon*, vii, 72–3.

province, rallying support, and crossed the marches, fending off attacks, before occupying Roxburgh.[3]

Edward's move south was prompted by the recovery of his enemies. The deaths of Mar and many other nobles had rocked the Bruce party, but by September there were new leaders and forces in the field. In early October Perth was recaptured from Duncan of Fife and another force harried Galloway and pursued Balliol. This campaign was led by the new guardian, Andrew Murray, King David's uncle, and though Murray was captured soon afterwards in a skirmish, his loss did not end the recovery. In December Archibald Douglas, brother of Sir James, John Randolph, son of Earl Thomas, and Robert Stewart, King Robert's grandson, led an attack on Balliol and his household at Annan. Many were killed and Edward and the rest were forced to flee to Carlisle. In the wake of the victory, its architect, Archibald Douglas, was named guardian. Like Wallace's appointment thirty-five years before, this choice reflected military needs. Douglas would be the first of a new generation of leaders whose skill in war won them political power.[4]

The expulsion of Balliol merely made that war bigger. As early as November Edward had sent adherents to the English parliament offering to perform homage in return for military aid. When parliament resumed at York in January 1333, the request was renewed. Despite continued opposition from his subjects, the young English king, Edward III, was keen to raise his rights to Scotland. Support was given to the Disinherited and from March attacks were launched into Scotland. Balliol himself marched to Berwick and laid siege to the town. When Douglas led a counter-raid, it was used by Edward III to justify open preparations for war. On 9 May the English king joined Balliol at Berwick. During the rest of the month, men, ships, supplies and siege engines flowed into his camp. In response Douglas raised an army from all over Scotland. In early July he led it in an audacious campaign through Northumberland, aiming to repeat his brother's success of 1319 and break the siege of Berwick. Now, however, it was the Scots who broke under pressure. Edward III maintained his siege and the defenders agreed to surrender if not relieved by 20 July. Douglas would not abandon Berwick. On 19 July he marched on the town. His enemies were ready. They had chosen their ground on Halidon Hill outside Berwick. When the Scots host tried to batter its way through, they were cut down by archery. The guardian, five earls, scores

[3] *Chron. Lanercost*, 269–74; *Scotichronicon*, vii, 72–81; Nicholson, *Edward III and the Scots*, 84–97; Webster, 'Scotland without a King, 1329–41', Grant and Stringer, *Medieval Scotland*, 223–38, 229–30.

[4] *Scotichronicon*, vii, 82–5; *Chron. Lanercost*, 274–5; Nicholson, *Edward III and the Scots*, 103–4; Brown, *The Black Douglases*, 33–4.

of barons and knights and thousands of footmen were left dead on the hillside. In a way unthinkable under King Robert's leadership, Douglas had risked battle for the sake of the defence of one town and he had met defeat. The scale of the loss remained to be seen.[5]

Edward III left to others the exploitation of the greatest English victory for a generation. Having secured Berwick, he returned south on 10 August. Instead Balliol resumed his quest for the kingdom, crossing Scotland to Renfrew before marching north to hold a parliament at Scone on 17 September. Though support from within the kingdom remained limited, Earl Duncan of Fife and Earl Malise of Strathearn pledged allegiance to Balliol. At the meeting the rights of the Balliols were proclaimed. Edward Balliol 'revoked and quashed all the deeds and grants of Robert Bruce who had forced himself on the throne'. The Disinherited were restored. Strathbogie received Atholl and Badenoch and the forfeited lands of the Stewarts, while Beaumont was named earl of Buchan. English and Disinherited received lands and promises in a display of patronage designed to commit them to an ongoing war. Over the next nine months magnates pursued their own claims and, as far north as Buchan and Badenoch and as far west as Bute, gained recognition and submission from local communities. However, Balliol was no longer acting alone. By September Edward III was seeking his price for military support. The terms were agreed in a second parliament, held at Edinburgh on 1 February 1334 and attended by English envoys. The Scottish king would perform liege homage for his realm to the king of England. Balliol owed military service to his lord but, in recognition of previous problems, was freed from the legal superiority of the English crown. However, the agreement was not limited to the issue of homage. Balliol would also surrender much of the south of his realm to Edward III's direct lordship. On 5 June 1334 Edward, king of Scots did homage at York and ceded to the English king lands and lordships in eight sheriffdoms south of the Forth.[6]

The treaty left Scotland divided between three kings. The kingdom, already disputed between the rival allegiances to Bruce and Balliol kings, was now partitioned between the lands ruled by Balliol as a vassal, and the Scottish lordships of Edward III. For the two Edwards the prospects of fulfilling their agreement must have appeared good. Balliol, aided by English resources and the private ambitions of the Disinherited, faced little opposition. However, instead of securing victory, the allies misjudged their position. Edward III's failure to campaign in Scotland

---

[5] *Chron. Lanercost*, 278–81; Nicholson, *Edward III and the Scots*, 106–38.

[6] *Chron. Lanercost*, 283–4; *Scotichronicon*, vii, 92–3, 102–3; *Rot. Scot.*, i, 261, 269–71; Nicholson, *Edward III and the Scots*, 139–62.

during late 1333 missed the chance to exploit Halidon fully. The next summer, though he appointed officials to run his Scottish lands, Edward did little to back up these English and Scottish adherents. Moreover, friction broke out over the division of spoils. The English king did not trust Balliol to honour his promises and even threatened to negotiate with the Bruce camp. Balliol himself became embroiled in a dispute with his supporters Strathbogie and Beaumont, which led to them failing to co-operate in the summer of 1334. Such disputes reflected a sense of overconfidence which was also manifest in the release of two prisoners, Andrew Murray and William Douglas of Lothian, who would prove to be their leading enemies in coming years.[7]

After Halidon this confidence was not surprising. The Bruce party put up little resistance to their opponents. Many of their leaders had been killed, removing local sources of command. Amongst the survivors, John Randolph was in France, whilst Robert Stewart was forced to flee from Rothesay in the face of Balliol's adherents. Stewart took refuge in Dumbarton, joining King David in one of the last Bruce strongholds. Had Dumbarton fallen in late 1333, the Bruce cause may have fallen with it. When Randolph returned to Scotland with the first indication of the French support which would be so vital, it was decided to send David to France for safety. In May 1334 the young king and his English queen set sail for the continent with a small household. Within weeks of David's departure his adherents renewed the active struggle. Bruce lords like Randolph and Stewart, whose lands had been distributed between their enemies, had no place in the Balliol regime and led the fight back. Stewart raised a fleet from Cowal and with it recovered Bute with the help of his unfree tenants and crossed to the mainland, where the tenants of the Stewarts and Bruces from Renfrew to Carrick rose in his support as they had backed his grandfather in 1307. The rule of Balliol and Edward III proved to be fragile. In Annandale and Lothian, communities that had been quiet over the winter began to cause trouble. Their leaders were local knights like William Douglas of Lothian, a cousin of James and Archibald, who gathered bands and harried the English. By late July the Steward and Randolph were acting as guardians and, aided by Douglas and other local leaders, were taking the war into Galloway. In the following months they exploited divisions in the enemy camp to tackle their chief foes in isolation. Beaumont, who had occupied Buchan, was besieged in Dundarg Castle and forced to leave Scotland, while Strathbogie was faced by his rival in the north, John Randolph. Strathbogie was brought to bay in Lochaber and in late September negotiated a submission. He entered the

---

[7] *Scotichronicon*, vii, 94–5.

Bruce allegiance, but his continued influence in the north meant the terms were generous and included restoration of lands and offices and his appointment as Randolph's lieutenant in the region.[8]

With the fall of his adherents, Edward Balliol fled to Berwick. Once again he was forced to seek English aid, but the English king's response was slow. With a small army he came north and wintered at Roxburgh, raiding surrounding districts before withdrawing in February 1335. His campaign did not halt defections to the Bruce camp. By early April the leaders of King David's cause were campaigning in Fife. However, like its enemies, the Bruce party was also split by rivalries. At a 'parliament' held at Dairsie near Cupar, a dispute erupted between David Strathbogie and William Douglas. Douglas was backed by Randolph, while Earl David had the support of the Steward. The dispute increased the rivalry between the two young guardians. After the council, a number of Stewart's men were removed from their offices and Robert refused to co-operate with Randolph.[9]

Such animosities came at a dangerous time for the Bruce cause. Following a French-brokered truce, the English king was, once more, at the border in July, this time backed by massive forces. While Edward III led one army north from Carlisle into Clydesdale, Balliol marched with a second from Berwick through Lothian to Glasgow. From there the two armies moved to the Forth, crossing with the aid of a fleet and making their base at Perth in early August. A second fleet then sailed from Ireland to harry the isles and coasts round the Clyde. In the face of this ambitious campaign, the leading Bruce partisans reverted to the precepts of their old master, avoiding battle and harrying their enemies' supply routes. This yielded one success, when Randolph captured Edward III's ally, the Count of Namur, at Edinburgh, but the gains from this were lost with Randolph's own treacherous capture soon afterwards. By August the pressure of Edward's advance was telling. Fife submitted to Balliol once again. John of Islay, head of Clan Donald, was already in talks with Edward III, and negotiations were now opened between Balliol and two leading Scots lords, Strathbogie and the Steward. An agreement was struck which guaranteed private interests but which was also concerned with protection for the laws, church and customary government of Scotland. In these respects the terms resembled the peace conditions brokered by John Comyn in 1304. While Strathbogie was probably keen to return to his allies, Stewart's defection was a response to military pres-

---

[8] *Scotichronicon*, vii, 102–9; *Scalchronica*, 97–8; Nicholson, *Edward III and the Scots*, 156–7, 163–73; Ross, 'Men for all seasons, 2', 10–11.

[9] *Scotichronicon*, 106–9; Penman, 'The kingship of David II', 82–5.

sure and the surrender of many lesser lords during the autumn may have encouraged Edward III and Balliol to expect a wider submission. By October both were on the road south, leaving Earl David to continue the war. With the backing of his family's continuing connections in the region, Strathbogie energetically pursued the remaining Bruce partisans in the north-east, earning a later reputation for tyranny.[10]

Despite defections, the Bruce party remained in the field. In Lothian local leaders like Douglas and Alexander Ramsay waged war from refuges in hills and deep valleys. Nearby were also bands under Andrew Murray and Earl Patrick Dunbar. These leaders had endured considerable pressure and in early November 1335 accepted a truce and opened peace talks with the English. Such negotiations bought time and, perhaps with the hope of making further gains in the north, Balliol's partisans were left out of the truce. In these circumstances, the Bruce captains recognised Strathbogie as the most immediate threat to their cause. News that the earl was besieging Murray's wife, Christina Bruce, in Kildrummy Castle led Andrew, acting once again as guardian, to gather a small army and march swiftly north. Beyond the Mounth he was joined by northern neighbours under Earl William of Ross. On St Andrews Day this host met Strathbogie's force at Culblean near the Dee. In a short bloody fight Earl David was killed and his followers scattered.[11]

Strathbogie's death removed the one magnate with the ability and influence to uproot the Bruce party from the north but, despite Culblean, King David's partisans still faced a major struggle. After the battle, Murray was able to campaign as far as Fife and summon a council at Dunfermline which confirmed him as guardian and recalled defectors, such as Stewart, to the cause. However, all parties spent the winter waiting on negotiations designed to end the conflict by recognising Balliol's rights as king with David Bruce as his heir. It was not until March that, with Philip of France's backing, David rejected the proposal. By then Murray was back in the north, seeking to confirm the region in Bruce allegiance. Murray was also responding to his enemies' preparations for a fresh campaign. In May Edward Balliol entered Perth which Murray had burned, and in June Edward of England arrived after

[10] *Chron. Lanercost*, 290-1; *Scalachronica*, 98-100; *Scotichronicon*, vii, 112-15; Adam Murimuth and Robert Avesbury, *Chronica* (London, 1889), 298-302; Nicholson, *Edward III and the Scots*, 203-28; Rogers, *War, Cruel and Sharp: English Strategy under Edward III*, 96-102.

[11] *Scotichronicon*, vii, 114-17; *Chron. Lanercost*, 294; Nicholson, *Edward III and the Scots*, 229-36. A different construction in which Atholl was the victim of collaboration between Balliol and the Bruce leaders has recently been suggested in Ross, 'Men for all seasons, 2', 11-12.

sending a second force to ravage Carrick and the Stewart lands. When he heard that Murray was besieging Lochindorb Castle in Badenoch, which was still held by Strathbogie's widow, Katherine Beaumont, the English king rushed north with a retinue. Edward relieved the castle, rescued the countess and, less romantically, devastated the province of Moray before burning Aberdeen on his return. Though the foray took Edward III as far north as his grandfather had ever reached, this was no campaign of conquest but a *chevauchée* aimed at the destruction of enemy land which could not be held. Edward was responding to a new threat. In France Philip VI was assembling a fleet to bring troops to Scotland. By burning Aberdeen and wasting the north, Edward hoped to deny it a base. The campaign marked a shift in strategy. In his own lands and Balliol's realm, Edward III rebuilt and garrisoned castles. Works were carried out at Edinburgh, Stirling, Roxburgh, Bothwell and elsewhere but the key stronghold was to be Perth. The town was fortified at the expense of local clergy and housed a small army. Around it were a network of garrisons from Kinclaven on the Tay to Dunottar on the coast, and at Cupar, Leuchars and St Andrews in Fife. Edward was seeking to defend the approaches to this defended pale from the, now hostile, north. Hopes of outright victory, still cherished in 1335, were now replaced by a defensive attitude. Though Edward III and Balliol secured a valuable ally in September when John of Islay paid homage to them, the English king was now seeking to contain his enemies. Anxieties about growing French support for the Bruce cause may have been partly responsible but Edward was not writing off his Scottish ambitions. He spent most of the second half of the year supervising the defence of these lands and interests.[12]

However, even before Edward's departure in December, his enemies were demonstrating the flaws in his strategy. As the earlier wars had shown, garrisons were expensive to maintain and easy to isolate by a determined foe. Andrew Murray was such a foe. For over a year from October 1336 the guardian waged a relentless war, following King Robert's approach to war but outdoing even him for the ruthless intensity of his campaign. After storming Dunottar and other castles in the Mearns, Murray based himself in Angus, fighting a bitter winter war which caused destruction across the province. In the new year, Murray made an unsuccessful attempt on Perth before moving into Fife with a growing army, taking St Andrews, Leuchars and Falkland but failing before Cupar. With spring the guardian moved south, capturing his own

[12] *Scotichronicon*, vii, 116–19, 122–3; *Chron. Lanercost*, 296–9; *C.D.S.*, iii, nos 1,182, 1,240, 1,307; *Rot. Scot.*, i, 386, 398, 411, 472; Munro and Munro (eds), *Acts of the Lords of the Isles*, nos 1–3.

castle of Bothwell, and briefly blockading Stirling. The summer was spent in the south where Murray even launched raids into England. The campaign ended in Lothian. Andrew took the temporary submission of the province and besieged Edinburgh in October and November before retreating as winter came on, leaving famine in his wake.[13]

Murray did not defeat the English in battle or siege. He had failed to take the major castles he assaulted and Edward III's commanders had kept up a strong defence. Relief forces had made Andrew retreat from Perth, Stirling and Edinburgh. Despite this, the campaign showed that Murray knew how to beat his enemy. He had picked off small garrisons, moved through the south without fear and strained Edward's resources to the limit. The guardian was ready to lay waste his lord's realm as retribution on Scots who had made peace and to make the land useless for the enemy. From the Mearns to the marches he condemned thousands of ordinary Scots to death and suffering through a winter of famine and starvation, but his remorseless efforts were a critical turning point for the cause of King David. If much of Scotland was exhausted, so was the guardian. Andrew fell ill during the siege of Edinburgh and travelled north to his 'own land' of Moray, where he died in early 1338. His campaign had ended the possibility of Edward III establishing stable lordship over southern Scotland. During early 1338 this was confirmed by the failure of an English army to take Dunbar Castle in a six-month siege. The efforts of the army were frustrated by the Countess of Dunbar, Agnes Randolph, who held the castle, and by the harassment of the besiegers by local knights, such as Alexander Ramsay and Laurence Preston, with their followers. Even in the marches, the English king's lands were under pressure. Like earlier Scottish leaders, William Douglas had established himself by 1338 in the uplands of Liddesdale, the Forest and the Pentlands, using these refuges to harry surrounding districts in English allegiance. North of the Forth the position of the Bruce party was consolidated during 1337 and 1338. An exchequer audit was held at Aberdeen in late 1337 and, after Murray's death, Robert Stewart was chosen as guardian. Balliol's hold on this part of his realm was limited to Perth and Cupar. In spring 1339 Stewart moved against them with a large host. Perth was blockaded by land and sea. Scottish and French pirates prowled the sea routes and the Firth of Tay, forcing English supply ships to stay at Berwick. On land the moat was drained and the walls mined, and in August the garrison, which included many Scots, finally surrendered. Cupar, under its wily captain, the cleric William Bullock, had already

[13] *Scotichronicon*, vii, 124–31; *Scalachronica*, 103; *Chron. Lanercost*, 301–8; *Rot. Scot.*, i, 489, 495.

capitulated. Bullock had struck a deal with William Douglas, guaranteeing him rewards for entering the Bruce allegiance.[14]

A later, pro-Stewart, writer reported that 'through the activity of Andrew Murray and . . . Robert Stewart the kingdom was rescued'. This ignored the crucial shift of Edward III's ambitions towards war with France which meant that, though the English king returned to Scotland in 1341, campaigns like those of 1335 and 1336 were not repeated. Concerns with continental diplomacy and war decisively eased the pressure on Scotland after 1338 but even before then the war had already entered a phase of dogged and bitter fighting which Edward did not relish. Despite this outcome, the war from 1332 had threatened to bring Scotland under the lordship of the Plantagenets. It was a culmination of half a century of political and military conflict. Scotland was divided between two crowned kings from the families which had claimed the kingship since 1290, and the claims of the English crown were once again pressed in war. The fighting exposed major differences in attitude to legitimate authority in Scotland. The Disinherited represented those families whose place within the realm had been denied by Robert Bruce. They found support in traditional heartlands like Buchan, Atholl and Galloway and from others disaffected with the Bruce regime. Magnates like the earls of Fife and Strathearn showed no difficulty in accepting Balliol as king and Edward III's garrisons were full of Scottish adherents. The alignment of Balliol's claim to be rightful king of Scots with the power of the English realm was a combination which came close to imposing its lordship on Scotland.

The defeats and deaths of 1332 and 1333 dealt hard blows to the Bruce party and weakened its hold on the kingdom. But, in this sustained crisis, it was the resilience of King David's cause that was most impressive. Aided by the mistakes of their enemies, a small group of leaders led resistance to attacks that were every bit as dangerous as those launched by Edward I. These leaders were bound to the Bruce cause by kinship and patronage and drew on the traditional adherents of the dynasty. Their ultimate success, however, rested on the wider achievement of King Robert. The old king's victory meant that for most Scots and most European princes his dynasty was now regarded as the legitimate rulers of Scotland. Inside the kingdom, the strong image of Robert as the restorer of the realm allowed his partisans to identify defence of the Bruce dynasty with the defence of the kingdom. Such claims were aided by Balliol's dealings with the English king. Balliol himself was probably

---

[14] *Scotichronicon*, vii, 128–45; *Rot. Scot.*, i, 567, 573; *E.R.*, i, 448; Penman, 'The kingship of David II', 94–5.

aware that these recalled his father's capitulations and weakened his legitimacy for many Scots. The leaders of David II's cause could call on a wider hostility to alien rule, rallying support not simply in the Bruce name but in the name of the Scottish realm and its liberties, symbolised by the royal lion.[15]

The gradual success of King David's cause did not mean a return to the status quo. The losses amongst the Scottish political class at Dupplin and Halidon had been unprecedented. They left huge gaps in the nobility which had already been disrupted by the forfeitures imposed by Robert I. These gaps were exploited not just by Balliol, but by Bruce adherents. Many of these saw success in terms of the defence of the kingdom and the increase of their own status and resources. During his brief guardianship, Archibald Douglas had taken the vacant lordship of Liddesdale into his possession, while during the siege of Perth in 1339 Robert Stewart had tried to forfeit the earl of Strathearn and had occupied his earldom. The actions of such guardians were copied by their deputies. From 1339 William, earl of Ross was acting as justiciar in the north without reference to Stewart, and in the south, where intense fighting continued, leadership in war conferred political power. Knights like William Douglas and Alexander Ramsay had built reputations and retinues through their martial exploits. In the absence of stable sources of authority, these captains provided the effective leadership of the Bruce party south of the Forth. Their importance was exemplified by the capture of Edinburgh in April 1341 by William Douglas through a ruse engineered by William Bullock. Douglas installed his brother as keeper, adding Edinburgh to his power-base. Unlike in the war waged by Robert I from 1306, it was through the efforts of such captains and in the absence of royal leadership that the Bruce dynasty had been sustained during the 1330s. They had fought for David's rights but would expect the king to recognise their own gains made in his defence.[16]

THE KING AND THE STEWARD (1341–57)

In early June 1341 David Bruce returned to his kingdom. With a small household he landed at Inverbervie after seven years in French exile. The seventeen-year-old king had passed his youth at Château Gaillard in Normandy but did not lack contacts with his realm. His tutors and

---

[15] English officials recorded Scots fighting not for Bruce or Balliol but for the '*Leone*' in 1336 (*Rot. Scot.*, i, 401).
[16] Brown, *The Black Douglases*, 34–9; Penman, 'The kingship of David II', 94–102.

councillors, servants of King Robert like Malcolm Fleming, David Barclay and Reginald More, provided a valuable link between the Bruce party in Scotland and the French court. By the late 1330s there was a flow of Scots to Château Gaillard. In 1338 William Douglas visited the king and returned to Scotland with a French contingent provided by David. On his release from captivity, John Randolph also made his way to the king before returning home. If Randolph and Douglas sought the king's trust, the same was not true of Robert Stewart. During the previous decade, rivalry had grown up between Stewart and Randolph. David's friendship with the latter was accompanied by mistrust of Stewart and his motives as heir to the throne and guardian. In early 1341 acts were issued in David's name and revenues sequestered for the king's use in preparation for the renewal of Bruce kingship.[17]

King David and his councillors were aware that this was not straightforward. In David's absence the leadership of the Bruce cause had been exercised by guardians and captains rather than the king. The establishment of his personal authority required the king to demonstrate an ability to run his realm, winning support and managing interests, and also to prosecute the continuing war against his enemies. David took an immediate role in both areas. In July he was at Stirling to receive the surrender of the castle which had been under siege since 1339. He had probably already sanctioned the appointment of Randolph, Douglas and Alexander Ramsay as march wardens, responsible for prosecuting the war in the south in the king's name. David's control of government was confirmed by a meeting of parliament at Scone in September. The estates agreed to raise a financial contribution to support the royal government and renewed their fealty to the king. David may also have initiated an inquiry into grants and assumptions of lands and rights which had occurred in his absence. Like his father, the young king recognised that control of patronage was central to the establishment of his authority. In the months after his return David made numerous grants of lands and offices. His 'foster-father' Malcolm Fleming was made earl of Wigtown, as a focus for Bruce allegiance in Galloway. William Douglas was granted or confirmed in a dozen or more important estates across the south as rewards for his services, while his family provided a number of royal sheriffs and constables. Douglas's henchman, William Bullock, was appointed as David's chamberlain, a post he had earlier held under Edward Balliol. The king also sought to widen his following. Maurice Murray, a cousin of Andrew and associate of Stewart, was shown favour by David in 1341 with grants of land and his appointment as keeper of Stirling. The young

[17] *Scotichronicon*, vii, 140–1, 148–51; Penman, 'The kingship of David II', 98–101.

king was using royal resources to build up his friends and recruit new adherents as a personal affinity.[18]

However, David's position was more complex than that of his father. Robert had built his party during years of personal leadership against his enemies. David was seeking to create his own following after a period of absence, and in competition less with Balliol than with men within in his own camp. During 1341 Robert Stewart had largely stayed away from court and was clearly outside the royal circle. David mistrusted his territorial ambitions in central Scotland and blocked Stewart's claims on Strathearn and Atholl. Even amongst recipients of royal favour there were tensions. William Douglas regarded David's patronage as the rewards for past services, not as a means for David to rein in the influence established in the king's absence. The limits on the king's position with regard to such men were illustrated in a council at Aberdeen in February 1342. David sought to demonstrate his authority. Having previously confirmed Douglas as earl of Atholl, a title coveted by Stewart, David now rejected the claim of Douglas to hold Liddesdale for his ward, the son of the ex-guardian, Archibald Douglas. Instead the border lordship was confirmed to Stewart. However, two days later Douglas and Stewart exchanged their lordships, increasing their regional power and openly defying King David.[19]

The episode encouraged the young king to take a more intrusive approach. He looked to balance Douglas's influence and renew the control of the war which his father had exercised. In spring 1342 David took part in a raid on northern England under John Randolph's leadership. When Alexander Ramsay captured Roxburgh Castle in March, the king exploited the situation and appointed him sheriff. Giving another leading captain official powers in the heart of the middle march was a direct challenge to Douglas. Though David sought to placate him, Douglas took the issue into his own hands. In June he broke up the sheriff's court at Hawick, dragging Ramsay to Hermitage Castle in Liddesdale where the captive was starved to death. The killing of one of the Bruce party's leaders by another was sparked by a competition for lordship, not by disputes over allegiance. It was also a violent rejection of the king's interference in the marches, and David was provoked into a violent response. The chamberlain, Douglas's associate William Bullock, was seized on royal orders and, in a repeat of Ramsay's fate, was

---

[18] *Scotichronicon*, vii, 144-9; *R.M.S.*, i, app. 2, nos 1,097-9 ; *R.R.S.*, vi, no. 39; Penman, 'The kingship of David II', 161-70; Brown, 'Development of Scottish border lordship', 12-13.

[19] Brown, *The Black Douglases*, 39-40; Boardman, *The Early Stewart Kings: Robert II and Robert III*, 7.

starved to death in Randolph's castle of Lochindorb. Douglas himself was harder to deal with. The king sent armed men into the south but these were merely caught up in bitter fighting between the followings of Douglas and Ramsay which raged for two years and left a bloodfeud lasting a decade.[20]

The conflict between Douglas and the king created a dangerous situation in a region still under threat from Edward III. During 1343 William entered negotiations with the English. Though the loss of Roxburgh and of men and castles in Galloway in 1342 had been fresh blows to Edward III and Balliol, the defection of Douglas to the English king's allegiance would have reversed this decline in the marches. Douglas ultimately used the negotiations only to threaten David and instead looked for allies within the Bruce party. They were not hard to find. Robert Stewart had seen the king lure away his tenants and adherents. In late 1343 one of these, Maurice Murray, received the earldom of Strathearn which Stewart coveted. The feud in the south, rivalry over Strathearn and the king's moves to check the independence of William, earl of Ross in the far north all created a growing sense of political crisis which David confronted at a parliament at Scone in June 1344. The meeting was a qualified success for the king, and his will prevailed on most issues. Stewart and Ross accepted curtailed positions and Douglas returned to David's peace. In return he was recognised as sheriff of Roxburgh. Late 1344 and 1345 saw David in apparent control, building a strong political following headed by lords like Randolph, Maurice Murray and Malcolm Fleming and drawing on the rising revenues of his kingdom. However, these gains were at the expense of poor relations with other magnates. Stewart, Ross and Patrick, earl of March regarded David as poaching from their retinues and limiting their lordship. Such lords would prove to be dangerously ambivalent towards the king.[21]

Once again the flaws in Bruce kingship were exposed in war. Though the successes of his partisans in recent years meant that David was not faced with a struggle for survival, war remained a central issue for the young king. There was still conflict between the Bruce dynasty and those who rejected its rights to the kingship. David needed to take a lead in the defence of his title. Beyond Scotland such leadership would emphasise the unity of the realm behind the king in fighting which now centred on

Anglo-French rivalry, while for the Scottish political class David's bellig-erence recalled his father's victories and would re-establish the Bruce king at the head of the war effort. In 1345 and 1346 David took part in *chevauchées* into England. Though these had limited military goals, for a young king raised in a martial tradition, war was not just duty but pleas-ure. It was events in France which prompted a change in the character of the war. Edward III's victory at Creçy in August 1346 and his subsequent siege of Calais led David's protector, Philip VI, to appeal for Scottish support. David was determined to repay his debt to the French king. He called together a large host which included magnates and contingents from across the kingdom. The army gathered at Perth in late September. While such a host seemed to demonstrate David's power, it was also a test of his authority. In it were many lords who were ambivalent towards the king's success, who cherished private goals and who nourished rivalries with other leaders. Two of the key commanders, the former allies John Randolph and William Douglas, were now at odds over the death of Ramsay and military strategy. Even more damagingly, William, earl of Ross used the muster at Perth as a means to eliminate his local enemy, Ranald MacRuairi. Having slain Ranald as he slept at Elcho Priory, Ross led his men home.

Such divisions would dog the campaign. The initial advance of the host was through Liddesdale and was criticised by Randolph as being in Douglas's private interest. This dispute and the king's inexperience may have led to the meandering route of the army from Carlisle to Durham. The strategy lacked the pace and direction of Robert I's cam-paign and allowed northern English prelates and lords to muster an army. On 17 October the Scottish host stumbled into this enemy at Neville's Cross outside Durham. The battle which followed was a hard-fought and confused mêleé between the English and the leading Scottish divisions led by King David and by Randolph and Douglas. The tide was probably turning against the Scots when their fate was decided by the retreat of the Scottish rearguard. The leaders of this force were Robert Stewart and Patrick, earl of Dunbar. Neither man had a great desire to risk their lives and men, only to increase the pres-tige and authority of a victorious king. Whether motivated by political opportunism, by a calculation of military prospects or a combination of these, Stewart and Dunbar led the rearguard from the field, leaving the rest of the host to defeat. In the rout, losses fell most heavily on David's closest adherents. Randolph and Maurice Murray were slain, while William Douglas and many of the king's household knights were cap-tured. Fighting alone and wounded in the face, David was taken pris-oner by an English squire. He was led from the field, defeated by the swords of his enemies but also by rivalries amongst his own vassals which his rule had intensified.[22]

For the other king of Scots, Edward Balliol, the defeat and capture of his enemy opened up new opportunities. Balliol, who had fought at Neville's Cross, followed up the victory by returning to Galloway and bringing the local captains into his service once more. Meanwhile the northern English leaders, Henry Percy and John Neville, campaigned in the marches, where the local communities of Teviotdale, Annandale and the Merse submitted to the English king. By May 1347 Balliol was ready to renew the war for his throne. Supported by Percy and the Gallovidians, Balliol ranged through Lothian, Clydesdale and Ayrshire, once again bringing war to the heart of Scotland. However, despite the loss of their king and many of his nobles, Neville's Cross would bring no new collapse of the Bruce party. Though southern communities would remain in Edward III's allegiance for decades, Balliol's campaign did not mark a return of major internal conflict. His efforts were thwarted by the attitude of Edward III, whose energies remained focused on the French war and the capture of Calais, but also by the resilience of his Scottish enemies. Balliol found his advance dogged and his people harried by local leaders in Carrick, Cunningham and Lothian. Unlike earlier efforts, his campaign brought no flood of defections. The confidence of his opponents remained high, based on the successes achieved by the Bruce party before 1346, won mostly in the absence of their king. Lesser nobles and freeholders adhered to their allegiance in the knowledge of past events and current leadership. The losses of Neville's Cross had fallen heaviest on David's own following. In Robert Stewart, Dunbar, Ross and others there was an alternative, experienced Bruce leadership. Far from submitting, such magnates were quick to stake their claims to lead David's people. In May 1347 they gathered at Perth and chose Stewart as lieutenant 'as he was most powerful of them all . . . and the common interest would be most strongly guarded by him'.[23]

As David's heir Stewart could be counted on to defend the 'common interest', the kingship and settlement of the Bruces, against Balliol and Plantagenet. The same was not true of David's personal lordship. Through the crisis since 1286, struggles over the central issue, the status

[22] Scotichronicon, vii, 252–65; Chron. Lanercost, 330–8. There have recently been a number of good studies of Neville's Cross. See in particular Prestwich, 'The English at Neville's Cross'; Grant, 'Disaster at Neville's Cross: The Scottish point of view' Rogers, 'The Scottish invasion of 1346', 51–82; Penman, 'The Scots at Neville's Cross', 157–80.

[23] Scotichronicon, vii, 268–71; Scalachronica, 115–16; Chron. Fordun, ii, 358–9; Chron. Lanercost, 337–8; Rot. Scot., i, 691–2.

of Scotland, were intermingled with factional and personal rivalries. Within the Bruce allegiance, Stewart could see David's capture as being to his personal advantage. It allowed him to resume the leading role in the Bruce camp he had played between 1338 and 1341 and to exploit it, less for the purpose of controlling royal government than of widening his private lordship in central and northern Scotland. This was a direct result of Neville's Cross. Like Halidon and Dupplin, the defeat cut through the higher nobility. The deaths of the earls of Strathearn, Menteith and of John Randolph, earl of Moray, and the capture of Earl Duncan of Fife removed the natural focuses of local government and allegiance in many regions between the Forth and the Spey. Freed from any royal super-vision, Stewart intruded his own men and influence into these lands. The new lieutenant employed alliance, threat and negotiation to create a loose personal hegemony over Menteith, Strathearn, Atholl and the surround-ing districts. Stewart was not alone. Ross resumed the office of justicar, stripped from him by King David, and acted as Stewart's rival in the north. In the south the capture of William Douglas of Liddesdale created another power vacuum. This was filled from 1348 by the return of Liddesdale's godson, ward and namesake from France. The younger William was the son of Archibald, the guardian of 1333, and was the nephew of James Douglas. He was the rightful heir to the massive border lordship of the Douglases, which Liddesdale had held in his name. The latter's removal allowed young William to establish his rights as lord of Douglas in a progress through Lothian, Clydesdale and into the marches. Such events might suggest that, with David's capture, Scotland had fallen prey to selfish aristocratic ambitions. Stewart certainly allowed the dissi-pation of royal revenues amongst great lords and held few great councils or financial audits. However, the actions of these magnates had a value beyond private power. In the absence of their own royal or noble leaders after the defeat, local communities were provided with new lords who could defend them and hold them to their loyalties. In the south, where the threat was greatest, the lord of Douglas quickly assumed his family's mantle as leader of the Bruce cause in border warfare. As had been the norm for much of the previous decades, the key to Scottish resistance lay in aristocratic leadership of the diverse communities which formed the realm.[24]

Left out of this picture was the captive king. While his magnates pursued personal ambitions and continued the war in alliance with France, David languished in England. The possibilities inherent in this

[24] Boardman, *The Early Stewart Kings*, 8–13; Brown, *The Black Douglases*, 43–5; Penman, 'The kingship of David II', 225–9, 238.

The Black Death

'God and Sen Mungo, Sen Ninian and Seynt Andrew scheld us this day and ilka day fro Goddis grace and the foule deth that Ynglesshe men dyene upon'. In the summer of 1349 the Scots reportedly prayed to be spared the horrors of pestilence which had fallen upon their neighbours. The unstoppable advance of the plague brought it from the east to the Italian trading cities in late 1347, from there through France during early 1348 and across to the British Isles during the following summer. Though its advance slowed in the winter, by May 1349 York and the north of England lay in the grip of the disease. English chroniclers told tales of Scottish bands gathering in the Forest to exploit their enemies' plight but being themselves struck down by the pestilence.

However, the onset of winter once again slowed the disease's spread. It was not until the spring of 1350 that Scotland beyond the marches experienced the effect of the plague. The near-contemporary account of John of Fordun spoke of those inflicted suffering from swellings of the flesh which killed most in two days. These symptomatic swellings or bubos had been identified by observers from Florence to London but while chroniclers in Ireland and England spoke of the mortality taking a half, two-thirds or even nine-tenths of the population, the consensus amongst Scottish writers was that one in three died. Though one later account recorded that twenty-four, perhaps two-thirds, of the canons at St Andrews succumbed, this crude comparison may indicate that Scotland suffered less heavily from the disease than England or English parts of Ireland. The cooler climate, relatively sparse population and limited urbanisation could provide reasons for any such disparity but should not obscure the fact that the plague probably killed far more in two or three years than half a century of war. Perhaps between a fifth and a third of the population, tens of thousands of Scots, perished. Most of these reportedly came from 'the common people' which may explain the lack of attention it received from chroniclers. Though shocking and terrible, the plague in Scotland left no stories of the powerful brought low or of whole communities obliterated. Amidst the dislocation of population and destruction of property brought to Scotland by warfare, the fear and flight which coloured accounts of plague in other realms may have seemed less unique. Yet it was a far smaller Scottish population which emerged from the pestilences of 1349–50 and the early 1360s.[25]

---

[25] Ziegler, *The Black Death*, 159–61; Horrox, *The Black Death*, 62–92.

captivity were not lost on Edward III. The Bruce king, the crowned ruler of Scotland and focus of hostility to Plantagenet lordship, was in his hands. David was not treated as a rebel and traitor, as his father would have been, or as some of his magnates were. He was Edward's brother-in-law and, for the English government, the potential key to securing a settlement of the conflict on advantageous terms. In 1349 David was offered his freedom. In return, he would be required to do homage to Edward and restore the Disinherited amongst other demands. These proposals would have made David a vassal king like Balliol. He refused them but during 1350 and 1351 discussions continued. By November 1351 the issue of homage had been dropped. David was to be released for a ransom of £40,000 and to promise to restore the Disinherited and act as Edward's ally, while Edward agreed to relinquish his Scottish lands. The key to the deal was an agreement that David would nominate Edward's son, John of Gaunt, as heir to his throne whilst he remained childless. The terms satisfied both kings. Edward secured peace and alliance with Scotland and had the possibility of acquiring the kingdom for his family. David, who was still in his twenties, regarded the succession clause as a price worth paying to secure his release and return to Scotland.[26]

To achieve these aims, David needed to secure acceptance of these terms by his subjects. In particular, he needed to overcome the opposition of Stewart to an agreement which would cost him his primacy and his place as David's heir. Though in England, David still retained powers and supporters as king of Scots and, in late 1350, whilst negotiations were continuing, he dispatched William Douglas of Liddesdale to argue his case. Within Scotland, David also found support amongst Stewart's rivals. By early 1351, with royal support, the earls of Ross and Mar and the lord of Douglas had supplanted Stewart as lieutenant. They called a parliament at Dundee to debate possible terms for David's release. Though the discussions were unpromising, the final proposals were carried north by David, who had been paroled to secure the acceptance of his subjects. However, if David thought his presence would prove decisive, he was wrong. In a second parliament in March 1352 the terms were rejected by the estates who said that 'whilst they wished to ransom their king, they would never submit themselves to the English'.[27]

There was a widely-held and natural reluctance to negotiate away rights and liberties which had been successfully maintained in war. David was apparently warned, on pain of losing his throne, to renounce

[26] Duncan, 'Honi soit qui mal y pense: David II and Edward III, 1346–52', 113–41; Boardman, The Early Stewart Kings, 9–10.
[27] Chron. Knighton, 121–6; Penman, 'The kingship of David II', 242–50.

his dealings with Edward. Such responses may show the hand of Robert Stewart. They certainly show that David overestimated his support and misunderstood his subjects' attitudes. He had counted on the self-interest of a group of magnates to counter Stewart but even his key agent, Douglas of Liddesdale, was more concerned with assassinating his enemies and competing for regional influence with the lord of Douglas. The Stewart sat tight, widening his own connection through the marriage of his daughter, Margaret, to John of the Isles, and showing an ability to direct events despite losing his lieutenancy. By spring 1352 there was a real possibility of civil war between the king and the Steward. Liddesdale had David's licence to act against rebels and a promise of English support. In the event David drew back, returning to England and captivity rather than confronting his subjects. Scotland was left to competing lords once more. Some rivalries were settled in conflict, some in agreement. In 1353 the lord of Douglas ended the eventful career of Douglas of Liddesdale, slaying him in an ambush in Ettrick Forest to secure his position in the south. In 1355 Stewart married the sister of the earl of Ross, settling the feud between the two magnates. Stewart's new wife, Euphemia, was the widow of another rival, John Randolph. The match brought Robert a stake in Randolph's huge province of Moray. The running of lands and communities in many parts of Scotland was now shaped by marriage or murder. Under Alexander III and, more recently, under Robert I, kings directed such issues of lordship and authority and regulated relations amongst their chief subjects. By the early 1350s, it had become normal for them to be worked out without royal intervention. The lieutenant was himself part of a political process which favoured him and the other great lords of the realm.[28]

Once more the king was on the outside. David still retained adherents, especially amongst the lesser nobility, but had to bargain for the support of magnates. In 1354, for example, he confirmed the lord of Douglas in his lands and as leader of the middle march, using the crown's powers to formalise such rights. Yet, rather than patronage, this was merely the ratification of gains made by Douglas by his own efforts. David still faced the difficulty of securing consent for his release. Though Edward III remained keen to secure a settlement and in 1354 offered fresh terms which made no mention of the succession, these proposals were still rejected. Lords like Douglas, Dunbar and even Stewart saw their interests and the traditions of the Bruce party as pointing not to negotiation but to continued war. In 1353 Douglas had ravaged Galloway, forcing Balliol's

---

[28] *Scotichronicon*, vii, 274–5; Brown, *The Black Douglases*, 45–7; Boardman, *The Early Stewart Kings*, 11–12; *A.L.I.*, no. B25.

leading adherents to submit at Cumnock. Though he brought these men into the allegiance of the Bruce king, Douglas's actions ran counter to David's personal interests. Such aggression was encouraged by the French king. At Easter 1355 a small French expedition reached Scotland, to be followed later in the year by a cash subsidy of about £10,000. Both were sent by John II of France to 'put the Scots in motion to make war against the English'. By the autumn Douglas, Dunbar and the French were harrying Edward III's men in the marches and, in November, a third magnate, Thomas Stewart, earl of Angus took Berwick by assault.[29]

The escalation of the war in 1355 brought swift repercussions. Already in late 1355 rivalries were evident between the Scots and French and amongst the collective leadership of the kingdom. The fall of Berwick and the presence of the French stung Edward III into action. In January 1356 the English king rushed north, raising an army which he led into Lothian. When his supply fleet failed to appear, Edward let loose his forces to burn and plunder, torching Edinburgh and Haddington in what was recalled as 'the Burnt Candlemas'. The return of major war to Lothian in the depths of winter caused many folk to flee to the hills and across the Forth, but despite divisions amongst the Scottish leaders, which led to the abandonment of Berwick, the campaign won little for Edward. As he retreated, his men were harried and in Teviotdale and Annandale his Scottish adherents came under fresh pressure from local lords and their forces. The 'Burnt Candlemas' would prove a final flurry, confirming for Edward the futility of such unrewarding campaigns. He would never return to Scotland at the head of such an army, focusing more than ever on the wars in France. The same was even true of some Scots. Concluding a private truce in the marches, the lord of Douglas led a contingent to join John of France's campaign in Aquitaine. They were present when the French king's host was catastrophically defeated by Edward, prince of Wales's smaller force near Poitiers in September. Though Douglas escaped, the French king was taken prisoner.[30]

Even before Poitiers, the established political patterns of recent years were changing. In January 1356 Edward Balliol, worn out by his efforts, had resigned his royal title and claims to Edward III. The latter issued charters as the successor of good king Alexander, but the real significance of the end of the direct Balliol claim was in clearing the way for a settlement with the house of Bruce. Poitiers and the prospect of victories in

[29] *Scotichronicon*, vii, 278–83; *Scalachronica*, 119; Penman, 'The kingship of David II', 254–6.
[30] *Scotichronicon*, vii, 286–93; *Scalachronica*, 120; *Chron. Knighton*, 136–8; Brown, *The Black Douglases*, 46, 211; Sumption, *The Hundred Years War: Trial by Fire*, ii, 143–249.

France spurred Edward to make new efforts to reach a settlement with Scotland. Events during 1356 also blunted the bellicosity of Scottish magnates. It was ironic that the capture of King John opened the way for the release of King David. Talks dragged on during the winter and through 1357 and terms were finally agreed at Berwick on 3 October 1357. The Scots would pay a ransom of £66,666 over ten years for the liberty of their king, surrendering nobles as sureties for the payment of this sum. Linked to the agreement was a ten-year truce and the possibility of a future final peace. Beyond this, however, the Scots delivered no hostages to fortune. Issues of lordship and homage, of the succession or of the claims of the Disinherited were not included. In contrast to the 1328 treaty, such omissions were not forced on a weak and partisan minority regime but were willingly accepted by Edward III. His readiness, for nearly a decade, to seek a settlement contrasted with the English crown's attitude during most of the preceding half-century. It would be this desire to secure stability and peace in the north, rather than fight for greater lordship in Scotland, that would characterise subsequent approaches to the northern kingdom. Issues of English lordship would remain and Anglo-Scottish warfare was not over. Full recognition of David's kingship was missing from the terms and Edward III continued to hold Scottish lands in his allegiance. However, the treaty of Berwick marked an end to the sustained wars over the status and survival of Scottish crown and kingdom which had been waged over the previous sixty years.[31]

---

[31] *Scotichronicon*, vii, 304–5; Penman, 'The kingship of David II', 259–63.

CHAPTER 12

Lord of the Isles

THE WAR IN THE ISLES 1286–1318

The years of crisis and war which engulfed the Scottish realm between 1286 and 1356 altered political relationships and power structures across the north and west of the British Isles. Nowhere were these changes of greater significance than in the isles and coastlands to the west of Scotland. The experience of this maritime region would be bound up with the course of events on the mainland, but needs to be understood as different in critical ways. Though the Hebrides and Man had been brought under the lordship of the Scottish king, the Isles retained their own traditions and identities. Through the coming decades politics in the Isles would be dominated by competing magnates, especially the lines descended from Somerled, the MacDougalls of Lorn, the MacDonalds of Islay and the MacRuairis of Garmoran, who still regarded themselves as heirs to his kingship over *Inse Gall*. As before the 1260s, lords of these dynasties would move between the lordship of greater kings, seeking protection and grants of authority as they had shifted between Scottish and Norwegian allegiance, without ever being absorbed wholly into one allegiance. The wars in the Isles had a strategic importance in the efforts of first the Plantagenets and then the Bruces to extend their lordship, but it would be the ambitions of the Islesmen themselves that would prove of greatest significance in reshaping structures of power in the far west.

As in Scotland, it was the death of Alexander III that began the process of change. With the removal of active kingship, the unity of purpose and resources that had allowed the old king to establish his lordship over the Isles was also removed. The roots of this lordship remained shallow. To neighbours and to exiles, the royal settlement of the 1260s was not necessarily the final word on the status and political structure of the Isles. However, it was not just the king's authority which had defined and contained the activities of the lords and communities of the Isles in the years since 1266. Hebridean magnates had been drawn into closer contacts with lords from western Scotland. From 1286 these links assumed a new importance. In September 1286 at Turnberry Castle, Angus Mor of Islay, head of Clan Donald, entered into a bond with a group of magnates, led by his neighbours James Stewart, Walter Balloch, earl of Menteith and Robert Bruce, earl of Carrick. These lords agreed to give mutual aid to two English magnates in Ireland: Richard de Burgh, earl of Ulster and Thomas de Clare. Those who broke this promise would be subject to attack by the others. Of those agreeing to the bond, Angus had the strongest connections in Ireland; these connections were, moreover, with members of the Ó Neill and Ó Domhnaill dynasties who were hostile to the earl of Ulster. The bond's purpose was to curtail Hebridean support for these Irish lords through an alliance of Scottish and Anglo-Irish nobles. Easy alignments between royal and aristocratic interests on both sides of the North Channel had been crucial in previous decades in putting pressure on Gaelic communities in Ireland and the Isles, but the years of such co-operation between different Anglicised communities was coming to an end.[1]

The Turnberry band indicates that, despite links to the Stewarts and Bruces, Angus Mor was regarded with suspicion by his neighbours. This was less the case with Alexander of Argyll and Clan Dougall. His interests on the mainland and his marriage to the sister of John Comyn of Badenoch had made the MacDougalls better-known and better-trusted in Scotland and secured Alexander's appointment as the king's agent in the Isles. However, during the later 1280s there was a shift in the character of such alliances. Instead of acting as the means by which leading Hebrideans could be bound into the king's allegiance, they assumed a more partisan significance. Alexander of Argyll's connections with the Comyns now made him a leading figure in their faction. Between 1289 and 1292 he was active in the kingdom's politics, emerging as a supporter of the Balliol claim. The value of winning allies in the Isles was not lost on rival magnates. The Stewarts and Bruces may well have begun cultivating their contacts with Angus of Islay. The marriage between Duncan, son of Earl Donald of Mar, and Christina, daughter and heiress of Alan MacRuairi of Garmoran, certainly provided Earl Donald, a northern rival of the Comyns, with a bond of kinship to the Hebridean line whose lands bordered Badenoch to the west. During the growing instability of the 1290s, the concern of Scotland's rulers would shift from the maintenance of

[1] Stevenson, *Documents*, i, no. 12; *Ann. Connacht*, 178-9, 182-5; Duffy, 'The Bruce brothers', 73-4; Simms, 'Relations with the Irish', 66-86, 70-1.

peace and stability in the west to the search for allies whose galleys and military retinues were a source of strength in troubled times.[2]

However, it is wrong to see the Isles in a purely Scottish context. As the Turnberry band revealed, the region continued to be a crossroads of interests and concerns for all the surrounding lands, in Ulster, Dublin, England and Norway as well as Scotland. The treaty of Perth only twenty years earlier did not shut off links which had lasted for centuries, nor did it rule out new shifts in the status of the Isles. The increased involvement of Eric II of Norway in Scottish politics may have raised the prospect of renewed Norwegian claims in their lost dominions but it would be Edward I of England who would prove the real threat to the status quo. To Edward, Scottish lordship over the Isles and, especially, in Man had been achieved during the English political crisis of the 1260s. In Wales Edward had reversed the gains made by Llywelyn of Gwynedd during that period of Plantagenet weakness and in 1290, as he negotiated the terms of his son's marriage to Lady Margaret, the king showed an interest in imposing his authority on the Isles. This concern had an immediate cause. By 1290 the Turnberry band had failed, and Clan Donald had resumed its activities in Ulster. With the Stewarts and Bruces preoccupied with Scottish politics and keen to retain Hebridean allies, their ability to restrain Angus Mor of Islay and his son, Alexander, was much reduced. During the year these Islesmen helped Domhnaill Ó Neill and other Gaelic lords to recover the leadership of their kindreds in opposition to the interests of Richard de Burgh, 'red earl' of Ulster. It may have been as part of an escalating conflict with the Islesmen that Earl Richard occupied Man. His actions drew in King Edward to aid his chief Irish vassal. In June 1290 the king sent an official to take custody of Man and despatched Anthony Bek to impose his peace on the Isles which were suffering 'war and discord'. Like his father in the 1250s, Edward was drawn into the region to safeguard the stability of Ireland. Significantly, however, his treatment of Man was not unwelcome to the inhabitants. The Manxmen petitioned Edward, complaining of recent desolation, misery and lack of protection, perhaps referring to the rule of Alexander III but more likely to the experience of attacks since 1286. Typically, Edward extracted a promise of good behaviour from the Manx, toying with establishing formal protection over the strategically-vital island.[3]

---

[2] *R.R.S.*, vi, 648; McDonald, *Kingdom of the Isles*, 141–2; Sellar, 'Hebridean sea kings', 208–10; Duncan and Brown, 'Argyll and the western Isles', 220, no. 5.

[3] *Ann. Connacht*, 182–5; Stevenson, *Documents*, i, nos 103, 107; *Foedera*, ii, 739; Duffy, 'The Bruce brothers', 74. Domhnaill Ó Neill was son of the Brian Ó Neill who had claimed the high kingship of Ireland in the late 1250s. Domhnaill was again expelled by Earl Richard in 1291.

Conflict was not limited to Ulster and Man. The 'war and discord' in the Isles referred to in 1290 included rivalries within the Hebrides which would escalate during the coming decade. At the centre of these would be competition between the descendants of Somerled. By 1291 an immediate cause for friction was a land dispute between Clan Donald and the MacDougalls. This overlay older antagonisms and ambitions for wider lordship in the Isles which re-emerged in the new political atmosphere. In July 1292 Alexander of Argyll and Alexander of Islay appeared at Berwick before Edward I, then acting as lord of Scotland. The two magnates were bound to keep the peace in the Isles and the 'foreign lands in those parts' and to bring the case to parliament in September. Edward sensibly delegated the issue to the guardians, John Comyn and James Stewart, using their influence with the two parties to contain conflict.[4]

In late 1292 John Balliol was made king of Scots, receiving back Man from Edward I early in 1293. The new king would not, or could not, copy Edward's even-handed approach. In February 1293, at his first parliament, John created three new sheriffdoms designed to bring Argyll and the Hebrides under formal royal administration 'for the peace and stability of the realm'. Though James Stewart was given authority over Kintyre, Bute and Arran, areas under his lordship, the other sheriffs were partisan creations. William, earl of Ross was made sheriff of Skye with powers over the northern Hebrides. Alexander of Argyll was appointed sheriff of Lorn to run much of Argyll and the isles of Mull, Jura and Islay. Two staunch adherents of King John were given power over their regional enemies. If John thought 'peace and stability' would result, he was wrong. A decade later the earl of Ross recalled that the Isles and their 'cheventeyns' had opposed King John, who ordered Ross to wage a costly war against them. The conflict was in reality an escalation of the feud between Ross and the MacRuairis for lordship over Kintail, Skye and the Uists. Though Ross won a temporary victory, the war was far from over. In the same way, the appointment of Alexander of Argyll turned his private dispute with the lords of Islay into a clash between the crown and Islesmen. Angus Mor and Alexander of Islay refused to do homage to the new king, and John sent his sheriff to force Clan Donald to enter his peace, without obvious success.[5]

By backing his own adherents, John merely escalated existing rivalries

---

[4] *Foedera*, ii, 761; *Rot. Scot.*, i, 21. The dispute was over the lands assigned to Alexander, son of Angus of Islay, through his marriage to Juliana, sister of Alexander of Argyll. Alexander of Argyll was required by Edward to bring the MacRuairis under the king's authority.

[5] *A.P.S.*, i, 91; Duncan and Brown, 'Argyll and the western Isles', 220, no. 6; *C.D.S.*, ii, no. 1,631.

into open war against his rule. Moreover, his enemies were not without political weapons of their own. By 1295 Alexander of Islay had appealed to Edward I for justice. Edward's overlordship was also the means for a wider challenge to the king of Scots' position in the Isles. A lady from the old Manx dynasty raised a claim to Man, while Malcolm MacQuillin, the head of a kindred in the earl of Ulster's service, sought to recover lands in Kintyre. As well as John's own actions, the legitimacy of the settlement of the 1260s was under scrutiny. When Edward initiated war against John in spring 1296, he would find allies in the Isles. In particular, to counter Alexander of Argyll, Edward appointed Alexander of Islay as his agent and, with King John's sheriffs caught up in the disastrous events of the summer, MacDonald was able to occupy Kintyre.[6] However, unlike most of the Scottish realm, Argyll and the Hebrides did not pass under Edward's lordship. Instead, events revealed the very different character of island politics. The submission of Stewart and the captivity of Ross and MacDougall did not end conflict even temporarily. Instead, warfare in the far west intensified. Alexander of Argyll's sons, John of Lorn and Duncan, maintained a forceful defence of their kindred. Further north, Lachlan and Ruairi MacRuairi, the half-brothers of Christina of Garmoran, launched savage attacks on the tenants of the crown in Skye and Lewis. Though enemies of King John's sheriff, these leaders saw Edward's victory solely in terms of Ross's removal and the chance to extend their lordship and to plunder. The imprisonment of Ross, the Comyns and Alexander of Argyll weakened the chances for stable lordship in the region. Edward recognised the need for a powerful lieutenant. In September 1296, seeking to control the MacDougalls, Edward sought to employ the Stewart connection which had considerable influence in Argyll and had recently come into his peace. James Stewart, the Campbells and the men of Argyll and Ross were ordered to support Alexander Stewart, earl of Menteith against John of Lorn. Hopes that the earl would impose Edward's authority were dashed even before the general collapse of that authority in the summer of 1297. Menteith's ally Colin Mor Campbell was killed by John of Lorn, and by April the king had tranferred powers in Argyll and Ross to Alexander of Islay and released Alexander MacDougall from custody.[7]

These actions were an admission of failure. Instead of using mainland magnates, Edward was reduced to dependence on the Islesmen, a course

---

[6] *Rot. Scot.*, i, 18, 21–3; Barrow, *Robert Bruce*, 58, 330. For the identity of Malcolm MacQuillin (referred to here as '*le fils Engleys*'), see Simms, 'Gaelic warfare in the Middle Ages', 99–115, 109–10.

[7] Stevenson, *Documents*, ii, no. 444; *Rot. Scot.*, i, 31–2; McDonald, *Kingdom of the Isles*, 165; Sellar, 'Hebridean sea kings', 212.

that, once again, resulted in increased warfare. Acting in Edward's name, Alexander of Islay pursued the MacRuairis and occupied Stewart's lands in Cowal following his rebellion, but the other kindreds regarded his efforts as a regional challenge. Lachlan MacRuairi joined the MacDougalls and the tenants of the Comyns in Lochaber in attacks on Clan Donald and other Islesmen which Alexander of Argyll encouraged after his release. With the defeat of Edward's government in Scotland, the war in the Isles was almost wholly a struggle between these kindreds for dominance, accompanied by Lachlan MacRuairi's continued attacks on the leaderless men of Ross. Without Edward I's active backing, the lord of Islay was vulnerable to the greater strength of Clan Dougall. In 1299 'Alexander MacDomhnaill . . . was killed with countless numbers of his people . . . by Alexander MacDubgaill'. Though private conflicts were part of the war in Scotland, in the Isles such feuds were the dominant issue, greater than allegiances to rival royal lordships.[8]

From 1296 onwards neither Edward I nor the guardians exercised effective lordship in the Hebrides. This did not mean, however, that the whole region was a backwater in the wider war. The English king in particular saw the western seas as a valuable route into the Scottish realm. In 1296 his adherents seized Man once more, and during his campaigns in Scotland in 1296, 1298, 1300 and 1301 the resources of his Irish lordship were employed on a large scale. Ireland was not simply used as a source of men and victuals. The contacts between Ulster and the Scottish realm were exploited to apply political leverage with exiles like Malcolm MacQuillin, John MacSween and Hugh Bisset returning in search of land. These exiles sought to renew claims arising from the disputes of the mid-thirteenth century and most had connections with Richard, earl of Ulster. The earl's importance in royal plans was demonstrated by the marriage of his sister to James Stewart in late 1296 in a move designed to bind the Scottish lord into Edward's allegiance. Though this attempt failed, by autumn 1301 Edward was ready for the direct extension of his lordship in the region. In conjunction with an ambitious land campaign in the south-west, a fleet was sent under Hugh Bisset and the gallowglass John MacSween into the Isles, joining up with Angus Og of Islay, one of the new leaders of Clan Donald. Its aim was to extract the submission of Alexander of Argyll and the MacRuairis, either by diplomacy or by war. Fighting occurred in Knapdale between MacSween and John Menteith, the latter backed by John of Lorn. This marked the renewal of a feud from the 1260s when Menteith's father, Walter Balloch, had driven MacSween from the lordship. However, the campaign of 1301 clearly had

---

[8]   Stevenson, *Documents*, ii, nos 444–5; *Ann. Connacht*, 198–9.

an effect. Though the Stewarts and their cousins the Menteiths did not submit, perhaps fearing the claims of the exiles, western lords like Robert Bruce, earl of Carrick, the earl of Lennox and the Campbells did come to Edward's peace. Bruce's new stance was accompanied by marriage to the earl of Ulster's daughter, Elizabeth de Burgh, a match designed to link him to the king's principal regional supporter. The MacDougalls and MacRuairis probably made terms soon afterwards.[9]

Having secured these submissions, Edward did little to alter the region's political balance. Rather than reward his adherents, he allowed the MacDougalls access to his favour and released the earl of Ross, appointing him lieutenant in the north. While it was unlikely that this return to the status quo would have brought lasting peace, as in the rest of the Scottish realm it would be the actions of Robert Bruce that would initiate fresh disruption. The Islesmen would play a central role in Bruce's coup and its aftermath. The response of the MacDougalls to these events was dictated by their strong ties to the house of Comyn. In July 1306 John of Lorn defeated Bruce's escort at Dail Righ, coming close to ending the war by taking or slaying the fugitive king. In the weeks which followed, however, it would be the actions of Clan Donald and the MacRuairis in aiding Robert which would prove of greater significance in both Scotland and the Isles. Despite Bruce's connections with these kindreds, there was no political alliance to match that between the MacDougalls and Comyns. The readiness of the Hebrideans to support Robert related to short-term circumstances. For the MacRuairis, the restoration of Earl William of Ross had been unwelcome. In 1304 the earl was already seeking to recover ground, asking for money to bring the Isles to the king's justice. Though Ross may have come to a temporary arrangement with Lachlan MacRuairi, for the whole kindred, and Christina of Garmoran its head, the signs were ominous. The leaders of Clan Donald may also have felt vulnerable. Like Bruce, Angus Og had supported Edward I without major reward. Edward's favour to the MacDougalls and his friendship with the Earl of Ulster suggested the future would be bleak for Clan Donald, whose strong links to the Gaels of Ireland made them suspect to the English crown and the Anglo-Irish.[10]

The alliance between Robert and Clan Donald was essentially a

[9] Stevenson, *Documents*, ii, nos 401, 610, 614–16; *C.D.S.*, ii, nos 1,238, 1,253–5, 1,275; Lydon, 'Irish levies in the Scottish Wars, 1296–1302', 207–17. Bisset was descended from the family exiled from Scotland by Alexander II and given lands in Ulster by Henry III. MacSween was probably son of Murchad Mac Suibhne who was driven from his lands in Knapdale by Walter Balloch (Stewart) in c. 1262.

[10] *C.D.S.*, ii, no. 1,632; iv, 400; Sellar, 'Hebridean sea kings', 213; Duncan, 'War of the Scots', 138; Barbour, *The Bruce*, 104–29; McDonald, *Kingdom of the Isles*, 170–4.

marriage of convenience for both parties. Though contact was probably made in March 1306, when Bruce's followers were active in Kintyre, it was Robert's expulsion from Scotland in the late summer which brought him together with Angus Og and his kin. Lack of effective authority in the Hebrides was now Edward's problem. He ordered Hugh Bisset from Ireland and John Menteith from Dumbarton to lead fleets into the Isles, but Robert was clearly able to move freely through the Hebrides, receiving the support of Christina of Garmoran, raising men and ships from Clan Donald and exploiting that kindred's connections with Gaelic Ulster to recruit Irish support. Kintyre was the base for the king's renewed campaign and, during the next eighteen months, his victories over his Scottish enemies were greatly aided by the efforts of Clan Donald and the MacRuairis. The Islesmen contributed directly to Bruce's forces. 'Men of the outer isles' under Angus Og's cousin, Donald of Islay, aided Edward Bruce's campaign in Galloway in 1308. Moreover, while Robert campaigned on the mainland, his Hebridean allies harried their mutual enemies in the Isles. Lachlan MacRuairi's challenge to Ross's authority in the west undermined the earl's ability to resist Robert in the east and encouraged his submission to the king. When the decisive campaign in the region was launched against the MacDougalls in August 1308, Alexander of Argyll reported that he was vastly outnumbered and attacked from land and sea. His neighbours to the south, the barons of Argyll, led by the Campbells, were against him, and the same was true of Clan Donald to the west. King Robert moved from the east, forcing the Pass of Brander and moving on to take the surrender of Dunstaffnage Castle in Lorn. Meanwhile, it is likely that the island lordships of Alexander were attacked by his Hebridean rivals. Faced by such concerted pressure, Alexander of Argyll sought peace, while his son, John of Lorn, probably fled to Edward II.[11]

The surrender of Alexander and of Earl William were victories not just for Bruce, but also for the king's allies and adherents, the enemies of these magnates. The results of the victory may not have been immediately clear. King Robert accepted both Ross and MacDougall into his allegiance. Ross was allowed to retain his lands and it seems likely that Alexander was hopeful of similar terms. Both attended the king's parliament at St Andrews in March 1309 but, by the end of the year, Alexander had fled Scotland and joined his son in English allegiance. His decision may have

---

[11] *Chron. Fordun*, ii, 335; *C.D.S.*, iii, no. 80; iv, 400; Barrow, *Robert Bruce*, 179–81; McDonald, *Kingdom of the Isles*, 174–80. McDonald suggests 1309 as an alternative date for the war in Argyll. Though there are problems with the evidence, all near contemporary indications suggest the fighting took place in 1308.

been prompted by continuing difficulties at the hands of his neighbours, keen to exploit his weakness. Donald of Islay and the barons of Argyll had also been at parliament, perhaps pressing the king to reward their support, while in the west MacDougall may have found his lands occupied by local enemies. In the aftermath of Alexander's flight, members of the Campbell kindred obtained lands held by the MacDougalls in Lorn and Benderloch, but Clan Donald gained most. Angus of Islay received a royal charter granting him Morvern and Ardnamurchan, while his nephew, Alexander Og, was granted Mull and Tiree. By comparison Clan Ruairi made few gains, perhaps because of internal shifts within the kindred. Robert confirmed changes which saw Lady Christina replaced in control of Garmoran by her half-brother, Ruairi. Though Ruairi recognised the rights of Christina's line and sought royal recognition, promising to provide galleys for the king's fleet, it is likely that the replacement of Robert's ally and kinswoman by a leader with a violent and chequered record was the result of family politics, not of royal policy. In other, more ominous ways, the king had to recognise limits to his rule in the far west. Lochaber was a key region, linking the Western Isles and coasts to Strathspey and the Great Glen. Its attachment to Badenoch in the thirteenth century had been a vital means of policing these routes and Robert continued the connection by including Lochaber in Thomas Randolph's earldom of Moray in 1312. However, the king seems also to have recognised the rights of Angus Og in the lordship. Allowing a Hebridean magnate control over Lochaber would not have served the interests of the crown in the north-west. Robert's grant, limiting Randolph's lordship, may have been wrung from him by Angus, and it may have recognised that, after the fall of the Comyns, Clan Donald had effectively occupied Lochaber. It would be an approach to the extension of power pursued across the west by the kindred in coming decades.[12]

The king's readiness to placate the Islesmen was born out of a knowledge of western politics. The MacDougalls remained a threat, joining the exiles in Ireland. Though Alexander of Argyll died in 1310, the Isles were still a weak flank for Robert, hard to police and easy to penetrate from Ireland. Edward II also grasped this and, like his father, sought to use these exiles to recover lordship. In 1310 John MacSween, 'stout of spear', led a fleet to attack his ancestral hold of Castle Sween from John Menteith, who was now in Bruce's allegiance. John of Lorn was also employed. In 1311 and 1314 he was named Edward's admiral in the west

---

[12] *A.P.S.*, i, 289–459–60; *R.M.S*, i, app. 1, no. 9; app. 2, nos 56–8, 351–3, 363, 653; *R.R.S.*, v, nos 239, 366. For Professor Duncan's alternative view of Christina's resignation, see *R.R.S.*, v, 67–8.

and given ships and men to recover his lands in the Isles and Argyll. Irish resources were assigned to these efforts. Richard de Burgh, earl of Ulster was once more the central figure, leading a list of over fifty English and Gaelic leaders summoned to serve in the expedition led by Edward II in 1314. The results of these campaigns were limited to sporadic fighting. The tide continued to be with the Bruces. In 1313 Edward Bruce secured Galloway, opening the way for the expedition which captured the Isle of Man in May. However, such gains were not secure. In February 1315, leading a fleet of Hebrideans, John of Lorn retook Man from Robert's garrison. A month later John was seeking submissions from Donald of Islay and other Islesmen.[13]

It was against this uncertain background that Edward Bruce landed on the Antrim coast at the head of an army in May 1315. The expedition was a reverse of those planned by the English in 1311 and 1314 and formed part of the Bruces' escalation of their war after Bannockburn. However, behind these strategic goals and the hopes of a realm based on kinship between Scottish and Irish Gaels, Edward's war was also part of established regional patterns that connected Ireland, Scotland and the Isles. As lord of Carrick and Galloway, Edward himself was part of such patterns, and south-west Scotland provided large contingents in his armies. But the ambitions of Hebridean magnates, and above all Clan Donald, also shaped the character and course of the war. It was amongst Angus Og's Gaelic kin and allies in Ulster that Edward found his strongest Irish adherents, led by Domhnaill Ó Neill. Ó Neill, a long-standing ally of Clan Donald, reportedly invited Edward's aid and made over his claim to the high-kingship to Bruce. It was also from the men of the Isles that Edward recruited his best soldiers. In 1315, 1317 and 1318 the Bruce forces in Ireland contained a strong Hebridean element, including both MacDonalds and MacRuairis and drawing on the experience of such gallowglass kindreds in Irish warfare. The influence of the Islesmen was also apparent in the goals of Edward's warfare. Bruce's initial efforts were directed against Domhnaill's enemy, Richard de Burgh, earl of Ulster. The earl had been central to English interventions in the Isles since the 1290, but he was also rumoured to be in talks with his old allies, the Bruces. While the defeat of de Burgh in 1315 made sense as a means of securing Edward a power-base, it served the interests of Ó Neill and Angus Og much more directly. They were free to challenge their Gaelic enemies, chief among them Aed Ó Domhnaill, who was supported by his

---

[13] *Rot. Scot.*, i, 118–24, 143–4; McNamee, *Wars of the Bruces*, 48–9, 52, 58, 60–1, 169. Gaelic verses were composed to record MacSween's efforts in 1310 (Clancy, *Triumph Tree*, 302–5).

own gallowglass led by the exile John MacSween. In Ulster and much of Ireland, the effect of Bruce's arrival was to intensify such local conflicts, supporting the interests of his allies and their gallowglass.[14]

Edward's links with the Islesmen and their Ulster allies committed him to war with de Burgh and the Anglo-Irish, made him dependent on Gaelic allies and bogged him down in the dynastic competitions which made up Irish politics. While it is unlikely that Bruce could have won support from the colonists, however disaffected they were with Edward II, his prospects were limited by the interests of his chief supporters. The end of his brief kingship at the battle of Fochart in 1318 certainly involved these supporters. Amongst the dead at Fochart were 'Mac Ruairi *ri Inse Gall* and Mac Domnhaill *ri Oirear Goidel* (Argyll)', perhaps Ruairi of Garmoran and Angus of Islay. In the aftermath, Domhnaill Ó Neill's son was killed at Derry with another MacDonald leader, conceivably Alexander Og, at the hands of Aed Ó Domhnaill. The fate of Edward's Irish ambitions and of Clan Donald's hopes of increased influence in Ulster were bound together in defeat. Since 1315 warfare had been waged with an intensity and on a scale not seen in the region for decades but, though this escalation was driven by direct competition between royal governments, the ambitions of Bruce and Plantagenet in the west still worked in conjunction with the interests of under-kings, magnates and even exiles like John MacSween. The Isles remained a world of many competing lords.[15]

CLAN DONALD AND THE KINGDOM OF SCOTS (1318–57)

The defeat of Edward Bruce at Fochart brought an end to one phase of conflict in the west. Despite the destruction, in terms of royal lordship little appeared to have changed. The English crown's hold on its Irish lordship was preserved, and in 1317 Thomas Randolph retook Man for the Bruces. However, amongst leading lords of the region there had been fundamental shifts. Though the deaths of Edward Bruce and his Hebridean allies left their marks, it was the fate of his enemies which had the greatest impact. In Ulster the earl had been driven into exile. Although he returned in 1318, he never recovered his old dominance. In

[14] Duffy, 'The Bruce brothers', *passim* and 70–6; Barbour, *The Bruce*, 666–75; *Ann. Connacht*, 248–51. Angus Og was married to Aine Ó Cathain, the sister of one of Ó Neill's vassals, Diarmait Ó Cathain, another Ulster adherent of Bruce. The MacRuairis were also active in local Irish conflicts (*Ann. Connacht*, 250–1).
[15] *Ann. Connacht*, 250–3.

the Isles and Scotland change was even more significant. In 1317 John of Lorn died a broken exile. His end confirmed the removal of Clan Dougall from a leading role in Argyll and the Isles. Alongside the fall of his kinsmen, the Comyns of Badenoch and Lochaber, this meant that the wars since 1306 had removed the two dynasties at the heart of western politics since the 1260s. It remained to be seen how their leadership in the region would be replaced.[16]

In the decade from 1318 that leadership was in the hands of King Robert. The change had begun earlier. In May 1315, as Edward Bruce gathered his allies and galleys at Ayr, Robert set sail with his own ships to Tarbert on Loch Fyne. There he had his galleys dragged in full sail across Kintyre, consciously fulfilling a prophecy that any who performed the feat 'should win the Isles'. Whilst he dwelt at the old castle at Tarbert, the king cemented his loose superiority in the Hebrides, confirming support for the Irish venture. This quest for effective rule in the far west was, ironically, aided by the bloodbath at Fochart. The deaths amongst the leaders and men of Clan Donald and Clan Ruairi would weaken and fragment these kindreds for over a decade. Robert was not a man to miss the opportunity to tighten his lordship. The king knew the west and its political traditions. His perspective on the region was that of his forebears as earls of Carrick and their kin and allies, the Stewarts, who regarded Argyll and the Isles as a frontier zone of threat and opportunity. As king, Robert recognised the importance of these western magnate houses. His son-in-law, Walter Stewart, accompanied him to Tarbert in 1315, perhaps receiving confirmation as lord of Kintyre. The Stewarts' kin and adherents, the Menteiths and Campbells, similarly played key roles in Knapdale and Argyll. Further north Robert sought to restore the structure of lordship so important for the thirteenth-century kings, and in 1324 Randolph's authority over Lochaber was confirmed, probably at the expense of Clan Donald. The proof of the king's approach was in his dealings with the earls of Ross. Earl William was Robert's personal foe, but the lordship he exercised was vital for the order and stability of the north-west. From William's submission in 1308 onwards, the family was treated with generosity designed to preserve this role. New lands were added to their holdings in the east, while their western lands were confirmed by royal grant. The marriage of William's heir, Hugh, to the king's sister, Maud, cemented an alliance which had guarded the crown's interests in the far north for a century.[17]

[16] Sellar, 'Hebridean sea kings', 217; McNamee, *Wars of the Bruces*, 184.
[17] Barbour, *The Bruce*, 564–5; *R.M.S.*, i, app. 2, nos 17, 49–50, 55, 61, 63–5; *R.R.S.*, v, 635; Barrow, *Robert Bruce*, 271–4.

Robert was not content to bolster the power of western magnates. More than any of his royal predecessors, he maintained a personal presence in the Isles and coastlands. This was especially true in and around the Firth of Clyde. Following his visit there in 1315, the king identified Tarbert as a key point in the region, and in 1325 work was begun to strengthen the old castle as a royal base. He raised the money and supplies for construction from Argyll, Arran, Islay and Kintyre. These sums were levied by royal officials, Dugald Campbell as sheriff of Argyll and John MacDonald as bailie of Islay. John was probably the son of Angus Og and in the coming decades would rise to dominate the region. In 1326, however, he acted as a royal agent on his family's home island. The Hebridean kindreds lacked established leaders and were faced by a king capable of dealing with unrest within the Isles. When Robert visited his castle at Tarbert in 1326 and again in 1328, he was entering a region that sat firmly under his authority.[18]

This authority was not limited to the Hebrides. From 1326 Robert's interest was drawn, once again, across the narrow seas. The death of his father-in-law, Richard de Burgh, left his earldom weak and vulnerable with a youth, Richard's grandson, William, as absentee heir. By the end of the year, the fall of Edward II in England meant the Dublin government was uncertain and isolated. Robert received messages from this government and at Easter 1327 he landed in Ulster, acting as the kinsman of the young earl and protector of his tenants. The king remained in Ireland until August, negotiating with the English. Though he left after the colonists formally recognised Edward III, he returned the next year. After the treaty with the minority regime, Bruce now came 'in peace'. In his train was his nephew, William de Burgh, earl of Ulster. Robert established the earl in his province, his actions contrasting totally with the events of a decade before. In the late 1320s Bruce was seeking to restore the situation of the previous century when English and Scottish crowns and magnates acted together to maintain their interests against the Gaels of Ireland and their gallowglass allies. The attack on de Burgh in 1315 had been a product of the Bruces' position and served the goals of their supporters in the Isles. It did not offer a basis for secure Scottish kingship in the region. Influence in Ulster as the sponsor of the young earl linked to effective rule in the Isles was more effective. This was no peripheral concern to Robert. The ailing king spent much of his last two years on

[18] *E.R.*, i, 52–7; *R.R.S.*, v, 136–7, 156–7. In 1325 'Roderick de Ile', an unidentified Hebridean lord, was forfeited in parliament, an indication of both tensions in the Isles and the king's determination to stamp his authority on the region (*R.M.S.*, i, app. 2, no. 699).

ship and shore seeking to cement his dynasty's hold in the region. The peace and stability of much of his realm was bound up with the management of the isles and coasts to the west.[19]

However, the security of Robert's lordship in the Isles depended on the peace between the English and Scottish realms and on the continuity of effective royal government in the region. The renewal of war between the kingdoms in 1333 shattered the brief era of cohabitation, confirming a very different political environment in Ulster and the Isles. Ireland was, once again, used as a source of men and supplies for the Scottish wars, and questions of internal politics were neglected by the English crown. In this atmosphere the problems of the Anglo-Irish intensified, especially in Ulster. In 1333 Earl William de Burgh was murdered by his own kinsmen, ending the male line of earls and leaving his English tenants under absentee lords and vulnerable to their Gaelic neighbours. The role of the earls of Ulster as figures with influence across northern Ireland and into the Isles was over. Robert's support of his nephew in 1328 had not repaired the damage done to the earldom in the Bruce name a decade before.[20]

The renewal of war brought a parallel change to the west of Scotland. Here too, the great magnate adherents of the crown experienced a crisis. Earl Hugh of Ross was killed, his son and John Randolph left the kingdom, and young Robert Stewart was chased from his lands by the Balliol forces. Conflict for lordship was brought directly into the region by David Strathbogie. David occupied Stewart's lands on the Firth of Clyde in 1333 and two years later carried his war against Randolph into Lochaber, which Strathbogie claimed as heir of the Comyns. Though Stewart drew heavily and successfully on his tenants in Bute and Cowal, the attacks of Balliol and Strathbogie prevented the leading Bruce adherents in the west from exerting influence in the Isles. In their absence, Robert's political settlement unravelled. Man was lost in 1333 and in the Hebrides new leaders emerged: Ranald, son of Ruairi of Garmoran, and John, son of Angus Og of Islay. John's rise was possibly at the expense of his cousins, the sons of Alexander, who took the exiles' route, becoming Ulster galloglass. By 1334, John was lord of Islay and the leading figure in the southern Hebrides. In the warfare between Bruce and Balliol partisans, his support was valuable. John's aims in this conflict represented the change in regional circumstances. His position was no longer shaped

---

[19] McNamee, *Wars of the Bruces*, 242–5, 253; Frame, *English Lordship*, 139–42.
[20] Frame, *English Lordship*, 144–6, 196–227; Nicholson, *Edward III and the Scots*, 196–7. Edward III abandoned a planned expedition to Ireland in favour of the Scottish campaign of 1333.

Ulster in the Fourteenth Century

The de Burgh earls of Ulster had played a central role in the politics of the Isles and north and north-west Ireland since the 1260s but they were the major regional casualty of the wars. Robert I's restoration of his nephew, William, earl of Ulster in 1328 proved to be in vain. The earl's attempts to renew his grandfather's authority over a wide region ended when he was murdered near modern Belfast by his own steward and retainers in June 1333. This precipitated a period of conflict and raised fears of a fresh Scottish descent on Ulster. Though the English king's officials restored order to the heart of the earldom in eastern Ulster where English urban and rural communities survived, beyond the river Bann the lordship of the earls over Irish kindreds disappeared for good. Political activity amongst these dynasties remained characterised by conflict between rival claimants, like that between Aed and Enri Ó Neill which lasted into the 1340s, but the balance of power had altered. By the 1350s inroads were being made into English Ulster by the Ó Neill and the Ó Cathain kindreds and by families from Scotland and the Isles. As gallowglass and as lords in their own rights, Hebridean kindreds like the MacQuillins in north Antrim and the MacSweenys in Fanad established themselves in this unstable environment.[21]

by rivalry with the MacDougalls. John of Lorn's son, Ewen, did return with the Disinherited, but his activities did not amount to a challenge to Clan Donald's hold on the Isles.[22]

By 1335 both the Bruce guardians and Balliol recognised John of Islay as a lord to be courted. John Randolph travelled to Tarbert, not like Robert to display his authority but to seek the support of John of the Isles. Randolph's move was in response to offers made by both Balliol and the English who wanted John to aid an attack on south-west Scotland from Ireland. Whether or not John actively participated in the campaign, the attractions of allegiance to Balliol and England clearly proved stronger. By recognising Balliol, John secured a free hand in the Hebrides. In September 1336 he entered into an indenture with that king which gave him fresh title to Clan Donald's heartlands on Islay and to the lands granted to the family by Bruce, but which added new lordships. John was given rights to hold Knapdale on the mainland, the isles of Skye and Lewis, and a new claim to Lochaber, though only as guardian for

---

[21] Frame, *Colonial Ireland*, 118–19; Nicholls, *Gaelic and Gaelicised Ireland*, 128–35; A. J. Otway-Ruthven, *A History of Medieval Ireland* (London, 1968), 248–53.
[22] Simms, *From Kings to Warlords*, 139; Sellar, 'Hebridean sea kings', 217.

Strathbogie's young son. This arrangement was confirmed by Edward III and during 1337 and 1338 John remained his adherent, receiving praise from the English king for having 'repeatedly curbed our many wicked enemies'. The 1336 indenture gave John claims on the lands of Stewart, Randolph and Ross, and the Islesman probably pursued these rights through war with three of the leaders of King David's party. The only magnate not challenged by John's new claims was Ranald of Garmoran. Instead, MacRuairi was drawn into an alliance with his kinsman, a relationship secured through a marriage between John and Ranald's sister, Amy, in 1337. By then, John clearly regarded himself as the leading Hebridean magnate and adopted the style *Dominus Insularum*, Lord of the Isles. This was a Latin rendering of the Gaelic *Ri Innse Gall* claimed by Somerled and several of his descendants. From the 1330s it would symbolise the lasting predominance of John of Islay and his kin over the Hebrides and much of the surrounding coastlands.[23]

In the late 1330s John represented a growing power, from Ulster to Lewis, outside the allegiance of the Bruce king. While they led an increasingly effective war against Balliol and his backers, Stewart and Ross were apparently unsuccessful in forcing John of the Isles into submission. After David II's return in 1341, the king attempted to undermine John by recognising the latter's cousin, Angus, as lord of Islay, but this too made little impression. John's resistance to the Bruce cause was not due to fixed loyalties to its enemies. Instead, it sprang from a determination to retain his recent gains, areas in which he had made inroads since 1336. In this John was assisted by the divisions between the king and his magnates. His poor relations with David II probably encouraged Earl William of Ross to seek friendly relations with John and Ranald of Garmoran in 1342. Evidence of the Hebrideans reaching a similar peace with King David only came in June the next year in a meeting at Ayr. John was recognised as lord over many of the isles and lands granted him by Balliol, including Lewis and Lochaber. Though Stewart's position in Kintyre and Knapdale and Ross's rights in Skye were also acknowledged, the grants confirmed the gains made in war by John of Islay at the expense of the Bruce party.[24]

David issued his charters for 'the good and peace of the realm and community'. Though the Islesmen clearly accepted David's distant

---

[23] *Scotichronicon*, vii, 110–11; Nicholson, *Edward III and the Scots*, 220–1; *Acts of the Lords of the Isles*, lxxiv–lxxv, nos 1–3; *Rot. Scot.*, i, 516, 534, 535.
[24] *R.R.S.*, vi, nos 72, 73, 485; *R.M.S.*, i, app. 1, no. 114; Penman, 'The Kingship of David II', 185. The accommodation between Ross and the Islesmen was sealed by the earl's marriage to John's sister, Mary, and his grant of lands in Kintail (under dispute between the two men) to Ranald (*A.L.I.*, app. B, no. B23).

authority, in reality the grant of mainland lordships to John of the Isles and Ruairi of Garmoran guaranteed not peace, but continued disruption. William of Ross clearly continued to find the MacRuairies and other kindreds difficult neighbours and vassals in the west. His response to the problem was to seize the chance presented by the mustering of the king's host at Perth to surprise and kill Ranald MacRuairi at Elcho Priory in early October 1346. The slaying of a dangerous enemy by treachery was a tactic used by numerous English lords against Irish rivals. Its value depended on the ability of the killer to exploit the disruption created by the deed, but Ross would continue to experience opposition from local kindreds. Instead, the death of Ranald allowed John of the Isles to extend his lordship further. Ranald was the last male leader of the MacRuairi kindred. As both his brother-in-law and the most powerful figure in the west, John of the Isles moved quickly to secure Ranald's lordships. Uist and Garmoran were added to the orbit of the lord of the Isles.[25]

Between the 1330s and the 1360s the power of this Hebridean magnate developed as a loose but effective hegemony. In islands and in mainland districts John acted as overlord of lesser kindreds, like the MacLeans on Jura and Mull, the MacLeods on Lewis and the MacKintoshes in Lochaber. These families, and later junior branches of John's own house, were formed into a political hierarchy. John exacted limited services from these adherents, most importantly military support. The MacLeans in particular would be identified as the leader of John's standing forces, soldiers paid in land and rents in the manner of galloglass septs who combined professional service in war to a lord with permanent landholdings. The wars in the Isles which had absorbed the energies of such warbands were now replaced by relative peace. The use of these troops would now be focused beyond the Hebrides.[26]

How had a region, long fragmented between rival dynasties and easily brought under Scottish royal authority in the previous century, been formed into a single great lordship? Most obviously, John's rise was a consequence of the crisis experienced by the Scottish kingdom since the 1280s. The Hebrides had never been effectively absorbed into Scottish political society. Loose royal overlordship and aristocratic connections were no substitute for real identification with the Scottish kingdom. Like English lordship in western Ireland, such predominance disappeared quickly in the face of setbacks. War and crisis from the 1280s and after 1332 meant that the means and will to bring a distant and diffuse region

---

[25] *Scotichronicon*, vii, 253. Garmoran was confirmed to John in the 1370s but was almost certainly in his possession from soon after 1346 (*R.M.S.*, i, no. 412).
[26] *A.L.I.*, xlii–xlviii, no. 4; Simms, *From Kings to Warlords*, 116–28.

like the Isles under effective external authority were lacking. In the wars
Hebridean magnates were sought as allies and themselves used the wider
war to fulfil their own goals in the region. The decisive passage of the conflict saw the downfall of Comyn lordship in Lochaber and of the
MacDougalls in Mull, Morvern and Lorn between 1307 and 1309.
Achieved by Bruce in alliance with Clan Donald, this would serve the
interests of the Islesmen much more than the king. The MacDougalls
were the most powerful Hebridean kindred, the dynasty most closely
bound into the structures of the kingdom and most susceptible to royal
direction. By contrast, Clan Donald and Clan Ruairi remained much less
closely linked to the Scottish polity and retained stronger Irish connections. They were never comfortable agents of the Scottish crown. Bruce
had destroyed the strongest ties of lordship between the Scottish elite and
the Islesmen.

Of equal importance were attitudes within the Isles. For Islesmen the
defeat of Alexander of Argyll and his kin was a decisive episode, not in
King Robert's war but in the sporadic but bloody conflict between the
descendants of Somerled for kingship over *Innse Gall*. This kingship was
ill-defined but nevertheless possessed real meaning, corresponding to the
different values and perceptions of the Islesmen. These were reflected by
the continuing strength of ties – political, military, cultural and social –
between the Hebrides and Gaelic Ireland. John of the Isles himself
retained links of kinship with those Gaelic kindreds which profited most
from the decline of the earls of Ulster. With this background John would
hardly see his lordship in a purely Scottish context, and during the
coming decades Hebridean kindreds, the MacSweens, the MacRuairi and
the MacAlasdair branch of Clan Donald, would continue to establish
themselves in Ireland, receiving the praise of bards, the employment of
lords and control of new lands. For the men of the Isles, while the Scottish
king's lordship was an external intrusion, John's primacy represented the
continuation of their customary identities and activities as a Gaelic, sea-
borne, militarised and aggressive society. His achievement revived and
redefined the islands and coastlands as a distinctive political society
within the Scottish realm but outside the effective orbit of the kings.[27]

Such developments had dangerous implications for the Scottish
kingdom. John's primacy ended much of the internal warfare which characterised the Isles, but the Hebrides remained a militarised society. Still
economically poor, the Isles exported their surplus military population in

---

[27] Clancy, *The Triumph Tree*, 309; Nicholls, *Gaelic and Gaelicised Ireland*, 87–9; Duffy,
'The Bruce brothers', 74. John's mother, Ainè, returned to Ireland in c. 1336 and
married into a branch of the Ó Neill, an alliance perhaps in her son's interests.

search of lands or money. They added a new and unpredictable element to the political society of the north.[28] John also represented a new element in Scottish politics. In 1350 the lieutenant of the kingdom, Robert Stewart, sought a personal alliance with John of the Isles through his marriage to Stewart's daughter, Margaret. During the 1350s John was linked to the leading magnates of northern and western Scotland, Stewart and Ross. However, these connections were of a very different character to those of the previous century. The Comyns and Stewarts forged ties with Hebrideans in the 1260s to aid the crown in bringing the Isles into its orbit. The contacts made in the 1350s were no adjunct to royal authority. Instead they were attempts by magnates to accommodate and manage the place of Clan Donald and its satellites in the politics of the mainland. The trends of the thirteenth century in the west had been reversed. The re-establishment of an effective sub-kingdom in the Isles altered the political balance not just of Scotland, but of the whole maritime world of the west. The relative unity of the Hebrides contrasted with the fragmentation of royal authority in both Scotland and Ireland and with the lasting divisions between lords in English and Scottish allegiance. In an atmosphere of lasting warfare, the ability of Anglo-Irish and Scottish magnates to contain the activities of the Islesmen, through alliances like the Turnberry band, was lost. In Ireland the result was the part played by Hebrideans in the weakening of English lordship in Ulster and Connacht. As a consequence of the Scottish wars, in the fourteenth century it would not be the rule of English and Scottish kings and nobles, but the lordship of John Mór that would hold sway in the Isles and span the narrow seas.[29]

---

[28] Boardman, 'Lordship in the north-east: The Badenoch Stewarts I, Alexander earl of Buchan, lord of Badenoch', 1–30; *A.L.I.*, xxxviii–xli.
[29] *A.L.I.*, app. B, no. B25. The lordship of Kintyre, which Stewart and John both claimed, may have been Margaret's dowry. It was confirmed to the couple by Robert as king in 1376 (*R.M.S.*, i, no. 568).

CHAPTER 13

Europe and the Scottish Wars

A EUROPEAN WAR

To understand fully the course of events and the issues involved in the wars of Scotland, it is necessary to look beyond the northern British Isles. From the succession crisis of the 1280s onwards, Scotland's fate involved princes and communities, temporal and spiritual, across the west, with which the kingdom and its inhabitants had social, economic and political connections. Obviously, the closest and greatest involvement was that of Edward I, king of England and his heirs. The interests and ambitions of the Plantagenets were a permanent external force, driving events in Scotland but also drawing them into the wider framework of the English crown's connections and concerns. Above all, from the 1290s onwards, Scotland would be one of a number of smaller lands caught up in the rivalry of the greatest rulers of north-west Europe, the kings of England and their lords, the kings of France. Like Flanders, Aquitaine and later Brittany, Scotland was one arena in this rivalry. The Scots' predicament in the face of internal and external threats and their responses to them were not without parallels in the actions of other communities in the west between 1280 and 1360. This chapter seeks to assess the influence of such external factors on Scottish attitudes and experiences during the long crisis.

The end of the male line of the Scottish royal house was an event of significance in northern and western Europe. However, the death of Alexander III was overshadowed by an earlier royal fatality. The previous autumn the greatest western ruler, Philip III of France, had died on return from a disastrous campaign in Spain. The French king's war against the house of Aragon had been an escalation of the war over the Sicilian realm which threatened to draw in the major rulers of Christendom. When the Scottish envoys carried news of their king's death to Edward I, they found him preoccupied with these affairs. Edward left for France to do homage for Aquitaine to his new lord, Philip IV of France, but also to take up a renewed role as arbitrator between the Aragonese and the French. Between 1286 and 1288 Edward's energies were focused on this. His efforts failed to secure a lasting settlement and antagonised the French king, but they confirmed Edward as a figure of European stature. This stature was extended when, in 1287, Edward took the oath of a crusader once more. His ambitions were genuine, though while he negotiated terms with Pope Nicholas IV, the last Christian-held cities in the Holy Land were lost. From 1286 the Scots were seeking the help of a ruler of enormous prestige and extensive interests, making Edward both more valuable and more dangerous as a participant in Scottish affairs. The English king was able to secure papal support for the marriage between his son and Margaret of Norway in 1289 and also had the pope's support for his use of crusading taxes raised in Scotland for his own expedition. They would later denounce his actions, but in 1291–2 neither the pope nor the French king would be likely to object to Edward's role in Scotland and his alteration of the status of the Scottish realm.[1]

Edward was involved much more closely with Scotland during the Great Cause, but the northern kingdom still remained only one amongst many concerns and one of which the resolution would release him to other issues. It was not only through Edward's involvement that Scottish affairs attracted European interest. For generations the Scottish royal house had forged ties with other European dynasties – Alexander III in particular had secured prestigious marriages for his children with the houses of Norway and Flanders – and from 1286 these would create problems. The old king's son, Alexander, had married Margaret, daughter of Guy, count of Flanders. Though she returned to the Low Countries after the death of her husband, the count claimed her dower of lands and rents worth £1,000. King Eric of Norway would lay a similar claim for the dowry of his wife, Alexander's daughter, which included rents worth about £466 a year. Eric also claimed the 100 mark annuity for the Western Isles which went unpaid after 1286. As father of the lady of Scotland, Eric could hope to secure these demands, but with his daughter's death he put forward a claim to the Scottish throne as her heir. The Great Cause was not just an Anglo-Scottish affair. Alongside Eric was Floris, count of

[1] Prestwich, *Edward I*, 318–33; Vale, *Origins of the Hundred Years War*, 177–8; Strayer, 'The crusade against Aragon', 107–22; Prestwich, 'Edward I and the Maid of Norway', 166–8.

Holland, a descendant of David I, whose actions delayed the case, perhaps in the interest of his patron, Edward I.[2]

The accession of John Balliol as king of Scots did not end the claims of neighbouring princes. Both Guy of Flanders and Eric of Norway

---

The Scottish Wars and the Scandinavian Realms

Anglo-French rivalry was not the only context for the Scottish wars. During the thirteenth century, the Scottish realm's most problematic neighbour had been the kingdom of Norway, the dominions of which still included Orkney and a claim on the Western Isles. The actions of King Eric between 1286 and 1296 suggested that the Norwegians would play a part in the Scottish wars. After the short-lived alliance with France, Eric sought to resume the traditional friendship with England, and after his death in 1299 his brother and successor, Hakon V, offered Edward I the services of a fleet in the Isles in return for consideration of his claims on Scotland. This intervention would have been a potent threat to the guardians, but Edward may not have wished another king in the north. In the event, Hakon's offer marked the end of active Norwegian participation in the wars.

After 1306 Hakon proved to be more sympathetic to the Scots. Robert Bruce's sister was dowager queen of Norway and Hakon sheltered refugees from the defeats of 1306 in his lands. In 1312 Hakon was the first king to conclude a formal alliance with Robert. As part of the treaty, Robert promised payment of the annuity owed for the Isles, the smallest of Hakon's claims from 1299, but the wider demands for land and money were dropped. Since 1299 a shift in the Norwegian crown's interests had occurred. From the early fourteenth century Norway looked less to the western seas and more to her neighbours in Scandinavia and north Germany. Hakon's daughter and heiress married a Swedish prince and, when Hakon died in 1319, Norway was united to her eastern neighbour in a royal union like that planned for Scotland in 1290 under a Norwegian queen. During the next century such dynastic links between Scotland and Norway were not to be repeated. Though a plan was drawn up in the late 1350s by King Waldemar III of Denmark, which saw Scotland as the base for a Franco-Danish attack on England, the likelihood of such schemes had receded. The decline of Scandinavian political interests in the British Isles removed one set of potential enemies and allies from the Scottish war.[3]

---

[2] Stevenson, *Documents*, nos 246, 247; Helle, 'Norwegian foreign policy', 148–52; Nicholson, 'The Franco-Scottish and Franco-Norwegian treaties of 1295', 120–2; Kossmann-Putto, 'Florent V, Count of Holland, claimant to the Scottish throne in 1291–2, 15–27.

[3] Helle, 'Norwegian foreign policy'; Larsen, *A History of Norway*, 159–97.

pressed for their financial rights. Their demands to enjoy a fair proportion of the crown's income were another source of difficulty for King
John. Eric's marriage to Isabella Bruce, sister of the earl of Carrick, in
1293 suggests an alignment between John's enemies inside and outside
Scotland. By 1294 Eric was demanding the surrender of the Isles for non-
payment of the annual rent. The terms of John's kingship meant that
such issues were not fully in his power. Both the Norwegians and Flemish
took their cases to Edward as John's lord and the Scots king authorised
payment of Margaret of Flanders' dower in 1294 on the advice of Bishop
Anthony Bek, Edward's henchman. By contrast, Edward allowed Eric's
claim to remain unsettled. The English king was not willing to see his
vassal harassed by other rulers, and he extended protection. His actions
were, however, influenced by wider concerns. In 1294 Edward was negotiating an alliance with Flanders which suddenly assumed a massive
importance when war broke out between England and France.[4]

The Scottish wars were launched and waged against the background
of sustained rivalry between the kings of France and England. Such
rivalry had largely been absent from events since the 1250s. Suddenly and
unexpectedly, in early 1294 Philip IV initiated war by confiscating
Edward's duchy of Aquitaine. The tension this created was never fully
settled. The war which the two kings waged from 1294 to 1298 was more
wide-ranging and expensive than any previous clash between the two
realms. Two increasingly ambitious and demanding royal administrations
mobilised the full resources at their disposal, raising huge armies and
seeking grand coalitions of allies. Trends towards the intensification of
royal authority were accelerated by the conflict. A war which began over
Edward's rights as duke of Aquitaine saw the demands of the competing
kings squeeze other princely vassals and lesser rulers. One of these was
John, king of Scots.[5]

The outbreak of Anglo-French war was crucial for Scotland. The conflict provided the motive and means for the onset of conflict between
Edward and the Scots. Edward included John in his demands for troops
to defend his French lands in 1294. The summons to Scottish magnates
turned a jurisdictional dispute into a wider issue involving the whole
Scottish political elite. This elite also recognised the possibility of escaping Edward's lordship through an alliance with Philip of France. In July
1295 an embassy was appointed to negotiate with Philip, and in October

[4] Stevenson, *Documents*, no. 323; Nicholson, 'Franco-Scottish and Franco-Norwegian
treaties of 1295', 126-8.
[5] Vale, 'Edward I and the French: rivalry and chivalry', 165-76; Prestwich, *Edward I*,
376-84, 401-18; Strayer, 'The costs and profits of war: the Anglo-French war of
1294-1303', 269-91.

a formal treaty was agreed at Paris. The treaty involved a planned marriage between John's son, Edward, and Philip's neice, Jeanne, daughter of the anti-English Charles of Valois. For Philip the alliance was part of a northern coalition, also involving Eric of Norway, designed to counter Edward's arrangements with numerous princes in the Rhineland and the Low Countries. The French hoped that the threat of a land and naval campaign in the British Isles would limit Edward's actions on the continent. Despite the failure of Norwegian support, in 1296 Philip's aims were achieved and Edward's attentions were drawn north. For the Scots, who hoped that the alliance would protect them against Edward, it was a lesson in dealing with great kings. John's defiance of Edward was followed by the swift collapse of Scottish resistance, while Philip's forces merely raided the Channel coast. The Scots were not alone in learning such a lesson. Floris of Holland was murdered in 1297 after resisting Edward's diplomatic approaches, while Guy of Flanders and his territories were also engulfed in war. Like John, Count Guy saw the war as a means of escaping the demands of his superior lord, in his case, Philip IV. He too sought an alliance with his lord's enemy and issued a formal defiance. Guy then experienced the dangers of such actions. In 1297 most of his lands were overrun by the French, and the Flemish nobles and cities submitted to Philip.[6]

Though direct participation in the war by the Scots in 1296 had similarly served to precipitate disaster, the continuation of the Anglo-French war remained critical to their fortunes. In 1297 Edward's determination to intervene in both Gascony and Flanders coloured all his decisions. He placed increased demands for money and manpower on his dominions to provide him with the resources for two major campaigns. In Scotland such unprecedented burdens focused and accelerated widespread revolt. In England they sparked a political crisis which lasted through the summer and autumn and which came close to initiating civil war. Edward's decision to persist with his departure for Flanders was a mark of his priorities during this fateful year. He neither provided effective aid for the Flemings nor maintained a hold on his interests in the British Isles. The failure of the Edwardian administration in Scotland during the summer of 1297 owed much to the diversion of the king's interest and resources to continental war.[7]

[6] A.P.S., i, 451–3; Nicholson, 'Franco-Scottish and Franco-Norwegian treaties of 1295', 132; Nicholas, Medieval Flanders, 186–90. Balliol's French lands were to be held by his son and Jeanne of Valois. For Charles, see Vale, 'Edward I and the French', 171–3.
[7] Prestwich, Edward I, 414–31.

Edward may have learnt this lesson. In late 1297 he agreed to a truce with Philip IV which, after nearly two years of papal negotiation, was extended into a formal agreement which left Edward the loser. Edward was, however, free to concentrate on the Scottish war. The armies he led north in 1298, 1300 and 1301 were products of the king's disengagement from his struggle with Philip. Despite this disengagement – perhaps because of it – the leaders of Balliol's cause continued to attach a huge importance to seeking the French king's diplomatic and military support. Bishop Fraser, the leader of the 1295 embassy, remained in Paris until his death in 1297 and two of his colleagues, John Soules and Bishop Crambeth of Dunkeld, stayed on for several years more. In 1298 the Scottish lords who had been made to serve in Edward's Flemish expedition returned home via Philip's court, and in late 1299 William Wallace was one of a group of Scots who received the king's gifts. The most important embassy, in 1302, included Bishop Lamberton, James Stewart and the earl of Buchan. In years of major warfare, a good number of leading Scots devoted their efforts to seeking French support, and their labours yielded results. In contrast to Edward's abandonment of the Flemings, the 1299 settlement did not end Philip's support for the Scottish cause. It was the threat of a new breakdown of relations with the French which probably prompted Edward to surrender King John into papal custody in 1298. Edward's fear and his Scottish enemies' hope was that Philip would send troops to Scotland. Though this continued to be unfulfilled, in early 1302 French diplomacy scored two successes. Talks with England led to a truce for nine months during the summer of 1302, while the pope agreed to release King John onto his lands in Picardy. Both sides anticipated Philip's direct involvement in the war.[8]

The guardians looked to a second source of support. As the spiritual leaders of Christendom, the papacy could exert considerable pressure on temporal rulers. During the preceding century popes had been, in theory if not always in practice, the protectors of Scotland's status as a distinct realm. Even before their alliance with the French king, in late 1294 the Scots had sought papal support for resisting Edward, appealing to Celestine V for absolution from their oaths to the English king. Aged and unworldly, Celestine was useless as a supporter. His successor, enthroned as Boniface VIII, was a very different figure. From 1296 he confronted both Edward I and Philip IV over their taxation of the clergy and yet, in 1298–9, was asked by the kings to arbitrate in their dispute. Boniface also took a robust approach to Edward's actions in Scotland. In response to

[8] *Scotichronicon*, iii, 398–9; Barrow, *Robert Bruce*, 80, 95, 110, 124, 344 n. 26, 345 n. 41, 350, n. 94; Prestwich, *Edward I*, 496.

the efforts of Scots at the curia, in 1299 the pope issued the bull, *Scimus Fili*, which rebuked Edward for his actions since 1290, his imposition of lordship, his cancellation of the treaty of Birgham and his war against a neighbouring realm. Edward was ordered to desist from war and to prove his rights in Scotland before the pope within six months. The bull was a recitation of the Scottish case, but though Balliol was in papal custody, little was said about his restoration. Instead, acting without precedent, Boniface claimed the Scottish realm was a vassal of the papacy. Such a claim was characteristic of Boniface's view of papal authority. *Scimus Fili* added to Edward's discomfiture. It sparked an exchange between English and Scottish agents at the curia and caused Edward to rewrite the records of his dealings with Scotland and trawl historical sources to justify his actions. Like Robert Bruce in 1320, the king issued letters on behalf of his nobles, declaring communal support for his rights. However, like Robert too, Edward was aware that, although embarrassing, the hostility of the papacy posed a limited threat, especially compared with the attitude of Philip IV.[9]

Between 1298 and 1303 the strategy of the guardians placed considerable faith in winning support from Philip and Boniface whilst they waged their defensive war. It is hard to see an alternative to their hopes of bringing Edward to negotiation by external pressure and financial exhaustion, but there were flaws in this approach. Despite his advocacy of King John, Philip IV showed no readiness to send forces to Scotland or renew war on the continent over the issue. For both Philip and Boniface, Scotland was only one of many concerns. Their policies and priorities were way beyond the abilities of Scots to influence. This was clear from 1302 when the revolt of Flemings against Philip's direct rule in May led to the decisive defeat of his army at Courtrai in July. To reverse this major blow to his prestige and authority, Philip strained his full resources and sought to remove all entanglements. Though the Scots sent a major embassy to plead for continued support, in May 1303 Philip and Edward agreed a treaty which, in practice, allowed the French king a free hand in Flanders and the English ruler the same in Scotland. Within a few months the Scots had lost their other protector. Boniface died after having been seized by Philip's agents in the course of a struggle between king and pope for control of the French church. That their main allies were at odds for much of the period was an indication of the difficulties facing the Scots in their search for effective aid from the western princes. In the absence of external pressure, Edward was free to spend fourteen months in Scotland. While Edward's campaign of 1303–4 dealt an apparently

[9] Stones, *Anglo-Scottish Relations*, nos 28–31; Barrow, *Robert Bruce*, 63, 338, n. 44.

decisive blow to his Scottish enemies, Philip IV was able to impose harsh terms on his Flemish opponents.[10]

The war which began in Scotland in 1306 was regarded in very different terms by the rulers of the west. Robert Bruce initiated conflict without powerful allies. It would be three years before his kingship was acknowledged by any major prince and, in contrast to John Balliol, Robert would be the subject of sustained papal hostility. Though he was greatly assisted by the series of political crises endured by Edward II in his English realm, in terms of European politics Robert's success was achieved in spite of, not because of, wider circumstances. This lack of external support was due, in part, to his seizure of the throne. Murder, sacrilege and usurpation were hardly the means to achieve the sympathy of the papacy or of King Philip, especially as King John was still living under French protection. Moreover, in the twenty years from 1304, neither the papacy nor the French crown had an interest in causing problems for Edward II in Scotland. The Anglo-French peace of 1303 held shakily and was actively supported by, first, Clement V and then John XXII, popes of Gascon birth based at Avignon and keen to prevent conflict between their royal neighbours. Robert's successes in Scotland did allow him to make some headway with the French king. In 1309 Philip IV at least referred to Robert, not John, as king of Scots and wrote to him in friendly language. However, the French king attempted to persuade Robert to make peace with Edward II in the interests of Christendom. Philip's letters referred to the previous alliance but did not offer to renew it. Robert's relations with the papacy were even more difficult. Excommunicated in May 1306, Robert found Clement V to be consistently hostile and pro-English, even refusing to allow Scottish business to come before the curia. The election of John XXII brought some initial improvement but he too regarded Robert's claims as a source of dangerous disunity within Christendom. The Scottish king's refusal to recognise the papal truce in 1317–18 led to a fresh sentence of excommunication on Bruce and his adherents, and to an interdict being imposed on his realm. Though the efforts of Robert and his agents led to these penalties being lifted, there was no sign of the earlier papal support for the Scottish cause.[11] Between 1306 and 1322, during what was the most important phase of the wars, Robert established his kingship in Scotland without the help of major external allies.

[10] Nicholas, *Medieval Flanders*, 191–5; Strayer, *The Reign of Philip the Fair* 336–7; Prestwich, *Edward I*, 397–8; Chaplais, 'Le duché-pairie de Guyenne: L'hommage et les services féodaux de 1259–1303', in Chaplais, *Essays in Medieval Diplomacy and Administration*, iii, 37–8.

[11] *A.P.S.*, i, 459; Barrow, *Robert Bruce*, 183; Vale, *Origins of the Hundred Years War*, 227–9.

BRUCE AND VALOIS

The Bruce dynasty only succeeded in winning formal allies with a fresh shift in relations between the kings of England and France. The brief war of Saint Sardos in Gascony from 1324 ended the period of peace between Edward II and his brother-in-law, Charles IV. Robert, who was already seeking the French king's goodwill, seized the opportunity to open negotiations, sending Thomas Randolph to Paris in the summer of 1325. The result was a formal treaty, agreed by King Charles at Corbeil and confirmed by Robert in July 1326. By its terms the Scots agreed to make war against England in a future Anglo-French conflict, and the French agreed to give 'help and advice' to the Scots in any Anglo–Scottish war. Truce or peace between one ally and England should include the other partner. Though unequal in its requirements, the treaty of Corbeil was a diplomatic victory for Robert. Its value would survive both peace with England and the accession of a new French king, Charles's cousin, Philip of Valois. Alliance with France and the subsequent peace settlement with Edward III's government were probably the key elements in the alteration of papal attitudes to the Bruce dynasty. Papal acknowledgement of Robert's royal title had finally come in 1324 but the culmination of Bruce's rehabilitation came in 1329 when John XXII granted the rite of coronation to the Scottish kings. This was recognition that Scotland's rulers were not subject to the superior lordship of the English crown and it marked the end of a dispute at the curia which stretched back a century.[12]

In the wars of the 1290s to 1320s, the fate of Scotland had been linked to the relationship between English and French kings. However, the causes of Anglo–French conflict and direct confrontation between their forces occurred far from Scotland, in Aquitaine and Flanders. When war returned to Scotland in the 1330s, its European significance would be far greater. More directly than Aquitaine or Flanders, Scottish affairs generated tensions between the greater realms which by 1340 had spiralled into a conflict between Edward III and Philip VI for the French throne. Without the Scottish war, such a conflict could have been long delayed. Philip VI (Philip of Valois) was certainly not seeking a quarrel in the early 1330s. His plans for a crusade to the east led him to seek Edward's goodwill, even agreeing to concessions on the vexed issue of Aquitaine. However, unlike his uncle, Philip IV, Philip of Valois did not find it easy to abandon his allies, even after the defeats of 1332 and 1333. The arrival of John Randolph and other Scots at the French court in late 1333 prompted Philip to offer sanctuary to the young David Bruce. With

[12] *R.R.S.*, v, no. 299; *Nat. MSS Scot.*, ii, no. 30.

The Bruce Cause and the Trading Towns

Though Robert I lacked the support of the pope and French king, he was not without active external support. His war in Scotland was assisted by the inhabitants of the trading and industrial towns of northern Europe from Flanders to the Baltic. Long-standing economic connections with Scotland translated into vital military support from 1297 onwards. Much of this support remained economic in character. The Flemish towns continued to be the principal market for Scottish wool and, despite the shifting alliances of princes, these markets remained open for most of the period, providing the Scots with access to funds and goods. Above all, Scots relied on these links to bring in armour and weaponry, a trade underway from the 1290s to the 1330s. The seafarers of these regions also preyed on English ships in alliance with Scottish privateers based in their ports. Robert's predecessors recognised the importance of this support. In late 1297 one of the acts of Wallace and Moray after Stirling Bridge was to write to the German cities of Hamburg and Lubeck informing them that the Scottish ports were open for trade. For Robert the crucial breakthrough was his capture of Aberdeen in 1308, allowing him access to the North Sea trade routes. Though Robert was assisted by German merchants, Flanders remained the crucial economic link. Ironically, in this relationship, Robert was aided by the Anglo-French peace of 1303. In the 1290s the Flemish had seized Scottish goods in the interests of their ally, Edward I. After 1303 neither the counts nor the cities had any interest in disrupting trade and, despite English pressure, Count Robert of Flanders refused to expel Scottish merchants. When Edward II placed an embargo on English trade with Flanders in 1315, the seas were flooded with Flemish merchants seeking to redeem their losses by piratic attacks on English shipping. Captains like John Crabbe gave King Robert vital aid in harassing English merchants and in his land campaigns, especially the capture of Berwick in 1318. Similar support at sea would again aid the Bruce partisans during the 1330s and 1340s. As a means to supply Scottish armies and disrupt English trading interests, merchants from across northern Europe played a key role in support of Scottish kings and guardians.[13]

David II on French soil, Philip then found it difficult to ignore Edward III's war in Scotland in his dealings with English envoys. At the last minute Philip demanded that Scotland be included in a planned Anglo-French treaty. His action was required by Corbeil but Philip's intervention represented a major shift in policy. From the summer of 1334 the

[13] Stevenson, 'The Flemish dimension of the Auld Alliance', 32–9; Simpson, 'Trade, traders and Scottish independence', 210–22; Stevenson, *Documents Illustrative of Sir William Wallace*, 159.

French king was a consistent upholder of the Bruce cause, first by diplomatic, then by military efforts.[14]

Philip's efforts during 1334 and 1335 were, however, stalled by the
actions of the English king and the papacy. While Edward prevaricated,
agreeing to a short truce during which he prepared his massive campaign of August 1335, Pope Benedict XII, the successor to John XXII,
intervened as arbitrator. Benedict's motive was not concern for
Scotland. He had been appalled by Philip's neglect of the crusade and
declared that the French king had no obligations to the Scots. Papal
envoys arrived in England in late 1335 and attempted to broker a settlement which would once again consider the rival claims of Bruce and
Balliol. While the beleaguered Bruce partisans in Scotland used this to
buy time over the winter, the rejection of the papal plan by David's court
in Normandy was unequivocal. This response was backed by the king of
France. By the winter of 1335–6, Philip had determined to intervene in
the Scottish war. The crusade was abandoned. Plans were laid for an
armada of over 200 transports and thirty galleys to sail from France and
carry an army of 6,000 men to north-east Scotland. Since the previous
summer French and Scottish ships had been using Norman ports to
harry English shipping and carry supplies to Scotland. News that this
fleet was assembling shaped Edward's Scottish strategy. His devastating
chevauchée through the north-east and the destruction of Aberdeen was
designed to deny the French an easy landing, while the fortification of
Scotland below the Mounth was a recognition of his diminishing
options. Edward's efforts and administrative problems delayed the
French expedition beyond the sailing season. The ships which had gathered were used to raid the southern and eastern English coasts. The
effect of this was electric. The Scots could harry northern England
without major political effect in the rest of the kingdom, but news of the
French raids sparked a crisis of confidence and prompted military preparations. The planned parliament at York in early 1337 was moved to
Westminster where its business was dominated by relations with the
French king. For his part, Philip was now looking not to the British Isles
but to Aquitaine, sensitive politically and vulnerable militarily to French
royal aggression. Though the armada of 1336 never sailed, it had played
a vital role in turning the Scottish war into a general struggle between
Plantagenet and Valois.[15]

[14] *Foedera*, ii, 860, 883; Sumption, *The Hundred Years War: Trial by Battle*, 132, 135–6;
Nicholson, *Edward III and the Scots*, 157–8.
[15] *Chron. Lanercost*, 295–6; Sumption, *Trial by Battle*, 142–6, 153–9, 162–3; Penman,
'The kingship of David II', 79, 89.

After 1337 Scotland never dominated this struggle in the same way. In May Philip VI confiscated Aquitaine and sent an army into the duchy. Even before this, Edward III was building a grand coalition of allies in the Low Countries and the Rhineland. The focus on the north-east frontier of France was confirmed by revolt in Flanders at the end of the year. In the early 1340s the war of succession in Brittany provided another theatre for a rivalry whose significance had increased when Edward III claimed the throne of France as Philip IV's grandson in 1340. The Scottish war was on the northern fringe of a much wider conflict, but it was not forgotten. Edward sent expeditions north in 1337 and 1338, while Philip maintained the flow of supplies to Scotland, culminating in the dispatch of ships and men with William Douglas in 1339. This French contingent and French and Flemish privateers aided in the capture of Perth in 1339. The strains of fighting on three fronts limited Edward's ability to hold onto his Scottish lordship. Murray's campaign in 1337 had stretched resources to the limit and the resistance of Dunbar to a sustained English siege in early 1338 prompted a rethink. Edward recalled the force from Dunbar to provide men and supplies for an army being equipped for Flanders. English priorities had shifted decisively.[16]

This shift was of vital long-term advantage to Scotland. For most of the century from 1340, the English monarchy was engaged in a hot or cold war with the Valois kings of France which absorbed the bulk of its external energies. The value of this in military terms was quickly clear between 1339 and 1342. The rapid capture of Perth, Stirling, Edinburgh and Roxburgh and the end of significant English lordship in the south-east occurred without a major response from Edward III. The men and victuals needed to maintain English lordship in Scotland were diverted to continental war and diplomacy which, like that of Edward I in the 1290s, provoked an internal crisis in England. However, for many Scottish leaders, the alliance with France was more than a marriage of convenience. The help given by Philip VI in the 1330s, in particular the sheltering of King David and other young nobles, left a legacy with the new generation of leaders, like William, lord of Douglas and Thomas Stewart, earl of Angus. Above all, David himself felt obliged to his royal protector. When, in early 1346, the French king appealed to 'the bonds of blood and friendship between us', David was keen to offer help. Additional letters reported Edward III's march through northern France which climaxed in his defeat of Philip at Creçy and it was to aid his ally that David led his

---

[16] *Chron. Lanercost*, 308–15; *Scotichronicon*, vii, 140–1. For the widening of the war between Edward and Philip, see Sumption, *Trial by Battle*, 185–410; Rogers, *War, Cruel and Sharp*, 127–216.

subjects into northern England in September. The defeat at Neville's Cross was, in part, the price paid for David's adherence to the French alliance beyond the immediate needs of his realm.[17]

The events of 1346 were proof of the dangers for a small realm in a major war. The same lesson was shown in a different way during the next decade. In 1355 a small French expedition and a large cash subsidy from King John II persuaded the Scots to renew the war in the marches after a truce. The leading roles in this warfare were played by border magnates – Patrick, earl of Dunbar, Thomas, earl of Angus and William, lord of Douglas, the latter two lords with French connections – and by Eugene de Garencières, the experienced French captain. The capture of Berwick town was a major victory for these men, but it initiated a military crisis. The presence of French troops in Scotland and the loss of his main Scottish base alerted Edward III to the renewed importance of the Scottish war. His campaign of early 1356, the 'Burnt Candlemas', achieved little beyond the recapture of Berwick, but it brought fresh destruction and misery to the south-east as a consequence of the French presence.[18]

Not surprisingly, Neville's Cross and the 'Burnt Candlemas', as well as Creçy and Poitiers, persuaded some leading Scots that the value of an active alliance with the French king was limited, now that Edward III's efforts were concentrated elsewhere. David II himself felt abandoned by Philip VI after his capture and increasingly saw his hopes of release and possibly the best interests of his kingdom as resting with a final peace with England. The reluctance of his subjects to agree terms with Edward's envoys in 1351–2 owed more to distrust of the English king than to the late and unsupported appeals to the French alliance made by John II of France. For his part, John was prepared to negotiate with Edward concerning a final peace without mentioning his Scottish allies. The defeat and capture of John at Poitiers in 1356 revealed the limits to the alliance. The situation of the French realm after the battle, kingless and prey to the English king, may have recalled the state of Scotland in the 1290s and 1330s, but it did not persuade Scottish leaders to step up their support. Instead, at Berwick in 1357 they agreed a ten-year truce and David's release for ransom, a settlement which revealed Edward's readiness to let slip the rights he claimed in Scotland in order to further the pursuit of those he now sought in France. It may have

[17] Penman, 'The kingship of David II', 203–9; Brown, *The Black Douglases*, 211–12; Sumption, *Trial by Battle*, 499–500, 503–4.
[18] *Scalachronica*, 118; *Scotichronicon*, vii, 278–83; Sumption, *The Hundred Years War: Trial by Fire*, 152–3, 162, 173–4, 187–90.

appeared that the Bruce dynasty was securing its future by abandoning its former protector.[19]

Such a verdict would be misleading. The efforts of the Scots were hardly a guarantee of French fortunes, and the events of the late 1350s would show that Edward III had reached the limits of his success. In 1360 he agreed the treaty of Brétigny with the French, securing major gains but relinquishing his royal claims. As part of these terms, the French consented to end the alliance with Scotland. Along with the treaty of Berwick, the treaty of Brétigny suggests the loosening of ties between the former allies. This would not be the long-term trend, however. Even during the late 1350s there were signs of continuing co-operation between the two governments, while on a personal level many Scots retained links with France. The decision of William, lord of Douglas to seek knighthood from John II of France and serve in his army at Poitiers with his retinue was clear evidence of identification with the French realm. Such affection for France was a legacy of the crucial aid provided by their ally at key points in the preceding half-century. Philip IV had played a significant role in Scottish resistance to Edward I, but greater assistance had been rendered by Philip VI. Honourable or naive, depending on the perspective, Philip of Valois' refusal to abandon the Bruce regime in 1334 and his decision to initiate war on Scotland's behalf in 1336 were key moments in the struggle of the 1330s. Without the first, David Bruce would conceivably have fallen into his enemies' hands; without the second, Scotland would have faced a far longer and more disruptive war against Edward III's full resources with no guarantee of success. Though the events of 1296, 1303 and 1346 were less happy for the Scots involved, the recognition and help of the French monarchy, and the wider context of Anglo-French hostility, greatly facilitated the long-term defence of Scotland, free from the English king's lordship. Despite the late 1350s, the alliance with France would remain a natural connection for the Scottish realm during the next two centuries.[20]

The Scottish wars could not be isolated from the wider world. Western Europe around 1300 was not a collection of separate national realms: despite the growing power of royal governments, it remained a single Latin Christian community, the identity of which transcended the rivalries of temporal lordships. War between Christian peoples was the concern of all. It was on these terms that successive popes sought to

[19] Penman, 'The kingship of David II', 232–4; Sumption, *Trial by Fire*, 149–52, 289–92.

[20] Le Patourel, 'The treaty of Brétigny, 1360', 24, 29; Brown, *The Black Douglases*, 47, 54–5, 211; Sumption, *Trial by Fire*, 228, 238–46.

influence English and Scottish leaders between the 1290s and 1350s, usually without much success. Amongst papal concerns was the damage done to the crusade, and the loss of the Holy Land in the 1290s made this an active issue. In this context the Scottish war was a distraction, consuming the time and resources of rulers, like Edward I in the 1290s or Philip VI in the 1330s, who had agreed to take the cross and lead eastern expeditions. The 'tyrant' Robert Bruce was criticised in particular as the disrupter of Christian peace and unity. Robert's envoy to the curia, Thomas Randolph, stressed to Pope John his lord's desire to go to Jerusalem, probably in an effort to deflect such criticism. In the barons' letter of 1320, the same issue was answered by the accusation that the English preferred to seek the conquest of their weak Christian neighbours than defend Christendom from the infidel. Beneath the diplomatic point-scoring, such issues mattered. Robert's desire to have his heart carried to the Holy places was perhaps born of the knowledge that, unlike his grandfather, he had spent his life fighting Christians without undertaking an expedition against the enemies of Christ. The expedition of James Douglas to Spain with Robert's heart may have come to a swift and bloody conclusion with Douglas's death at Teba de Ardales in 1330, but James's progress to Spain via Flanders and France was a way of displaying the piety of the Bruce party, so long the subject of attack, before a European audience. In practice, even while Robert was excommunicant, his position in Scotland and influence over the Scottish clergy made it necessary for him to be involved in the affairs of Christendom. The suppression of the Templars in 1308 was an example of this. The papacy required the clergy of the Scottish province to assemble to enquire into the order and judge its members. The general council of the Scottish church met on the outskirts of English-held Dundee in February 1310. It was exploited by Bruce and his clerical advisors to re-issue the so-called Declaration of the Clergy, this time for the benefit of Pope Clement V and the council of the whole church which was due to meet at Vienne in October 1310. Robert's rightful place as king of Scots was made plain to a European audience.[21]

Just as Scotland's fate was bound up with wider events and policies across the west, so the experiences of Scots in the late thirteenth and early fourteenth centuries shared significant features with those of neighbouring communities. The issue of Scotland's status, its freedom from, or subjection to, the superior, sovereign lordship of the English crown was the central theme of the conflict. This issue of defined sovereignty was symptomatic of wider trends in government, especially in France where

[21] MacQuarrie, *Scotland and the Crusades*, 72-5.

the Capetian kings achieved formal recognition of their authority over principalities like Aquitaine, Brittany and Flanders. Even where this sovereign lordship had been accepted in theory, its practical application tended to initiate conflict. The intrusion of external jurisdiction and, even more, the demands for services in the interest of the superior lords, which sparked the Scottish wars, lay behind conflicts between the French crown and its princely vassals. Royal demands even caused unrest in lands accustomed to direct rule. The criticisms of the crown's exactions from the English community, under Henry III in the 1250s, against Edward I in 1297 and faced by Edward II for most of his reign, and, in a more limited way, the formation of leagues of mutual defence in parts of the French royal demesne to oppose the king's policies in 1314–15, were manifestations of such unrest against novel or excessive demands. In lands where such demands were made by rulers and officials perceived to be foreigners, there was an additional element. The rising of the Sicilians against Charles of Anjou and his French regime in 1281 or that of the citizens of Bruges against Philip IV's officials in 1302 were attacks against 'alien' oppressors. They were motivated not just by the actions of the government in question, but by the desire to remove foreigners from positions of lordship and authority in secular and ecclesiastical spheres. Hostility to foreign customs and personnel were elements in creating forceful reactions to French rulers and administrations in Sicily, Flanders and, later, in Brittany which were exploited and manipulated by leaders to sustain resistance on behalf of native communities. Similar attitudes towards the English crown, officials and clergy were strong elements in Scottish attitudes, especially in 1297.[22]

The desire to obtain formal recognition of Scotland's status as a realm 'without subjection' to the English crown developed as a response to demands for defined, sovereign lordship. The ambiguous situation tolerated, and even encouraged, by Alexander III was no longer a valid position. The direct rejection of English lordship which characterised the position of the Bruce party from the 1320s had parallels elsewhere in Europe. Amongst these, ironically, were the claims of Edward I and his heirs to rule Aquitaine with similar freedom from the jurisdiction of the French crown. In 1360 Edward III secured the recognition of these claims in the treaty of Brétigny, a document which can be compared with the 1328 treaty of Edinburgh-Northampton. In the course of their own internal and external struggles, Bretons and Flemings voiced a similar desire

[22] Pirenne, *Histoire de Belgique*, i, 416–19; Dunbabin, *Charles I of Anjou*, 99–113; Brown, *Politics and Institutions in Capetian France*, v, 109–37; Gaillou and Jones, *The Bretons*, 217–22.

to withdraw from the sovereignty of the kings of France. In an era of legalistic and assertive monarchies, lesser kings and princes, like the kings of Scots, needed their own legal protections, though even these could not guarantee lasting protection from greater rulers. In motivations and aims, as well as in their course and connections, the Scottish wars were a European conflict.[23]

[23] Rogers, *War, Cruel and Sharp*, 419–20; Le Patourel, 'The king and the princes in fourteenth-century France', 155–83; Rogers, 'The Anglo-French peace negotiations of 1354–1360 reconsidered', 193–214.

CHAPTER 14

Allegiance and Identity

THE SCOTTISH CAUSE

The status of Scotland and the identity and rights of its rulers were at the centre of the military and political struggles in the northern British Isles between the 1280s and 1350s. The end of the old royal dynasty led to rival claims to the kingship of the Scots, while successive kings of England sought to establish sovereign lordship. The – ultimately successful – opposition of Scottish kings and guardians to this external pressure resulted in a series of wars from 1296 to 1357. However, the struggle was never simply one of conquest and coup by these leaders. Through the various phases of the wars, any who sought to establish their title to Scotland needed to obtain the acceptance of their authority from the *commune* of Scotland, the political class of the kingdom. As discussed earlier, though this group was dominated by fifty or so great magnates and prelates, it included a much wider body of men and women, laity and clergy, whose places and attitudes formed a network of relationships inside and outside the realm. Both practical power and legitimate authority rested in the recognition of the people of Scotland.

It was through such recognition that the rival rulers of Scotland sought to restore the bonds that had held the thirteenth-century kingdom together. At the heart of these bonds was the oath of fealty sworn by Scottish tenants-in-chief to the crown. This act represented their obedience to the king's authority and the promise of personal support and service to their royal lord. In the years of peace these oaths had signified a fixed and stable relationship between the royal line and its vassals. From 1286, however, the days of such settled and relatively-undemanding allegiance by the political class to their natural and uncontested lord were at an end. Through the next seventy years, oaths of fealty were given, willingly or unwillingly, to rival royal lords whose rule lacked full or lasting acceptance. In the years of crisis and war the performance of homage was coloured by the instability and conflict which was now involved in questions of loyalty and political direction. The decade from Alexander III's death saw issues of conflicting fealty and lordship assume a dominant place in the kingdom's political life. From 1286 the old king's vassals swore fealty to a succession of lords, culminating in the homages given to Edward I on the Ragman Roll in 1296. The onset of sustained warfare from 1297 made competition for allegiance and changes of allegiance a lasting feature of politics. Rival royal lords recognised this. Throughout most of this period both English and Scottish leaders accepted, and actively courted, the negotiated submission of enemy lords. On both sides, such moderation was the mark not of flexibility on questions of rights and authority (hardly to be associated with Edward I), but of the acceptance of the need to win and retain support from political society in general and, in particular, from those leading figures who could deliver the support of the local communities which made up the kingdom.[1]

The actions and attitudes of such men explain the course of the wars as much as the ambitions of Plantagenet, Balliol and Bruce. They create a picture which is not easy to disentangle. During the long periods of open war most members of the political class were involved in at least one change of allegiance. The submissions to Edward I in 1296 and 1304–5 and to his grandson in the 1330s, the continuing support given to the Balliol cause from the 1290s to the 1350s, and the rise and success of the Bruce party from 1306 created an atmosphere in which magnates, lesser nobles and even freeholders had to break and remake bonds of fealty with competing rulers. The reasons that informed such changes were central to the wars and their outcome, combining individual hopes, needs and obligations with the pull of collective values and identities.

Changes in sworn allegiance did not occur in a political vacuum. Nor were they made solely in response to coercion. Scotland's political class in the 1280s and their successors in subsequent decades possessed a developed sense of shared values and structures. As has been shown, the thirteenth-century kingdom rested on these values which, if neither uniform nor exclusive, provided the framework of political life. For its inhabitants, Scotland was identifiable as a kingdom, a province of the Latin church and it could be claimed as the homeland of a single people. Questions and limits existed for all these definitions but it is clear that the uncertainty and disruption of the period from 1286 did not remove their importance. Instead they were recognised as the liberties of Scotland, the rights and customs of the kingdom and the various communities within

[1] For a discussion of this, see Barrow, 'The aftermath of war', 103–25.

it. Successive Scottish regimes placed defence of these liberties at the centre of arguments used to justify resistance to English kings and seek recognition from the papacy. Between the 1290s and 1350s a series of statements were issued in the name of the Scots which contained common elements. As a realm, a community, a nation and a church, it was claimed that Scotland 'rejoiced in every kind of liberty' and 'lived in freedom and quiet'. They had been ruled by 'kings of our native and royal stock' who had never been justly subjected to their neighbours, and the separate status and rights of their church enjoyed the special protection of the papacy. These rights and the peace of the land had been broken solely by Edward I. He 'was not acknowledged as lord of the Scots except only through fear at a time when the kingdom was vacant'. Later, when the Scots sought to recover 'former liberties', Edward unleashed war, not as rightful lord but as a 'foreigner' inflicting savage damage on church and people. Scottish submissions had been made through 'force and fear' and, despite them, the Scots continued to adhere to their ancient liberties, remaining loyal to kings chosen according to 'the laws and customs of the realm' with 'the consent and assent of all the people'. Rather than 'rebels' as their enemies claimed, the Scots were united in defence of king, church and established liberties.[2]

The language used would have been recognisable within the kingdom. The defence of 'ancient liberties' was a potent and well-understood concept in contemporary Europe. Its use by Scottish advocates was not baseless propaganda nor the abstract ideology of a clerical elite but was born out of well-established patterns of allegiance and identity within Scotland. The appeal to past rights and status sanctioned resistance to Plantagenet claims to sovereign lordship over the kingdom in forms understood by most Scots. The desire to preserve well-understood liberties shaped Scottish political attitudes at both Birgham in 1290 and Norham in 1291. This was the defence of both collective and individual interest and of Scotland's status as a separate society, free from the demands of a superior lord. It was in opposition to such demands that John defied Edward in April 1296, citing 'harm beyond measure to our liberties and our kingdom'. After Robert Bruce's seizure of the throne and renewal of war, he and his adherents similarly presented their activities in terms of the rights of kingdom and inhabitants. In 1309 Robert was

---

[2] The Scottish case was presented in two documents of 1301 and the famous barons' letter (also known as the Declaration of Arbroath) of 1320. All were preserved in the fifteenth-century *Scotichronicon* compiled by Walter Bower (*Scotichronicon*, vi, 132–89; vii, 5–9). For the background to this material see Simpson, 'Declaration of Arbroath revitalised', and with a different emphasis Cowan, 'Identity, freedom and the Declaration of Arbroath', 38–68.

identified as acting to 'reform the deformities of the kingdom' and restore 'the kingdom of Scots . . . to its former liberties' while seventeen years later Robert claimed that he 'had sustained many hardships for the recovery and protection of the liberties of them all'. Whatever doubts remained about his legitimacy, success in war allowed Robert to act as the defender of his subjects' rights. His recognition by Edward III as the ruler of a kingdom 'divided in all things from the realm of England and . . . without subjection [or] servitude' both confirmed Robert's rights and added to the identification of the Bruce dynasty with a separate and sovereign Scottish realm. Throughout the quarter-century of war which followed Robert's death the maintenance of a realm 'without subjection' remained at the heart of resistance to the lordship of Edward III and Edward Balliol. In the 1350s and 1360s it was argued that the 'full liberty' of Scotland depended on its status as a realm with its own king. The wars which began in 1296 to defend the interlinked rights of both king and community in Scotland remained focused on the same issue over six decades.[3]

Some, at least, of these arguments could be regarded as the language of political manifesto and diplomatic exchange. However, even these forms, which placed stress on legal concepts and precedents, needed to relate to the hard choices involved in taking up, or remaining in, arms. The sense of a Scottish cause, relating to the rights and interests of the people of Scotland, was clearly an element in decisions taken by a wide group of Scots. In 1297 the broadly-based reaction to Edward I's administration suggests the desire to resist the material threats posed by the new regime merged with a willingness to carry arms, in Wallace's reported words, 'to free our kingdom'. The subsequent war waged by guardians acting in King John's name still depended on a wider identification of his cause from political society. Similar support was almost certainly an element in King Robert's success. 'The goodwill of the people' referred to in an English assessment of Robert's position in 1307 should be read less as a belief in the rightness of the Bruce claim, than the continuing attraction of a leader in arms against the English king and those in his allegiance. The support received by Robert remained limited and patchy for over a decade but, even so, Bruce showed an ability to win assistance from knights and freeholders in localities where his personal influence was limited.[4]

The ability to articulate support for a Scottish cause certainly spread amongst these groups. In 1308 a bond between Neil Campbell, Alexander

[3] Stones, *Anglo-Scottish Relations*, nos 23, 41; *A.P.S.*, i, 289, 475–6; *S.H.S. Misc.*, xii, 29, no. 9. For discussions of this theme, see Watson, 'The Enigmatic Lion 18–37; Barrow, 'The idea of freedom', 26–32.

[4] Barrow, 'Idea of freedom'; Grant, 'Aspects of national consciousness', 82–8.

Seton and Thomas Hay committed each to support King Robert and to defend the liberties of the realm, while on two occasions, Scots claimed to be fighting for the 'Lion'. The second of these occasions, in early 1336 was the complaint of an English official that certain Scots were continuing the war in breach of a truce. These men were 'refusing to serve anything but the *Leone*'. By the 1330s it was possible to use the Lion, the symbol of the realm, to justify and sanction unceasing warfare against the English in defence of Scottish liberties without reference to an individual king. This language recalled the barons' letter of 1320 which placed the freedom of the Scottish realm from the English king's lordship above the authority of their own ruler. While, in practice, Robert I did not regard his powers as subject to new communal limitations, from the 1330s the atmosphere may have changed. For most of this renewed period of warfare the Bruce party operated without an active royal leader. In the early 1350s, when David II was seeking the support of his subjects for his release, their response was to reject any terms that they considered threatened the status of the kingdom. Even if this was a justification with a partisan motive, it was also an expression of a sense of collective rights belonging to the kingdom.[5]

Yet the wars of Scotland were never simply about the defence of the liberties of realm and people. Identification with these liberties did not automatically fix the actions and loyalties of individuals or communities, and throughout the period from 1296 a changing but always significant part of the Scottish political class was in the allegiance of the kings of England. This reflected different factors but symbolised fundamental divisions within the community of the realm which gave the period the character of a civil war as much as a struggle to defend collective rights. The principal cause of these divisions was the rivalry between the Balliol and Bruce families for the Scottish throne. The course of this rivalry was as important as the issue of Plantagenet lordship in shaping the warfare and politics of these decades. Competition and tension turned into open dynastic warfare which culminated in the 1330s with rival Bruce and Balliol kings fighting to bring political society into their allegiance. Though the Balliol claim ended in 1356, the divisions in allegiance on dynastic grounds had shaped Scottish political attitudes.

Even before warfare began, it was clear that factional issues divided the kingdom's leaders. That Bruce supporters accused two guardians and 'the part of the community' which adhered to them of seeking Balliol as

---

[5] Barrow, 'Idea of freedom'; *Rot. Scot.*, ii, 401; *Chron. Knighton*, 136–8. The first reference to the Lion, reported in a northern English chronicle, had the defenders of Stirling Castle in 1304 claim to be holding out 'for the Lion' (*Scalachronica*, 25).

king in late 1290 speaks of a split within the political class beneath the apparent unity at Birgham. The defence by the community of its shared liberties was expressed alongside, and undermined by, competition for the kingship. This remained true once war had begun. In 1296 and from early 1302 Robert Bruce chose adherence to Edward I over the defence of Balliol's kingship. However, it was Bruce's own seizure of the throne that confronted the whole political class with a similar issue. To accept Bruce's kingship required people to forget those loyalties to Balliol which had been at the heart of resistance to Edward I for a decade, and to recognise the claims of a dynasty which had already been rejected. Not surprisingly, this act transformed the Scottish cause and its presentation inside and outside the kingdom. In the case argued before the curia in 1301, John Balliol was claimed as king 'by hereditary right . . . justly and legitimately according to the . . . customs of the kingdom'. By 1309 it was announced that the Bruce family had always been recognised as rightful kings by 'the faithful people'. Balliol's kingship was an error which had brought disaster on the land. In the barons' letter of 1320 the Balliol name was omitted, though it clearly remained a factor in Scottish politics. The hijack of the Scottish cause by the Bruce cause required the rights of King John to be airbrushed from historical arguments. It is not surprising that the French and papal courts, which had defended these rights, were reluctant to recognise the man who, as much as Edward I, had trampled on them. Though Bruce's actions and run of victories gradually won him the homage of many, for a number of lords who had led resistance to Edward I before 1304, Robert's success did not justify his political crimes. Some, like the Comyns, made an instant choice. Others, perhaps a wide group of nobles, were caught between the desire to take their place within a restored Scottish realm and their dislike of the new order based on a king they regarded as a usurper and on the ascendancy of his followers. From 1306 to 1332 the alternative to Bruce was to pay homage to the kings of England and join their wars against Robert, incurring forfeiture and exile rather than recognising the 'tyrant'. However, the return of Edward Balliol meant that in the 1330s a choice was presented to political society between a Balliol king with a better claim to be rightful heir by descent and a Bruce king whose rule was free from the homage that Balliol had paid to Edward III. Victory for David Bruce and his cause was a test of Scottish allegiances but its outcome was in doubt for many years.[6]

---

[6] Stones, *Anglo-Scottish Relations*, no. 14; *Scotichronicon*, vi, 186–7; *A.P.S.*, i, 289. In the 1301 pleading at the curia the Bruces were probably those identified as 'one group of magnates . . . belonging to a party which had no right in the kingdom of Scotland' who aided Edward I (*Scotichronicon*, 176–7).

The right of rival kings to the leadership of their people was not simply an obstruction to the successful defence of Scottish liberties. For contemporaries it could not be ignored. A claim based on the verdict of war alone was not the basis for kingship but a recipe for tyranny. Robert I worked hard to portray his victories as proof of rights based on descent and consent. Yet factionalism was not just a negative factor. Ambition and competition possessed their own dynamic. The crucial period of the wars from 1306 was initiated not as a reaction to Edwardian government as in 1297, but as a political coup to secure the throne for one man. That this inevitably involved the rejection of Edward I's lordship and harnessed latent resentment to it should not obscure the fact that for the next seven years Robert waged war against Scots to encourage the recognition of his kingly authority and title. His victories, and the patronage which followed them, solidified the loyalty of many to both the Bruce party and to a realm free from the English king's lordship. The liberties of Scotland would ultimately be secured and shaped by the interest of a faction.

To this picture of divided loyalties must be added the lordship exercised by the kings of England. Despite Scottish propaganda, Edward I and his successors were not simply 'foreigners' but rulers who had well-established connections to the Scottish kingdom. As has been discussed, in the thirteenth century there existed no sharp distinction between the political elites of England and Scotland. Overlaps of family, land and service made the border between the two royal lordships permeable, and Scottish magnates were accustomed to regarding Edward I as more than an outsider. This did not preclude these magnates from acting within the Scottish community in defence of shared rights, as many did in 1290 and 1291. However, open defiance of Edward was more problematic. To magnates with interests in both kingdoms, war meant a choice of allegiance, risking forfeiture for rebellion in one of the two realms. The years from 1296 to 1322 repeatedly asked such questions of magnates, widening the sense of civil war beyond Scotland. The lordship of Edward I and his heirs was the most obvious means of preserving family connections and landed interests which spanned the Anglo-Scottish border. The English crown fostered these links with new marriage alliances, like those between the family of Richard, earl of Ulster and the Stewarts and Bruces, seeking to add to the material attractions of Plantagenet lordship.

Such connections meant that, especially before the 1320s, it was not unthinkable for Scottish magnates to enter the allegiance of the king of England. The events of 1291 to 1296 had, after all, involved paying homage to Edward I, and most nobles and prelates did so again between 1301 and 1305. Many must have felt, like the earl of Strathearn in 1306, that it was wrong to break sworn oaths of fealty as easily as shattering a glass. Scottish landowners with strong English interests, like Gilbert Umfraville, earl of Angus and the elder Robert Bruce found it easiest to adhere without a break to the English crown. Others, like Alexander Balliol of Cavers and Alexander Abernethy, chose to serve Edward I and Edward II, placing personal allegiance above arguments about the defence of Scottish liberties. When the enemies of Bruce similarly accepted the English king's lordship, they were not entering unknown territory. The 1314 statute, by which Robert forfeited those landowners who had not paid him homage, would ultimately establish and formalise the division of political society between those in Bruce allegiance and those who remained at the English king's peace.[7]

Between 1296 and the 1350s adherence to English kings was not simply the resort of renegades and political refugees. Nor did it mean the total rejection of the liberties of the Scottish realm. For all Edward I's determination to extract recognition of sovereignty from the Scots, he was aware of, and could be careful about, the customs and practices of that kingdom. Though he abandoned this approach, ignoring both Scottish custom and personnel in setting up his short-lived administration in 1296, the reaction he experienced taught him a lesson. In 1302 the king was urged by his officials to promise the Scots 'to maintain and govern them in the laws which were used and customary in the time of King Alexander', and this sentiment was present in the negotiation and settlement of the war between 1304 and 1305. Edward II similarly sought to maintain diminishing Scottish support by posing as a good lord to the *commune* of Scotland, but the greatest move in this direction was Edward III's recognition of Edward Balliol as king of Scots, albeit as his vassal and with a grant of southern Scotland to the English king. For his part, Edward, king of Scots was ready to guarantee the liberties of his kingdom, promising to preserve the rights of church, the laws of King Alexander and the access of Scots to the offices of his government. In 1356, when Balliol resigned his rights to his lord, Edward III responded by issuing his own confirmation of the customs and liberties of those Scots in his allegiance. Against the claims of the Bruce dynasty, the kings of England learned to present themselves, in a limited fashion, as the upholders of the rights, customs and laws of good King Alexander's Scotland and as the defenders of the community. Though they would not accept a kingdom which was not under their lordship in some form, the Plantagenets, and Edward III in particular, were looking to find a basis for their authority within a Scottish political environment. Though reduced

---

[7] For the issue of the Disinherited, see Cameron and Ross, 'Treaty of Edinburgh and the Disinherited'.

in its geographical limits, Edward III's lordship in Scotland would continue in open opposition to the rights and claims of the Bruces.[8]

Yet, for all the claims to be defenders of Scottish liberties, the English crown's lordship always depended on their coercive power. While individuals identified Edward I and his successors as their lords, the community as a whole never did so with enthusiasm. The course of the wars, the damage inflicted on the land by forces of the English king, the language of conquest employed by the Edwardian administration and by English writers, and clear Scottish resentment of lost rights and status all encouraged resistance. The English kings resorted to war to compel recognition of their rights and end this resistance. Their most successful campaigns, in 1296, in 1303–4 and in 1335, did not require success in battle but the submission of the enemy in the face of persistent pursuit. Victory did not mean the total defeat of a political class. Though death in battle, execution for treason and lasting loss of lands were fates experienced by some of those who took up arms against the English kings, most survived to negotiate surrenders which secured their lives and lands. The material power of the enemy, rather than their promises, convinced Scots to submit. Such acts were born of pragmatism and frequently proved shortlived, but they were also the basis on which, given time, English kings hoped to establish their authority.

The Plantagenets were not alone in seeking to extract allegiance by force. Especially after Bruce seized the throne, much of the campaigning by leaders of the Scottish cause was against fellow Scots. Many had to be compelled to leave English allegiance by Robert I. In 1306 Earl Malise of Strathearn was pursued and his lands plundered until he acknowledged Bruce's kingship. After the latter's defeat, the earl then suffered a spell of imprisonment by Edward I for his defection. Between 1307 and 1314 many lords and communities faced similar hard choices. Robert waged war to undermine allegiance to the English king. The effects were recognised as early as 1307 when the English king's officials reported that 'there are many people living well and loyally at his [Edward's] faith provided the English are in power, otherwise they say they must be at the enemy's will through default of the king'. In the north-east and Lothian, Robert demonstrated the 'default' of English protection. His campaigns in Lothian showed Bruce's coercive power to be greater than that of Edward II and prompted local communities to buy truces and, ultimately, enter his allegiance. The same goals were behind Andrew Murray's campaigns

---

[8] *Nat. MSS Scot.*, no. 7; Watson, 'Settling the stalemate', 135–7; *C.D.S.*, ii, nos 186, 337; Adam Murimuth and Robert Avesbury, *Chronica* (London, 1889), 298–302; *Rot. Scot.*, ii, 794.

in Angus, Perthshire, Fife, Clydesdale and Lothian from 1336 to 1338. Adherence to the Bruce cause was won not by appeals to legitimacy and liberty alone but by demonstrations of military primacy, the ability to punish and protect.[9]

Allegiance and political action were not dictated solely by public issues or coercion. For the figures at the top of political society, such factors were balanced by private and individual concerns. Ties of marriage created the political bond which linked the Comyns to the Balliols and MacDougalls, and later bound the Stewarts and Bruces together. The desire to preserve lands and status encouraged Robert Bruce to submit to Edward I in 1302, while in 1308 William, earl of Ross paid homage to Robert to safeguard his earldom and receive secure title to other lands. Robert's readiness to restore and even reward lords who entered his allegiance reflected the value of such private generosity in winning support. Edward I was more sparing, giving offices, payments and places in his household to Scots rather than lands. In 1306 Edward's fury was partly provoked by the perceived ingratitude of lords 'to whom we showed such courtesy', when they joined Bruce. Bruce's own actions were, in part, a reaction to the drying-up of Edward's favour, while James Douglas joined Robert after the English king refused to restore him to the lands his father had forfeited. Patronage was not a certain art, depending as it did on the interplay of magnates' greed, jealousy and idealism. Such factors often conflicted. The activities of the Strathbogies between the 1280s and 1330s were heavily influenced by successive rivalries with the Comyns, Edward Bruce and the Randolphs. Even lords like Robert Stewart and William Douglas of Liddesdale, whose birth or careers bound them to the Bruce cause, changed allegiance, albeit temporarily, in reaction to disputes for land and lordship with rivals. In all these issues adherence to the liberties of the realm did not necessarily take precedence. Loyalty to the cause of Bruce or Balliol dynasty, obligations to family and friends and concerns of status and power all had their own well-understood significance, even legitimacy, in the eyes of leading Scots.[10]

THE PEOPLE OF SCOTLAND AND THE WARS

The importance attached to the concerns of a few great lords reflected their place in Scotland. Below the king the magnates were the natural

---

[9] Neville, 'The political allegiance of the earls of Strathearn', 143–4; *C.D.S.*, ii, no. 1,926.

[10] *A.P.S.*, i, 477; Nat. MSS Scot., ii, no. 14.

leaders of the community. As the thirteenth century had shown, the major nobles and leading churchmen were the principal agents and advisors of the crown and, in the absence of an active ruler, possessed the status to act collectively in his place. With the notable exception of Wallace, all the guardians of Scotland from 1286 to 1357 were magnates or bishops, while justiciars, regional lieutenants and sheriffs had baronial, if not magnate, backgrounds. The leading figures in warfare and politics during the wars were almost all from a small secular and ecclesiastical elite. The decisions taken by such magnates about allegiance often determined the loyalty of a much wider group of people, altering the course of the war regionally or even across the realm.

However the link between these great lords and lesser figures was a two-way process. Late thirteenth-century Scotland was a complex community in which involvement in politics was spread well beyond a small elite. In an era of shifting loyalties and local or general war, this wider participation assumed a new importance. As has already been identified, when Edward I sought the homage of over 1,500 Scots in 1296 he was recognising the significance of these individuals in questions of loyalty and authority. The next year an even larger group, referred to by the term '*le menzane d'Ecosce*', the middle people, were identified with the uprisings against the Edwardian administration. The concerns of this group seem to have included antipathy towards the English-dominated regime and social and economic anxieties about Edward's policies. Fears about financial exactions or being forced to go 'across the sea' in the king's armies were strong amongst Scots who were rich enough to be targeted for these services but vulnerable to the costs and other dangers they involved. The group likely to share these fears was wide and varied, including burgesses, free tenants of the crown and great magnates amongst others. Along with lesser knights and serjeants, these people had a long recognised importance in the kingdom's political and military structure, providing the key level in the common army, the local administration of justice and the followings of greater lords.[11]

That the concerns of this group were a factor in the risings of 1297 indicates their ability to identify and articulate their political interests. Their military importance was demonstrated in the subsequent fighting when, under the leadership of one of their own number, William Wallace, many such men took up arms without significant magnate direction, serving as 'the army of Scotland'. Aside from the lack of magnate leaders, this was hardly revolutionary. Wealthy freeholders, serjeants and burgesses had long provided the best-equipped part of the host and probably

[11] Stevenson, *Documents*, ii, no. 452; Grant, 'Aspects of national consciousness', 86–8.

served as the leaders of the 'foot followers'. They would continue to act in this way throughout the wars, adding local political importance to their purely military role. Their allegiance and active support was sought by all kings, lieutenants and guardians. On several occasions Edward I specifically instructed his officers to receive the submissions of 'knights and middle people', and his son took pains to satisfy the grievances of burgesses and local landowners in his peace. The leaders of the Bruce cause likewise attached significance to elements of this group. Freeholders, burgesses, and free tenants of the crown and of earldoms were associated with letters issued by Robert to illustrate the depth of support for his rights, and they were involved in parliaments, indicating a growing sense of their collective importance. The language of liberties and customs which all sides employed was aimed not just at magnates and prelates, but also at many lesser figures to whom such terms still had both material and ideological importance.[12]

However, these people were a diverse and dispersed group across Scotland. Despite 1297, they did not form a coherent class acting in concert. Instead, as in the thirteenth century, their loyalties and actions were shaped by the varied connections and communities with which they were involved. In particular, the involvement of lesser nobles, freeholders and others in political events was normally shaped by their relations with greater figures. The political and military uncertainties of this period meant that the protection and leadership of the powerful assumed an even greater importance. As before 1296, lesser men were drawn to the followings of magnates for a variety of reasons: kinship, political alliance and, above all, landholding. The story of the freeholders of Douglasdale giving their manrent to their disinherited lord, James Douglas, on his return in 1307 may have been idealised, but it also captures the spirit of fealty and service at a level below the obligations to the crown. Such obligations remained important and the followings of magnates like the Comyns, Stewarts and Strathbogies were dominated by their knightly vassals who probably brought their own tenants with them into the political connection. However, the needs of war increasingly led to less formalised types of lordship. By the 1330s minor nobles like Alexander Ramsay and Douglas of Liddesdale were able to attract affinities of other knights and lesser men. These bands were drawn together as military companies, limited in size but effective in war and, increasingly, giving political importance to their leaders. Though harder to identify before the 1330s, companies of armed men, like the one led by Wallace in 1304–5, clearly

---

[12] C.D.S., ii, no. 1,244; Stevenson, Documents of William Wallace, 191–2; Grant, 'Aspects of national consciousness', 88–9.

existed and throughout the wars were an unpredictable element in the conflict.[13] As this suggests, in times of sustained war the military character of lordship predominated. The campaigns of 1299, of Culblean and even of Neville's Cross showed that Scottish hosts were frequently composed of groups of lords leading their 'people' to a general muster and dispersing during or after the fighting. In these years the political and military functions of affinities became inseparable. In the south such militarised lordship was synonymous with the Douglas family. By 1347 the Douglas name could raise military support not just from the family's estates, but from a much wider following, and this military character was formalised by David II's grant of the leading of the men of Clydesdale and the middle march to the lords of Douglas. Especially in the absence of royal leadership, the war effort depended on the ability of magnates to recruit and lead their own retinues.[14]

Such political groupings were not simply about the interests of magnates. If lordship developed a new importance, it was primarily because it had advantages for those who sought aristocratic leaders. The profit motive, derived from plunder and from blackmail, may have been an attraction for many in a period of major disruption and regular raiding. However, the need for protection may have been a stronger attraction. Effective lordship depended on the ability to safeguard the lives, lands and goods of adherents from direct attack or from political punishment. In 1296, for example, the earl of Atholl and John Comyn acted as sureties for their followers who were held prisoner by Edward I, while, following his own submission in 1302, Bruce secured the restoration of his tenants to their forfeited estates in England. It was normal for magnates negotiating their own submissions to secure the lands and lives of their men. But ties of lordship could survive the loss of lands and status. In 1320 tenants of William Soules and the Mowbrays fled into exile following their lords' conspiracy against Robert I, and former retainers of the Strathbogies and Comyns could be found amongst Edward III's Scottish adherents as late as the 1370s. Yet other evidence shows that the obedience and support of lesser men to their lords was not unconditional. Magnates could not ignore the interests of their followers. In 1297 Robert Bruce failed to persuade his father's Annandale tenants to risk their lands and lives by following him into revolt, while James Stewart may have taken up arms in the same year to satisfy the demands of his own men. The closest contemporary account of the risings during that summer suggests that 'the retinues of the magnates' adhered to Wallace and Moray, acting independently of their lords

[13] Barbour, *The Bruce*, 204–6; Brown, 'Development of Scottish border lordship', 6–9.
[14] Brown, *The Black Douglases*, 43–9.

who remained with the English. The experience of Robert Stewart in 1334, forced to flee from his lordships of Renfrew and Kyle while his tenants did homage to David Strathbogie, showed the link between protection and lordship. So too, in a different way, did the failure of Patrick, earl of March to lead his vassals in Lothian, which allowed some of these tenants, Alexander Ramsay and others, to assume leading roles in the area in the late 1330s. In seeking new leaders or refusing to follow their own lords, lesser men could make political choices of considerable importance in the course of warfare and politics.[15]

In many parts of Scotland patterns of political behaviour remained focused on the provinces which were so important in the fabric of the kingdom. The earldoms of northern and central Scotland and the Gallovidian province were communities with their own traditions of lordship, law and local politics. Of greatest significance, the leaders of these areas possessed powers to raise and lead provincial armies, and Robert Bruce, for one, called out his men of Carrick both as part of the common army and as a private force. The military significance of such provinces to their lords was revealed repeatedly during the wars. Carrick was Bruce's stronghold and recruiting ground when he returned to Scotland in 1307, and his grandson, Robert Stewart, used his lordships of Cowal and Bute in the same way in 1334. Their enemies also relied on such resources. Buchan and Ross opposed Bruce from their provinces in 1308, and in the 1330s and 1340s Edward Balliol received support from his family's lordship of Galloway. The long list of lesser men from the Lennox who accompanied Earl Malcolm to Bruce's inauguration in 1306 was further proof that the key to provincial allegiances was normally the leadership of the earl. Yet the power of these lords to direct their men was not automatic. Earl Malise of Strathearn was compelled to submit to Robert I by a force that included one of his chief tenants, and William of Ross sought peace with Bruce in 1308 'at the entreaty of good men', probably those in his earldom who had suffered heavily from the king's attacks. However, Bruce's devastation of Buchan and subsequent dismantling of the earldom was the act of a man who recognised the lengths necessary to break the bonds of hostile provincial identity.[16]

---

[15] C.D.S., ii, no. 940; iii, nos 721, 724, 731; Chron. Guisborough, 298–306; Scotichronicon, vii, 96–7, 102–3; Ross, 'Men for all seasons, 1', 1–30, 5–8; Brown, 'Development of Scottish border lordship', 7.

[16] Melrose Lib., i, no. 351; Barbour, The Bruce, 176, 196–201, 242–3; Scotichronicon, vii, 102–5; Chron. Lanercost, 269–74; A.P.S., i, 477; Grant, 'Aspects of national consciousness', 89; Barrow, Robert Bruce, 155–6, 171–2, 270–1; Neville, 'Political allegiance of the earls of Strathearn', 137–9, 144; Young, 'The earls and earldom of Buchan', 182–8; Young, Robert the Bruce's Rivals: The Comyns, 203–6.

Galloway and the Wars of Scotland

No part of Scotland experienced more warfare than the province of Galloway. The attacks of the Bruces on their regional enemies in 1286 proved a foretaste of sustained rivalries which focused on provincial loyalties and interests far more than identification with any Scottish cause. The location and character of Galloway as an upland region close to England and guarding access to Ayrshire and Clydesdale also gave it major significance and made the region a centre of sustained campaigning. In 1298, 1300 and 1301 Edward I and his son led major armies through the region while, in his absence, the guardians sought to win the allegiance of the local men. The murder of John Comyn in Dumfries in 1306 initiated another period of intense conflict. Robert and Edward Bruce waged a violent struggle against their enemies in Galloway which lasted until 1313. When Edward Balliol returned to Scotland in 1332, he found ready support in Galloway. The next decade saw renewed warfare in the region between partisans of Balliol and Bruce until David II secured the homage of leading local captains in 1343. After Neville's Cross, Balliol was able to recover some support in eastern Galloway and it was only in 1353 that William, lord of Douglas forced the submission or exile of Edward's last adherents.

The allegiances of the captains of Galloway were shaped by the traditions of the province. In 1296 Edward I released the hapless Thomas of Galloway, the defeated native heir of Galloway, who had spent sixty years as a prisoner. Edward's efforts to re-activate loyalties to the old dynasty did not win major support, but a natural antipathy towards the Scottish crown was a factor in Gallovidian attitudes. This was further coloured by provincial loyalties. If their identification with the Balliols as their legitimate lords was not always certain, the readiness of local men to support the Balliol cause after 1306 and from 1332 must be related to this connection. Above all, there was a consistent hostility towards the Bruces. As earls of the rival province of Carrick, the Bruce family were hereditary enemies, and the defeat of Robert's brothers in 1307 by the MacDowells escalated the blood feud. The failure of Bruce efforts at pacification between 1313 and 1332 may have been partly due to the absence of provincial lordship after Edward Bruce's death but it also reflected lingering enmity. It was left to the Douglas family to 'cast down the captains' and draw Galloway into their lordship.[17]

Though the impact of war would alter the character of many provinces, for most of these decades the earls retained their natural place as the leaders of provincial societies. However, as in the thirteenth century, earldoms were more than just estates, providing their lords with men and

[17] Oram, 'Bruce, Balliol and the lordship of Galloway', 29–47.

resources. When 'the communities of the earldoms' were recorded as attending Robert I's parliament in 1309, the phrase was not simply a device to conceal the continuing absence of several earls from the Bruce party. Instead it was a recognition that the men of an earldom formed a distinct community, with defined rights, customs and status and capable of acting collectively without their lord. The most extreme example of this on the Scottish mainland was provided by Galloway, where the wars had their own distinct course. Leadership in the province was provided by the captains of the local kindreds, and rival rulers competed to win their adherence. The confirmations of the laws and customs of Galloway and the status of the captains issued by Robert I, David II and Edward III were attempts to maintain support from a community with an extremely strong sense of provincial identity. Elsewhere, the attempt by Macduff to raise the men of Fife in 1297 and 1298 was based not on private lordship but on his status as head of the comital kindred, while Gilbert of Carrick and his kin acted in a similar role beneath their earl in 1306–7. Despite the changes of allegiance and internal disruption experienced by most provinces, as across the kingdom, the bonds of provincial community remained a real, though perhaps a diminishing, factor governing the choices and attitudes of many Scots.[18]

The political heartlands of the thirteenth-century kingdom were local-ities where the lordship of major nobles was not the traditional focus of political life. The sheriffdoms of the south and east retained their charac-ter as communities of lesser barons, minor royal tenants and burgesses. Used to direct royal administration and the source of much of the king's revenues and many of his servants, these sheriffdoms contained the main royal castles and the largest burghs in the realm. To rulers seeking to establish themselves as the successors of Alexander III, effective control of these communities was vital. This importance is clear from the events of 1296. Edward I's campaign of that year progressed through royal Scotland, securing the crown's castles, burghs and thanages, and con-cluded with the formal submissions of about 1,500 Scots, the vast major-ity of whom were minor royal tenants from these sheriffdoms. In the wars that followed, Edward and his heirs installed garrisons in the centres of royal government from Jedburgh to Inverness but especially in the south, using them as the bases of their own administration. These garrisons, and the sheriffs and constables who led them, gave a military character to Edwardian rule, and from 1297 onwards their acts could arouse local hos-tility by their enforcement of the English crown's policies or, more often,

[18] *A.P.S.*, i, 289, 459; *R.M.S.*, i, app. 1, no. 59; app. 2, no. 1,012; *Rot. Scot.*, i, 788; Bannerman, 'Macduff of Fife', 38.

by their ill-disciplined harassment of the local population. Complaints of 1313 that the garrisons of Berwick and Roxburgh plundered local men and visiting merchants and held them to ransom were indicative of the inevitable tensions which existed between foreign-led soldiers and the urban and rural populations forced to live in their shadow and accept their rule.[19]

However, this picture of occupied and downtrodden communities is too simple. Garrisons were maintained at huge cost to control the surrounding area but, with only a few exceptions, they numbered between a score and 200 men, hardly enough to hold a whole community quiet without local acquiescence. Instead their role was to maintain the allegiance of Scottish communities which had already entered the peace of the English king. The complaint of 1313 was sent to Edward II by Scottish burgesses and local landowners who clearly expected a response from their lord, the king of England. Particularly in the south, there were many examples of full participation by locals in the Edwardian administration, both judicial – by attending the sheriff's court – and military – serving in forces levied by the English king's officials. Such duties were owed as vassals and, though a significant number of such tenants suffered forfeiture rather than perform their services to an English administration, the majority of local lords in Lothian and the marches accepted Edwardian rule in the 1300s and 1330s. In part, this was the acceptance of local realities but many Scots were more actively involved in the new regime. Both before 1314 and after the mid-1330s, English garrisons contained significant numbers of Scots. Like Richard Rutherford, Simon Howden and Thomas of Traquair in the Roxburgh garrison in 1312, many were local men, probably attracted by Edward II's wages, while the defenders of Perth in both 1313 and 1339 contained a high proportion of Scots from the surrounding region, and from the burgh itself. In a similar vein, though much was brought in from England, the market for supplies represented by such garrisons would have drawn in merchants and would have proved profitable for the neighbouring burgh. Despite the difficulties caused to trading by the presence of soldiers and the threat of attack from outside, the picture was not simply one of separate, hostile populations.[20]

In sheriffdoms where English lordship enjoyed a period of relative stability, questions of loyalties and attitudes were complex. In Lothian and the marches, Robert I had to launch repeated, damaging attacks to

[19] Stevenson, *Documents*, ii, no. 152; Grant, "Thanes and thanages', 64–5; *C.D.S.*, iii, no. 337.

[20] *C.D.S.*, iii, 405–8; Barbour, *The Bruce*, 334–42; *Rot. Scot.*, i, 537. For garrison sizes in the period 1298–1304, see Watson, *Under the Hammer*, 69–75.

The Lost Burgh: Berwick and the Wars

The first and, in some senses, the greatest casualty of the wars was Berwick. The thirteenth-century burgh, recognised as the largest, richest and most important urban settlement in the realm was effectively destroyed as a Scottish community. Its vulnerability in war with England was obvious. In early April 1296 Edward I's troops broke through the flimsy defences of the burgh and slaughtered thousands of its inhabitants. When the king returned to Berwick in August plans, were laid for the establishment of a new town populated by English burgesses after the fashion of his north Welsh boroughs. For the next two decades Berwick served as the centre of Edwardian administration in Scotland and as a military base.

Its fall to Robert I in 1318 marked the end of this role. Robert sought to restore Berwick as a Scottish centre, refortifying the burgh in contrast to his normal policy, raising money for the town's repair and using it as a royal centre in the south. He encouraged local Scots to settle in the burgh and confirmed these new burgesses in the old privileges, including their trading monopoly and their guild. Though these efforts restored Berwick's wealth and status, they depended on peace. In war Berwick was an obvious target and in July 1333 it came into Edward III's hands. During the next year Scottish burgesses were forfeited and replaced by English, amongst them perhaps some deprived by Robert I. Berwick once again acted as the administrative and military centre of Plantagenet government. However, questions of allegiance did not disappear. Scots remained within the burgh and in 1335 it was feared that these would ally with local refugees to betray the town to the enemy. In response some townsmen were shipped off to Newcastle for safekeeping.

The critical phase in Berwick's decline came in the two decades from 1335, not as a result of storm and sack but through strangulation. While the burgh remained an English base, its hinterland in Berwickshire became a district disputed between men of rival allegiances. Severed from the vast bulk of Scotland by war and with no economic role in north-east England, Berwick dwindled to a garrison town. By 1347 the 'Alexandria of the north' was described as 'like a desert for want of people.' Its brief tenure by the Scots in 1355–6 only increased the burgh's problems. Sixty years of conflict and attempted colonisation had left Berwick an isolated outpost of the English king's lands.[21]

---

[21] Barrow, *Robert Bruce*, 301–2; *R.R.S.*, v, ed. Duncan no. 163; *Rot. Scot.*, i, 266–8, 366, 281.

make these local communities accept his lordship, despite the absence of major English armies. This suggests that the English crown's hold on the south-east, which lasted from 1298 to 1314, had laid down some roots. After 1335 another local war was waged for the allegiance of the south-east and Teviotdale, and much of Berwickshire remained in Edward III's allegiance beyond 1357. The key to Plantagenet lordship was the ability both to coerce and to protect the local community, and this depended on garrisons. When Roxburgh fell in 1314 and 1342 and when Edinburgh was taken in 1314 and 1341, the surrounding country sought peace with the Bruce king of Scots. It was hardly surprising that Robert I demolished Edinburgh and Roxburgh castles or that Edward III rebuilt them as strongholds. These collective changes of allegiance in response to external pressure were a feature of the wars, but the local knights, freeholders and burgesses of these sheriffdoms did not merely adapt to shifting circumstances. As individuals and groups, such people could have a major impact in their localities. In 1297 the burgesses of Inverness, led by Alexander Pilche, played a key part in the risings against the English in Moray, and later accounts enshrined the actions of lesser men in support of the Bruce cause. The roles played by Philip, the forester of Platen, in the fall of Forfar Castle in 1308, and by William Fairley, a burgess of Edinburgh and man at arms in the garrison, in the capture of Edinburgh Castle in 1341 are just two such examples which show minor local figures taking crucial political and military decisions. Between 1335 and 1342, unlike the period before 1314, the leadership of the Bruce party in Lothian was taken by minor barons and knights from the area. If other locals still preferred to enter Plantagenet allegiance, the refusal of a significantly larger group to work with Edward III's officials may suggest the hardening of loyalties after two decades in settled Bruce allegiance.[22]

Those are scattered examples but the attitudes of such individuals and groups is striking. They do not show universal or automatic hostility to English lordship across the period but they do suggest the fragility of allegiances to the Edwardian administrations. There is a contrast with the apparent stability of sheriffdoms, especially beyond the Mounth, which were under the control of the guardians between 1297 and 1304, and of the Bruce regime for most of the period after 1308. Except for the submissions of 1303–4, and periods of warfare in 1307–8 and 1334–5, these local communities seem to have been less troubled by questions of allegiance during the wars. This was not simply a matter of warfare but also involved questions of loyalty and identity. The officials of the English

---

[22] Barbour, *The Bruce*, 386–7; *Scotichronicon*, vii, 144–7; *C.D.S.*, iii, nos 1,521, 1,670, p. 361; Barrow, 'The aftermath of war', 103–25; Ewan, *Townlife*, 125, 154–5.

king always found it difficult to establish the legitimacy of their rule over communities whose links with Scottish royal government made them acutely aware of the traditions and customs of the kingdom. Though the presence of garrisons and even attempts to appeal to these Scottish liberties locally, for example by appointing Scots as sheriffs, provided the basis for periods of effective administration in the south, the continued vulnerability of English control in these sheriffdoms to both external and internal pressure suggests that the Plantagenets and their officials were never able to convince enough Scots to accept their lordship as a natural feature of political life.[23]

The sense of a Scottish cause, which was, in part at least, responsible for encouraging continued resistance to the English king's rule, was associated above all with one group within the land. The Scottish church and especially the clerical elite had become experienced in defining and defending its rights against English clergy and ecclesiastical institutions well before the onset of crisis and war. Disputes about the freedom of the Scottish ecclesiastical province from the claims of the archbishops of York and from efforts to collect crusading taxes by English officials, or attempts to restrict the activities of English clergy in the direction or staffing of religious houses had accustomed the leaders of the Scottish church to the defence of their liberties. With the loss of effective royal protectors, Scottish prelates were clearly vulnerable to greater interference, a fact witnessed by Edward I's diversion of crusading taxes raised from Scotland into his coffers. Efforts to limit the influence of a Plantagenet ruler of Scotland, in the treaty of Birgham, by insisting that the election of prelates took place in Scotland, were an indication of the church's vulnerability to the intrusion of English clergy. After 1296 English kings would press for the election of their clerical supporters to Scottish sees, and they would fill a large number of lesser benefices with English clergy as a means of increasing their authority over both church and realm. The establishment of Edwardian rule would have meant the domination of the Scottish church by foreign clergy within a generation. In the light of this, it was natural that Scottish prelates took a leading role in the defence of the rights of a separate Scottish realm as well as the church. The rights, liberties and customs of secular political society were defended by churchmen: by Bishop Wishart at Norham in 1291, by

---

[23] As well as Edward I's 1305 ordinance which named Scottish sheriffs in many sheriffdoms, in the 1330s Edward III appointed Scottish adherents like John Stirling, Eustace Maxwell and Geoffrey Mowbray as sheriffs in the south (*C.D.S.*, iii, no. 1,204, pp. 317–18, 327–9). For examples of Scottish government in the north-east, see Watson, *Under the Hammer*, 116; Penman, 'The Kingship of David II', 81–4.

Bishop Crambeth at the French king's court, by Baldred Bisset at the curia and, above all, by the group of clerical servants around King Robert. The ideology of nation, realm and community was elucidated, initially at least, by the clergy.[24]

The support provided by this group went beyond writings and legal arguments. Bishops Wishart, Lamberton and Sinclair and others provided political and even military leadership and, throughout these decades, clergy played a vital role in sanctioning warfare to the wider population. This was never more vital than in the months and years after Robert Bruce's seizure of the throne. A usurper, a homicide and an excommunicant, Robert's qualifications as a royal leader were hardly those conventionally supported by the church. However, in February and March 1306 Wishart legitimised Bruce's claim to the kingship, absolving him of his sins, administering an oath in which Robert promised to follow 'the direction of the clergy of Scotland', and producing from his wardrobe and treasury the vestments and royal banner used in the inauguration of the new king. During the following months the bishop spoke on behalf of Robert, according to English accounts, 'encouraging the people who he attracted to the party of the earl [Bruce] . . . that it was just as meritorious to take the part of the earl and wage war against the king of England . . . as to go in the service of God to the Holy Land'. The alliance between Bruce and the Scottish church was not total or immune from tensions but it was a crucial element in his political and military success. The king's ability to maintain the support of his prelates despite papal sanctions between 1317 and 1320 is striking. It rested not just on ideological issues but on the powers of patronage, protection and coercion which a king possessed. Such support was as decisive as his military victories in allowing Robert to pose inside and outside Scotland as the legitimate king. The church councils which met under his rule in the 1320s were the manifestations of that legitimacy and his renewal of royal protection and patronage of the church.

The charge that Scottish clergy associated the war against Edward I and his heirs with crusading was not new in 1306. In 1296 it was said that prelates and preachers 'corrupted the ears and souls of rich and poor . . . so that they turned against the king [Edward I] . . . falsely asserting that this was more just than fighting the saracens'. These accusations were possibly designed to blacken Scottish clergy as harming the interests of Christendom. However, they also show the importance of preaching in

---

[24] Barrow, *Robert Bruce*, 263–9; Barrow, 'The Scottish clergy in the War of Independence', 1–22. For examples of Edwardian presentations to Scottish benefices, see *C.D.S.*, iii, nos 653, 657, 658, 659.

stirring opposition to Edward I and his successors. The friars were specifically associated with activities which related to their normal duties, and they were probably amongst the 'false preachers from Bruce's army' who encouraged support for the king in 1307 with prophecies and, perhaps, pardons, causing major anxiety to his enemies. The Franciscans in particular were accused of opposition to the English king, as were their counterparts in Ireland during Edward Bruce's campaigns. In 1333 Edward III sought permission to expel the Franciscans of Berwick to England, replacing them with English friars. He argued that the continuation of the wars was due in part 'to the preaching of certain religious Mendicants of the Scottish nation, who, under the cloak of sanctity, encourage the Scots in their tyranny'.[25]

Yet it is important to avoid exaggerating the unity or consistency of clerical support for the Scottish cause. Even prelates who were the apparently committed defenders of the Scottish cause were not driven by concerns for collective liberties alone. In their accusations against Wishart in 1306, the English could point to the numerous occasions on which the bishop had paid homage to Edward I and promised loyal service to the king. Also a captive of the English in 1306, William Lamberton spent the period from 1308 as an active agent of Edward II, only returning to Bruce's camp in 1314. William Sinclair similarly spent time in English allegiance and may even have been promoted to the see of Dunkeld as Edward II's candidate before recognising Bruce as lord after the latter had taken Perth. Though Sinclair was close to Robert I in the rest of the king's reign, in 1332 he presided over the coronation of Edward Balliol. The lack of effective episcopal leadership for the Bruce party during the 1330s was a striking contrast to the roles played by earlier bishops and, though this was due to the qualities of individual churchmen, this fact provides a warning against assuming that the clergy were the natural leaders of any Scottish cause. That compromises were made by individual bishops should not be surprising. Like most magnates, Lamberton, Sinclair and other prelates were concerned to protect their lives and their status in difficult circumstances by their choices of allegiance. Bishops were political figures, and Lamberton and Wishart were motivated not just by an impartial attachment to the rights of their church, but by their alliances with the Bruce family. In a similar way, Sinclair's defection to Bruce probably coincided with the submission of his Lothian-based kinsmen to the

[25] Stones, *Anglo-Scottish Relations*, nos 34, 35; *Chron. Lanercost*, 165–6; Palgrave, *Documents*, 347–8; *Rot. Scot.*, i, 258; MacQuarrie, 'The idea of the Holy War in Scotland, 1296–1330', 83–92; Ash, 'William Lamberton, bishop of St Andrews, 1297–1328', 44–5; Mackenzie, 'A prelude to the War of Independence', 111–13.

king, while the poor relations between Robert I and Bishop Henry Cheyne of Aberdeen owed much to the role played by the bishop's family in opposing the king in the north-east and his links to the disgraced Strathbogie family.[26]

As a counterpart to such variations of behaviour amongst the leading secular clergy, the attitudes and actions of most monastic orders contrast with those attributed to the friars in Scotland. The occupants of rich and vulnerable abbeys with wide lands and rights and a cosmopolitan outlook and population, most monastic communities were concerned more with peace and protection than with the defence of the liberties of the Scottish church province. Linked to their mother houses, many of which were English, monks did not naturally share the views of such liberties with other clergy. There were some indications of internal conflict. Abbot Richard of Kelso was expelled from his house as a 'rebel and a traitor' by the English in the 1290s, while English inhabitants of abbeys were driven out when their communities came under Scottish lordship, like the abbot and canons of Jedburgh who were exiled in 1314. A more typical example was Melrose Abbey. The community here sought aid and protection from both Bruces and Plantagenets and received generous help from these patrons. By the 1340s they were even given dispensation to hold estates in both allegiances. Yet, the tales of looted and damaged buildings and of estates plundered and occupied by their tenants and neighbours provide proof of the immediate concerns of the monks, which preoccupied them far more than issues of temporal allegiance. However, despite these provisos, it seems likely that many clergy tended to be more susceptible to arguments about both the material and ideological advantages of the removal of English lordship from Scotland. The view of Edward II was certainly that it was 'the prelates of Scotland who encourage the nobility, gentry and estates in their evil acts'.[27]

The variations and inconsistencies that emerge in any discussion of Scottish political attitudes and actions during these years of war are understandable. The kingdom had always been, and remained, a diverse collection of communities, and the impact of internal divisions and the changing pressures of warfare increased such differences of outlook and experience. Yet a clear sense of common values did survive from the thirteenth-century kingdom. An understanding of collective liberties and

[26] Palgrave, *Documents*, 347–8; Ash, 'William Lamberton', 44–5; Barrow, *Robert Bruce*, 266; *R.R.S.*, v, no. 140 and n.

[27] *C.D.S.*, ii, nos 817, 1,087, 1,981, 1,982; iii, nos 509, 893–4, 1,561; Brown, *The Black Douglases*, 184–7; Goodman, 'Religion and warfare in the Anglo-Scottish marches' 245–66; Barrow, *Robert Bruce*, 250.

traditions was a key factor in shaping attitudes to allegiance and legiti-macy. Most obviously, such values encouraged continuing resistance to the claims of English kings to exercise sovereignty over the Scottish realm, and they made the establishment of secure lordship over the kingdom and its local communities a difficult and expensive task. However, though the outlines of this Scottish cause were rehearsed and developed between 1290 and 1360, they did not provide an easy template for the political choices forced upon Scots in these years. A range of other pressures had an influence on decisions of allegiance and action, amongst them those of family, lordship and the weight of physical coercion. Moreover, it was also easier for Scottish lords and lesser men to identify the language of the Scottish cause than to distinguish its legitimate lead-ership, especially in the years after 1306. If the case made by the Bruce party concerning its rights is best known, it is clear that their enemies, not just Balliols but Plantagenets, made their own claims to be the protectors of Scottish liberties. Even though these latter claims involved subjection to the direct or indirect lordship of the English crown, they were still accepted by many Scots who paid homage to the three English Edwards or to Edward Balliol. These acts of homage were born from many motives, with fear of force almost always amongst them, but they should not be seen as gestures empty of meaning. In the full or partial homage of the political class lay the means to establish Plantagenet dominion over Scotland. The maintenance or renewal of alternative structures of royal lordship in opposition to the English crown was vital to the defence of a kingdom without subjection, but it was not an inevitable product of pre-war allegiances.

The attitude of Scots to the competing claims of Bruce, Balliol and Plantagenet was neither nor universal or unchanging. It varied greatly between localities according to differences in past traditions and contem-porary realities. It also varied greatly over time. The leadership of the kingdom by the Bruce dynasty and its adherents, which seemed natural and secure by the end of the period, was not the obvious outcome of the struggle to re-establish the thirteenth-century kingdom. In the 1300s, and even in the 1330s, the Bruce cause depended on relatively small groups of partisans for its survival, and defections from even this core under the pressure of war meant that a collapse of the Bruce party, like that of the Balliol regime in 1304, was not impossible. In questions involving the per-sonal and collective decisions of a whole kingdom and political class during an era of dynastic crisis and major war, it is right to be cautious. As for most Scots of the time, it is often hard to chart a clear and consis-tent path through the tangle of events to reveal patterns of certain and immutable allegiance. However, rather than reducing the achievement of the leaders of the Bruce party, the doubts and dangers facing the community as a whole and the wide range of political responses to them from Scots make the ultimate success of Robert I and his cause even more striking. That even men like Bruce, Lamberton, and Douglas of Liddesdale submitted to the lordship of the English crown is an indication to historians of the dangers of drawing conclusions about the course of these wars and their outcomes.

CHAPTER 15

The Legacy of War: Scotland in the 1360s

A LAND AT PEACE?

In the six decades before 1357 Scotland had been a land of war. While the ten years from 1322 provided an interlude of relative peace, the overall character of the period was set by conflict. The impact of these wars stretched far beyond the actual campaigning, and meant that much of Scottish society had altered to meet the needs of ongoing warfare. The treaty of Berwick in 1357 might have brought a period of truce between English and Scottish kings which, in the event, lasted for a quarter of a century, but any clear break with the past was limited. The issues arising from the years of major war would continue to dominate events and attitudes in Scotland throughout the late 1350s and 1360s. The result of the period was to see the working-out of the legacy of war, confirming and making plain the changes to the kingdom and community.

The most immediate impact was physical. The 'Burnt Candlemas', Edward III's devastating campaign through south-eastern Scotland in early 1356, was only the latest episode in a brutal war of *chevauchée* and raid by both sides. The English king burned a swathe through Lothian in his ten-day march, destroying Haddington and Edinburgh and a large area of surrounding country. The local inhabitants had been forced to hide in caves, woods and bogs, or to flee beyond the Forth. In Galloway and the marches, the scars caused by war were equally fresh and, though the lands north of the Forth had been spared in recent years, they too had experienced savage campaigning in earlier periods. The people of Buchan were reported to be still suffering from the effects of Bruce's 'herschip' in the late 1350s, and it might be expected that the warfare of the late 1330s had left similar damage behind them. Strathbogie's harassment of minor royal tenants in the north-east, Edward III's destruction

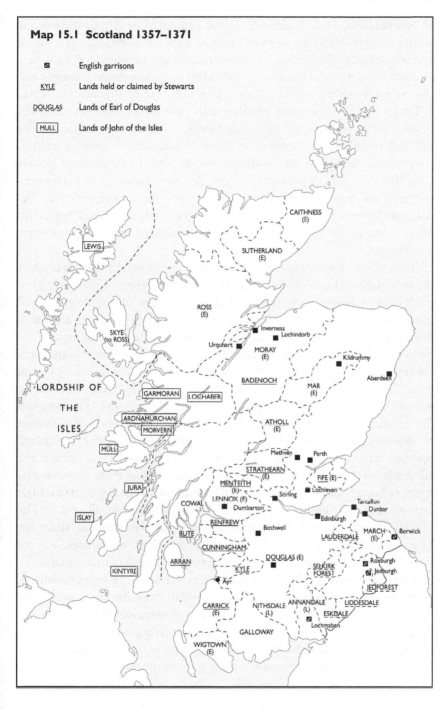

Map 15.1 Scotland 1357–1371

English garrisons

KYLE   Lands held or claimed by Stewarts

DOUGLAS   Lands of Earl of Douglas

MULL   Lands of John of the Isles

of Aberdeen in 1336, Murray's brutal campaign in Angus during the winter of 1336–7 and the siege of Perth in 1339 which brought starvation and, reportedly, cannibalism to the surrounding country suggest a legacy of disruption north of the Forth. Added to such man-made disasters was the recurring horror of the plague. The outbreak of the late 1340s was followed by a second major pestilence in 1361, at its most severe in the south, and it has been estimated that between a fifth and a third of the Scottish population succumbed in these disasters. Such massive mortality probably added to the confusion of displaced and migrant people who, like the Lothian peasants in 1356, sought temporary or permanent refuges. The economic effect of these events was compounded by the damage done to Scottish trade, especially in wool, which had been shut off and preyed on by English shipping for most of the quarter-century before 1357.[1]

The effect of war, famine and plague on the wealth and economic organisation of the Scottish kingdom is hard to gauge. Apparently clear evidence of relative wealth is provided by the review of taxable goods and rents carried out in 1366. Including church benefices, crops and most livestock, this assessment recorded the current 'true value' alongside the 'old extent', the sum due in thirteenth-century records. The results of the survey showed a major drop in taxable wealth to about half its pre-war level. The fall was least in the eastern Lowlands from Lothian to Kincardineshire, while Argyll, the central Highlands and Galloway saw the greatest decline. The sheriffdoms in the south, from Dumfriesshire to Berwickshire, which were amongst the richest in the thirteenth century, were also greatly impoverished and included areas outside the allegiance of the Scottish king. The fall in the value of these marcher districts is borne out in English records which show estates in Teviotdale losing between 80 and 100 per cent of their worth as a result of war. The overall decline in assessed wealth had apparently occurred since the 1320s, encouraging the view that plague, rather than war damage, was the principal reason for the change. It is certainly plausible that a major fall in the population, allied to a gradual deterioration in climatic conditions, bringing shorter summers and higher rainfall from the last years of the previous century, led to the abandonment of marginal land, marsh and upland, during the years before 1366. Interestingly, it was on upland estates in the Cheviots that land was recorded as utterly worthless in 1357, having been previously valued at nearly £50. In the territory under David

[1] Rogers, *War, Cruel and Sharp*, 339; Grant, *Independence and Nationhood*, 75–7; *Scotichronicon*, vii, 286–97; Mayhew, 'Alexander – a silver age?', 60–1, 65; Ewan, *Townlife*, 68–9.

II's lordship too, a smaller population, cultivating less land inevitably meant a smaller tax base.[2]

Such contraction was not the same, however, as a general economic decline. The prosperity of those who had survived the plague may not have fallen, but rather the reverse. In particular, it seems likely that the economic impact of war was a temporary phenomenon. This is suggested by the rapid recovery of northern England from Scottish raiding between 1311 and 1346, and by evidence of a similarly swift increase in royal income in Scotland in the 1320s, early 1340s and again between the late 1350s and 1370. The income from customs and fermes collected by David II's officials rose from just over £2,000 in 1358 to over £10,000 in 1370. Even in 1360 the burghs of Edinburgh and Haddington, burned down only four years before, were providing over £1,500 to the king's coffers. The suggestion of rapidly reviving fortunes extended to individual burgesses, like Roger Hogg of Edinburgh who loaned the king £172 between 1358 and 1364, and it was during the period of peace after 1357 that Edinburgh secured the position of being Scotland's principal trading town, a position held before 1296 by Berwick. The customs revenues paid by burghs were also an indication of wider economic growth linked principally to the export of animal hides and wool. Wool was the main source of Scotland's income from abroad. The revival of the trade from the late 1350s continued through the next decade and reached a peak in the early 1370s when 7,600 sacks were exported from Scotland. This represented a significant injection of funds into the country, and it benefited not just the royal government or the wool merchants but also the producers, from great magnates and prelates to freeholders and peasants. Evidence of nobles receiving licences to import foodstuffs and luxury goods during the 1360s may suggest a rise in the wealth of the kingdom and its leaders. Though the growing market and rising prices would not last beyond the early 1370s, the years between 1357 and 1371 were ones of recovery and general prosperity for the smaller Scottish population.[3]

This prosperity had political as well as economic implications. The evidence of increased wealth is drawn from the records of the king's government. Both customs revenue and the assessment of taxable values

---

[2] McNeill and MacQueen, *Atlas of Scottish History*, 302–3; Mayhew, 'Alexander – a silver age?', 60–5; *Rot. Scot.*, i, 825; *C.D.S.*, iii, no. 1,641; iv, nos, 1, 62.

[3] Lanark and Linlithgow seem to have replaced the 'lost burghs' of Berwick and Roxburgh in the parliament of the four burghs alongside Edinburgh and Stirling, but in the 1340s Edinburgh, Perth, Dundee and Aberdeen were referred to as 'the four great towns of Scotland'. Penman, 'The kingship of David II', 295–303; Ewan, *Townlife*, 121, 127, 144, 147, 150–3; Grant, *Independence and Nationhood*, 236–7; McNeill and MacQueen, *Atlas of Scottish History*, 244–53.

reflected the needs and reach of that government and were part of the principal political theme of the period, the efforts of David Bruce to establish an ascendant monarchy. These also occurred against the background of the recent war, which had reshaped Scotland internally and externally. David had to grapple with the consequences of changing circumstances and political attitudes. Most directly he returned to Scotland bound to pay a ransom of £100,000 to Edward III. David regarded the payment of this sum as a necessity to wipe out the humiliation of 1346 and restore his full status as king of Scots. However, his ability to raise the ransom depended on David's authority in his realm, part of the wider problem he faced. David had spent eleven years as the English king's captive and, out of twenty-eight years as king, he had only ruled in person between 1341 and 1346. His realm and his adherents had grown used to operating in the absence of an active king. David returned to Scotland to find the financial and political resources of the crown greatly reduced. The crown's lands had been dissipated in decades of military and political necessity and, in particular, by their use as a means of buying support by embattled kings. Robert I had been most lavish in this regard but David had copied his father in the early 1340s, further reducing the number of thanages, especially in the north-east, by his gifts. Added to this, the years from 1346 to 1357 had seen many remaining royal estates occupied by nobles, while magnates continued to dominate the offices of the crown. Robert Stewart had been lieutenant, his cousin Thomas, earl of Angus was chamberlain, while William Douglas and the earl of Ross were the justiciars. The sheriffdoms were largely administered by the retainers of these men. Magnates and their connections thus controlled the royal establishment and its ability to collect revenues. In 1358 and 1359 little of these funds reached King David, and his lack of political weight was evident in the widespread non-payment of the taxation ordered to pay the ransom.[4]

The recovery of financial resources and political authority depended on the re-establishment of royal lordship. Despite David's lack of funds, he still possessed considerable advantages as king, and he used them to good effect. To Scots in his allegiance David had always been the ultimate source of legitimacy in the land. In a limited sense, this was understood as the means by which magnates could secure their hold on lands and titles, receiving confirmation of dubious rights. In the aftermath of his return, David acted in this fashion, recognising Robert Stewart as earl of Strathearn and Patrick, earl of Dunbar's claims to Moray through his

---

[4] Duncan (ed.), 'A question about the succession, 1364', xii, 1–57; Penman, 'The kingship of David II', 296–301; Grant, 'Thanes and thanages', 66–7.

wife, Agnes Randolph. He also created an earldom of Douglas for Lord William, uniting his lands into a single regality. Such acts hardly increased the king's strength, and David's view of his office required much more than this limited role. Despite his absence, or even because of it, there remained support for a more assertive monarchy. David could call on the remnants of his following from the early 1340s and on the traditional powers of Scottish kingship. As king, David held authority over his whole realm and people and possessed a natural claim to be the guarantor of peace and order. These principles were stressed in the legislation issued by his parliaments and undoubtedly appealed to many Scots keen to enjoy the fruits of peace after their experience of war and instability. Especially among the clergy, burgesses and lesser nobility, the ideological pull of kingship would prove stronger than aristocratic lordship.[5]

David could back these claims with a reservoir of patronage which, despite recent setbacks, was still beyond that of the greatest nobles. Moreover, unlike such lords, the king had less fear of raising other nobles to new lands and titles. During the early years of his renewed rule, David won the support and service of many knights and barons. Most of these were wooed from the followings of magnates. Stewart retainers from the south-west and Strathearn, Lothian knights who had followed Douglas's banner, and the tenants and neighbours of earls like Dunbar, Mar and Angus were attracted into David's connection. Many were well rewarded for their support. Most spectacularly, William Cunningham from Ayrshire was made earl of Carrick and William Ramsay was created earl of Fife. Though these grants proved short-lived, more concrete gains in lands and money were distributed amongst the lesser nobility. The bulk of these adherents came from Lothian, Fife, Angus and Perthshire and many were experienced soldiers. Many too were junior kinsmen of magnates, like George and John Dunbar and James and Archibald Douglas. Archibald was the bastard son of Robert Bruce's Good Sir James Douglas. Known as Archibald the Grim, he was a veteran soldier and, thanks to King David, he rose from being a landless knight to a great baron by marrying Joanna, daughter and heiress of Maurice Murray. His loyalty to the king recreated the bond between their fathers and saw Archibald employed as sheriff of Edinburgh and march warden. By the early 1360s David had established his followers in the principal offices of royal government and the efforts of these king's men and the growing appreciation of his authority allowed David to tap into the wealth of his realm. His tripling of the customs levy and

⁵ Boardman, *Early Stewart Kings*, 11–16; Brown, *The Black Douglases*, 49, 53–60; Penman, 'The kingship of David II', 285–6.

recovery of burgh rents produced an income of over £7,500 by 1362 and allowed David to amass a hoard of over £3,000 for his private use.[6]

The king's wealth and power had been established at the expense of the leading magnates. These lords had seen their offices removed, access to royal resources shut off and their influence over lesser nobles reduced. Like Douglas of Liddesdale in the early 1340s, such magnates regarded royal recognition of their standing as a right, and saw displays of royal superiority as interference. They also had direct fears. Earl William Douglas saw the favour given to the heirs of his dead rival, Douglas of Liddesdale, as a threat to his leadership in the south, while Stewart's anxieties were even greater. To a history of tensions arising from David's first period of rule, from Neville's Cross and from the negotiations over the king's captivity, could be added clashes between the two men's adherents in Fife and Strathearn. Behind all these issues was the question that had dogged the Bruce dynasty since its seizure of the throne: the succession. From David's birth, Robert Stewart had been his presumed heir and, while the king remained childless, this gave the rivalry between uncle and nephew a huge significance. David had made moves to favour his sisters' offspring but his principal hopes rested on a child of his own. His queen, Edward III's sister, Joan, had chosen to remain in England after 1357, while David returned with an English mistress, Katherine Mortimer. The murder of Katherine at Soutra in 1360 suggests fears of her influence and David's plans for even an illegitimate child. Her killer, Thomas Stewart, earl of Angus, was Robert's ally, and David reacted by imprisoning Thomas until his death from plague in 1362. The plague also claimed Queen Joan, freeing David to marry his new mistress, Margaret Logie. Margaret's family connections in Strathearn made her an enemy of Stewart. The prospect of her as queen and mother of the royal heir increased animosities between David and Robert.

David's intervention in north-eastern politics in late 1362, which resulted in his humiliation of Thomas, earl of Mar and temporary confiscation of his earldom, proved to be the spark for a reaction. Stewart was joined by Mar's brother-in-law, William earl of Douglas, and by Patrick, earl of Dunbar in raising rebellion in the early spring of 1363. Beneath issues of private lordship and complaints of David's financial misrule, the conflict pitted the Bruce king against the heirs of his family's principal backers, Stewart, Douglas and Randolph. From a royal perspective, the clash was about the confirmation of David's authority over the aristocratic group which had headed his cause between the 1330s and the 1350s.

[6] For a detailed account of David's patronage and income between 1358 and 1363, see Penman, 'The kingship of David II', 284–94, 335–56.

The actual rebellion demonstrated the material strength of David's position. The king relied on his baronial and knightly followers, sustained by his hoarded money. Faced with this combination, Stewart abandoned his allies and promised loyalty on pain of forfeiting his lands and rights to the succession. Douglas was more determined. He waged war on royal supporters in Lothian, Fife and Clydesdale before defeat at Lanark forced him to make peace.[7]

In an immediate sense, David's easy victory confirmed his achievements and allowed the continuation of his policies. None of the leading rebels suffered loss of life, lands or liberties but David married Margaret Logie and pursued ambitious plans for the succession involving Edward III. He also diverted extensive patronage to his adherents. The effective leader of the church, William Landellis, bishop of St Andrews had his episcopal rights confirmed, while burgess adherents like Roger Hogg were similarly rewarded. From 1363 the king was also able to establish his supporters as magnates in their own right. In the late 1360s the inheritance of Ross was diverted to the crusading veteran, Walter Leslie, Archibald Douglas was created lord of Galloway, and George Dunbar inherited his family earldom on the death of his great-uncle, Earl Patrick. The king was creating rival lords to balance the heirs of his father's adherents. In financial terms too, David was clearly in the ascendant. The king was able to call on a variety of sources of income. As well as the customs rate, now four times its 1357 level, a statute was passed in 1367 revoking all grants made since the death of King Robert nearly forty years before as a means of extracting payments for fresh entry into these lands by their owners. In the same year David debased the coinage, increasing the money which could be made from the available precious metal. Alongside these means of raising royal wealth, David was able to extract taxation from his subjects. In July 1365, for example, parliament agreed to raise 8,000 marks (over £5,000) for David's needs, while the customs revenue was assigned to pay the ransom. In 1370 the regular income of the crown alone produced £10,200, allowing David a surplus of £1,300. Despite the low assessment of taxable wealth in 1366, David Bruce was a rich and powerful ruler whose resources and real authority appeared to make him equal to, or even greater than, his thirteenth-century forerunners.[8]

David certainly regarded his rights and powers in terms which matched his predecessors. However, beneath the tide of royal success, fundamental flaws remained in the position of the Bruce dynasty. Some

---

[7] *Scotichronicon*, vii, 330–3; Duncan, 'The "Laws of Malcolm MacKenneth"', 239–73; 263–70; Boardman, *The Early Stewart Kings*, 17–19; Brown, *The Black Douglases*, 57–8; Penman, 'The kingship of David II', 357–80.

[8] Penman, 'The kingship of David II', 444–50, 461–4, 505.

History and Propaganda in Fourteenth-Century Scotland

The end of major warfare from the later 1350s initiated a golden age in the writing of Scottish history. The earliest products of this came in the 1370s with the composition of the epic poem *The Bruce* by John Barbour and the compilation of *Chronica Gentis Scotorum*, a history of the Scottish people, by John of Fordun. However, at least some of the impetus for these later histories came from earlier works which survived, embedded within them. In discussing both the ancient pedigree of the Scots and the struggles of the recent past, such works reflect a desire to proclaim and celebrate their rights and achievements as a people. In this sense, historical perspective was being deployed to repeat and amplify the statements of Scottish liberties made before 1357.

Historical writing also involved another form of propaganda. Discussions of events since 1286 also had the aim of stressing the legitimacy and achievements of recent Scottish leaders. Most obviously, the opportunity was taken to demonstrate the rights of the Bruce dynasty and its backers and to denounce those Scots who had opposed it. However, the divisions within the Bruce party since 1329 also left their mark. In an account of this period composed at St Andrews before 1371 and incorporated into Fordun's chronicle, the impression is created of Robert Stewart as a man unfitted to rule Scotland and of King David as the just and compassionate guardian of his people. In the 1360s such views may well have been current in the king's party but there is evidence of an opposite tradition. Material included in early fifteenth-century chronicles, but originally composed earlier, elevated Stewart as the saviour of Scotland between the early 1330s and the mid-1350s, whose career had echoes of that of his grandfather. In this 'Anonymous chronicle', David is a largely absent and ineffective figure. The two accounts conflict directly in their version of Neville's Cross. While the St Andrews account implies that Stewart abandoned his king, in the 'Anonymous' it is the recklessness of David that led to a defeat from which Stewart saved his own command. It is easy to imagine these competing views of recent history being replayed during the 1360s and recorded for future generations. As in other ways, it took David's death to clarify matters. The way was cleared for the development of a Stewart view of Scotland's recent past, most notably in the state-sponsored writing of Barbour's *Bruce*.[9]

---

[9] Boardman, 'Chronicle propaganda in late medieval Scotland: Robert the Steward, John of Fordun and the "Anonymous Chronicle"', 23–43; Broun, 'A new look at *Gesta Annalia* attributed to John of Fordun', 9–30.

were personal and unavoidable, like the absence of an obvious heir to continue David's work. Though a point of weakness, the king could hardly
be blamed for this, and the favour shown to the Steward's eldest son,
John, who was married to the queen's niece and made earl of Carrick,
suggest efforts to heal the rift within Robert I's descendants. However,
compared with earlier kings, David's financial position was also uncertain. Unlike Alexander III, David could not rely on the resources of a
network of royal estates as the basis of his income. Instead his revenues
came from the high customs charges he imposed, from dubious short-
term measures like revocation and debasement of the coinage, and from
one-off grants of taxation levied on goods and rents. Rather than traditional and undemanding sources of income, David's exactions depended
on the acquiescence of his subjects and the temporary high volume and
returns obtained from wool exports. From being a low-key issue in the
thirteenth century, royal finance had assumed major political significance,
colouring David's relations with the wider community of his kingdom.

ESTATES AND MAGNATES

The ways in which the relationship between king and kingdom developed
illustrated major changes in the structure of Scottish political society from
the preceding century. David presided over a polity which was more
complex and difficult to manage than the pre-war kingdom. War and
dynastic instability had emphasised the ability of the community as a
whole and its component parts to function and make political choices
independent of royal government. Since the late 1280s interregnum, conquest, rebellion, usurpation and long years of warfare had forced Scots to
develop and define their sense of identity and modes of political behaviour
beyond the simple equation of the earlier thirteenth-century: that the
Scottish realm and people was the creation of the royal dynasty and that
the principal unifying factor was the lordship of the king. Ideas of allegiance to the Lion, voiced on occasion during the preceding years, suggest
an understanding of obligations to the Scottish realm above loyalty to the
king as an individual. While such examples were rare and extreme, similar
ideas were also involved in the stress placed by all sides on the laws,
customs and liberties of the Scottish kingdom and people. The Bruce
dynasty had taken the throne as the self-proclaimed defenders of these
rights. Their subjects would judge them on their efforts, in terms of the
sovereignty of the kingdom, but also in their rule over its people.
    One manifestation of this new atmosphere was the role of parliament.
The Scottish perception of parliament as a formal body with a set

composition had developed during the long crisis in royal government. Both King John and King Robert had called assemblies under the name of parliament to emphasise their legitimacy. Parliament was increasingly understood as the source of consent for the actions of the king. Though its origins lay in the great councils of earlier kings, from the early 1290s the body acquired public authority and included new groups, both of which were lacking from thirteenth-century assemblies. Robert summoned burgesses and freeholders to several of his parliaments and in 1357, when David II called parliament, the division into three communities, or estates, of clergy, nobles and burgesses was stated for the first time. It was understood that this collection of individuals acting as parliament possessed the authority to express the communal will. David, like his father, recognised that this body was the legitimate method of seeking taxation. The unprecedented number of contributions demanded by David may have augmented his income but it cemented the place of parliament in Scottish government. As English kings of this period also discovered, grants of taxation came at a political price. David was forced to answer complaints and petitions concerning his financial policies, his maintenance of internal peace and his management of patronage. Though the king sought to control parliament by shifting its business onto a smaller committee, opposition to royal policy from his subjects could be potently expressed in this forum as when the estates discussed David's plans for the succession at Scone in 1364. Neither the dependence of the crown on the consent of its chief subjects nor the experience of criticism from the same group were unknown before 1286, as Alexander III's succession plans and the reaction to Patrick of Atholl's murder showed. However, in the fourteenth century the need to obtain communal assent had developed a formal place and structure.[10]

The significance of communal consent went beyond meetings of the estates. It is striking that contemporary accounts of the 1363 rebellion spoke of the magnates drawing up a petition bearing their seals. This accused King David of misrule by following 'evil council' and squandering the money raised by the community for his ransom. The rebels justified their attack on the king by appealing to the interests of the wider community, demanding the reform of government in their name. Such language and attitudes owed much to the experience of preceding decades when the defence of these interests was employed to establish the rights of the Bruce party. The aims of the rebels also reflected recent Scottish developments. It seems likely that the king would be replaced by aristocratic deputies, guardians or lieutenants, whose place in the kingdom was

10   A.P.S., i, 491.

well understood. For over half of the sixty years before 1357 Scotland had been ruled by one or more guardians. It had become normal for these guardians to have their authority established in meetings of the community and to safeguard the peace of the realm and, more importantly, provide leadership in war in the king's place. Up to the late 1350s this vice-regal authority had only been used in the absence of an adult ruler but the possibility existed of guardians being appointed as a means of removing power from a king, justified by an appeal to the wider community. David may have been threatened with such a challenge in 1359 and certainly faced one in 1363. Ironically, it would be Robert Stewart, the most likely candidate for guardianship in 1363, who twenty years later would find himself supplanted by a lieutenant whose powers were probably confirmed by the estates.[11]

David II had to work with a community which possessed greater expectations of its rulers and had developed means to articulate criticism and take action against them. However, as in the thirteenth century, the key to political life was the relationship between the king and a small group of great nobles. In a single-chambered parliament the interests of these magnates influenced the estates and, in peace and war, it was from these men that guardians were chosen. Yet, if the importance of crown-magnate relations remained constant, the character of the higher nobility altered greatly. The ranks of earls and territorial lords who had headed the nobility in the 1280s were much reduced. Many established families, among them the Balliols of Galloway, the Comyns of Buchan and Badenoch, the Strathbogies of Atholl and the native earls of Strathearn and Fife, became extinct in the male line, as did the Randolph earls of Moray. Such extinctions could be a natural phenomenon, but from the 1290s the rate of change was accelerated by disinheritance and death in battle. While exceptions existed, like the Lennox, where the native line survived largely unscathed, the unstable fortunes of many houses had an effect on their provinces. So too did the passage of warfare through the realm which, inevitably, drew earldoms and lordships more fully into the wider politics of Scotland through demands of service and loyalty. The interference of the Bruce kings in provincial affairs was one sign of this. Robert I's indenture of 1315 with Earl Duncan of Fife, while seeming to confirm the importance of the comital dynasty, was also an example of the king meddling with the running of, and succession to, an ancient province. The weight of Bruce intervention was also felt in numerous other provinces, from Galloway to Buchan.[12]

[11] *Scalachronica*, 172–4; Fordun, ii, 269–79.
[12] *R.R.S.*, v, no. 72.

The Rebuilding of Scotland

The peace of the 1360s witnessed the first stage of a period of major archi-tectural activity which lasted into the fifteenth century. The aim of much of this was to repair the ravages of war on both secular and ecclesiastical buildings. Though work was planned at Melrose Abbey and elsewhere, the efforts of this first decade were centred on the residences of the great secular figures in the realm. King David himself led the way, constructing a new royal residence within Edinburgh Castle. David's Tower was a massive tower-house, a style of building which would become widespread in subsequent generations. While the king's adherent Archibald Douglas built a similar castle at Threave in his lordship of Galloway, most great castles of the 1360s followed different models. Douglas himself turned the ruins at Bothwell into a crude, fortified enclosure, while his cousin, Earl William, built a massive fortress on the cliffs at Tantallon in East Lothian. Perhaps the most sophisticated residence, however, was that begun at Doune for Robert, second son of the Steward, in his earldom of Menteith. This castle combined a fine tower-house with an attached great hall and was intended to stretch round an internal courtyard. What linked Bothwell, Doune, Threave and Tantallon was the desire of their owners to construct castles which cemented their hold on newly-acquired lands.[13]

Yet the most important changes in the higher nobility occurred in the absence of active kingship. Especially between 1314 and 1350 the rapid turnover of earls in many provinces created situations where the local community was left without a head, or was in the hands of an heiress or a figure with no local pedigree. Such circumstances meant a lack of effec-tive lordship at provincial level. In the absence of this, local leadership devolved onto lesser men and families, often junior kinsman of the old comital lines, like the Menteith or Atholl (*Clann Donnachaidh*) families, or leading tenants like the MacDowells in Galloway. Competition between such groupings was a cause of increased local feuding, for example the bitter struggle in Menteith and Strathearn between the Drummonds and Menteiths in the early 1360s. This feud drew in King David and Robert Stewart on opposite sides and showed how such con-flicts, though local in origin, could be of significance at the highest level, reflecting the breakdown of cohesion in provincial societies. Instead of earls and lords with defined authority in a single province as in the thir-teenth century, by the late 1350s the greatest nobles exercised lordship

[13] Fawcett, *Scottish Architecture from the Accession of the Stewarts to the Renaissance 1371–1560*, 3–58.

which was more widely based but was less stable and deeply rooted. Such structures had grown out of war and political upheaval. Stewart's involvement in Menteith and Strathearn was part of interests which had been built up since the late 1330s in central and northern Scotland and was based on the occupation of lands left vacant through deaths and forfeiture. Robert exploited his position as lieutenant to legitimise these actions and established loose predominance by finding local allies or inserting his lesser adherents into new provinces. In the far north, Earl William of Ross copied these tactics in Caithness and Sutherland, but it was the Douglases who provided the closest parallel. Like Stewart, the power of William, earl of Douglas was based on personal links with men from a wide area and was not confined to a single province or sheriffdom. Like Stewart too, Earl William could point to his family's links with Robert I and its role in the defence of Scotland. By the 1350s the Douglases had established a tradition of lordship based on both public authority as justiciars and march wardens and as private lords in a region which had shifted from a relatively peaceful royal heartland to a militarised and disputed march. When David II returned to Scotland in 1357, his greatest subjects were not a score of lords whose power centred on a single earldom but a smaller group of much more powerful figures whose regional influence and place in the Bruce establishment challenged his kingship. David had to compete with Douglas, Stewart and others to extend his own authority, and even after 1363 the Bruce king lacked the means or will to uproot magnates whose power was inextricably linked to the Bruce cause. The structures of regional lordship they had formed would continue to characterise political society in Scotland for much of the next century.[14]

In the north and west these shifts in the exercise of provincial lordship were part of wider changes that would have an even greater impact on the development of Scotland. The lands from Argyll, through the upland districts of Lennox, Menteith, Strathearn, Atholl and Mar to the interiors of Moray and Ross had long been outside the direct orbit of the royal government. They were run by provincial magnates, the Comyns and others, whose lordship rested on loose superiority over local lords. However, despite this, these Gaelic-speaking, upland communities were not regarded as a problem by the crown or its agents. Differences of political, economic and cultural behaviour were not remarked upon and were probably regarded as acceptable variation within a diverse kingdom. From the 1230s and 1240s these lands were in the peaceful allegiance of the king through their lords; they were natural, if not central, parts of the realm.

---

[14] Boardman, *The Early Stewart Kings*, 7–8, 16; Brown, *The Black Douglases*, 48–9.

Figure 15.1. Tantallon Castle. A fifteen-metre high wall created an enclosure on a promontory surrounded by cliffs. The simplicity of the basic defensive scheme was augmented by extensive tower lodgings and hall ranges which made Tantallon a fitting residence for the earls of Douglas.

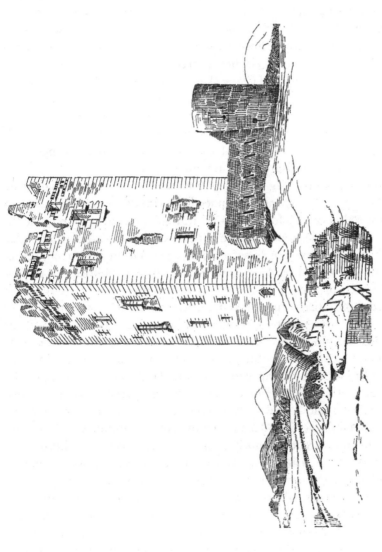

Figure 15.2. Threave Castle provided an alternative model of fortification based on equally simple principles. Threave was actually an island refuge in the Dee. The massive tower-house provided the focal point of a complex of halls and ancillary buildings which provided a base for Archibald Douglas in eastern Galloway.

By the 1350s the situation was very different. The disruption of provincial lordship, which saw the disappearance of many principal magnate houses in these lands and the failure of the families, like the Randolphs in Moray or the Campbells in Atholl, who had been given the role of replacing them, was a key element in this change. In Badenoch, Atholl and Lochaber this failure of lordship severed the principal political links between local communities and the kingdom as a whole. As in lowland societies, this vacuum was filled by lesser lords. However, in the central Highlands, these lords emerged as the heads of Gaelic kindreds, like the MacKintoshes in Badenoch and Lochaber and *Clann Donnachaidh* in Atholl. Though before the 1300s such families had probably been the tenants and officials of Anglicised magnates like the Comyns and often traced their ancestry to these mid-thirteenth century forebears, from the 1330s these lords developed as predatory and independent leaders of militarised followings ready to exploit a period of disorder and fragmentation.[15]

Such changes probably represented the renewal of traditional structures of power at the expense of connections with the values of the Anglo-French world. Even landowners from an Anglicised background, like the Grants of Freuchie, took on elements of Gaelic lordship, while Clan Chattan, a confederacy of lesser kindreds centred on Badenoch, represented the use of kin-based structures to form new political groupings. The primacy of local lords, who expressed their power in terms of extended family ties, real or invented, was a feature of Gaelic political culture. The new attraction of such kin-based units of lordship in the Highlands was not simply driven by the removal of established magnate superiors. The effects of war, plague and worsening climate since the 1290s had a special importance in the central Highlands. A fall in population allied to the difficulty of raising crops in upland areas meant that estates in these regions held by the church or secular landowners from surrounding regions were harder to turn to profit. Combined with the collapse in the structures of authority which would protect the rights of these landowners, these changes worked to the advantage of local kindreds which relied on the herding of cattle as one of their two principal activities. The other was raiding. Raids within the Highlands and into surrounding districts were led by nobles backed by bands of retainers, described by the Gaelic word, *ceathern*, Anglicised to cateran. Lightly armed and armoured, these semi-professional troops were ideal plunderers of cattle. Their emergence represented the militarisation of the Highlands. This process did not occur in isolation. From before the 1330s

---

[15] For changes in the Highlands, see Boardman, 'Lordship in the north-east: The Badenoch Stewarts I', 2–10; Grant, *Independence and Nationhood*, 200–9.

Hebrideans developed military and political interests in the north and west. The Isles were a reservoir of heavily-armed men, ready to serve lords permanently for land or money. Up to the 1230s such forces were found amongst the northern enemies of David I's heirs while Robert I employed them as the hard core of his armies. However, by the 1330s and 1340s the rise of John, lord of the Isles put a different complexion on the military role of the Hebrideans in Scotland. Instability in Lochaber, Badenoch, Atholl and Wester Ross provided an opportunity for the Islesmen from John down. In Lochaber John established his direct lordship by allying with local kindreds like the MacKintoshes but also by imposing his Hebridean satellites, particularly the MacLeans, in the province to bolster his position. During subsequent decades Clan Maclean would be identified as the vanguard of Clan Donald's lordship, the two kindreds extending their lordship up the Great Glen. Such indirect influence was a feature of Clan Donald's presence in mainland Scotland. In Moray, Wester Ross and even Atholl, Hebridean lords could be found occupying the lands of other lords or receiving grants of territory.[16]

The Islesmen were not regarded as enemies by lords and kindreds in the Highlands but as allies, mercenaries and superiors. Magnates like William, earl of Ross and Robert Stewart sought accommodation with John and his adherents as a means to maintain their own lordship in the region. Stewart, in particular, was skilled at exploiting shifts in the character of the region. In Atholl his orbit drew in the local kindred of *Clann Donnachaidh* and Hebridean incomers, like Ewen MacRuairi of Glentilt. Further north, Stewart also exercised lordship over kindreds in Badenoch, and his third son, Alexander, built his own personal connections with the men and women of the lordship, siring the eldest of his children who were raised with gaelic-speaking families. The Stewarts could present their lordship in ways recognisable to their northern satellites. If the lieutenant of the kingdom adapted to change, by the 1360s a less sympathetic attitude was evident. From 1366 David II regarded the bringing of these 'northern regions' into 'the peace and service of the community and the realm' as a priority. In the parliament of July 1366 the arrest of 'certain rebels . . . from Atholl, Argyll, Badenoch and Lochaber' was ordered, and the refusal of the lords of these provinces to allow them to be assessed for taxation increased tensions. David regarded control of these regions and access to their resources as being his right and he identified the problems with the followings of his rivals. The penalties of the 1367 revocation were imposed heavily on Badenoch, Lochaber and Garmoran, where Stewart and John of the Isles were charged large sums

[16] *A.L.I.*, xxxviii–xli.

for occupying lands in the king's absence. The next year Stewart was associated with a plan to force John, Gillespic Campbell and the men of the Isles and Highlands into the king's 'peace and obedience', but the reluctance of Robert to give his support led to his arrest, along with his son, Alexander, and their imprisonment in Lochleven Castle during 1368. Stewart's spell in custody was a mark of David's seriousness. In November 1369 the king travelled north to Inverness and received John of the Isles's submission. John promised that he and his men would 'obey and support' the king and his officers and perform 'all services' as under Robert I, handing over hostages for his good behaviour.[17]

David was acting to establish the primacy of the crown over his magnates but his efforts probably had a wider motivation and support. The statutes of 1366 and 1368 concerning 'rebels' suggest the involvement of elements in the kingdom whose lands and property had suffered at the hands of Highland kindreds. John's promise in 1370 that he 'would make amend for all damages, injuries and crimes' done by his liegemen and to 'pursue rebels' who 'show contempt for [the king's] laws' suggest local disorder was at the heart of the issue. The activities of John's 'liegemen' were the product of major changes in the structures of authority and society in the north and west. They would not be halted by a single royal campaign and David was only the first king to fail to recognise that Clan Donald was not just another magnate house. John's dominance in the Hebrides was bound up with the continuing opportunities for plunder and lordship in surrounding lands which provided the Islesmen with employment. His and Stewart's positions in the Highlands were as loose overlords, and much disorder was generated at a lower level. Attitudes to this disorder were already hardening within the communities that bordered Atholl and Badenoch. Local knights, burgesses and especially clergy articulated a growing hostility to their neighbours in what was increasingly regarded as a distinct Highland zone. The declining place of the Gaelic language in these north-eastern lowlands during the medieval period, and the contrast between the relative stability of these lands from the late 1330s and the continuing fragmentation and disruption of Highland lordship meant that the inhabitants of upland Moray and Atholl seemed a distinct group to their neighbours. The intrusion of men of the Isles increased the sense of a powerful and assertive Gaelic world posing a threat to the landowners and burgesses of lowland Scotland beyond the Tay. During the coming decades such fears and prejudices would harden, and events in this region would reshape the internal identities and political character of the kingdom.

---

[17] Boardman, 'Lordship in the north-east: The Badenoch Stewarts I', 9–10; *A.P.S.*, i, 499–501; Penman, 'The kingship of David II', 452–4, 463, 467, 492–5, 506.

The anxieties of the Anglicised communities in northern Scotland about their neighbours, and the forceful responses of the crown to a perceived political problem during the 1360s were part of a wider picture. In Edward III's lordship of Ireland there had been growing complaints about the weakening and contraction of royal government and dependable structures of aristocratic rule. A sense of racial difference and antagonism between English and Gaelic Irish communities had been a long-term element in relations within Ireland, but since the late thirteenth century the increased effectiveness and independence of Irish leaders in Ulster, Connacht, western Munster and even in the bogs and mountains of Leinster had prompted appeals for aid from English settlers. As in northern Scotland, the involvement of Hebrideans had been a major element in shifts in the political and military character of many regions. After 1360, however, the cessation of major warfare against Scotland and France allowed Edward III to divert resources to Ireland. The next year an army led by his second son, Lionel, duke of Clarence and earl of Ulster, was sent to restore royal authority. Lionel's efforts paralleled those of David II in the later 1360s. The link between events in the Plantagenets' Irish lordship and the Bruces' dominions in the Isles and the west was recognised in 1365 when the possibility of a force from Scotland or the Hebrides supporting Clarence's efforts in Ireland was considered.[18]

However, while before the 1290s such co-operation between the kings of England and Scotland and their magnate adherents against leaders of the Gaels or the Islesmen was not uncommon, by the 1360s the situation was very different. The effect of sixty years of warfare involving Scotland, the Isles, Ireland and northern England was to disrupt and fragment the alliances of land and family which formed the aristocratic world of the thirteenth-century British Isles. Most directly divisions were created between the nobilities of Bruce Scotland and those of the Plantagenet dominions by the refusal of Edward I and his successors to recognise the legitimacy of Robert and David Bruce's claim to the Scottish throne. As Robert I's statute of 1314 forfeited those holding lands in Scotland who refused him homage, and as Edward II and his son normally regarded such homage as an act of treason, this political division inevitably severed the connections of landholding which were the basis of Anglo-Scottish aristocratic ties. Many families, knights and burgesses as well as great barons who possessed estates in the two realms were forced into a choice. Though the Bruces, Dunbars, Douglases and earls of Fife were amongst the group that forfeited their English estates, greater significance was

---

[18] Frame, *Colonial Ireland*, 129–34; Lydon, *The Lordship of Ireland*, 215–25.

attached to those lords who were deprived by the Bruces in Scotland. Such disinherited nobles could appeal to the sympathy of English kings who regarded themselves as also having been denied their rights in Scotland. As has been apparent, these Disinherited were a mixed group of English, Scots enemies of the Bruces and even French adventurers. Their involvement in the conspiracy of 1320 and the wars of the 1330s and as part of continuing diplomatic debate into the 1360s was a mark of the tensions left by widespread royal interference with rights of land and inheritance. Plans to restore these lords were discussed, especially in the peace talks of 1327–8 but, though the issue was on the agenda, Robert was clear during negotiations 'that nobody in the allegiance of the king of England . . . can demand land within the realm of Scotland'. Although, during the 1360s, Scots nobles visited England on pilgrimage, for tournaments and on shopping expeditions, and could serve in Edward III's armies on the continent, the key permanent connection created by land-holding and liege homage had been cut.[19]

During the 1360s, the finality of this break was not clear to any of the parties. The question of the Disinherited and of cross-border lordship was one of the issues at stake between David II and Edward III. Though open warfare never broke out, the relationship between the crowns and realms of the British Isles remained unsettled. As since 1289–90, the ambitions of the Plantagenets in Scotland exerted a major influence on events in the northern realm. The treaty of Berwick in 1357 had left aside questions of Scotland's status. David had been released for a ransom accompanied by a ten-year truce, guaranteed by hostages from the Scottish nobility. However, this arrangement did not mean that Edward had abandoned wider ambitions. The possibility of a final peace between the realms and the terms on which Edward would agree to this remained of crucial importance and debates on the issue were set against the background of Edward's ascendancy in France after the victory at Poitiers. The English king was concerned to maintain pressure on the headless French kingdom and in 1360 he was able to extract favourable terms in the treaty of Brétigny. Edward would abandon his claim to the French crown but would receive an enlarged duchy of Aquitaine in full sovereignty and a promised ransom of £500,000 for King John. If not total victory, the terms satisfied the English king's consistent demands since the 1330s and may have encouraged him to pursue a settlement in Scotland.[20]

[19] Stones, *Anglo-Scottish Relations*, nos 40–1; Frame, *Ireland and Britain*, 166–9.
[20] For the treaty of Berwick, see *A.P.S.*, i, 19. For events in France between 1356 and 1360, see Rogers, *War Cruel and Sharp*, 385–426; Rogers, 'The Anglo-French peace negotiations of 1354–1360 reconsidered', 193–214; Sumption, *Trial by Fire*, 250–454.

Events in France certainly coloured Scottish attitudes. In 1359 David may have approached the French but found little real support for a renewal of the earlier alliance. The Anglo-French peace left the Scots with the danger of facing a hostile Edward III in isolation as they had done in the 1300s and early 1330s. With Edward III at the height of his power, the need for a peace that prevented fresh warfare was clear. In the months after his defeat of the 1363 rebellion, David initiated plans for peace with Edward, and in late October he journeyed south to meet the English king, the first willing visit south by a Scottish king since the early 1290s. David probably offered to recognise one of Edward's younger sons, Lionel of Clarence or John of Gaunt, as his heir should he die childless. In return, David would be freed from the ransom and peace would be established between the realms. Such terms had been agreed by David and Edward in 1351 but were rejected by the Scottish community. The Bruce king was now in a position to direct his subjects but found Edward seeking more. In early December 1363 Edward proposed to cancel the ransom, surrender his Scottish lands, compensate the Disinherited and restore David to the estates of Alexander III in England in return for recognition of himself as heir to the Scottish throne. David was pressured into agreeing to place these terms before his subjects. In March 1364 he held a parliament at Scone where these proposals were debated. The succession of the English king was rejected but, though Stewart and others may have wished no deal that compromised their rights, David remained ready to make concessions for peace. The estates certainly feared that rejection would provoke a war, but by 1364 Edward was increasingly preoccupied with the attempt to secure his interests in France. The English government needed funds and offered 'progress' on the issue of peace if the Scots would pay the ransom, offer a sum to recover the English-held castles in the marches, restore the Disinherited and provide military assistance. David responded with an offer of limited military aid in Ireland, the satisfaction of the Disinherited and a plan to enfeoff a younger son of Edward with Galloway and Man.[21]

The flurry of proposals continued into 1366 whilst discussions were also held on the payment of the ransom. However, the death of the captive French king and the determination of his son, Charles V, to reject the treaty of Brétigny created fresh problems for Edward and reduced Scottish fears. In 1367 and 1368 there was local warfare in the marches and David suspended payment of the ransom. In 1369 David returned to London, this time striking a deal to pay a reduced ransom during a

---

[21] Duncan, 'A question about the succession, 1364', 7–12; Penman, 'The kingship of David II', 332–5, 392–415, 432–7.

fourteen-year truce to last until 1384. Peace proposals were offered by the English in 1370 but David simply parried them. The dispatch of a Scottish embassy to France, while not seeking a formal alliance, marked David's increased confidence and security.[22]

Though ultimately without positive results, the diplomacy of the 1360s was of pivotal importance in confirming the status of the Scottish realm. It provided an insight into the varied attitudes and priorities of Scots concerning their rights and interests. These show that the severing of ties to the Plantagenet dominions in previous decades was not necessarily final. The Bruce king himself proposed to restore disinherited families like the Mowbrays, Beaumonts, Percys and Strathbogies as Scottish lords and to grant provinces like Moray and Galloway to English magnates of royal blood. Such actions would have re-established major cross-border families with obligations of allegiance to both English and Scottish kings and would have been accompanied by military support for the Plantagenets in the British Isles. This return to a stable, peaceful relationship with the English realm without formal subjection to Plantagenet lordship would have been attractive to David and perhaps to many Scots. However, the involvement of the succession in the discussions raised a prospect of far greater connections between the kingdoms. If David remained confident of producing offspring who would render such negotiations irrelevant, his subjects were right to take a less sanguine view. The discussions of 1363 to 1366 raised the real possibility of Plantagenet kingship in Scotland, either through the direct succession of the English king or its acquisition by one of his younger sons. The terms on which this was offered in 1363 would deliver tangible gains to the Scottish community in the form of peace and territory. The proposed succession would also have been accompanied by guarantees like those of 1290. Scotland's parliament, church and royal government would remain separate. The kingdom's elites were promised security of land, access to office and freedom from new taxes and demands for military service beyond what was normal. When these terms were debated by the Scottish estates in 1364, their proponents argued that, unlike in previous decades, a peaceful Plantagenet succession would safeguard the achievements of the wars. It would secure the kingdom's peace and prosperity without loss of honour and status and provide kingship which would be preferable to a 'tyrant and plunderer' whose rule was based solely on superior power, perhaps a reference to Stewart's lieutenancy. The Scottish realm was without French support, burdened by the ransom and weakened by the

---

[22] Duncan, 'A question about the succession, 1364', 13–20; Penman, 'The kingship of David II', 440–6, 509–13; Sumption, *Trial by Fire*, 455–539; MacDonald, *Border Bloodshed: Scotland, England and France at War, 1369–1403*, 9–23.

losses of past battles. Its people should not risk defeat but should accept peace on terms welcomed by their forefathers in 1290. Though Edward III might not be welcome as king, the rule of a son who could ensure family ties with England but retain Scotland's separate status was considered a realistic prospect.

However, the account of the debate of 1364 showed how attitudes had changed in Scotland since 1290 as a result of war and political upheaval. As well as arguing that the Scottish position was not as weak as was claimed, that the realm possessed good leaders and was rich enough to pay the ransom, and that Edward's resources were stretched on the continent and in Ireland, resistance to the succession plans was shaped by the language and experience of the previous sixty years. Much of this was expressed as mistrust of the English royal dynasty. Edward III had broken the peace of 1328, why should he not do the same in this case? Examples of Wales and Ireland where people were treated 'like slaves', 'so that the name and nobility of the Welsh has altogether vanished', were cited as warnings to the Scots. In itself, this reveals a shift in attitudes from the previous century, when the focus was on membership of a common Anglo–Scottish elite at odds with Welsh and Irish leaders, to identification with those in opposition to the English crown and people. Edward's promises of good lordship were also suspect. His promise to rule without taxation or increased customs would leave him 'with nothing of his own', prompting the king 'to live by robbery', 'despoil the people' and dispossess the lords, especially those of royal blood. Underlying this mistrust was a sense of collective interest developed since 1290 but shaped by Bruce leadership. This was now threatened by the planned settlement. A Plantagenet king of Scots would have placed Scottish bishops under the archbishop of York. He would direct patronage to English lords and would restore the Disinherited to their Scottish lands. A king whose office was clearly subordinate to the English crown would forfeit the rite of coronation, becoming a lesser king, like those of Ireland. The church, nobility and monarchy would be irrevocably undermined by a settlement that, once done, could not be undone.[23]

Such arguments must have tapped into widely-held attitudes in Scotland. The claims of Robert Stewart to the throne were threatened. Magnates and lesser men must have feared the loss of lands and influence won under Bruce leadership to the Disinherited and to English lords. Despite the close relations between William Landells, bishop of St Andrews and King David, many clergy must have retained anxieties

---

[23] Duncan, 'A question about the succession, 1364', 2–5, 24–57. Though the record of the 1364 debate was written well after the event, its language and outlook suggest that it was an accurate, though perhaps partial, account of proceedings.

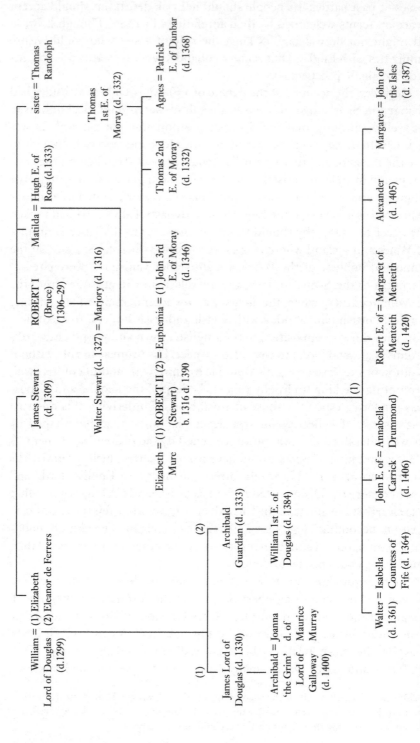

Table 15.1. Stewart, Douglas and Randolph

about their prospects in a realm ruled by a Plantagenet prince. Most of the political class debating the succession in 1364 had defended these rights and interests in David's absence between 1346 and 1356. Their status as individuals and as part of a community had developed in Scotland in resistance to Plantagenet claims and in support of King Robert's line and its rights. Despite the threat of renewed war, it is unlikely that resistance to a settlement that challenged this would have been less in 1364 than when presented to them before, in 1351. Though the debate revealed that the rewards of peace were attractive and could divide the estates, it is likely that it took the authority of a politically ascendant king to present an effective case for a Plantagenet succession.

Ironically, it would be the end of the Bruce dynasty that would mark the end of this long era of insecurity. Despite divorcing Margaret Logie and planning to marry a third wife, Agnes Dunbar, King David was still childless when, in February 1371, he died suddenly at Edinburgh. His throne was taken by his nephew, Robert Stewart, who had first been named as heir over fifty years before. After David's efforts to bypass his claims, Robert did not accede to the kingship without opposition. William, earl of Douglas led a challenge to the legitimacy of the new king and the new dynasty, and had to be bought off before Stewart's coronation at Scone. Despite this and despite the fact that Robert II was hardly a new figure at the head of the realm, his accession did much to end remaining uncertainties. In 1372 the throne was entailed on the male line of the Stewarts. As Robert had five adult sons, this act ended the chain of anxieties over the succession which stretched back to 1284. Though the truce with England and the late king's ransom were not repudiated, Robert sent envoys to France in 1371 who negotiated an alliance with Charles V. Meanwhile, in the marches the earls of Douglas and Dunbar and Archibald, lord of Galloway began local campaigns against those lands in Edward III's lordship. The entail and the French alliance were the key actions of a regime with roots that stretched back to 1306. There would be no Plantagenet succession, no peace and alliance with England and no restoration of cross-border ties of lordship or land. Scotland's royal dynasty, its nobility and church would remain separate in personnel and allegiance from the dominions of the English kings. The thirteenth-century sense of Scottishness which defined the Scottish cause of the 1290s to 1350s was now coloured deeply by this conscious separation from, and rejection of, the rule or influence of the English crown.[24]

[24] Penman, 'The kingship of David II', 517–22; Boardman, *The Early Stewart Kings*, 39–62, 108–13; MacDonald, *Border Bloodshed*, 23–74.

Conclusion: A United Kingdom?

The years between the mid-thirteenth and mid-fourteenth centuries represented a pivotal period in the history of Scotland. The strengthening of the ideological and material power of the crown and the extension of royal lordship under Alexander II and Alexander III brought the kingdom to its high medieval peak. However, their successes were part of general western European trends which favoured the tightening of central jurisdictions over those of lesser rulers and subjects. These trends also increased the possibility of Scotland itself being drawn into the close orbit of a greater royal lordship, that of the Plantagenet dominions. The thirteenth-century status quo between the two realms remained ambiguous and, in the legalistic atmosphere of the time, it may have been inevitable that such ambiguities were exploited by English kings seeking formal authority over Scotland. Though it was driven by the dynastic catastrophe of the early 1280s, it would have been neither unnatural nor unthinkable for Scotland to have been absorbed into the lordship of the English crown at the turn of the fourteenth century. Had such an absorption occurred, the close dynastic relations and aristocratic connections between the two realms would have appeared as the natural precursor to this process. Between 1290 and 1370 varied routes to this absorption were proposed, by dynastic union between the two ruling lines, the succession of a Plantagenet prince to the Scottish throne, the exercise of superior lordship by the English crown over the kings of Scots, or the direct subjection of Scotland to the king of England.[1]

The establishment of Plantagenet lordship by any of these methods would have hugely altered the development of Scotland. Whether ruled

---

[1] For excellent discussions of high and later medieval Scotland from a broad perspective see R. Frame, 'Overlordship and reaction, c.1200–c.1450' in Grant and Stringer (eds), *Uniting the Kingdom? The Making of British History*, 65–84; K. J. Stringer and A. Grant, 'Scottish Foundations', in Grant and Stringer *Uniting the kingdom?*, 85–110.

by the English kings directly or through their rights as superior, Scotland would have joined Ireland, Wales, Aquitaine and England as a part of their family dominions. The status of Scotland as a separate unit of temporal and ecclesiastical government would have dwindled to that of a satellite of the English crown. The ultimate focus of political life would have shifted south to the king of England's court, and the influence of English models on the practices of law, government and church would have received an enormous new impetus. At the very least, the personnel of the political elite, the royal administration, nobility and church, would have been subject to a continual influx of men with primarily English interests and perspectives. Despite the guarantees given in 1290, 1305, 1335 and 1363 about the access of Scots to the offices of church and state in their land, slowly or quickly it is likely that Plantagenet lordship would have led to the merging of the already connected elites of the two realms.

With a longer perspective, such a merger might seem only to predate the unions of 1603 and 1707. However, if these changes had occurred over three centuries before, it would have had enormous significance. The development of a late medieval state in Scotland with its own sense of ideological and historical development would have been stifled. Distinct institutions of royal government, separate judicial practices, traditions of financial management and the development of the Scottish parliament would all have been arrested at an early stage. Rather than a kingdom with internationally-recognised status and rights and with a place as an enemy and ally in the warfare and diplomacy of late medieval and early modern Europe, Scotland would have been merely one of the English kings' territories, like Aquitaine or Ireland. The Irish parallel is, perhaps, illuminating. As in Ireland, the presence of a central administration receiving its political direction from the English crown and likely to interpret matters of law and custom from a starkly-Anglicised perspective would have opened up greater cultural and political divisions between English and Gaelic-speaking communities. The absence of a native political centre from Scotland would have had profound effects on the development of political society and identity in that realm.

Scotland never passed under the lordship of the Plantagenets. The failure of the efforts of Edward I and his successors to extract settled recognition from the Scottish community had implications across the British Isles. The wars from the 1290s to the 1350s contributed to the weakening of English lordship in Ireland, and ended with the fragmentation of the common aristocratic world of the thirteenth century into two hostile and exclusive allegiances. The lessons of the conflicts after 1296 seem to be that the Medieval English state lacked the material and ideological power to subject another established royal lordship. The Scottish kingdom was too large and developed to be dismantled by force. This view certainly encapsulates the problems experienced by Edward I and Edward III in cementing their apparent grip on the realm. However, too much depended on chance, on individual choices of allegiance, on personal leadership and on wider patterns of events for people to be overly sanguine about the survival of the Scottish realm. Without the sudden death of Margaret of Norway, Scotland would have passed peacefully under Plantagenet rule. It was Bruce's decision to seize the throne and his survival of defeat in 1306 which challenged Edward I's settlement of 1304–5. The unexpected breakdowns in Anglo-French relations in 1294 and 1336 provided critical assistance for the Scots at key moments. The significance of these events also depended on the maintenance of a Scottish cause. From 1290 onwards it is possible to identify this as a sense of distinct Scottish interests and practices and the recognition, even during periods of peace, that the king of England represented a threat to these. This was a mark of the achievement of Alexander III and his forebears. Their formation of a political hierarchy, associated efforts to develop the identification between the realm and its inhabitants, and the definition of rights of crown and church in opposition to external interference would all inform attitudes at work amongst Scottish communities between the 1290s and 1360s.

Yet while these characteristics of the thirteenth-century Scottish polity can be recognised as exercising vital influence on forthcoming events, there were major alterations in the way Scotland functioned. The social and political links between the elites of the Scottish kingdom and those of England had also been an integral element in pre-war identities and loyalties, but these were severed along arbitrary lines. Peace and a shared aristocratic society were replaced by war and separation. The ways in which this occurred caused many Scots to feel uncomfortable as late as the 1360s. The internal character of Scottish political life was also subject to major change. Thirteenth-century Scotland was characterised by the exercise of effective, but mostly undemanding, royal government in the sheriffdoms of the east and south, and by more indirect management by the crown in established and defined provincial societies with their own rulers. The shared interests of kings and the magnates of the north and west were the basis by which the crown extended its lordship into the far west and the Hebrides during the century up to 1286.

Crisis and war interrupted many of these processes. Political activity in the Hebrides remained focused on its own traditions and swiftly moved beyond the effective reach of Scottish kings and magnates. Instead, the Islesmen were an element in the disruption of the structures of provincial rule in the north. The relative stability of these mainland provinces from the 1220s to the 1290s was replaced by the fragmentation of authority and competition for lordship. Similar shifts took place in the south where areas subject to direct royal lordship became a disputed and militarised marchland. In both regions by the late 1350s magnate houses combined public and private powers to secure wide but ill-defined support from local men and communities. Though such aristocratic power structures were not entirely new, in the fourteenth century the crown was forced to compete with magnates for effective lordship. While David II still possessed material and ideological advantages in such competition, the long periods of rule by guardians had undermined the natural rights of the crown to leadership. Kingship remained central to the status and identity of Scotland as a distinct political society and took pride of place in all efforts to articulate the Scottish cause. However, the wars had also required the defenders of this cause to develop other structures to maintain their interests in the absence of royal leadership. Alongside the clear statements of these years about Scotland's rights as a realm and community, the structures of lordship and government in the realm were becoming less defined and stable. The late medieval kingdom of Scotland was a product of war and division which had formed a realm both more coherent and more fragmented than it had been in the mid-thirteenth century.

Table of Events

1214–49		**Reign of Alexander II**
1214	5 December	Inauguration of Alexander II at Scone
1215	June	Defeat of Donal Ban MacWilliam
	22 October	Alexander receives homage of northern English rebels
	November	Opening of the Fourth Lateran Council
1216	January	John, king of England campaigns in Lothian
	September	Alexander pays homage to Louis of France at Dover
	October	Death of King John. Accession of Henry III as king of England
1217	September	Scotland placed under an interdict by the papal legate
	December	Alexander pays homage to Henry III
1218	2 February	Absolution of the Clergy
1220	August	Agreement between Alexander and English government
1221	June	Alexander II marries Joan, sister of Henry III, at York
	3 October	Marriage of Margaret (I), sister of Alexander II, and Hubert de Burgh
1222	May–June	Alexander leads expedition into Argyll
	11 September	Killing of Bishop Adam of Caithness
1223–9		Conflict between Ranald and Olaf over Man and the Isles
1230	May	Norse fleet in the Isles. Attacks Rothesay
1233–4		Rebellion of Richard Marshal against Henry III
1234	2 February	Death of Alan, lord of Galloway
1235	July	Alexander II leads army into Galloway
1237	June	Death of John, earl of Huntingdon
	22 September	Treaty of York between Henry III and Alexander II
1239		Harald, son of Olaf, named as king of Man by Hakon of Norway
	15 May	Marriage of Alexander II to Marie de Couci at Roxburgh
	17 June	Birth of Edward, son of Henry III
1241	4 September	Birth of Alexander, son of Alexander II, at Roxburgh
1242–3		Henry III's Poitevan campaign
1242	May or June	Killing of Patrick of Atholl at Haddington
	26 November	Alexander II exiles the Bissets

1244	August	Confrontation between Alexander II and Henry III at Newcastle
1247		Death of 'MacSomhairle' (Dugald MacRuairi) at Ballyshannon
1248		Drowning of King Harald on return from Norway
1249	June–July	Alexander II leads expedition into Lorn
	8 July	Death of Alexander II on the Isle of Kerrera.
1249–86		**Reign of Alexander III**
1249	13 July	Inauguration of Alexander III at Scone
1250	19 June	Translation of Saint Margaret in Dunfermline Abbey
1251	26 December	Marriage of Alexander to Margaret, daughter of Henry III
1253–4		Henry III in Aquitaine
1253	26 April	Death of David Bernham, bishop of St Andrews
1255	14 February	Election of Gamelin as bishop of St Andrews
	10 August	Seizure of Alexander III by earls of Gloucester and Dunbar
	20 August	Henry III meets Alexander at Roxburgh
1256–7		Llywelyn ap Gruffydd's initial campaigns in Wales
1257	29 October	Alexander III seized at Kinross by Walter Comyn and allies
1258	January	Henry III summons host for expedition against Scotland
	18 March	Alliance between Scottish magnates and Llywelyn ap Gruffydd
	April–June	Emergence of baronial opposition to Henry III in England
	November	Death of Walter Comyn. Henry recognises new council
1259	13 June	Pope consecrates John Cheam as bishop of Glasgow
	4 December	Henry III pays homage for Aquitaine to Louis IX of France under terms of treaty of Paris
1259–61		Dispute over the earldom of Menteith
1262		William, earl of Ross harries Skye
1263–7		Barons' Wars in England
1263	summer	Hakon of Norway in the Isles (dies in Orkney, 16 December)
1264	21 January	Birth of Alexander, son of Alexander III
	summer	King Magnus of Man submits to Alexander III at Dumfries
1265		Death of Magnus of Man. Lands annexed by Alexander III
1266	2 July	Treaty of Perth
1267	29 September	Treaty of Montgomery between Henry III and Llywelyn ap Gruffydd
1270–1		Crusades led by Louis IX and Lord Edward
1274		Council of the church at Lyons
	19 August	Alexander III attends the coronation of Edward I
1275		Manxmen revolt against Alexander III's rule
1277	January–November	War between Edward I and Llywelyn ap Gruffydd
1278	28 October	Alexander pays homage to Edward for lands in England
1281	14 August	Marriage of Margaret, daughter of Alexander III, to Eric II, king of Norway
1282–3		Edward I's second Welsh war. End of line of Gwynedd

1284	29 January	Death of Alexander, son of Alexander III
	February	Barons recognise Margaret of Norway as Alexander's heir
1285	14 October	Marriage of Alexander III to Yolande de Dreux
1286	19 March	Death of Alexander III at Kinghorn
1286	29 March	Funeral of Alexander III. Envoys sent to Edward I
	late April	Assembly at Scone. Possible choice of guardians
May 1286–August 1289		Edward I in France
	20 Sept	Turnberry Band
	c. November	Bruces attack royal and Balliol castles in the south-west
1289	10 May	Edward I seeks dispensation for marriage of Margaret of Norway and Prince Edward
	September	Murder of Earl Duncan of Fife
1290	June	Edward takes custody of Man
	18 July	Treaty of Birgham
	late September	Death of Margaret in Orkney
1291	10 May	Meeting of Edward I and Scots at Norham
	early June	Submission of claimants to Edward I
	early August	Opening of the Great Cause at Berwick
1292	July	Edward I's parliament at Berwick
	17 November	Judgement given in favour of John Balliol

1292–   **Reign of John**

1292	30 November	Inauguration of King John at Scone
	26 December	John pays homage to Edward I at Newcastle
1293	8 February	John holds parliament at Scone
	early October	John at Edward I's parliament. Submits to his authority
1294	19 May	Philip IV, king of France confiscates Aquitaine from Edward I
	29 June	Edward summons John to perform military service
	September	Outbreak of rebellion in Wales
	late	Scots seek absolution for oaths to Edward I from Pope
1295	5 July	Scots send embassy to negotiate alliance with French
1296	March	Scottish army harries English marches
	30 March	Edward I sacks Berwick
	27 April	Battle of Dunbar
	early June	Surrender of King John. Resigns kingdom to Edward I
	28 August	Parliament at Berwick. Submission of Scots
1297	spring	Uprisings in the south-west and north. Fighting in the Isles
	June	Capitulation of Bruce and Stewart at Irvine
	July–October	Political crisis in England
	August–March	Edward I in Flanders
	11 September	Battle of Stirling Bridge
	3 November	Election of William Lamberton as bishop of St Andrews
1298	early	William Wallace named as guardian
	22 July	Battle of Falkirk
1299	27 June	Boniface VIII issues the bull *Scimus Fili*
	December	Edward I fails to lead campaign to relieve Stirling

1300	July–August	Edward I takes Caerlaverock and enters Galloway
1301	July–September	Edward I and Prince Edward campaign in southern Scotland
	summer	John released into French custody
1302	January	Anglo-Scottish truce agreed at Asnières.
	11 July	Battle of Courtrai. Defeat of French in Flanders
1303	May	Peace between Edward I and Philip IV of France
June 1303–July 1304		Edward I leads army through eastern Scotland
1304	20 July	Fall of Stirling Castle
1305	23 August	Execution of William Wallace
	15 September	Ordinance for the government of Scotland issued
1306	10 February	Robert Bruce kills John Comyn at Dumfries

1306–29		**Reign of Robert I**
1306	25 March	Inauguration of Robert I at Scone
	19 June	Battle of Methven
	september	Flight of Robert from Dunaverty
1307	February	Robert returns to Carrick
	10 May	Battle of Loudon Hill
	7 July	Death of Edward I at Burgh by Sands
Autumn 1307– summer 1308		Robert campaigns against his northern enemies
1308	23 May	Battle of Inverurie
	summer	Campaigns in Argyll and Galloway
1309	16 March	Parliament held at St Andrews
1310	February	Church council at Dundee. Suppression of the Templars
1312	29 October	Treaty between Robert and Hakon V of Norway
1313	January–September	Capture of Perth, Dumfries, Man and Linlithgow
1314	23–24 June	Battle of Bannockburn
	November	Cambuskenneth parliament
1315	27 April	Assembly at Ayr. Throne entailed on Edward Bruce
	May	Edward Bruce leads army to Ireland
1316	spring?	Birth of Robert, son of Walter Stewart and Marjory Bruce
1318	1 April	Capture of Berwick
	June	Robert excommunicated and Scotland placed under interdict
	14 October	Battle of Fochart. Death of Edward Bruce
	December	Parliament at Scone
1320	6 April	Letters from Scottish community to Pope John XII issued
	4 August	Black Parliament at Scone
1322	early	Civil war between Edward II and his baronial opponents
	August	Edward II leads expedition into Scotland
	20 October	Battle of Byland
1323	30 May	Thirteen-year truce between England and Scotland
1324	5 March	Birth of David and John, sons of Robert I and Queen Elizabeth
1326	May	Treaty of Corbeil between Robert I and Charles IV of France
	July	Parliament at Cambuskenneth

1327	20 January	Deposition of Edward II
	Easter	Robert in Ulster
	July–August	Weardale campaign
1328	17 March	Treaty of Edinburgh-Northampton
	12 July	Marriage of David II and Joan of England
1329	7 June	Death of Robert I at Cardross

1329–71		**Reign of David II**
1329	13 June	John XXII gives the Scottish kings the right to coronation
1331	24 November	Coronation of David II at Scone
1332	6 August	Edward Balliol and the Disinherited land at Kinghorn
	11 August	Battle of Dupplin Moor
	24 September	Edward Balliol crowned king of Scots at Scone
	November	Edward Balliol offers homage to Edward III of England
1333	March–July	Siege of Berwick by Balliol and Edward III
	20 July	Battle of Halidon Hill
1334	May	David Bruce sent to France
	5 June	Edward Balliol does homage to Edward III at York
	July	Robert Stewart and John Randolph act as guardians
1335	July–October	Edward III leads army to Perth
	30 November	Battle of Culblean. Death of David Strathbogie
1335–6	winter	Attempt at Papal arbitration fails. Philip VI of France plans to send fleet to Scotland
1336	May–June	Edward III fortifies Perth and ravages the north-east
	September	Agreement between Edward Balliol and John of the Isles
October 1336–October 1337		Andrew Murray campaigns against English and Balliol garrisons in Angus, Fife, Clydesdale and Lothian
1337	May	Philip VI confiscates Aquitaine from Edward III
1338	c. March	Death of Andrew Murray. Robert Stewart named as guardian
1339	17 August	Perth surrenders to Robert Stewart
1341	16 April	Edinburgh captured by William Douglas
	2 June	David II returns to Scotland from France
	September	Parliament held at Scone
1342	February	Parliament held at Aberdeen
	June	Killing of Alexander Ramsay
1343	June	David II receives Islesmen into his allegiance
1346	26 August	Battle of Creçy. Defeat of Philip VI by Edward III
	17 October	Battle of Neville's Cross
1347	May	Robert Stewart named as guardian at Perth
		Balliol leads expedition into southern Scotland
	summer	Plague reaches England and Ireland
1349	autumn	Plague arrives in Scotland
1351	May	Parliament meets at Dundee to discuss release of David II
1352	February–March	David attends parliament at Scone. Release terms rejected
1355	Easter	Arrival of French expedition in Scotland
	November	Franco-Scottish army captures Berwick
1356	January–February	'Burnt Candlemas'. Edward III harries Lothian
	19 September	Battle of Poitiers. Defeat and capture of John II of France

1357	3 October	Treaty of Berwick. Release of David II
	6 November	Council held at Scone
1360	October	Treaty of Brétigny. Anglo-French peace.
1363	early	Rebellion of Stewart, Douglas and Dunbar against David II
	c. April	Marriage of David to Margaret Logie
	14 May	Submission of Stewart
	October	David II goes to London
1364	March	Parliament at Scone to consider peace proposals
	April	Death of John II of France in London
1366	July	Parliament at Scone. Tax assessment initiated. Arrest of 'rebels' in north and west ordered
1368		Arrest and imprisonment of Robert Stewart at Lochleven
1369	summer	Renewal of Anglo-French warfare
	18 June	Agreement between David and Edward III at Westminster
	November	David II at Inverness. Submission of John of the Isles
1371	22 February	Death of David II at Edinburgh
	26 March	Coronation of Robert II
		Alliance between Robert II and Charles V of France
1373	April	Parliament at Scone. Entail of the throne on the male line

Guide to Further Reading

1. SURVEYS AND REFERENCE WORKS

The tendency to divide later medieval Scottish history at about 1300 has been reflected in previous general histories. Thus, Duncan's magisterial *Scotland: The Making of the Kingdom* gives way circa 1286 to Nicholson's pacier but still hugely impressive treatment of the fourteenth and fifteenth centuries in *Scotland: The Later Middle Ages*, while *Independence and Nationhood* by Alexander Grant commences its excellent analysis of late medieval Scotland at the moment of crisis in 1306. The alternative to this approach has been to attempt the full coverage of the whole history of medieval Scotland in a single, often slim, volume. The most recent, and among the best, of these general surveys is Barrell's *Medieval Scotland*. An indispensable aid to both surveys and to more detailed discussions now exists in the second edition of *The Atlas of Scottish History to 1707* by McNeill and MacQueen. In over 400 maps and plans, this illustrates most of the main issues of medieval and early modern Scottish history and has provided the basis for the maps in this volume.

2. POLITICS AND POLITICAL SOCIETY 1214–86

Detailed analysis of politics in the reigns of Alexander II and Alexander III is surprisingly thin on the ground. The excellent volume on *The Reign of Alexander III* edited by Norman Reid illustrates this, devoting only one of its chapters to politics and government. The author of this, Alan Young, has also produced in his study of *Robert the Bruce's Rivals: The Comyns* the most recent attempt to cover these two reigns in detail, though the weight of his coverage is post-1286. The only exceptions to this limited coverage are the political crises of the 1240s and 1250s. Here Young's discussion builds on earlier work by Duncan, and by Watt in his article 'The minority of Alexander III'.

Interestingly, as Young's focus on the Comyns illustrates, more attention has been accorded to the Scottish nobility than to their royal masters in the thirteenth century. Central to such studies is the work of Keith Stringer. His *Earl David of Huntingdon*, and 'Periphery and core: Alan son of Roland, lord of Galloway and constable of Scotland', as well as other essays shed considerable light on the character of the nobility and on Scottish (and British Isles) politics. In terms of regional political societies, works by Oram on *The Lordship of Galloway*, Neville on Strathearn, and Young on Buchan illustrate the continued provincialism of the kingdom, while Grant's study of 'Thanes and thanages' is an excellent analysis of the traditional roots of royal lordship.

3. SUCCESSION CRISIS AND WAR 1286–1329

Though it is now nearly forty years since its first appearance, Professor Barrow's *Robert Bruce* remains a complete and compelling account of the events involving the Scottish kingdom from 1286 to 1329. For the same amount of time, the works of Professor Duncan have provided an alternative perspective in terms of coverage and outlook. Duncan's *Regesta Regum Scottorum* volume on Robert I, his heavily annotated edition of Barbour's *Bruce*, and his numerous articles continue to increase understanding of the complexities of government and politics in this period. His recent book *The Kingship of the Scots, 842–1292: Succession and Independence* is a detailed study of the law of succession (and other elements of monarchy) from the ninth to the thirteenth centuries, which provides an exhaustive analysis of the Great Cause and its background, and sheds indispensable light on the legal approaches of the participants. Additions to this bipolar debate, beyond general and popular histories, have been rather more limited. However, the recent appearance of two works which regard events from a different perspective to Barrow has enlivened debate. Watson's study of Edward I and Scotland, *Under the Hammer*, provides a valuable analysis of the critical decade from 1296 based on the records of Edwardian rule, while McNamee's *The Wars of the Bruces* is an excellent study of the period of Scottish military ascendancy after 1314 and its effects in Ireland and England. Similarly, recent articles on the Soules conspiracy by Penman, on the Strathbogies by Ross, and on Wallace's reputation by Fraser are indicative of interesting new perspectives on this critical era.

4. FOURTEENTH-CENTURY POLITICAL LIFE

The fourteenth century after the death of Robert I has tended to be neglected by Scottish historians. With the notable exceptions of Nicholson, whose *Edward III and the Scots* was, for a long time, the only serious study of the post-1329 era, and Webster, who produced the *Regesta Regum Scottorum* volume for David II's long reign, there was limited discussion of the period. In recent times this has altered. Recognition of the crucial importance of the renewed war and diplomacy involving Scotland is reflected in its prominent place in recent works on the origins of the Hundred Years War by Rogers and Sumption, and Duncan's article on David II and Edward III and edition of the 1364 debates, 'A question about the succession', made clear the importance of the issues at stake from the 1330s to the 1360s.

Scottish internal politics have also received increasing attention. Steve Boardman's excellent *The Early Stewart Kings* opens with a discussion of the rivalry between Robert Stewart and David Bruce, while my own *The Black Douglases* provides an account of the development of aristocratic power structures in David's reign. A full analysis of this long and vitally important period has, at last, been provided by Michael Penman whose study of David II is forthcoming.

5. NATIONAL IDENTITY

While discussions about national identity in medieval England have only recently been recognised as a valid and vital focus of research, historians of high medieval Scotland have long recognised their importance. Scottish national identity, the sense of Scotland's existence as a people and a distinct political unit, has been closely linked to the debates about the course and outcome of the Wars of Independence. Such themes have recently been explored with reference to the two centuries before 1286 by Dauvit Broun in his *The Irish Identity of the Kingdom of Scots* and his article 'Defining Scotland and the Scots before the Wars of Independence'. Issues of identity and national ideology also inform much of Barrow's writings on this subject and provide the principal theme of his 'The idea of freedom in late medieval Scotland'. More recent treatments of the same topic have been produced by Reid in his 'Crown and community under Robert I', and by Watson in 'The Enigmatic Lion: Scotland, kingship and national identity in the Wars of Independence', while Goldstein's *The Matter of Scotland* takes as its theme the use of historical literature in a 'war of historiography' with England. Discussion of the best-known expression of Scottish nationhood, the Declaration of Arbroath, has produced a literature of its own with articles by Duncan, Simpson and others and Professor Cowan's new book seeking to place this document in its short-term and wider context.

6. THE CHURCH

There is a keen need for a full survey of the Scottish church covering the thirteenth to fifteenth centuries and assessing its full role in the life of the realm and society of Scotland. In the absence of such a work, the study of ecclesiastical affairs tends to be patchy. The thirteenth century has received some good treatment, especially in the works of the late Marinell Ash (see particularly her essay in Reid, *Scotland in the Reign of Alexander III*), and in the detailed study of *Medieval Papal Representatives in Scotland* by Ferguson, which provides an excellent discussion of the character of the Scottish church's relations with both the papacy and English prelates in the thirteenth century. The chief authority on this subject remains D. E. R. Watt whose study of *Medieval Church Councils in Scotland* and articles on Baiamond's Roll and on university men shed much light on aspects of ecclesiastical life. Watt has also produced a vital reference work on the church of these centuries in his *Biographical Dictionary of Scottish Graduates to A.D. 1410*. This provides biographies of almost all of the leading churchmen of the thirteenth and fourteenth centuries and is indispensable for understanding the character of the clerical elite. Despite this monumental work, the fourteenth-century Scottish church has not received the detailed study it deserves. Its role in the wars and diplomacy of the period needs further study. Barrell's monograph on *The Papacy, Northern England and Scotland, 1342–1378*, detailing papal influence in northern Britain is the only recent and detailed study of the Scottish church in this later period.

7. SCOTLAND AND THE BRITISH ISLES

The last twenty years has seen a growing appreciation amongst historians that events within the Scottish kingdom between 1214 and 1371 were deeply affected by the range of contacts between Scotland and neighbouring lands and regions in the British Isles. This archipelagic perspective has taken Scottish history a long way from older approaches which looked no further than England for external comparisons. In *Domination and Conquest* and *The First English Empire*, Rees Davies discusses common and overlapping patterns of royal and aristocratic lordship across the British Isles, while Robin Frame develops similar themes in a number of articles reprinted in *Ireland and Britain*. It is striking that the lead in this approach has been taken by historians of thirteenth and four-teenth-century Wales and Ireland, lands more directly involved with the Plantagenet dominions than Scotland and Ireland. Scottish involvement in this political society, especially at aristocratic level, has, however, been examined in detail by Stringer in a number of works and in his survey article in Grant and Stringer's *Uniting the Kingdom?* Attempts to take Scottish links with the British Isles beyond the major wars of the early fourteenth century and look at the process of disengagement are limited to Alexander Grant's excellent essay in the same volume.

Such new perspectives have been valuable in developing judgements on the contacts between Scotland and the Irish Sea region to the west. The relations between the Scottish realm and the kingdom of the Isles has, in particular, been the subject of recent work. McDonald's book on *The Kingdom of the Isles* is a full study of the region from a largely western perspective and is complemented by the article on 'Hebridean Sea kings' by Sellar. Both of these remain largely focused on Scotland and the Hebrides. The full range of maritime connections in the west is devel-oped by Duffy in his seminal article 'The Bruce brothers and the Irish Sea World' which looks back from the campaigns of Edward Bruce, explaining them in the light of long-standing contacts spanning the Isles, Scotland and Ireland.

Frustratingly, all these accounts draw to a close in the early fourteenth century. Coverage of the development of John of the Isles's lordship is much more limited, despite the edition of *The Acts of the Lords of the Isles* by the Munros. The best, though brief, accounts of the early lordship and its role in western Scotland come from Grant in *Independence and Nationhood* and his article in Davies (ed.), *The British Isles*, and from Boardman, 'The Badenoch Stewarts'. Of value as direct comparisons are the two principal works on Gaelic Ireland in the late middle ages: Nicholls, *Gaelic and Gaelicised Ireland* and Simms, *From Kings to Warlords*.

Bibliography

The Acts of the Parliament of Scotland, T. Thomson and C. Innes (eds), 12 vols (1814–75).

Altschul, M., *A Baronial Family in Medieval England: The Clares* (Baltimore, 1965).

Anderson, A. O. (ed.), *Early Sources of Scottish History 500–1286*, 2 vols (Edinburgh, 1922).

Anderson, A. O. (ed.), *Scottish Annals from the English Chroniclers 500–1286* (London, 1908).

Anderson, A. O. (ed.), *The Chronicle of Melrose* (London, 1936).

Ash, M., 'William Lamberton, Bishop of St Andrews, 1297–1328', in G. W. S. Barrow (ed.), *The Scottish Tradition* (London, 1974), 44–5.

Ash, M., 'David Bernham, Bishop of St Andrews, 1239–53', in D. McRoberts (ed.), *The Medieval Church of St Andrews* (Glasgow, 1976), 32–44.

Ash, M., 'The diocese of St Andrews under its "Norman" bishops', *S.H.R.*, 55 (1976), 106–26.

Ash, M., 'The church in the reign of Alexander III', in N. Reid (ed.), *Scotland in the Reign of Alexander III, 1249–1286* (Edinburgh, 1990), 31–52.

Balfour-Melville, E. W. M., 'John de Cheam, Bishop of Glasgow', *S.H.R.*, xxvii (1948), 176–86.

Bannerman, J., 'The King's Poet and the Inauguration of Alexander III', *S.H.R.*, 68 (1989), 120–49.

Bannerman, J., 'MacDuff of Fife', in A. Grant and K.J. Stringer, *Medieval Scotland. Crown, Lordship and Community* (Edinburgh, 1993), 20–38.

Barbour, John, *The Bruce*, ed. A. A. M. Duncan (Edinburgh, 1997).

Barnes, P., and G. W. S. Barrow, 'The movements of Robert Bruce between September 1307 and May 1308', *S.H.R.*, 69 (1970), 46–59.

Barrell, A. D. M., *The Papacy, Northern England and Scotland, 1342–1378* (Cambridge, 1995).

Barrell, A. D. M., 'The background to *Cum Universi*: Scoto-Papal relations, 1159–1192', *Innes Review*, 46 (1995), 116–38.

Barrell, A. D. M., *Medieval Scotland* (Cambridge, 2000).

Barron, E., *The Scottish Wars of Independence* (reprinted New York, 1998).

Barrow, G. W. S., 'The Scottish clergy in the War of Independence', *S.H.R.*, 41 (1962), 1–22.

Barrow, G. W. S., *The Kingdom of Scots: Government, Church and Society from the eleventh to the fourteenth century* (London, 1973).

Barrow, G. W. S., 'The aftermath of war', *T.R.H.S.*, 28 (1978), 103–25.

Barrow, G. W. S., 'The idea of freedom in late medieval Scotland', *Innes Review*, 30 (1979), 26–32.

Barrow, G. W. S., *The Anglo-Norman Era in Scottish History* (Oxford, 1980).

Barrow, G. W. S., 'Wales and Scotland in the Middle Ages', *Welsh History Review*, 10 (1980–1), 302–19

Barrow, G. W. S., *Robert Bruce and the Community of the Realm of Scotland*, 3rd edn (Edinburgh, 1988).

Barrow, G. W. S., 'Badenoch and Strathspey, 1130–1312, 1, Secular and political', *Northern Scotland*, 8 (1988), 1–15.

Barrow, G. W. S., 'Badenoch and Strathspey, 1130–1312, 2, The Church', *Northern Scotland*, 9 (1989), 1–16.

Barrow, G. W. S., 'The army of Alexander III's Scotland', in N. Reid (ed.), *Scotland in the Reign of Alexander III, 1249–1286* (Edinburgh, 1990), 132–47.

Barrow, G. W. S., 'A kingdom in crisis: Scotland and the Maid of Norway', *S.H.R.*, 69 (1990), 120–41.

Barrow, G. W. S., and A. Royan, 'James Fifth Stewart of Scotland, 1260(?)-1309', in K. J. Stringer (ed.), *Essays on the Nobility of Medieval Scotland* (Edinburgh, 1985), 166–94.

Bartlett, R., *The Making of Europe, Conquest, Colonization and Cultural Change 950–1350* (London, 1993).

Boardman, S., *The Early Stewart Kings: Robert II and Robert III* (East Linton, 1996).

Boardman, S., 'Lordship in the North-East: The Badenoch Stewarts I, Alexander Earl of Buchan, Lord of Badenoch', *Northern Scotland*, 16 (1996), 1–30.

Boardman, S., 'Chronicle propaganda in late medieval Scotland: Robert the Steward, John of Fordun and the "Anonymous Chronicle"', *S.H.R.*, 76 (1997), 23–43.

Bower, Walter, *Scotichronicon*, ed. D. E. R. Watt, 9 vols (Aberdeen, 1987–97).

Broun, D., 'Defining Scotland and the Scots before the Wars of Independence', in D. Broun, R. Finlay and M. Lynch, *Image and Identity. The Making and Remaking of Scotland through the Ages* (Edinburgh, 1998), 4–17.

Broun, D., *The Irish Identity of the Kingdom of the Scots* (Woodbridge, 1999).

Broun, D., 'A new look at *Gesta Annalia* attributed to John of Fordun', in B. E. Crawford (ed.), *Church, Chronicle and Learning* (Edinburgh, 1999), 9–30.

Broun, D., 'The seven kingdoms in *De Situ Albanie*: A record of Pictish political geography or an imaginary map of ancient *Alba*', in E. J. Cowan and R. A. McDonald, *Alba, Celtic Scotland in the Medieval Era* (East Linton, 2000), 24–42.

Broun, D., R. Finlay and M. Lynch, *Image and Identity. The Making and Remaking of Scotland through the Ages* (Edinburgh, 1998).

Brown, E. A. R., *Politics and Institutions in Capetian France* (Hampshire, 1991).

Brown, M., 'The development of Scottish border lordship', *Historical Research*, 70 (1997), 1–22.

Brown, M., *The Black Douglases: War and Lordship in Late Medieval Scotland* (East Linton, 1998).

Brown, M., 'Henry the Peaceable: Henry III, Alexander III and royal lordship in the British Isles, 1249–1272', in B. Weiller and I. Rowlands (eds), *England and Europe in the Reign of Henry III (1216–1272)* (Aldershot, 2002), 43–66.

Calendar of Documents relating to Scotland, ed. J. Bain et al., 5 vols (London, 1881–1986).

Cameron, S., and A. Ross, 'The Treaty of Edinburgh and the Disinherited (1328–32), *History*, 84 (1999).

Campbell, J., 'England, Scotland and the Hundred Years War in the fourteenth century', in J. R. Hale, J. R. L. Highfield and B. Smalley (eds), *Europe in the Late Middle Ages* (London, 1965), 155–83.

Campbell, N. D., 'MacEwens and MacSweens', *Celtic Review*, 7 (1911–12), 272–84.

Carpenter, D. A., *The Minority of Henry III* (Berkeley, 1990).

Carr, A. D., 'The last days of Gwynedd', *Transactions of the Caernarvonshire Historical Society*, 43 (1982), 7–22.

Chaplais, P., *Essays in Medieval Diplomacy and Administration* (London 1981).

The Chronicle of Lanercost, 1272–1346, trans. H. Maxwell (Edinburgh, 1913).

Chronicon de Lanercost, Bannatyne Club (Edinburgh, 1839).

Chronicle of Walter of Guisborough, ed. H. Rothwell, Camden Society (London, 1957).

Clanchy, M. T., *England and its Rulers 1066–1272* (London, 1983).

Clancy, T. O. (ed.), *The Triumph Tree, Scotland's Earliest Poetry* (Edinburgh, 1998).

Cosgrove, A. (ed.), *A New History of Ireland, II. Medieval Ireland 1169–1534* (Oxford, 1987).

Cowan, E. J., 'Norwegian sunset, Scottish dawn: Hakon IV and Alexander III', in N. Reid, *Scotland in the Reign of Alexander III, 1249–1286* (Edinburgh, 1990), 103–31.

Cowan, E. J., 'Identity, freedom and the Declaration of Arbroath', in D. Broun, R. Finlay and M. Lynch, *Image and Identity. The Making and Remaking of Scotland through the Ages* (Edinburgh, 1998), 59–61.

Cowan, E. J., *'For Freedom Alone': The Declaration of Arbroath, 1320* (East Linton, 2003).

Cowan, E. J., and R. A. McDonald, *Alba, Celtic Scotland in the Medieval Era* (East Linton, 2000).

Cowan, I. B., and D. J. Easson, *Medieval Religious Houses: Scotland* (London, 1957).

Cowan, I. B., P. H. R. Mackay and A. Macquarrie, (eds), *The Knights of St John of Jerusalem in Scotland*, Scottish History Society (Edinburgh, 1983).

Crawford, B. E., 'The Earldom of Caithness and the Kingdom of Scotland, 1150–1266', in K. J. Stringer (ed.), *Essays on the Nobility of Medieval Scotland* (Edinburgh, 1985), 25–43.

Davies, R. R., *The Age of Conquest: Wales 1063–1415* (Oxford, 1987).

Davies, R. R. (ed.), *The British Isles 1100–1500* (Edinburgh, 1988).

Davies R. R., *Domination and Conquest. The Experience of Wales, Ireland and Scotland, 1100–1300* (Cambridge, 1990).

Davies, R. R., *The First English Empire: Power and Identities in the British Isles, 1093–1343* (Oxford, 2000).

Denholm-Young, N., *Richard of Cornwall* (Oxford, 1947).

Dilworth, M., 'The Augustinian chapter at St Andrews', *Innes Review*, 25 (1974), 22–5.

Documents and Records illustrating the History of Scotland, ed. F. Palgrave (London, 1837).

Donaldson, G., 'The pope's reply to the Scottish barons in 1320', *S.H.R.*, 29 (1950), 119–20.

Donaldson, G., 'The rights of the Scottish crown in episcopal vacancies', *S.H.R.*, 45 (1966), 27–35.

Dowden, J., 'The appointment of bishops during the medieval period', *S.H.R.*, 7 (1909–10), 1–20.

Duffy, S., 'The Bruce brothers and the Irish Sea World, 1306–29', *Cambridge Medieval Celtic Studies*, 21 (1991), 55–86.

Duffy, S. (ed.), *Robert the Bruce's Irish Wars* (Stroud, 2002), 71–88.

Dunbabin, J., *Charles I of Anjou* (London, 1998).

Dunbar, J. G., and A. A. M. Duncan, 'Tarbert Castle, a contribution to the history of Argyll', *S.H.R.*, 50 (1971), 1–17.

Duncan, A. A. M., 'Documents relating to the Priory of the Isle of May, c.1140–1313', *P.S.A.S.*, 90 (1956), 52–80.

Duncan, A. A. M., 'The community of the realm of Scotland and Robert Bruce', *S.H.R.*, 45 (1966), 184–201.

Duncan, A. A. M., 'The early parliaments of Scotland', *S.H.R.*, 45 (1966), 36–58.

Duncan A. A. M., *The Nation of Scots and the Declaration of Arbroath* (Historical Association, 1970).

Duncan, A. A. M., 'The making of the Declaration of Arbroath', in D. A. Bullough and R. L. Storey (eds), *The Study of Medieval Records* (Oxford, 1971), 174–88.

Duncan, A. A. M., *Scotland: The Making of the Kingdom* (Edinburgh, 1975).

Duncan, A. A. M., *Formulary E: Scottish Letters and Brieves* (Glasgow, 1976).

Duncan, A. A. M., '*Honi soit qui mal y pense*: David II and Edward III, 1346–52', *S.H.R.*, 67 (1988), 113–41.

Duncan, A. A. M., 'The Scots invasion of Ireland, 1315', in R. R. Davies (ed.), *The British Isles 1100–1500* (Edinburgh, 1988).

Duncan, A. A. M., 'The War of the Scots, 1306–1323', *Transactions of the Royal Historical Society* (1992), 125–51.

Duncan, A. A. M., 'The "Laws of Malcolm MacKenneth"', in A. Grant and K. J. Stringer (eds), *Medieval Scotland. Crown, Lordship and Community* (Edinburgh, 1993), 239–73

Duncan, A. A. M., 'The Bruces of Annandale, 1100–1304', *Dumfries and Galloway Transactions*, 69 (1994), 89–102.

Duncan, A. A. M. (ed.), 'A question about the succession, 1364', *Scottish History Society Miscellany*, xii (Edinburgh, 1994), 1–57.

Duncan, A. A. M., 'The process of Norham, 1291', in P. R. Coss and S. D. Lloyd (eds), *Thirteenth-Century England*, v (Woodbridge, 1995), 207–30.

Duncan, A. A. M., 'John King of England and the Kings of Scots', in S. D. Church (ed.), *King John: New Interpretations* (Woodbridge, 1999), 247–71.

Duncan, A. A. M., *The Kingship of the Scots, 842–1292: Succession and Independence* (Edinburgh, 2002).

Duncan, A. A. M., and A. L. Brown, 'Argyll and the Western Isles in the early Middle Ages', *P.S.A.S.*, 90 (1956–7), 192–220.

Everard, J., *Brittany and the Angevins: Province and Empire* (Cambridge, 2000).

Ewen, E., *Townlife in Fourteenth-Century Scotland* (Edinburgh, 1990).

Ewen, E., 'An Urban Community: The Crafts in Thirteenth-Century Aberdeen', in A. Grant and K. J. Stringer, *Medieval Scotland. Crown, Lordship and Community* (Edinburgh, 1993), 156–73.

Facsimiles of the National Manuscripts of Scotland, 3 vols (Edinburgh, 1867–72).

Fawcett, R., 'Ecclesiastical architecture in the second half of the thirteenth century', in N. Reid, *Scotland in the Reign of Alexander III, 1249–1286* (Edinburgh, 1990), 148–80, 148–80.

Fawcett, R., *Scottish Architecture from the Accession of the Stewarts to the Renaissance 1371–1560* (Edinburgh, 1994).

Fawcett, R., *The Scottish Cathedrals* (London, 1997).

Ferguson, P. C., *Medieval Papal Representatives in Scotland: Legates, Nuncios, and Judges-Delegate, 1125–1286* (Edinburgh, 1997).

Fisher, A., *William Wallace* (Edinburgh, 1986).

Foedera, Conventiones, Litterae et Cuiuscunque Generis Acta Publica, ed. T. Rymer, 20 vols (London, 1704–35).

Fordun, John of, *Chronica Johannes de Fordun, Chronica Gentis Scottorum*, 2 vols, ed. W. F. Skene (Edinburgh, 1871–2).

Frame, R., 'The Bruces in Ireland', *I.H.S.*, 24 (1974), 3–37.

Frame, R., *Colonial Ireland* (Dublin, 1981).

Frame, R., *English Lordship in Ireland, 1318–1361* (Oxford, 1982).

Frame, R., *Ireland and Britain, 1170–1450* (London, 1998).

Fraser, J., '"A swan from a raven", William Wallace, Brucean propaganda, and *Gesta Annalia II*', *S.H.R.*, 81 (2002), 1–22.

Freeman, A. Z., 'Wall-breakers and river-bridgers,' *Journal of British Studies*, 10 (1970), 1–16.

Gaillou, J., and M. Jones, *The Bretons* (Oxford, 1991), 193–220.

Genet, J.-P., 'Which state rises?' *Historical Research*, 65 (1992), 19–33.

Gillingham, J., *The English in the Twelfth Century: Imperialism, national identity and political values* (Woodbridge, 2000).

Goldstein, J., 'The Scottish mission to Boniface VIII: a reconsideration of the context of the *Instructiones* and *Processus*', *S.H.R.*, 70 (1991), 1–15.

Goldstein, J., *The Matter of Scotland: Historical Narrative in Medieval Scotland* (Lincoln and London, 1993).

Goodman, A., 'Religion and warfare in the Anglo-Scottish marches', in R. Bartlett and A. MacKay (eds), *Medieval Frontier Societies* (Edinburgh, 1989), 245–66.

Gray, Thomas, *Scalachronica*, trans. H. Maxwell (Glasgow, 1907).

Grant, A., 'Earls and Earldoms in late medieval Scotland (c.1310–1460)', in J. Bossy and P. Jupp (eds), *Essays Presented to Michael Roberts* (Belfast, 1976), 24–40.

Grant, A., *Independence and Nationhood: Scotland 1306–1469* (London, 1984).

Grant, A., 'Thanes and thanages, from the eleventh to the fourteenth centuries', in Grant and K. J. Stringer (eds), *Medieval Scotland. Crown, Lordship and Community* (Edinburgh, 1993), 39–81.

Grant, A., 'Aspects of national consciousness in medieval Scotland', in C. Bjorn, A. Grant and K. J. Stringer, *Nations, Nationalism and Patriotism in the European Past* (Copenhagen, 1994), 68–95.

Grant, A., 'Disaster at Neville's Cross: The Scottish point of view', in D. Rollason and M. Prestwich (eds), *The Battle of Neville's Cross* (Stamford, 1998), 15–35.

Grant, A., 'The province of Ross and the kingdom of Alba', in E. J. Cowan and R. A. McDonald, *Alba, Celtic Scotland in The Medieval Era*, (East Linton, 2000), 166–86.

Grant, A., and K. J. Stringer, (eds), *Medieval Scotland. Crown, Lordship and Community* (Edinburgh, 1993).

Grant, A., and K. J. Stringer, (eds), *Uniting the Kingdom? The Making of British History* (London, 1995).

Greeves, R., 'The Galloway lands in Ulster', in *Dumfries and Galloway Transactions*, 3rd ser., xxxvi (1957–8), 115–21.

Hallam, E., and J. Everard, *Capetian France 987–1328*, 2nd edn (London, 2001).

Hary's Wallace, ed. M. P. McDiarmid, Scottish Text Society, 2 vols (Edinburgh, 1968–9).

Haskell, M., 'Breaking the stalemate: The Scottish campaign of Edward I, 1303–4', *Thirteenth-Century England*, vii, 223–42.

Hayes-McCoy, G. A., *Scots Mercenary Forces in Ireland (1567–1603)* (London, 1937).

Helle, K., 'Anglo-Scandinavian relations in the reign of Hakon Hakonsson (1217–63)', *Medieval Scandinavia*, 1 (1968), 101–14.

Helle, K., 'Norwegian foreign policy and the Maid of Norway', *S.H.R.*, 69 (1990), 142–56.

Holt, J. C., *The Northerners* (Oxford, 1961).

Holt, J. C., *Magna Carta* (Cambridge, 1965).

Horrox, R., *The Black Death* (Manchester, 1994), 62–92.

Huyshe, W., *Dervorgilla, Lady of Galloway and her Abbey of the Sweetheart* (Edinburgh, 1913).

Johnsen, A. O., 'The payments from the Hebrides and the Isle of Man to the crown of Norway', *S.H.R.*, 58 (1969), 18–34.

Kaeuper, R. W., *War, Justice and Public Order: England and France in the Later Middle Ages* (Oxford, 1988).

Kossmann-Putto, J. A., 'Florent V, Count of Holland, claimant to the Scottish Throne in 1291–2: his personal and political background', in G. Simpson (ed.), *Scotland and the Low Countries, 1124–1994* (Aberdeen, 1996), 15–27.

Larsen, K., *A History of Norway* (New York, 1948).

Lawrence, C. H., *Medieval Monasticism: Forms of Religious Life in Western Europe in the Middle Ages* (London, 1984).

Lawrence, C. H., *The Friars: The Impact of the Early Mendicant Movement on Western Society* (London, 1994).

Le Patourel, J., 'The treaty of Brétigny, 1360', *T.R.H.S.*, 5th ser., 10 (1960), 19–39.

Le Patourel, J., 'The king and the princes in fourteenth-century France', in J. R. Hale, J. R. L. Highfield and B. Smalley (eds), *Europe in the Late Middle Ages* (London, 1965), 155–83.

Linehan, P. A., 'A fourteenth-century history of Anglo-Scottish relations in a Spanish manuscript', *Historical Research*, 48 (1975), 106–22.

Lustig, R., 'The treaty of Perth: a re-examination', *S.H.R.*, 58 (1979), 35–57.

Lydon, J., 'Irish levies in the Scottish Wars, 1296–1302', *The Irish Sword*, 5 (1961–2), 207–17.

Lydon, J., *The Lordship of Ireland in the Middle Ages* (London, 1972).

Lydon, J., 'The Bruce invasion of Ireland', in S. Duffy (ed.), *Robert the Bruce's Irish Wars* (Stroud, 2002), 71–88.

Lynch, M., M. Spearman, and G. Stell, (eds), *The Scottish Medieval Town* (Edinburgh, 1988).

MacDonald, A. J., *Border Bloodshed: Scotland, England and France at War, 1369–1403* (East Linton, 2000).

McDonald, R. A., *The Kingdom of the Isles: Scotland's Western Seaboard c.1100–1336* (East Linton, 1997).

McDonald, R. A., 'Rebels without a cause: The relations of Fergus of Galloway and Somerled of Argyll with the Scottish Kings, 1153–1164', in E. J. Cowan and R. A. McDonald, *Alba, Celtic Scotland in the Medieval Era* (East Linton, 2000), 166–86.

Macdougall, N., *An Antidote to the English: The Auld Alliance, 1295–1560* (East Linton, 2001).

Mackenzie, W. M., 'A prelude to the War of Independence', *S.H.R.*, 27 (1948), 105–13.

McKerral, A., 'West Highland mercenaries in Ireland', *S.H.R.*, 30 (1951), 1–29.

McNamee, C., 'William Wallace's invasion of Northern England, 1297', *Northern History*, 26 (1990), 40–58.

McNamee, C., *The Wars of the Bruces* (East Linton, 1997).

McNeill, P. G. B., and H. L. MacQueen, *Atlas of Scottish History to 1707* (Edinburgh, 1996).

McNeill, T., *Anglo-Norman Ulster* (Edinburgh, 1980).

Macquarrie, A., 'Notes on some charters of the Bruces of Annandale, 1215–1295', *Dumfries and Galloway Transactions*, 58 (1983), 72–9.

MacQuarrie, A., 'The Idea of the Holy War in Scotland, 1296–1330', *Innes Review*, 32 (1981), 83–92.

MacQuarrie, A., *Scotland and the Crusades* (1985).

MacQueen, H. L., 'Scots Law under Alexander III', in Reid, *Scotland in the Reign of Alexander III*, 74–102.

MacQueen, H. L., 'The Laws of Galloway: a preliminary study', in Oram and Stell (eds), *Galloway: Land and Lordship*, 131–43.

MacQueen, H. L., *Common Law and Feudal Society in Medieval Scotland* (Edinburgh, 1993).

MacQueen, H. L., 'The Kin of Kennedy, "Kenkynnol" and the Common Law', in Grant and Stringer (eds), *Medieval Scotland*, 274–96.

Maddicott, J. R., *Thomas of Lancaster* (Oxford, 1970).

Maddicott, J. R., *Simon de Montfort* (Cambridge, 1994).

Mayhew, N., 'Alexander III – A silver age? An essay in Scottish Medieval economic history', in Reid, *Alexander III*, 53–73.

Munro, J., and Munro, R. W. (eds), *Acts of the Lords of the Isles*, Scottish History Society (Edinburgh, 1986).

Neville, C. J., 'The political allegiance of the Earls of Strathearn during the War of Independence', *S.H.R.*, 65 (1986), 133–53.

Neville, C. J., 'A Celtic Enclave in Norman Scotland: Earl Gilbert and the Earldom of Strathearn, 1171–1223', in T. Brotherstone and D. Ditchburn (eds), *Freedom and Authority Scotland 1050–1650: Historical and Historiographical Essays presented to Grant G. Simpson* (East Linton, 2000), 75–92.

Nicholas, D., *Medieval Flanders* (London, 1992).

Nicholls, K., *Gaelic and Gaelicised Ireland* (Dublin, 1972).

Nicholls, K., 'Anglo-French Ireland and After', *Peritia*, 1 (1982), 370–403.

Nicholson, R., 'The Franco-Scottish and Franco-Norwegian Treaties of 1295', *S.H.R.*, 38 (1959), 114–32

Nicholson, R., 'A sequel to Edward Bruce's invasion of Ireland', *S.H.R.*, 42 (1963–64), 34.

Nicholson, R., *Edward III and the Scots* (Oxford, 1966).

Nicholson, R., *Scotland, the Later Middle Ages* (Edinburgh, 1974).

Oram, R. D., 'Fergus, Galloway and the Scots', in R. D. Oram and G. P. Stell (eds), *Galloway: Land and Lordship* (Edinburgh, 1991), 117–30.

Oram, R. D., 'In obedience and reverence: Whithorn and York, 1128–1250', *Innes Review*, 42 (1991), 83–100.

Oram, R. D., 'Bruce, Balliol and the Lordship of Galloway: South-west Scotland and the Wars of Independence', *Dumfries and Galloway Transactions*, 67 (1992), 29–47.

Oram, R. D., 'A family business? Colonisation and settlement in twelfth and thirteenth-century Galloway', *S.H.R.*, 72 (1993), 111–45.

Oram, R. D., 'Dervorgilla, the Balliols and Buittle', *Dumfries and Galloway Transactions*, 73 (1999), 165–81.

Oram, R. D., *The Lordship of Galloway* (Edinburgh, 2000).

Oram, R. D., and G. P Stell. (eds), *Galloway: Land and Lordship* (Edinburgh, 1991).

Penman, M., 'The kingship of David II', unpublished PhD thesis (University of St Andrews, 1998).

Penman, M., 'A fell coniuration agayn Robert the douchty king: the Soules conspiracy of 1318–20', *Innes Review*, 50 (1999), 25–57.

Penman, M., 'The Scots at Neville's Cross', *S.H.R.*, 80 (2001), 157–80.

Phillips, J. R. S., *Aymer de Valence Earl of Pembroke* (Oxford, 1972).

Pirenne, H., *Histoire de Belgique* (Brussels, 1929).

Prestwich, M., *Edward I* (London, 1988).

Prestwich, M., 'Edward I and the Maid of Norway', *S.H.R.*, 69 (1990), 157–73.

Prestwich, M., 'The English at Neville's Cross', in D. Rollason and M. Prestwich (eds), *The Battle of Neville's Cross* (Stamford, 1998), 1–14.

Prestwich, M., *English Politics in the Thirteenth Century* (London, 1990).

Registrum Episcopatus Moraviensis (Edinburgh, 1837).

Registrum Magni Sigilli Regum Scottorum, ed. J. M. Thompson et al., 11 vols (Edinburgh, 1882–1914).

Regesta Regum Scottorum, vol. 2, *The Acts of William I*, ed. G. W. S. Barrow (Edinburgh, 1971).

Regesta Regum Scottorum, vol. 5, *The Acts of Robert I*, ed. A. A. M. Duncan (Edinburgh, 1988).

Regesta Regum Scottorum, vol. 6, *The Acts of David II*, ed. A. B. Webster (Edinburgh, 1982).

Reid, N., 'The kingless kingdom: The Scottish guardianship of 1286–1306', *S.H.R.*, 61 (1982), 105–29.

Reid, N., 'Margaret "Maid of Norway" and Scottish Queenship', *Reading Medieval Studies*, 8 (1982), 75–96.

Reid, N. (ed.), *Scotland in the Reign of Alexander III, 1249–1286* (Edinburgh, 1990).

Reid, N. 'Crown and community under Robert I', in A. Grant and K. J. Stringer (eds), *Medieval Scotland. Crown, Lordship and Communty*, (Edinburgh, 1993), 203–22.

Reid, W. S., 'Trade, traders and Scottish independence', *Speculum*, 29 (1954), 210–22.

Reid, W. S., 'Sea-power in the Anglo-Scottish war, 1296–1318', *Mariners' Mirror*, 46 (1960), 7–23.

Reynolds, S., *Kingdoms and Communities in Western Europe, 900–1300* (Oxford, 1994).

Reynolds, S., 'How different was England?', in M. Prestwich, R. Britnell and R. Frame (eds), *Thirteenth-Century England*, vii (Woodbridge, 1999), 1–16.

Rickard, P., *Britain in Medieval French Literature* (Cambridge, 1956).

Rixson, D., *The West Highland Galley* (Edinburgh, 1988).

Rogers, C. J., 'The Scottish invasion of 1346', *Northern History*, 34 (1998), 51–82.

Rogers, C. J., *War, Cruel and Sharp English Strategy under Edward III* (Woodbridge, 2000).

Rogers, C. J., 'The Anglo-French peace negotiations of 1354–1360 reconsidered', in J. S. Bothwell, *The Age of Edward III* (Woodbridge, 2001), 193–214.

Rollason, D., and M. Prestwich (eds), *The Battle of Neville's Cross 1346* (Stamford, 1998).

Ross, A., 'Men for all seasons? The Strathbogie Earls of Atholl and the Wars of Independence, c. 1290–1335, I', *Northern Scotland* 20 (2000), 1–30.

Ross, A., 'Men for all seasons? The Strathbogie Earls of Atholl and the Wars of Independence, c. 1290–1335, 2', *Northern Scotland*, 21 (2001), 1–15.

Rotuli Scotiae in Turri Londonensi et in Domo Capitulari Westmonasteriensi, ed. D. MacPherson, 2 vols (London, 1814–19).

Sayles, G. O., 'The guardians of Scotland and a parliament at Rutherglen in 1300', *S.H.R.*, 24 (1927), 245–50.

Scammell, J., 'Robert I and the North of England', *E.H.R.*, 73 (1958), 385–403.

Scotichronicon, see under Bower.

Scott, W. W., 'Abbots Adam (1207–1213) and William (1215–1216) of Melrose and the Melrose Chronicle', in B. E. Crawford (ed.), *Church, Chronicle and Learning in Medieval and Early Renaissance Scotland* (Edinburgh, 1999), 161–72.

Scoular, H. M. (ed.), *Handlist of the Acts of Alexander II* (Edinburgh, 1959).

Sellar, W. D. H., 'The origins and ancestry of Somerled', *S.H.R.*, 45 (1966), 123–42.

Sellar, W. D. H., 'Family origins in Cowal and Knapdale', *Scottish Studies*, 15 (1971), 21–37.

Sellar, W. D. H., 'Hebridean sea kings: The successors of Somerled, 1164–1316', in E. J. Cowan and R. A. McDonald, *Alba. Celtic Scotland in the Medieval Era* (East Linton, 2000), 187–218.

Shead, N., 'The administration of the diocese of Glasgow in the twelfth and thirteenth centuries', *S.H.R.*, 55 (1976), 127–50.

Shead, N., 'The household and chancery of the Bishops of Dunkeld, 1160s–1249', in B. E. Crawford (ed.), *Church, Chronicle and Learning* (Edinburgh, 1999).

Simms, K., *From Kings to Warlords: The Changing Political Structure of Gaelic Ireland in the Later Middle Ages* (Woodbridge, 1987).

Simms, K., 'Gaelic warfare in the Middle Ages', in T. Bartlett and K. Jeffrey, *A Military History of Ireland* (Cambridge, 1996), 99–115.

Simms, K., 'Relations with the Irish', in J. Lydon (ed.), *Law and Disorder in Thirteenth-Century Ireland* (Dublin, 1997), 66–86.

Simpson, G., 'The claim of Florence count of Holland to the Scottish throne, 1291–92', *S.H.R.*, 36 (1957), 111–24.

Simpson, G., *Handlist of the Acts of Alexander III, the Guardians and John* (Edinburgh, 1960).

Simpson, G., 'The Declaration of Arbroath revitalised', *S.H.R.*, 56 (1977), 11–33.

Simpson, G., 'The familia of Roger de Quincy, Earl of Winchester and Constable of Scotland', in K. J. Stringer (ed.), *Essays on the Nobility of Medieval Scotland* (Edinburgh, 1985), 102–29.

Simpson, G., 'Kingship in miniature: a seal of minority of Alexander III, 1249–57', in A. Grant and K. J. Stringer, *Medieval Scotland. Crown, Lordship and Community* (Edinburgh, 1993), 131–9.

Simpson, G. (ed.), *Scotland and the Low Countries, 1124–1994* (Aberdeen, 1996).

Simpson, W. D., 'Castle Tioram, Moidart, Inverness-shire; and Mingary Castle, Ardnamurchan, Argyll-shire', in *Transactions of the Glasgow Archaeological Society*, 13 (1954), 70–90.

Smith, J. B., *Llywelyn ap Gruffydd, Prince of Wales* (Cardiff, 1998).

Smith, J. B., 'England and Wales: The conflict of Wales', in M. Prestwich, R. H. Britnell and R. Frame (eds), *Thirteenth-Century England*, vii, (Woodbridge, 1999), 189–205.

Stell, G., 'The Balliol family and the Great Cause of 1291–2', in K. J. Stringer (ed.), *Essays on the Nobility of Medieval Scotland* (Edinburgh, 1985), 150–65.

Stevenson, A., 'The Flemish dimension of the Auld Alliance', in Simpson (ed.), *Scotland and the Low Countries*, 28–42.

Stevenson, J., *Documents Illustrative of Sir William Wallace, his life and times* (Glasgow, 1841).

Stevenson, J. (ed.), *Documents Illustrative of the History of Scotland*, 2 vols (Edinburgh, 1870).

Stones, E. L. G., 'The English mission to Edinburgh in 1328', *S.H.R.*, 27 (1949), 97–118.

Stones, E. L. G., 'The Anglo-Scottish negotiations of 1327', *S.H.R.*, 30 (1951), 49–54.

Stones, E. L. G., 'The Treaty of Northampton, 1328', *History*, 38 (1953), 54–61.

Stones, E. L. G., 'The submission of Robert Bruce to Edward I, c. 1301–2', *S.H.R.*, 34 (1955), 122–34.

Stones E. L. G., *Anglo-Scottish Relations, 1174–1328* (Oxford, 1965).

Stones, E. L. G., and G. G. Simpson, *Edward I and the Throne of Scotland*, 2 vols (Oxford, 1978).

Strayer, J. R., *Medieval Origins of the Modern State* (Princeton, 1970).

Strayer, J. R., 'The costs and profits of war: the Anglo-French war of 1294–1303', in H. A. Miskimin, D. L. Herlihy and A. L. Udovitch (eds), *The Medieval City* (New Haven, 1977), 269–91.

Strayer, J. R., *The Reign of Philip the Fair* (Princeton, 1980).

Strayer, J. R., 'The crusade against Aragon', in J. Strayer (ed.), *Essays in Medieval Statecraft and the Perspectives of History* (Princeton, 1981), 107–22.

Stringer, K. J., *Essays on the Nobility of Medieval Scotland* (Edinburgh, 1985).

Stringer, K., *Earl David of Huntingdon. A Study in Anglo-Scottish History* (Edinburgh, 1985).

Stringer, K., 'Periphery and core in thirteenth-century Scotland: Alan son of Roland, lord of Galloway and constable of Scotland', in A. Grant and R. J. Stringer (eds), *Medieval Scotland. Crown, Lordship and Community* (Edinburgh, 1993), 82–112.

Stringer, K., 'Identities in thirteenth-century England: Frontier society in the far north', in C. Bjorn, A. Grant and K. Stringer (eds), *Social and Political Identities in Western History* (Copenhagen, 1994), 28–66.

Stringer, K., 'Nobility and identity in medieval Britain and Ireland: The De Vescy Family, c. 1120–1314', in B. Smith (ed.), *Britain and Ireland* (Cambridge, 1999), 199–239.

Stringer, K., 'Reform monasticism and Celtic Scotland: Galloway, 1140–1240', in E. J. Cowan and R. A. McDonald, *Alba, Celtic Scotland in the Medieval Era*, (East Linton, 2000), 127–65.

Summerson, H., *Medieval Carlisle: the City and its Borders from the Late Eleventh to the Mid-sixteenth Century*, 2 vols (Kendal, 1993).

Sumption, J., *The Hundred Years War: Trial by Battle* (London, 1990).

Sumption, J., *The Hundred Years War: Trial by Fire* (London, 1999).

Taylor, S., 'The coming of the Augustinians to St Andrews and version B of the St Andrews foundation legend', in S. Taylor (ed.), *Kings, Clerics and Chronicles in Scotland 500–1297: Essays in honour of M. O. Anderson* (Dublin, 2000), 115–23.

Thompson, J. M., 'A Roll of the Scottish Parliament, 1344', *S.H.R.*, 35 (1912), 235–40.

Treharne, R. F., *The Baronial Plan of Reform, 1258–1263* (Manchester, 1932).

Treharne, R. F., and Sanders, I. J., *Documents of the Baronial Movement of Reform and Rebellion, 1258–67* (Oxford, 1973).

Tuck, A., *Crown and Nobility* (London, 1985).

Vale, M., 'Edward I and the French: rivalry and chivalry', *Thirteenth-Century England*, ii (Woodbridge, 1988), 165–76.

Vale, M., *The Origins of the Hundred Years War: The Angevin Legacy* (Oxford, 1996).

Vincent, N., *Peter des Roches, An Alien in English Politics, 1205–1238* (Cambridge, 1996).

Warren, W. L., *King John* (London, 1961).

Watson, F., 'Settling the stalemate: Edward I's peace in Scotland, 1303–1305', in M. Prestwich, R. Britnell and R. Frame (eds), *Thirteenth-Century England*, vi (Woodbridge, 1997), 127–43.

Watson, F., *Under the Hammer: Edward I and Scotland, 1286–1307* (East Linton, 1998).

Watson, F., 'The Enigmatic Lion: Scotland, kingship and national identity in the Wars of Independence', in D. Broun, R. Finlay and M. Lynch (eds), *Image and Identity. The Making and Remaking of Scotland Through The Ages* (Edinburgh, 1998), 18–37.

Watt, D. E. R., 'The minority of Alexander III of Scotland', *Transactions of the Royal Historical Society*, 5th ser. 21 (1971), 1–23.

Watt, D. E. R., *A Biographical Dictionary of Scottish Graduates to A.D. 1410* (Oxford, 1977).

Watt, D. E. R., 'Scottish University Men of the Thirteenth and Fourteenth Centuries', in T. C. Smout (ed.), *Scotland and Europe* (Edinburgh, 1986), 1–18.

Watt, D. E. R., 'The provincial council of the Scottish Church, 1215–1472', in A. Grant and K. J. Stringer, *Medieval Scotland. Crown, Lordship and Community* (Edinburgh, 1993), 140–55.

Watt, D. E. R., *Medieval Church Councils in Scotland* (Edinburgh, 2000).

Watt, D. E. R., 'Bagimond di Vezza and his "Roll"', *S.H.R.*, 80 (2001), 1–23.

Waugh, S. L., 'Tenure to contract: Lordship and clientage in thirteenth-century England', *E.H.R.*, 101 (1986), 811–39.

Webster, A. B., 'Scotland without a King, 1329–41', in A. Grant and K. J. Stringer, *Medieval Scotland. Crown, Lordship and Community* (Edinburgh, 1993), 222–38

Whyte, I. D., *Scotland before the Industrial Revolution: An Economic and Social History, c. 1050–c. 1750* (Harlow, 1995).

Williamson, D. M., 'The Legate Otto in Scotland and Ireland, 1237–1240', *S.H.R.*, 28 (1949), 145–73.

Wood, C. T., '*Regnum Francie*: a problem in Capetian administrative usage', *Traditio*, 22 (1967), 117–44.

Wyntoun, Andrew of, *The Original Chronicle*, Scottish Texts Society, 6 vols (Edinburgh, 1908).

Yeoman, P., *Pilgrimage in Medieval Scotland* (London, 1999).

Young, A., 'Noble families and political factions in the reign of Alexander III', in Reid, *Scotland in the Reign of Alexander III, 1249–1286* Edinburgh, 1990), 1–30.

Young, A., 'The Earls and Earldom of Buchan in the Thirteenth Century', in A. Grant and K. J. Stringer, *Medieval Scotland. Crown, Lordship and Community* (Edinburgh, 1993), 174–202.

Young, A., *Robert the Bruce's Rivals: The Comyns, 1212–1314* (East Linton, 1997).

Young, A., 'The North and Anglo-Scottish relations in the thirteenth century', in J. C. Appleby and P. Dalton (eds), *Government, Society and Religion in Northern England 1000–1700* (Stroud, 1997), 77–89.

Young, A., 'The Comyns and Anglo-Scottish Relations (1286–1314)', in M. Prestwich, R. H. Britnell and R. Frame (eds), *Thirteenth-Century England*, vii (Woodbridge, 1999), 207–22.

Ziegler, P., *The Black Death* (Stroud, 1997), 159–61.

Index